The Conservative Crack-Up

R. EMMETT TYRRELL, JR.

SIMON & SCHUSTER

New York   London   Toronto   Sydney   Tokyo   Singapore

SIMON & SCHUSTER
Simon & Schuster Building
Rockefeller Center
1230 Avenue of the Americas
New York, New York 10020

Coyright © 1992 by R. Emmett Tyrrell, Jr.

SIMON & SCHUSTER and colophon are registered trademarks
of Simon & Schuster Inc.

Designed by Irving Perkins Associates, Inc.
Manufactured in the United States of America

10 9 8 7 6 5 4 3 2 1

Library of Congress Cataloging in Publication Data
Tyrrell, R. Emmett.
    The conservative crack-up / R. Emmett Tyrrell.
        p.   cm.
        1. Conservatism—United States. 2. United States—Politics and government—1981–
1989. 3. United States—Politics and government—1989– I. Title.
JK271.T96   1992
320.5'2'0973—dc20   91-46641
                                                                     CIP

ISBN: 0-671-66038-1

*For Anne and Katy and P.D., with hope,
and for Jenny Woodward, with gratitude.*

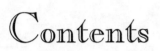
Contents

Acknowledgments

THIS BOOK BLOSSOMED from the op-ed page of *The Wall Street Journal*. On the morning of March 27, 1987, the *Journal* published my essay, "A Coming Conservative Crack-Up?"; and before lunch my astute editor at Simon & Schuster, Bob Asahina, once a movie critic for *The American Spectator*, was on the telephone to me, merrily urging that I drop plans for a book on Washington and instead apply myself to this impending crack-up. Thus I freely acknowledge Bob's nudge and, of course, my debt to Robert Bartley and his guerrilla band in *The Wall Street Journal*'s editorial department. The learning, good sense, and boldness that Bartley and his colleagues bring to their outpost, five days a week, year in and year out, have made it one of the great institutions in American journalism and one of the reasons that we can hope for high intellect and individuality to return to what is now a pretty dismal profession.

I always take the utmost delight in pinning the donkey's tail on almost any prof, but entre nous those profs who know their stuff are among the Republic's worthiest citizens. They are staunch sentinels of civilization, and so let me acknowledge that in writing this book I have readily called upon several learned profs for their broad knowledge, rigorous judgment, and insight. On this side of the ocean I thank Jacques Barzun, Alonzo Hamby, Hugh Kenner, Kenneth S. Lynn, and James Q. Wilson. At the London School of Economics I thank Maurice Cranston and Kenneth Minogue. Finally, let me heave an especially gaudy bouquet to Ernest van den Haag, who has been on call twenty-four hours a day with sage

9

counsel and an invitation to dine at any of a dozen Manhattan restaurants where he keeps lax waiters in terror.

Among Washington's wise coves let me acknowledge the help of former Under Secretary of Defense Fred Ikle and former Secretary of the Navy John Lehman. My colleague at *The American Spectator*, Vic Gold, is an inexhaustible source of facts, keen insights, wit, imagination, and . . . well, encouragement. Bill McGurn of *National Review*, and Fred Barnes of *The New Republic* have had their pockets picked for ideas. I know they will not prosecute, nor will John O'Sullivan of *National Review*, Andy Ferguson, currently with the White House, and Bob Novak, the dean of Washington's conservative press corps. Other valued friends on this project have been Martin Anderson, Terry Eastland, Peter Hannaford, Karlyn Keene, Penn Kemble, Michael Ledeen, Adam Meyerson, P.J. O'Rourke, Dan Quayle, Al Somers, Whit Stillman, Patricia Tyrrell, and my agent, Lois Wallace.

I am grateful for the early assistance of *The Washington Post*'s Don Graham and Meg Greenfield in launching my syndicated political column. It has kept me alive to daily events that I might not otherwise have followed. And I am grateful to the later assistance of *The Washington Times*'s Arnaud de Borchgrave, Wes Pruden, and Mary Lou Forbes. The competition between these two papers is more beneficial to the Republic than Thomas Jefferson's occasional doses of insurrection, and *The Washington Times*'s joie de vivre is a national treasure. Finally, let me acknowledge my debt to William Randolph Hearst, Jr., for his support and verve.

Back in New York I have learned much from the comments of the incomparable Tom Wolfe, that superb economics journalist James Grant, and a properly rewarded student of business, Theodore J. Forstmann— they all got the 1980s right. I want to thank Eric Breindel at *The New York Post* for his challenging views and Peter Kalikow for his efforts at keeping the *Post* vigorous. Andrew Whist of the Libertad Foundation has sharpened my perceptions of the world beyond our shores, and as always I am indebted to my first editor and gracious friend, Midge Decter. I must admit that I have learned from certain friends among the loyal opposition: Kathleen Kennedy Townsend, who has my vote; her husband, the learned David; and E.J. Dionne of *The Washington Post*. And let me acknowledge my debt to the wisdom and eloquence of two distinguished British journalists whose counsel and example have fortified me for nearly two decades: Colin Welch and Peregrine Worsthorne.

I note that practically all the above, with obvious exceptions, have been associated with me in one way or another through *The American Spectator*, now in its twenty-fifth year. Surely it is fitting to acknowledge my gratitude for the long-time support of Dick Scaife and his wise associates Dick Larry and Dan McMichael, of Randolph Richardson, of William Simon and his assistant James Piereson, and of Mike Joyce, the philosopher and political connoisseur in residence at the Bradley Foundation. For more than two decades *The American Spectator* has been able to muster and sustain hundreds of writers, their many books, and their even more numerous articles, thanks in large part to such independently minded benefactors.

Which brings me to the staff of the magazine. In reflecting on the many staff members who during a quarter of a century have served the magazine and passed on, I am struck by certain wonderful constants. Cheerfulness, selflessness, tirelessness, and high intelligence have characterized almost every staff member from my first associates, Ron Burr and the unsinkable Baron Von Kannon, both of whom improve with age, to the latest interns. During the writing of this book, managing editor Wladyslaw Pleszczynski has been adviser and friend day and night. Assistant managing editor Christopher Caldwell has plowed through the text with a shrewd editorial eye, and my indefatigable and cheery executive assistant, Jenny Woodward, is suitably remembered on another page. As always, Miss Myrna Larfnik brilliantly guided a research staff that has included Ken Kleinfeld, Mark Miller, Kevin O'Scannlain, Marcia Cristoff-Kurop, and Ed McFadden, whom I forgive for making off with a handful of my pre-Castro Cuban cigars the night the President stopped by.

I have always been assisted by first-rate associates, but I want to pause to express special thanks to Ron Burr, who has run the business side of the magazine with tireless ingenuity; and I want to end by saluting former managing editor Erich Eichman, an unusually gifted intellect.

"In politics the influence of imponderables is often greater than that of either military power or money."
—Otto von Bismarck: Speech in the Reichstag,
February 1, 1868

"I hold them [politics] to be subject to laws as fixed as matter itself, and to be as fit a subject for the application of the highest intellectual power."
—John C. Calhoun: Speech in the Senate,
February 15, 1833

Ladies and gentlemen, the choice is yours.
—RET

Prologue

THE PRESENT ANXIETIES in the body politic are understandable
even as an attack of morning sickness is understandable, occurring some
time after the female of the species has engaged in sexual congress unattended by the customary prophylactic machinery. Remember, our tireless
politicos have been having their way with the American electorate for
many years. Nausea and anxiety should have been expected. What has
worsened our present condition, however, is the fact that the usual sources
of therapy for the body politic, Liberalism and conservatism, are in a bad
way. Both of the latter are in a state of physical and even psychological
crack-up. The crack-up of Liberalism was apparent years ago, and I analyzed that phenomenon as charitably as I could in my 1984 book, *The
Liberal Crack-Up*. Today the evidence of a Conservative Crack-Up is
inescapable, and I have endeavored to face this contretemps with equal
analytical rigor, even though my heart is with the conservatives. In fact,
in the following narrative I have been able to throw in personal anecdotes
that were unavailable to me in my book on Liberalism. I have never been
a Liberal, not even in the blush of youth, not even in fetal repose, but I
have been an active conservative, and since college I have been a member
of the movement that came from the sidelines of American politics to
dominate the 1980s and shape the 1990s. Consequently, my analysis of
the Conservative Crack-Up can frequently be illuminated by personal
experiences, which I survived with only minor flesh wounds.

At the end of this book I shall tender a solution to what is obviously
another deadlock of democracy. I suspect that my solution will surprise

many Liberals and conservatives, but for now let me merely note that we are at the end of an era. The politics of the Left and the Right are bereft. The Liberals have not had a new idea since the last Ice Age; and nowadays the mark of a true Liberal is not so much his adherence to a coherent agenda but the intensity of his angers and the alacrity with which he urges impeachment proceedings against a conservative president at the least provocation. Congressman Henry Gonzalez began proceedings against Ronald Reagan as early as 1983, and there are Liberals ready to have at George Bush for a dozen esoteric infamies right now. Conservatives have coherent ideas but they have very few gifted pols. The conservatives' relish for politics is only sporadic and almost wholly dependent on their perception that some zany reformer has become a threat to home sweet home. Given the crack-up of the Left and Right, perhaps the time has come for American government to be jobbed out to professionals; and considering the immensity of the Washington bureaucracy, perhaps it has been.

I date the Conservative Crack-Up as beginning on the afternoon of July 1, 1987, when President Ronald Reagan stepped to the microphones and with ill-considered joviality announced Robert H. Bork of the United States Court of Appeals for the District of Columbia as his nominee to replace Associate Supreme Court Justice Lewis F. Powell, Jr. That did it. The loyal opposition was not in a very good humor to begin with. Now they went into a capital fury. Neither the President nor his fellow conservatives seemed to notice.

Possibly, a future Thucydides or Gibbon will take issue with me on this date. There is a body of opinion, most recently represented by *The Washington Post's* E.J. Dionne, that holds that there were portentous fissures in conservativism from its very founding in the 1940s, when its fractious alliance of traditionalists, libertarians, and anticommunists could put one in mind of the Austro-Hungarian Empire in its last irritable days. Other students of conservatism will date the Conservative Crack-Up from November 4, 1986, when the Republicans lost control of the Senate, or from November 12, 1986, when the Iran-Contra hullabaloo was auspicated. And perhaps others will hold that the real crack-up came during the Clarence Thomas fiasco, when the White House advised this conservative judge to conceal his ideas and principles and present himself as cleverly inane.

Nonetheless, I am sticking with July 1, 1987. The Bork hearings represented a watershed. Conservatism's time of greatest strength preceded that date, and it has been a rocky road ever since. What is more, all the conservatives' imperfections, as I diagnose them in the following pages, could be detected in their futile maneuvers during the Bork hearings. Their response was no concerted effort comparable to the political campaign being mounted against him and later against Judge Thomas. Some conservatives were complacent. Others thought a political campaign for a Supreme Court nominee unseemly. The conservatives' political libido is only slowly roused. They form few coalitions. They reach out to others only reluctantly. Their first urge is to exclude, rarely to include, which is the first impulse of the political virtuosi. Finally, in the Bork hearings the conservatives again demonstrated a failure of the imagination that has dogged them since their early days when they marched forth with their free market economists, their philosophers, many businessmen, some politicians, but almost no literary talent. When the opposition portrayed Judge Bork as an imperious fogy, the conservatives were utterly incapable of dramatizing his well-known wit and heartiness or of even recognizing the high drama of one man standing alone against the Senate's kangaroo court, presided over by real kangaroos.

And there is another reason for citing the Bork hearings as a watershed. The hearings typified battles that conservatives are now increasingly losing to Liberals. Despite vast support from the electorate, conservatives have few redoubts within the culture from which they can shape the public discourse. Their intellectuals' voices are easily ignored. As their protagonists' views are transmogrified into grotesques the conservatives sit in frustration watching as their positions are blatantly misrepresented and as legitimate points are simply ignored. Such is the Liberals' dominance of our culture that a conservative judge with a distinguished record passed upon by the Senate Judiciary Committee just five years before could now be transformed into a figure of scandal without any outcry from those provinces where fair play, tolerance, and all the other high-minded ideals of our society are enshrined. Only later, after Judge Bork's defeat, could it be admitted, as the *Boston Globe*'s Ethan Bronner did in *Battle for Justice: How the Bork Nomination Shook America*, that Judge Bork's opponents "shamelessly twisted Bork's world view."[1] They gave themselves over to innuendo, misrepresentation, and slander; and the conservatives sat quietly by with the rest of the American people witnessing an increasingly lurid spectacle.

It was an astonishing display of cultural power. Judge Robert Bork, a highly educated scholar, a graduate of the University of Chicago, a former professor from the Yale Law School, sat alone before a Senate panel that included a plagiarist, two campus cheats, various drunks, womanizers, a parking lot tycoon, and that towering hill ape, Senator Howell Heflin, who actually queried Judge Bork about his beard and later commented that the Judge had "a strange lifestyle"[2] and was "some kind of right-wing freak."[3] For weeks the republic echoed with such ludicrous sonorities as that of the senior senator from Massachusetts, who rumbled: "Robert Bork's America is a land in which women would be forced into back-alley abortions, blacks would sit at segregated lunch counters, rogue police could break down citizens' doors in midnight raids, school children could not be taught about evolution, writers and artists could be censored at the whim of government, and the doors of the federal courts would be shut on the fingers of millions of citizens."[4] Whammo, right on the fingers!

As Suzanne Garment summed it up in *Commentary*, Liberals did not oppose Bork "honestly, by saying that they hated Bork's ideas. Failing a scandal of the usual sort, they decided to present Bork's philosophy as itself a scandal. . . . They were saying that Bork's were not the sort of ideas that should be met through the normal give-and-take of serious argument."[5] But then, this is increasingly the way the Liberals have been framing their political struggles with conservatives, and the conservatives remain as nonplussed today as they were during the struggle for the Bork nomination. As all the Liberal interest groups rallied to the campaign against Judge Bork the conservatives wavered. They had grown complacent and bored with politics. When they did respond, the White House cautioned them against a forthright defense of Bork. "When the White House finally fought back," Judge Bork's wife later wrote, "it was too late. Here was my husband in the impossible position of being a sitting judge nominated to the highest Court facing a well ginned up political campaign against him, unable to speak in his own defense except at hearing, while the White House used none of its resources outside the usual preparation for a hearing on behalf of the nominee. I don't understand such ineptness. . . ."[6] Mrs. Bork, here is my explanation.

Kitty Hawk, North Carolina
November 15, 1991

CHAPTER 1

Pasta and Politics
A Yankee Conservative on
Via Cassia

I<small>T WAS IN</small> R<small>OME</small> in the summer of 1979 that I received the bad news. The sun was departing, dusk was creeping in, and there within the illuminated rectangle of a doorway leaned Luigi Barzini, swarthy but soigné, a cigarette in hand, his dark eyes cast downward towards the gravel of the driveway. The old sage looked like nothing so much as a venerable Sicilian don. He flicked the ash of his Philip Morris and straightened to face me and the wall of foliage at my back. That wall of foliage was his last line of defense from the noise and the fumes of the Via Cassia a few hundred yards beyond. The other lines of defense between his home and the ancient roadway were a field of flowers and fruit trees, a wall of shrubs, and immediately adjacent to the highway a tall tangle of laurel and olive trees—all cared for by an irritable gardener whose ceaseless warfare with Luigi was a perfect reflection of contemporary Italian labor relations. Once past the gardener's jurisdiction, all that protected Luigi's peace of mind from raucous modernity was this solemn line of trees. Luigi sucked on his teeth and enunciated ceremoniously: "*This* is your moment in history." Flicking his ash once again he waved me in.

Frankly, he had caught me off guard. I was anticipating a nice risotto, a bottle of Pinot Grigio Santa Margherita, and far into the Roman night the obbligato accompaniment of Luigi's lively and learned conversation, for this proud gentleman, the author of many wonderful books, the most wonderful of all being his masterpiece, *The Italians*, was a celebrated raconteur and wit. As for his pronouncement that this was my moment in history, well, in the words of the late Sam Goldwyn, "include me out." I had other things in mind. Since founding *The American Spectator* in my country's heartland late in the 1960s and becoming its editor-in-chief-for-life, I had sought no promotions and anticipated no career changes. In the early 1970s I had escaped Vice President Spiro Agnew's request that I join him in the historic business of writing speeches to inflame the spirit. Now history would again have to wait. I was pleasantly occupied with satisfying literary labors. Besides, back at the hotel I had taken aboard a drink or two. Perhaps the booze had impaired my judgment, but by the time I arrived at Luigi's the world looked unusually gay to me. I was without care. Nor was I really dressed for such a momentous occasion: no top hat, no morning coat, not even a press agent or a hairdresser in my entourage—in fact, no entourage.

My moment in history? Truth be known, current events frequently bore me. Days could pass without my ever as much as opening a newspaper were it not that a deep sense of social obligation made the odious business imperative. Along with my literary tasks at *The American Spectator* I had in the late 1970s begun a syndicated newspaper column that filled me with a sense of high purpose. Not only did it appear in such famed cities as Los Angeles, New York, and San Francisco but it appeared every Monday morning in *The Washington Post*, where its illuminations were urgently needed. Washington is the capital of our great Republic, and by the late 1970s its elites were as isolated from the West's free flow of ideas as their peers in such other capital cities as Sofia, Bulgaria or Ulan Bator, Mongolia. Of course, some of the Bulgar elites recognized their isolation and felt bad; Washington's elites were generally very content, believing the whole wide world to be composed of people just like them. Well, each Monday morning I felt duty-bound to file a caveat.

The column caused amazing distress throughout metropolitan Washington. Pluralism is all well and good, but this does not mean that pluralists will tranquilly entertain disagreement from the pluralizers. Actually, if one disagrees as frequently as I am wont to do, the champions of pluralism are apt to take up weapons against you, usually the telephone. Meg Greenfield, editor of the *Post*'s editorial page, once told me that before my arrival on her op-ed page her afternoons were punctuated by indignant telephone calls from Capitol Hill protesting the unorthodox views of Evans and Novak. Now, according to Meg, I had replaced Evans and Novak as the jinni of their vexed minds. She also received vituperative complaints for carrying my column from such latter-day Comstocks as Alexander Cockburn, who reproached her in the *Village Voice*, and from less forthright columnists of greater prominence, who chastised her covertly by telephone or *pssst* behind the hand on the cocktail circuit. It particularly peeved the prominent columnists when I would reproduce one of their Solomonic judgments from yesteryear, now rendered laughable by events: for instance, solemn prophecies that, once the American Army departed, Vietnam would become a peaceful democratic nation, or that Fidel's Cuba was about to become a model social democracy, or that the Soviet economy was as healthy as a Swiss milk cow!* I was asked to stop this uncharitable quoting. It annoyed them. Anthony Lewis was particularly offended. My penchant for quotation marks represented a new low in journalism: blackening a person's reputation by quoting him.

In Juan Manuel Fangio's *Fangio: My Racing Life*—a book I highly recommend, particularly to Washington policy analysts and university professors—the great Formula One champion writes of the delicious sense of excitement that seized him on race day. A similar excitement seized me every week on column-writing day, partly from a sense of sport but also from the excitement of fulfilling the American journalists' credo, "afflict the comfortable." I suppose it was foolish of me, but I took this piece of rodomontade seriously. Hence I composed my feuilletons with the utmost care, always with an eye for maximum effrontery. It meant that I must needs be au courant with all manner of news story.

Were it not for my weekly journalistic mission, daily political perturbations would rarely attract my notice. Which is not to say I lived remote from politics. Though politicians frequently appall me, for some reason I have been mixed up in politics for over two decades. Three presidents have been friends, two vice-presidents, scores of lesser politicians, innumerable political writers, and ideologues of every type; and I shall long remember the perfume of a woman of easy virtue who worked for the public television station in New York City, but more about her another time. Suffice it to say, however, that this involvement with politics has not been wholly to

---

*My urge to quote is unscotchable. Behold this observation from the greatest economic savant of his day, economist John Kenneth Galbraith, writing on the Soviet economy six months before Mikhail Gorbachev took power and pronounced his economy in crisis: "That the Soviet economy has made great material progress in recent years," Galbraith reports from affluent Russia, ". . . is evident both from the statistics . . . and from the general urban scene. . . . One sees it in the appearance of solid well-being of the people on the streets, the close-to-murderous traffic, the incredible exfoliation [sic] of apartment houses, and the general aspect of restaurants, theaters, and shops. . . . Partly, the Russian system succeeds because, in contrast with the Western industrial economies, it makes full use of its manpower. . . ." "Reflections: A Visit to Russia," *The New Yorker*, September 3, 1984, pp. 54, 60–61.

my liking. My basic sympathy is with Mencken's old pal George Jean Nathan, who in the early 1920s recalled that "On that day during the world war when the most critical battle was being fought, I sat in my still, sunlit, cozy library composing a chapter on aesthetics for a new book on drama. And at five o'clock, my day's work done, I shook and drank a half dozen excellent aperitifs."[1]

To my mind George had spent a perfect day, and dinner with one of his beauteous ingenues would have made a perfect night. But George and I have lived in different times. Perhaps if the battle that raged while he wrote and sipped aperitifs had gone differently the times through which I have lived would have been less troubled in all departments. Then this might be a book on aesthetics, and it would not matter all that much whether my judgments were right or wrong. No one in this century that I know of has ever been put to death for a bad play or for the Bauhaus style, though I have my nominees. Politics, however, is another matter. Enormous suffering has been occasioned in this century by political ideas and the lust for power. More so than any other century in history, the twentieth century has been dominated by politics, and political misjudgments have meant concentration camps for millions, torture and death for millions more. Anyone who cares for freedom is obligated to defend it, and so during the last third of this century I have fallen in with some of the major participants in the era's political debates. My associates were for the most part conservatives, for I have found them to be freedom's most reliable defenders.

In earlier books I directed fire toward those whom I did not personally know: the Liberals, so-called. In this book I am talking about the behavior of people I know well: the conservatives, so-called. The terms have been sorely abused by sophists, so much so that if a reader lacks the knowledge to distinguish a conservative from a Liberal in America I am not sure I can provide much illumination except to say that a Liberal generally trusts the state as an instrument for almost any good purpose and the conservative—certainly if in pristine condition—is allergic to the government as an instrument for almost any good purpose.

At any rate, having written earlier books belaboring Liberal error and now this monograph on conservatism, I suppose it is going to be pretty hard to get anyone to turn out for my book party. My early books analyzed behavior and ideas. This, too, is a book of political analysis, but it is also a narrative. I was with the conservatives as they emerged from the pages of a few intellectual reviews; from various think tanks, law offices, and college faculties; from remote congressional districts and from the governor's office of California. Over the years they transformed themselves from sour adherents of what Clinton Rossiter once called "the thankless persuasion" to the dominant political critics of the 1970s. Perhaps by 1979 we had indeed arrived at what Luigi called conservatives' moment in history. Luigi had studied history, written journalism, and for a while practiced politics. He appraised contemporary politics with an historian's eye. In fact, to me he was a kind of exemplar as were his politics; but whereas his nineteenth-century liberalism with its ardor for liberty and reason was still defunct in Italy, it was poised for a revival in America.

AS BEFORE, THE JOURNEY to Luigi's had begun at the top of the Spanish Steps with the delicate business of engaging an Italian taxi driver. First I had to impress on him that I knew all the streets of Rome and every alleyway—so no unnecessary excursions. Second, that I knew the currency as well as the Pope's banker—so correct change or no tip. Finally, that a war wound made sexual congress unfeasible; his good offices with the town's trollops could be saved for the next visiting dignitary. Our contract having been agreed upon, we squalled out the Via del Babuino, into the swirl of the Piazza del Popolo, out the Via Flaminia, and eventually past a relic from my youth, the pool built for the 1960 Olympics.

It was in that Olympiad that I would have vanquished the world's fastest 200-meter breaststrokers were it not for the sad fact that some twenty American breaststrokers had slipped past me in the summer's National AAU Outdoor Championships. The 1960 Olympic team did include several swimmers whom I was destined to team up with a year later when I entered Indiana University; and one, Al Somers, would be with me in most of the political revelry that lay ahead. In 1960, Al briefly dominated the sports news by demonstrating a fundamental conservative principle, to wit: innovation is usually the work of crackpots or charlatans and should be greeted with extreme hostility. The Olympics had been politicized in the past by Nazis and Communists; Al's austere demonstration was probably the only time true conservatism ever insinuated itself into the Olympic Games. Not surprisingly, eight years later he was writing music reviews for the magazine I was to found. He remains a member of its board of directors. His skepticism is a salient trait of the true conservative.

What Al did in the 1960 Olympics was this: he refused to shave any hair from his body that was not on his face. Glassy-eyed progressives had convinced Olympic coach Gus Stager that if one shaved one's body comprehensively from crown to heel one's body would cut through the water like a knife. Stager was an excellent coach and a very amiable gentleman, but his credulity was unfortunate. When I had swum for him the summer before, I—though a mere child—had had no difficulty whatsoever in convincing him that deafness prevented me from participating in 1,500-meter heats. Those were grueling exercises, and when he called us for them I would miss out every time, by simply falling fast asleep on a diving platform 10 meters above the pool deck, the glorious sun shining above me, Gus hollering somewhere below. He grew so concerned about my condition that he eventually sent me off for hearing tests. Thus I missed still more of his grueling workouts. Of course, I also missed the Olympic team, but the point is that Gus was as trusting as a Cub Scout.

Now humbugs had convinced him to reject what puberty had ordained; and Al, citing science and right reason, led the forces of reaction against the ignominy of the Total Shave. He made headlines on sports pages around the world with his protest, and he made headlines again in the preliminary heats of the 400-meter freestyle when he broke the Olympic record and stood athwart history triumphant. Alas, as the slave reminds the Roman general, all fame is fleeting; and in the finals five clean-shaven racing machines stroked effortlessly past Al's soggy, sinking body. He argues to this day that body hair cannot possibly affect a swimmer's performance. That all swimmers now shave everything but their eyebrows has no impact on his fierce argumentation whatsoever. We conservatives recognize that the burden of proof always rests with the innovator—and for a very long time.

But back to that other exemplary conservative, Luigi Barzini. Once we had driven past the pool of my unfulfilled youth, we crossed an astonishing bridge whose garishness, so vulgar and bizarre, would not be tolerated today even in Hollywood, California. The bridge, Ponte Flaminio, is as gaudy as a sheik's seraglio and as much of a ruin as the sheik's quarters will someday be—sooner rather than later if the feminist fevers reach his contented ladies. Pillars rise from it, but they hold nothing up. Odd lumps of stone are scattered about, steps ascend to nowhere but blue sky, and there appear to be pedestals—though they exalt only empty space. There are massive eagles with chipped wings, pathetic fountains, and oppressive links of wrought-iron chain. All, save this chain, is of a ponderous and especially stupid local stone called *travertino*; no steel can be seen anywhere in support of this monstrosity. The bridge was designed by a Fascist architect in the 1920s but not built until after the war, sometime in the 1950s. For some reason the bourgeois who had ultimately beaten the Fascists lacked the heart to prevent this pompous vulgarity from spanning the Tiber, though perhaps this is not so surprising. In Europe traces of evil endure through all the generations of virtuous erasures. The same holds true in America, of course, though in America there have been fewer erasures and fewer traces of evil, America being younger by almost a hundred generations.

A few miles past Ponte Flaminio, a solitary stone pillar, erect since Roman times, decays before a stand of laurel trees and thick bushes. Behind these verdant walls, on a foothill of seven acres, half of which had long been canopied by ancient cypresses, Luigi built his home. He built it in 1948, having acquired the land for a song thanks to the turbulent forces of history and to one of turbulence's faithful twentieth century accessories, il Partito Comunista Italiano. The Cold War was upon Europe. Alarmed by the Berlin blockade, Europeans anxiously anticipated the beginning of World War III. In Italy the Communist party appeared poised to take over the country. It had a militant constituency, was disciplined in the Stalinist mold, and maintained shadow military formations armed with vast stores obtained during the war. Vivid memories of the recent past's bully-boy politics spurred Italy's propertied classes to unload their immovable property for gold, and Luigi was ready to buy. In the American journal *Foreign Affairs* he had read George Kennan's 1947 Mr. X assessment of Soviet ambitions and concluded that World War III was unlikely.

Luigi had wanted to be able to see the rooftops of Rome from his rural retreat and so he only moved seven or eight miles out this old consular road, which for more than 2,000 years had linked Rome with the North. In the late 1940s his rural serenity was secure, the old roadway being traveled only by an occasional herd of sheep or a caravan of mules. Since the late 1940s, however, Rome's population had doubled, and along the Via Cassia the urban clamor of traffic, apartment houses, and shopping centers steadily advanced towards the house he had built for his children, a comfortable villa after the manner of a Campagna farmhouse. Modernity rattled along the old road a few hundred yards from his front door. Housing developments and their noisy inhabitants accosted him on the left and on the right, but the glaciers and volcanoes that had creased and cracked the Italian boot millions of years before had left a lovely valley behind and below his lands, a little stream for his children to swim in, and an unob-structed view of Rome. The valley was green all winter, and free of urban contamination. The land across the valley had been owned for centuries by the Ospedale di Santo Spirito. It would not be sold. Thus nature and the Church, two of Italy's most venerable institutions, were cooperating to ensure that from his garden Luigi would see the same view of rolling lands and distant Rome that centurions returning from the north had seen centuries before. For Luigi that element of timelessness was a digitalis to his imagination.

Postwar urban sprawl, then, would not deny him his country life, though what in the 1940s had been a ten-minute drive to the center of Rome was now an hour-long ordeal. The reason Luigi had wanted to live close to Rome was that he wanted easy access to the drama of politics and to the amenities of a great city. Yet he wanted his home to remain a country house, abundant with the earthy delights that he loved: orchards and gardens exuberant with flowers, fruits, herbs, and vegetables. The land even provided him with olive oil and a serviceable wine.

Although he had not known it at the time, Luigi had built his home on old Roman grounds. The pillar in front of his house was the remnant of a Roman monument and apparently there had been villas in the region, for soon after Luigi moved in his children discovered the ruins of a Roman house with a mosaic floor, coins, and a Roman head without a nose. Contrary to Dr. Marx's ludicrous observation, it is part of man's nature to be acquisitive. Humans since the dawn of time have been amassing private property, and so energetic are they in their acquisitiveness that remnants of their possessions remain long after their own extinction. Rome is one of the world's oldest refuse heaps; hence today's Romans are not surprised to turn up imperial pottery and other debris while spading their gardens. Luigi displayed his noseless head in a pond. After a year or so, the head was pinched and now, perhaps, has become the proud possession of a New Jersey furrier or a newly made entrepreneur in Riyadh. All over the world antiquity's knickknacks flow into the hands of the affluent, brought to them by thieves. Triflings that would have been discarded by Caesar's stable boy now appear under glass cases in Beverly Hills or on mantels illuminated by recessed lights. Their celebrated owners pose proudly in front of them, a fashion designer with a shard of ancient bedpan over his right shoulder, a real estate tycoon beaming with two fragments of Mesopotamian junk on either side of his skull.

Luigi had been born in Italy but his curiosity about the future of *Homo sapiens* and his enthusiasm for liberty kindled in him a fascination with America. He always had high hopes for it. When he died, late in the winter of 1984, a friend going through his books noticed that in Thoreau's essay "Walking" Luigi had marked the lines: "My needle is slow to settle, but it always settles between west and south-southwest. The future lies that way to me, and the earth seems more unexhausted and richer on that side. . . . Eastward I go only by force; but westward I go free." Those were

Luigi's thoughts, too, at least since the 1920s when his father, Italy's greatest journalist, brought the family to New York, where he endeavored to establish a newspaper for the Italian-American community. In fact, Luigi's first bout of higher education began at Columbia Journalism School where so many journalists have ended their educations forever.

Luigi's education continued throughout his life. Even on his deathbed the curious Barzini surely learned something. His rule was to read six hours a day whether those around him approved or not. He maintained a spacious, panelled library with ladders to the topmost bookshelves. History, biography, political thought, the lesser humanities, all such books could be found by his reading chair, along with the finest intellectual reviews of the West. What he did not learn from books he learned from experience.

He was an inveterate traveler. In his last year, stooped by age and an ominous cough, he inveigled an invitation to faraway Bloomington, Indiana, where he took his usual anthropological soundings. Behind a facade of cosmopolitan badinage he collected samplings of the Americanos' progress. He never had a chance to put this information to use.

That cough of his was the growl of a cancer that would soon kill him with merciful suddenness. I suspect he knew what the cough portended and measured out his last year or so always with the intention of savoring life and putting off the quacks until he had come to such a pass that their intrusion into his pleasant life would be brief. Returning from the American Midwest in 1983 he reported that America was a little shabbier but getting over the problems of the 1970s. Then he fell ill. Three months later he died at home, but a month before his death he was delighted to receive a get-well message from the president of the United States. Through most of his life Luigi was more honored in America than in Italy. That message from Ronald Reagan was not matched by greetings from Italian statesmen. But then Luigi had told the truth as he perceived it about both countries, and the American capacity for self-criticism is not shared by other peoples.

Unlike any contemporary journalist I know of, Luigi had made systematic studies in various disciplines, though he was curiously uninterested in undertaking a disciplined study of art, and music totally eluded him. He had a style, however. Cyril Connolly esteemed him one of the finest stylists of English in this century; the style was wry, earthy, learned, and elegant. It inhered throughout his thought as well as his prose. Drawing on a well-stocked sense of the past, he grandly faced the future and with panache. For him the future was to the west. He was a good friend of America, which is not to say that he let us off easy.

Americans are well aware of Europe's anti-American intellectuals, but there are also European intellectuals who are fascinated by us, admiring our devotion to liberty, our energy, our optimism. They are all basically nineteenth-century liberals who survived into the twentieth century and who recognize America's sense of tolerance, its pursuit of excellence, its absorption with justice, its touching belief in progress. Certainly Luigi has to be numbered among these pro-American Europeans. They recognize America's embarrassing proclivity for excess, but they also recognize that America remains the heir to the best of the nineteenth century's promise.

My discussion of the American conservative movement begins in Europe with Luigi because his values were pretty much the values of American conservatism and because he had two great gifts. If more American conservatives had possessed these gifts their moment in history would have endured for years, untroubled by the uncertainties of the late 1980s. Those gifts are imagination and a sense of drama.

My "MOMENT IN HISTORY"? Luigi was a member of the Partito Liberale Italiano. He had served for some years in the Italian Chamber of Deputies. As a self-conscious nineteenth-century liberal, he watched the steady *reductio ad absurdum* of one species of that point of view in America, the Democratic Liberals, and the rise of another species of it, the Republican conservatives. Now, in the summer of 1979, he knew that the Republicans were almost certain to win the next election. Owing to American Liberalism's collapse into so many futile enthusiasms, America's conservatives were about to be presented with their first opportunity to have an historic influence on the polity. Fifteen years after the catastrophic defeat of Barry Goldwater, his political heir, Ronald Reagan, was on the threshold of the presidency. For the same reason that he had anticipated peace in the late 1940s, Luigi now anticipated the conservative victory. He had not restricted his reading to the usual socially approved intellectual stuff. He read everything he could get his hands on about America, and so he knew more about the coming election than almost any European journalist—or, for that matter, almost any American journalist. The Europeans were really in the dark.

The truth about America travels across the Atlantic about as well as Corton-Charlemagne. Of course, those Americans who consume Corton-Charlemagne hope they are getting a good bottle. Europeans who consume news about America do not particularly care about its quality, so long as it keeps them stewed. The problem originates with the Europeans. America alarms them. It is too harum-scarum. Things move too fast here, and so many a European journalist takes refuge from America's perplexing inquietudes by retreating into a well-sozzled fantasy world of reassuring falsehoods and shared prejudices. In the European journalists' drunken vision of America the great Republic is a fabulous realm of crassitude, material excess, and dunce piety. Reporting accurately on the ever-changing American scene demands too much of average European journalists, some of whom are amazingly indolent and timid. They look for the most dismal news from America and gladly pass on their hallucination: an America whose excesses never change. The jokes about cowboys and tycoons ceaselessly amuse them. Many American journalists share this vision and diligently reinforce it. Consequently familiar prejudices and falsehoods are transported back and forth across the Atlantic. Only the accents are different.

But the America beheld by these besotted scriveners does not actually exist. It is a delusion. In 1979, happily socked away in that delusion, the European journalists whom I encountered were convinced that Ronald Reagan was a second-rate actor without a chance against the incumbent bungler, Jimmy Carter. Think of it! The economy was a disaster. The misery index combining inflation and unemployment rates was above 20%. Domestically the Carter Administration's accomplishments registered negligible to ruinous. Its foreign policy was downright dangerous, especially for those carrying American passports. Soon the polls would prove what logical deduction already suggested, to wit, the American electorate was at the limits of its patience with late 1970s Liberalism. Ronald Reagan's honeyed phrases did not win conservatism the 1980 election. To understand the change of administrations about to take place, one must recognize a time-honored truth: in America an election is the incumbent's to lose. By 1979 all indicators revealed that the incumbent was going down fast. Liberalism had cracked up. American conservatism was coming to power by default. I had little doubt that conservative policies would work. I only wondered about the competence of our conservatives.

The imminence of the conservative ascendancy had no place in the delusory vision of Europe's Americanologists. Before arriving at Luigi's I had stopped off in London, and Alexander Chancellor, then the editor of the British *Spectator*, laid on a splendid lunch with some of his cleverest writers. Neither when sober nor once squiffed could the assembled conceive of the possibility of the forthcoming Reagan presidency. It was the same throughout Europe—the news of America passing back and forth across the Atlantic was thoroughly contaminated by prejudice.

Only in a few Paris ateliers had the truth penetrated that American Liberalism had run amuck, transforming itself into the Liberalism of the New Age and thereupon parting company with the voters. Whether owing to serious reflection or French nationalism, the French had become weary of Marxism's false prophecies and alarmed by the Red Army to their east. They took Solzhenitsyn's chronicles of the Gulag more seriously than did most Europeans. Raymond Aron and Jean-Francois Revel's eviscerations of Marxist bibblebabble shook a generation of French intellectuals into undertaking a defense of liberty. In France the drunken certitudes of Western journalism had limited appeal. Still, intellectuals in other European countries preferred the dark. At the end of the 1970s they would rather remain ignorant of the approach of American conservatism. Think of it! Jimmy Carter had brought the American economy to the mortician's door. His foreign policy had made the United States the butt of derision worldwide. His was a hopeless presidency. Still, pundits in both Europe and America considered the election of the conservative opposition unlikely.

Luigi knew better. That night in Rome he was eager to discuss what the change would mean for America. During the past decade I had grown to intellectual maturity with the American conservative movement; Luigi knew that and wanted to compare notes. Had he not returned to Italy after studying at Columbia our conservative movement might have been his movement too. Ever since 1957 when he favorably appraised an ambitious analysis of modern society, *The Fabric of Society*, written by one of the early members of the American conservative movement, Ernest van den Haag, he had kept an eye on American conservatives. Yet he was coy about his commitment. He understood another fundamental of the American scene, namely, Liberalism's sway over the culture, and he recognized how dangerous the cultural monopoly could be. In Italy, where his espousal of individualism and of cool reason had made him as unsavory to the bovine intelligentsia as such dangerous enthusiasms were to make William F. Buckley, Jr. over here, his independence had cost him dearly. The culture of Italy's intelligentsia was conformist left, and years before, when the proprietor of *Il Messaggero* attempted to make Luigi the paper's editor, mutiny in the newsroom denied him the job.

Thus he knew something American conservatives had yet to learn, namely, that politics is waged in the culture as well as at the polls. Unless a political point of view gains influence in the culture of a country, victory at the polls and control of government remain provisional.

Luigi had a sufficiently broad acquaintance with America's large number of Liberals and small number of conservatives to recognize that the Liberal Crack-Up was here, but could a Conservative Crack-Up lie ahead? Our ideas were sound and certain to be therapeutic. But what about our fellow conservatives? Did they have Luigi's imagination and sense of drama? Could they influence the culture? These were the questions to be discussed that evening with Luigi, but as the wine flowed we got sidetracked onto other earthier matters. I wish I had pursued my questions with him that night at the onset of the conservatives' moment. After dinner I left Luigi's house on the Via Cassia full of hope and Pinot Grigio. As my yellow Fiat taxi began the ride back to Rome, it beamed a tunnel of light through the haze over Luigi's long driveway. Twenty-five yards ahead two glistening eyes bounded into view, stared at us, and bounded on into the dark. What sort of omen was this? On the night the *onorevole* Barzini announced conservatism's moment in history a Roman fox crossed my path.

CHAPTER 2

The Conservatives' Revolt
Up from Rooseveltism

"IF YOU DISAGREE WITH an American intellectual," Jacques Barzun has noted, "it *disturbs* him." Doubtless we have all experienced our painful moments with disturbed intellectuals. In America intellectuals on the left and the right share an insecurity that easily moves them to a dispendious wrath.

Though enjoying palmy days immediately after World War II, Liberals could never rest easy that the marvels of the New Deal and of progressive education might not someday be demolished by the agents of the National Manufacturers Association or by insurrectionary movements from within the bourgeois tribes of the suburbs. When organized protests against the Liberals' orthodoxy did appear in the 1940s, the Liberals' indignation was colossal. The protestors, who soon united into what was called "the conservative revival" and later "the conservative movement," were met with rhetorical violence of an almost incomparable ferocity by Liberals who, though aware of the concept of a loyal opposition, could never get the hang of its praxis. One of the enduring constants of American political life during the twentieth century's last five decades has been the stupendous indignation that American conservatism triggers among Liberal humanitarians. Since their initial outbursts the Liberals have never calmed down or even paused to adjust their terms of abuse to changing times—as my persistent citations will demonstrate.

This ideological violence that America's Liberals bring down on conservatives and that conservatives are quick to reciprocate is one of the amazing aspects of American life. Back in the Old World, say in Paris, the leftist whose roots trace to the fall of the Bastille and the rightist whose roots trace even further back, having caused him perhaps to lose a few ancestors after the Bastille's fall, might both wonder why the two groups of Yankee republicans seemed to hate each other so. By European standards they had much in common, little to quarrel over, and only an insignificant record of blood feuds. Nonetheless, after 1945 hostilities between conservatives and Liberals intensified and, magnified by the insecurity that Barzun describes, endured.

The "conservative revival" or "movement" began at the end of World War II after certain disparate ideas took to the air, pollinating in the minds of those no longer comfortable with New Deal Liberalism. In 1945 most New Dealers were very satisfied with the world. They had saved it from Nazism and Fascism. They were establishing a world government insulated from the errors of the old League of Nations. They were going to banish colonialism and rationalize American society. Only a few, such as Dean Acheson and George F. Kennan, glimpsed the dangers ahead.

Those who would eventually be categorized as "movement conservatives" were not in such a celebratory frame of mind. Drawn from various sectors of society by various concerns, they were worried: some over the drift of government and the economy, others over developing social arrangements, and still others over the huge Communist tyranny bestriding Eastern Europe and Asia. There were, then, three groups that eventually coalesced into the conservative movement: the libertarians, the traditionalists, and the anticommunists. Members of the first group were devoted to personal liberty and to free enterprise. Members of the second were devoted to traditional Western values. And members of the third group saw Communism as a threat to world peace and to Western civilization as cataclysmic as Nazism.

All three elements had existed in the United States in both political parties throughout most of the twentieth century. But now ideas summoned them to action. Generally the ideas could be found in recently published books, few of which ever summoned their readers to sustained political action, and this I take to be another reason for the original conservatives' maladroitness at the political arts. Politics was not encouraged by the movement's political masters.

The libertarians were roused by the publication in the spring of 1945 of *The Road to Serfdom* by Friedrich Hayek, an Austrian economist who astonished Liberals with his thesis that the planned society ends in dictatorship. In the 1940s the Liberals had great hope for planning at all levels of society, but Hayek argued that "the direction of economic activity" inevitably demands "suppression of freedom." And lest Liberals miss his drift, Hayek went on to argue that "the rise of fascism and Nazism was not a reaction against the socialist trends of the preceding period but a necessary outcome of those tendencies."[1] Hayek's sense of politics was rather high-flown, but at least he allowed for its usefulness. Other advocates of classical economics who joined Hayek in his critique of collectivism were less sanguine about the political impulse, most notably an American essayist, Albert Jay Nock.

Nock's *Memoirs of a Superfluous Man* stressed anti-statism, educational traditionalism, and a disdain for the masses—views very congenial to many Americans after the War. In the 1950s these Nockian values fetched many of those who were beginning to see themselves as members of a conservative movement intent on political action. His writings bridged the gulf between anti-statist economists and many advocates of traditional American values. He appealed to them and to all non-leftists then in revolt against Liberalism with his notion that they might comprise a "saving Remnant." Aside from members of the Remnant, all were beyond hope. The idea was a fine euphoriant to one's self-esteem, but in a democratic society the concept was bound to dampen one's ardor for political action. If the majority was beyond hope, it surely was beyond for political influence unless one had access to a private army, which was out of the question even for wealthy conservatives. From its earliest days, then, the conservative movement's capacity for political action was handicapped by some of the same sages who had galvanized it. Consider Richard Weaver.

Though only an obscure University of Chicago professor, he was another formative influence on traditionalist conservatives. His 1948 book, *Ideas Have Consequences*, became a revered text for generations of movement conservatives. In it he remonstrated against "the dissolution of the West," which he believed was the natural consequence of the West's abandonment of transcendental values or "universals" and of its cordiality toward relativism. Weaver stimulated a sense of urgency in all three conservative groups; though when he extolled immutable principle, hierarchy, and restraint, he surely lost a few libertarians, and provoked Liberals to one of their first displays of white-hot indignation against conservatism. In fact, Weaver's work inspired Liberals to condemn conservatives as authoritarian, a false charge that, but one they were to level against conservatives for decades.

In the aftermath of World War II Liberals were habitually condemning opponents on their right as authoritarians, usually with no more justification than was provided by the writing of Weaver. His idealized world of moral absolutes, if unleavened by tolerance, might indeed lead to authoritarianism, but so too might the Liberal's pragmatic, secular world of moral relativism. Both conservatives and Liberals are capable of an obsessive pursuit of the ideal that tramples individual rights. To be sure, Weaver's theocrat is potentially a threat to human freedom, but so is the president of Stanford University. Of course, decades after Weaver's book we have yet to see his right-wing theocrat come to power in America. At Stanford a Liberal regime of Virtue imposes "politically correct" values on students, banishes unwelcome dissent, and throughout the 1980s politicized college curricula to the point where many of the great minds of Western civilization were exiled because they were white and male.

The harmful side effect of Weaver on conservatism was not his encouragement of authoritarianism but his encouragement of a sense of political futility similar to that inhering in Nock. If, as Weaver was to assert, "the dissolution of the West" began in the late fourteenth century when Western man made the "evil decision" to accept the nominalism propounded by William of Occam (d. c. 1349), what the hell could be done about it? And note that reference to old Occam: both Weaver and Nock encouraged a quirkiness among conservatives that made them occasionally quite unreliable. Following Weaver, generations of conservative pedants gave Occam a bum rap, presenting him as the Eleanor Roosevelt of the fourteenth century when in point of fact he was one of those thinkers who opened the way for modern science. Weaver's dismal scholarship had its virtues. He directed his readers to important things, the nature of man, the quality of men's souls; but the bad news is that his writing was more likely to move his readers to political despair than to enthusiastic, back-slapping political action.

The pessimism of Nock and Weaver could also be found in the somber humors of the third group contributing to conservatism after the war, the anticommunists. They feared that Liberalism was insufficiently tough-minded in its opposition to Communism and frequently they despaired of ever seeing red flags hauled down in the East. The evaporation of Communism in 1989 and thereafter was beyond their imaginations. Alarmed by Communist espionage at home* and subversion abroad, the anticommunists frequently went off on pessimism binges. Surely the works of

---

*Espionage that has now been verified by Soviet sources, for instance, *Khrushchev Remembers: The Glasnost Tapes* (Boston: Little Brown, 1990).

Weaver and Nock could only encourage the anticommunists' sense of imminent catastrophe as they contemplated a Cold War that could very easily be lost, thrusting Western civilization into the past forever.

Most of the leading anticommunists had themselves experimented with Marxist potions in the 1930s and 1940s. The career of James Burnham was typical. He became a major anticommunist theoretician only after dabbling in Trotskyism. The 1939 Nazi-Soviet pact, however, disabused him of the hope that the Soviet Union was going to become a progressive "workers' state," and in time he came to the position that the Soviet Union was essentially "exploitive and imperialist." He urged the West to resist it. In an outpouring of lucid books and essays Burnham criticized Liberal foreign policy vis-à-vis the Soviet Union while making the conservatives' case for worldwide resistance to communism. His writing was learned, realistic, and comparatively hopeful. Unfortunately he was not the most popular of the anticommunist conservatives.

That title went to another former Communist, Whittaker Chambers. Once a senior editor of *Time*, Chambers became the man chiefly responsible for exposing Alger Hiss, thus beginning one of the most bizarre controversies in American history, the Hiss case, that decades-long debate over what Hiss, a well-connected State Department bureaucrat, was up to in the 1930s and 1940s when some intolerably stupid upper-class American humanitarians moonlighted for Stalin. Chambers insisted that he had known Hiss as a fellow Communist in the 1930s. Hiss magisterially denied the charge, sued Chambers for slander, was eventually convicted of perjury, and jailed. Hiss protested his innocence forevermore, though he never came up with sufficient exculpating evidence to win his case in court and the best scholarship found him guilty as charged.* Somehow Liberals transformed Hiss into a legend, another mythic victim of American civilization as worthy of their sympathy as the Plains Indian, the whooping crane, and the California redwoods.

Chambers, an elegant albeit melodramatic writer, wrote an 800-page book—part autobiography, part anticommunist polemic, and part chronicle of his engagement with Hiss. Its popularity among conservatives was instant and enduring. To him, the West was engaged in an epic struggle for survival. Published in 1952, *Witness* outlined the full catastrophe, arguing that modern society could only escape the totalitarian boot if it

---

*The charges received fresh substantiation from the Soviet side with the publication of *KGB: The Inside Story of Its Operation from Lenin to Gorbachev*, by Christopher Andrew and Oleg A. Gordievsky (New York: HarperCollins, 1990).

chose God over man and recognized that secular, pragmatic Liberalism was but a way station on the road to Communism. Once again a seminal conservative tome groaned with heavy themes of pessimism, and its recommendation of prayer over politics was but another impediment to conservative action.

Chambers was himself so fastidious about his participation in politics that, notwithstanding his alarm over Communism, he was only a sporadic supporter of those anticommunists who in the 1950s gathered behind William F. Buckley, Jr.'s *National Review.* As for Senator Joseph McCarthy's campaign to ferret out subversives in government, it horrified him. Most anticommunists sided with McCarthy, and here was one of the first fissures in the "conservative revival," for, notwithstanding their abhorrence of Communism, most of Hayek's advocates of the free society opposed barring Communists from government and the universities, a policy many anticommunists favored.

During the 1950s more divisions developed in the movement. Frank S. Meyer, an influential editor of *National Review* and an ex-Communist, became a libertarian and began to deprecate traditionalists for lacking "clear and distinct principle." Russell Kirk, a leading traditionalist whose 1953 book *The Conservative Mind* became a best-seller, responded that libertarian principles were mere "abstractions" unsupported by history or experience.[2]

Conflicts like this became a preoccupation with conservatives, who occasionally displayed more relish for sectarian debate than for taking on the Liberals whose errancies had originally sparked their ardor. In fact, there were times in the 1950s and 1960s when the right's doctrinal quarreling grew so intense that peace-loving spectators wondered if this ideological hairsplitting was actually a dodge to avoid serious political action. The debates frequently were over such extreme questions that they might not become issues in American politics for decades, if ever. Libertarians argued that highways ought to be sold to private corporations. Traditionalists argued for reforms in education that would revive the curriculum of the medieval monastery. Some Catholic traditionalists led by L. Brent Bozell argued that the true conservative position was to reform the American Republic into a theocracy consistent with the fantasies of some revered Spanish monk of a distant century.

The whole 1960s conservative establishment, viewed in the light of historical perspective, reminds me of nothing so much as the Austro-Hungarian Empire in its final agonies, not a very promising model on which to launch a political movement. The old Empire had been in a boil of querulousness from its earliest days when its founders had such names as Frederick the Warlike and Henry the Quarrelsome. Centuries later the quarrelling had become terminal and the Empire collapsed into a pother of brawls: the Czechs against the Slovaks, the Croats against the Serbs, and the Magyars forever in a stew. Monarchists gouged the middle class. The Church clamped down on the liberals. And the socialists heaved against all the above. How long could American conservatism avoid such an ignominious end?

By the 1960s the American conservatives were riven by strife, and lest their own predisposition for feuding prove insufficient they had imported anticommunist emigrés from Eastern Europe whose talents for weird sectarian skirmishes were legendary. The American conservatives attracted hundreds, perhaps thousands, of former inhabitants of the old Austro-Hungarian Empire, including real Austrians: the formidable Hayek, Ludwig von Mises, and even Otto von Hapsburg himself, the pretender to the Austrian throne. The would-be emperor wrote for *National Review*, causing something of a public relations problem. At the time two of Liberalism's favorite complaints against the conservatives were that they were un-American and smitten by monarchism. In fact, Arthur Schlesinger, inspired by the conservatives' admiration of Edmund Burke's organic order, accused conservatives of yearning for "the ethical afterglow of feudalism," and being irrelevant to the "non-feudal, non-aristocratic, dynamic, progressive business society of the United States."[3] Imagine, here was a man who dreamed in public of Rooseveltian dynasties and of Kennedys as romantic as King Arthur and his knights. Think of it; Professor Schlesinger was accusing others of archaicism.

Not that conservatives did not embrace the quaint and the ridiculous at times, but they had their charm. Arthur should have met one of the conservatives' most amusing Austrians, an odd old bird from the Tyrol named Erik von Kuehnelt-Leddihn. He wrote for conservative periodicals and made annual lecture tours to America. Tall, courtly, and Old World, he had a habit of folding his pink hands over the hull of his stomach and patting it contentedly while retailing the immensities of the conservative canon to rapt audiences filled with dimwits. Without protest he saw himself billed as "the world's greatest authority," and few who actually survived one of his hypnagogic lectures ever complained. Supposedly he spoke eight languages, thus allowing him in scores of countries to order breakfast in bed. Doubtless he was another of poor Occam's critics. Erik was a curiosity, and in the early days there were so many others that a perfectly sensible reason for joining the movement was its immense entertainment value.

I can remember spending many happy times observing the arrivals and departures of college boys with monocles, walking sticks, capes. They always livened up receptions and dinners, to say nothing of seminars and street demonstrations. I remember one fellow whom I found particularly amusing. He was an inveterate user of snuff, which he delicately picked from ornate little boxes and jammed into his soiled nostrils, whereupon he would sneeze uncontrollably into a filthy handkerchief. I dreaded his presence at dinner parties and prayed that he would be seated next to some hypochondriac other than me. There were libertarians with huge bronze dollar-sign medallions hanging from their necks and dozens, possibly hundreds, of pretentious Anglophiles imitating Winston Churchill. Occasionally one encountered an epigonous Lord Byron. I cannot actually report having spotted a young squire wearing a powdered wig, but doubtless there will come a day. Every few years a new conservative prodigy would pop up and be the honored guest at a conservative assemblage, then he would disappear, never to be seen again. It happened all the time. I could never understand their rise, so I could never understand their fall.

I recall one who cast a large shadow at the movement's yearly conference of conservative intellectuals, the Philadelphia Society. Of a sudden he was before us at the speaker's dais, learnedly explicating modern political philosophy. He spoke well, and had arresting points to make about freedom and order. More to the point, he had orange hands! This was no genetic accident. He had striven diligently to acquire orange hands! He was another American health-food adept, and had become a disciple of the salubrious carrot. Some charlatan whose name and theories time has forgotten had sold him on *Daucus carota* as the key to longevity and vigor. The key was to consume carrots, tremendous quantities of carrots, and one knew one had consumed enough if one's hands attained the full color of a jack-o'-lantern. This he accomplished through disgusting daily menus of carrot juice, carrot pâté, carrot cake, and so on. There I was with a man who at one instant had been holding forth thoughtfully on *The Federalist Papers* and who later over drinks demonstrated quite convincingly that he was a genuine nutcase, with the table manners of Bugs Bunny.

The whole temperamental assemblage of brilliance and mediocrity, individualism and pedantry, sages and misfits, caused stupendous alarm amongst Liberals in the 1950s. As I have mentioned earlier, the Liberals' indignation could not possibly have been caused by the abyss between their values and those of the conservatives. The abyss was not that wide. As the historian Daniel Boorstin has noted, both sides admired the Constitution and the values of the founding fathers. Both the conservative anticommunists and the Liberals abhorred Communism. All they disagreed on was *how* to oppose it. Both libertarians and Liberals shared the fundamental political principle of freedom. Both traditionalists and Liberals were advocates of the same great tradition of Western thought. Over the nature of man a serious disagreement could be posited, with Liberals subscribing to a sunny view of man's nature and conservatives subscribing to a more inclement view. Yet even here the division did not always hold. Not all Liberals were so optimistic about mankind's nature; some conservatives were. Anyway, America has never really been the kind of country where the citizenry differs over an issue as divisive as man's nature.

What triggered the Liberals' outrage was not a conflict in values. It was the inherent insecurity of the American intellectual coupled with a quirk not wholly confined to the Liberals but still quite rare among true sophisticates. As Liberalism aged it developed a passion for sameness. To veer from the Liberal position on almost any issue or value invites endless exhortations to rethink that issue or value. If in the postwar decade one did not share the Liberal position on sex education, arms control, the environment, or dozens of other matters, it was, the Liberal always explained, because of one's insufficient understanding; and so the Liberals were always engaged in educating dubious nonconformists to their enlightened positions. Remember the peace movement of the early 1980s? It was typical of so many progressive campaigns. One of its fundamental beliefs was that those who disagreed with the movement were ignorant and in need of "education." This was actually a somewhat magnanimous response. Earlier Liberals often accused those who dissented from Liberalism of insanity, as we shall see.

In the 1940s and early 1950s the three currents of conservatism grew, each propelled by its particular concerns, all united by the insight that Liberalism was drifting away from its historic concern for personal liberty, individual responsibility, and an internationalist role for the United States. But the conservatives needed a communications center to allow them to coalesce into an enduring movement. That communications center was provided in 1955 by William F. Buckley, Jr., when he founded *National Review*, his meticulously edited, immensely engaging fortnightly. *National Review* united the three currents of conservatism. In the words of George Nash, the most knowledgeable and judicious historian of modern conservatism, "if *National Review* (or something like it) had not been founded, there would probably have been no cohesive intellectual force on the Right in the 1960s and 1970s. To a very substantial degree, the history of reflective conservatism in America after 1955 is the history of the individuals who collaborated in [*National Review*]."⁴ Presently the conservative movement established other institutions—endowed chairs at major universities, think tanks such as the American Enterprise Institute, and student organizations such as the Intercollegiate Studies Institute and Young Americans for Freedom. By the early 1960s all the institutions were in place for the establishment of a conservative counterculture to oppose the Liberal culture; and over the next two decades that counterculture grew, attracting more adherents, more think tanks, more publications, more politicians and more voters.

Despite the fact that the conservative counterculture remained small in comparison to the Liberal culture and despite the odd behavior of some of its adepts, its politicians and intellectuals proved the soundness of their beliefs. The libertarians' defense of the free market gained cogency as the planned society—once an essential of Liberal dogma—revealed its bugs, the final bug being Liberal government's utter inability to enforce any plan opposed by some constituent of the New Age, say militant blacks or Hispanics. Conservatism's anticommunism was vindicated as the brutality of Communism was exposed, along with its singular economic imbecility. The depiction of the Gulag Archipelago presented by Alexander Solzhenitsyn became the locus classicus of Communism's cruel consequences, and the Cambodian holocaust served as a practical demonstration. After these revelations no decent person could any longer hold out hope for Dr. Marx's bulls. At the end of the 1970s even such an untutorable hind as Jimmy Carter was abjuring earlier pert remonstrances against America's "inordinate" fear of Communism. Conservatism's traditionalists were by the 1980s being validated, thanks to the pathetic results of the social engineers. The traditionalists had been alarmed by the emergence of a secular, rootless, mass society, devoid of fixed values and utterly toothless against the perverse and the inhumane. After three decades of inveterate reformers, social engineers, and mountebank therapists, the evidence of the traditionalists' good sense was all over the place: incessantly jumping out windows, dying of drug overdoses, and writhing in numerous other social pathologies.

Yet the ideological jihad begun by the indignant Liberals in the late 1940s against the conservatives never abated or, for that matter, even changed tunes. The conservatives were to grow more latitudinarian in the 1970s. The Reagan Administration left the American welfare state pretty much untouched. The right overcame such bugaboos as its alarm over foreign aid, and, throughout the 1980s as the Soviet condition evolved, its resistance to negotiating with Moscow. Still the Liberals continued to execrate the conservatives with the same curses that they had used in prior decades. Their fulminations never changed.

"Today, the politics of the radical right is the politics of frustration," Daniel Bell wrote in 1964, "—the sour impotence of those who find themselves unable to understand, let alone command, the complex mass society that is the polity today."[5] Bell said that in the same year that "the radical right" in its "sour impotence" was wresting control of the Republican Party from the Eastern Liberals who had dominated it for decades. The conservatives' candidate was nothing more discreditable than a duly elected United States Senator from Arizona, Barry Goldwater. That, however, is not how the Liberals saw things. Goldwater's colleague Senator William Fulbright swore that "Goldwater Republicanism is the closest thing in American politics to an equivalent of Russian Stalinism." The Rev. Martin Luther King, Jr., had even more unpleasant nightmares. According to him, "We see dangerous signs of Hitlerism in the Goldwater campaign." And Edmund G. Brown, governor of California, shared King's experience: "All we needed to hear [at the Republican convention] was 'Heil Hitler.'"[6] The historian Richard Hofstadter diagnosed American conservatism as "the paranoid style in American politics" and he adjudged it incurable.[7] Twenty-four years later, after nearly eight years of conservative government, all free of Ku Kluxian policy initiatives or Nazi memorabilia, Ronald Reagan handed the scepter over to George Herbert Walker Bush, and the Liberals were still sounding the same alarums. In assessing Vice President Bush's 1988 campaign, Congressman Richard Gephardt dusted off the 1964 theme of Brown and King to declare: "Hitler would have loved these people."[8] Building, perhaps, on the late Prof. Hofstadter's occult researches, the Rev. Jesse Jackson announced that Bush's campaign was "designed to create the most horrible psycho-sexual fears," and in *The New York Times*, Anthony Lewis charged the Republican campaign with "nativism," "McCarthy tactics," "lying," and being susceptible to "the extreme right"—he was referring, I kid thee not, to a *Wall Street Journal* editorial.[9]

This stupendous, enduring, changeless indignation had a very beneficial effect for the Liberals as many theologians, particularly various Islamic theologians, might have anticipated. It scared hell out of those Liberals in danger of backsliding, and it marginalized the conservatives, causing many to feel they had absolutely no role at the center of American culture. I remember an encounter I had in the early 1980s with surely one of the brightest and most capable of the conservative activists, Phyllis Schlafly, who, by the way, was prettier by far than any feminist generalissimo ever engaged in feminism's guerrilla war against sexual congress. Schlafly was fresh from her tremendous victory over the Equal Rights Amendment and should have been in high spirits. Perhaps she was, but the day of our encounter she had just read my syndicated column in the *Washington Post*, and it gave her no pleasure. In fact she considered it prima facie evidence that I was "selling out." As with other conservatives, her years of abuse from Liberals made her only a reluctant participant in the central forums of national affairs in the 1980s. At the outset of the decade I had gotten a sense of how the conservatives' small vision might hobble them when my lawyer, Bill Casey, sent me on a political mission to Europe in the summer of 1980.

Casey, who was to become a colossus in the Reagan Administration, had not always been a Reaganite conservative. His philosophical metamorphosis was illustrative of the personal political evolutions that took place as conservatism grew and Liberalism went to seed. In the aftermath of World War II, when he became active in aiding refugees from Nazism and Communism, Casey was only a moderate Republican. He had no reflexive opposition to government action and no academic conception of the free market, as was *de rigueur* with so many conservatives in the emerging movement. At one point in the 1960s he even challenged the seat of a Goldwater supporter, New York Congressman Steven Derounian. Later he became a Nixon supporter, which was still pretty Liberal by most movement conservatives' calculations. Yet as Liberalism fled its international responsibilities, such foes of totalitarianism as Casey were left to find support in the conservative camp. By the late 1970s, Bill was a Reagan supporter and in the spring of 1980 he took over the Reagan campaign. That summer he asked me to join with one of his former OSS colleagues, Bert Jolis, in lining up European intellectuals receptive to the Reagan candidacy for a series of dinners with Bill and Reagan's top foreign policy advisors.

Jolis was an international businessman, as cosmopolitan as lunch at the Ritz, which we naturally charged to Casey. Jolis and I got on easily. He handled the practical details. I corralled the intellectuals. Things went well. We set up meetings in Paris and London. Perhaps we set one up in Rome; I do not recall. But two matters I do recall presaged the problems that lay ahead for those conservatives who had been marginalized by Liberal indignation.

Before leaving for Europe we were telephoned by some movement conservatives from the Reagan campaign and given the names of their favorite European conservative intellectuals whom we were to invite to our forthcoming dinners. As it turned out, this was not going to be easy, for many now resided in cemeteries and those who were not among the deceased were among the vaguely visible, having faded to the outer reaches of European politics. At the time, the same political disturbances that in America were bringing longtime figures from the left into alliance with conservatives were having a similar effect in Europe, but the movement conservatives monitoring our trip knew nothing about this process in Europe and did not want to learn. They were not eager to become acquainted with central figures in Europe's changing constellation of intellects. Rather, for Casey's visit to Europe they wanted graves robbed and exiled rightists returned from Stromboli or wherever the hell they were then resident. Moreover they had grown suspicious that this fellow Jolis might be preparing to make some sort of power grab.

Eventually we set up the required dinners and retired from the field, leaving the ideological squabbles in Casey's capable hands. Later one of the French writers whom we had mustered, Jean-François Revel, reported his admiration for Casey and for Jeane Kirkpatrick, who accompanied him to Paris; but when it came to the lesser fish around them he was not impressed. He sensed that something was missing. For years I had a similar feeling. The original members of the conservative movement were frequently most remarkable. Intelligent, perceptive, audacious, and they were concerned about important things: the direction of historic events, human dignity, freedom, and the just society. But others, obsessed as they were with petty turf battles and so frequently flat stupid about the world around them, well, in these fellows something did indeed seem to be missing. It took me years to put my finger on it. As we shall see, it had to do with this extraordinary indignation agitating our Liberals and with the conservative temperament.

CHAPTER 3

The Idealists and Us
They Had the Dope and
We Had the Future

Wℋᴇɴ ɪɴ ᴛʜᴇ ᴍɪᴅ-1960s I entered the world of conservative politics I came as a stranger from a background so foreign to my new associates
and so intense for me that we were immediately uneasy with each other.
This unease has probably made me a keener critic of all the ideological
flutters from both ends of the spectrum, but at times it leaves me lonely.

I came to cultural politics after a youth spent not in scholarly study or
in student activities but in a swimming pool, where my teammates and I
would go through three- to six-mile workouts daily. Sending all those
calories up in smoke every day gives one a more philosophic outlook on
life. To this day I do not fully trust a man who does not end his day in a
gym. For me, in the fullness of middle age, a two- to three-hour workout
in the pool has given way to a one-hour workout on the handball court.
It beats afternoon tea as either a recreation or a stimulant, and so I greet
my evenings with relish whether they be devoted to work or to more
convivial pastimes.

The last team I swam for was my college team, Indiana University.
Participating on it gave one—dare I say it—a sense of history. In part this
was because the team made a historic mark on our sport but also because
our coach was a serious teacher and a historic figure in his own right. He
made us aware of what we were achieving in the pool, and he provoked
those of us so inclined to peer deeper into passing events. During workouts

43

he slipped in references to art, ideas, and politics, and stirred the imagination.

The fates decreed that he was to be my neighbor for a quarter of a century and close observance of his political evolution allowed me a prevenient sense of how political developments were shaping up from the 1960s through the 1980s. Doc Counsilman began as a New Deal Liberal, but Doc was one of those Liberals who recognized that time had not stopped after World War II with the dawn of Liberal triumph. In subsequent years student riots, the politicization of the university, the Vietnam War, the fragmentation of the Democratic party, and other disturbing developments moved Doc into the conservative camp. He came to admire Ronald Reagan and when he retired in 1990 President George Bush and Vice President Dan Quayle both sent the ex-Democrat letters of congratulations. I read them myself to an audience of his ex-champions including Mark Spitz and a half dozen others whose achievements were not far below Spitz's. It was a fitting scene. Doc had contributed to the world of sports, ideas, and politics. Training under him had been an excellent preparation for the ideological battles of the decades ahead.

I went to Indiana in search of world records. Unfortunately others who were more buoyant did too, yet my efforts in the pool were well compensated outside the pool. In sport one learns to train and to compete. One gains a sense of the finality of victory or defeat. Carved in stone above the entrance to the Indiana University swimming pool was the line, inexplicably inverted, from the Roman poet Juvenal, *"In Corpore Sano Mens Sana,"* or "A sound mind in a sound body." As the years drag me further out toward dotage and dust, I grow in the conviction that the Roman poet had something there. Not only does one learn from sports the value of competition, but one also learns the requirements of victory and the irrevocable nature of a defeat—no true competitor believes defeats can be erased or appealed to some higher authority. On a gayer note, through sports one picks up a swell form of recreation, allowing one to indulge in some less salubrious recreations with minimum side effects. Finally, from sport one can learn that there are in life truths that can be verified—for instance, one trains hard or one performs badly.

A background in sports is a splendid corrective for the delusions of politics and *la vie intellectuelle*, two areas of human endeavor that can revolve wholly upon fraud. An athlete cannot dupe a stopwatch. In politics and in the life of the mind one can go far on a honeyed tongue and plastic principles. Sufficiently blessed with guile, a politico or an intellectual can avoid the truth for a very long time; some of the greats have been able to drive out the truth altogether. But in sport one's efforts are submitted to a final arbiter—the stopwatch, the finish line, the left hook to the jaw—the judgments of which are pretty much indisputable.

In the early 1960s, when the conservative movement was taking shape, I was swimming six or more miles a day on a legendary athletic team, an Indiana University swimming team that held three-quarters to four-fifths of all world records in men's swimming. No Olympic team in the world was superior to our college team; and there were years in the 1960s and early 1970s when all the world's Olympic teams combined could not beat us in a dual meet. I entered the conservative movement from an athletic background in which I had never been on a team (not even a high school team) that had lost a championship or even a dual meet. On those teams all of us were accustomed to training and to winning; and we all knew precisely where we stood in national and world standings—again, thanks to the irrefutable message of the stopwatch.

The members of the conservative movement whom I came to know were frequently hard-working, and many were keen competitors, but they were usually appalling fatalists. They did not expect to win. Possibly this was because they had lost so often to the century's waves of reformers or because totalitarianism was on the march and appeared so formidable or because, as we have seen, many of their founding evangels, such as Albert Jay Nock and Richard Weaver, actually scorned politics. Whatever the reason, many were afflicted with an obstinate fatalism. They had a soft spot for the defeatist themes of Whittaker Chambers, the drift of which Russell Kirk imparts when he laments: "I am a conservative. Quite possibly I am on the losing side; often I think so. Yet out of a curious perversity I had rather lose with Socrates, let us say, than win with Lenin."[1]

Well, the hell with that! By the summer of 1961 I was beginning most mornings by rising with the sun and heading for morning workout with Doc and the team. As the cock crowed and vapor wafted from the surface of our fifty-meter outdoor pool my teammates would stretch out over the water to begin a three-mile workout of kicking and stroking across the steaming water—all before breakfast. It was a grand way to begin the day. Through the remainder of the morning we would rest in the cavernous old fraternity house we rented, and most of us would read. Perhaps because the Cold War was still upon us and because the Second World War was not far behind, much of what we read was political and literary: Orwell, Aldous Huxley, and gigantic tomes on Nazism, the War, and Communism. As sports teams go, this team was a veritable salon; our grade-point average was usually well over 3.0. At noon we would work out again, and in the late afternoon we would go out into the Indiana hills to the deserted limestone quarries where, with trees and green hills all around, one could swim for a quarter mile without a turn while looking ten and twenty feet down through the glassy water to the ghostly stone works below.

But morning workouts were the best. While America slept we churned along the pool lanes; the sun replaced the moon in the Hoosier sky, and we trained to defend our National Amateur Athletic Union outdoor title. So superior were many Indiana swimmers in the early 1960s that they set unofficial world records in practice! At the outset of a workout we shoved off like a human flotilla, twenty or so of us, many with American or world records to their credit. Off to the right of me at about one o'clock would be the three fastest breaststrokers in the world, a fact that would have been much more thrilling to me had I not been a breaststroker, too. Also in front of me were the world-record holders in the backstroke, the butterfly, and the individual medley. So many Olympians and veterans of other national teams were in the pool that our relay teams usually were faster than national Olympic teams. In the summer of 1961 my roommate, Chet Jastremski, broke the world record in the 100- and 200-meter breaststroke practically every time he swam those events. Often I was in the same heat, though as Chet finished I would be so far behind that it seemed as if I were just coming up over the horizon.

If competitive athletics is a superb training ground for life, Doc made the IU team a splendid laboratory for studying the evolution of Liberalism. Himself a former world-record holder and by the 1960s one of the most venerated coaches in sport, Doc remained, during my undergraduate years, a faithful Liberal, a believer in progress, science, reason, and the need for America to institute social welfare agencies similar to those that bejeweled all Europe. The metamorphosis that his views underwent over the next two decades was made easier for Doc because, unlike those Liberals in the humanities who moved to the right, Doc worked in a profession where performance could be verified by objective measurements. Doc was a scientist. Having earned a Ph.D. in physiology, he experimented with new training techniques and alterations in stroke mechanics. To this day, no other swimming coach has equalled the number of his innovations. While we were working out, he took notes for the scholarly papers that he would write on "lift," "acceleration," and some aspect of "Bernoulli's law," about which I cannot comment except to say that if it improves the quality of Chianti I am for it.

THE IDEALISTS AND US 47

Via Doc all Indiana swimmers were the recipients of frequent lectures on the miraculous powers of education, and we were discreetly nudged in the direction of the arts, particularly music. During workouts Mozart or Puccini might lilt over the public address system of the Indiana University indoor pool, instilling a fear in many of the nearby students of physical education that homosexuals had taken the place over. As a Liberal in the effulgent, can-do days of American Liberalism, Doc prescribed knowledge as a cure for all mankind's ills—particularly if it was dispensed by enlightened Liberals like him.

For some inscrutable reason swimmers are often eccentrics, but Doc was tolerant. True to his Liberal values, he always held out hope for each of his athletes despite the many times their misbehavior threatened to make them more celebrated for their mischief than for their athletic accomplishments. Among the staff kept on duty for the Indiana University swimming team there should have been at least one criminal lawyer. Though as sports go, swimming is about as violent as badminton, the Indiana swimmers were given to wild scrapes. There were bills for hotel rooms that we left in ruins, and for the mascots of opposing teams that frequently disappeared under mysterious circumstances. Once one of Doc's world-record holders became agitated upon discovering halfway through a race that he was swimming the wrong stroke. In his embarrassment, he fled the pool and took a strategic position atop a nearby telephone booth from which he pitched occasional Coke bottles into the pool until his mood brightened. All this and more Doc accepted, fortified by the oldest idea known to man, philosophical acceptance of the inevitable. Henry Adams had Augustus Saint-Gaudens symbolize it in the statue he commissioned for his wife Clover's grave. It was one of Doc's favorite pieces of American art.

In demeanor and philosophy Doc could have passed for the model from which Steinbeck fashioned his tolerant and reasonable "Doc" in *Cannery Row*. As Liberalism drifted into unreason, anti-Americanism, and visions of utopia, Doc parted company with his old label and called himself a conservative, though he needed to make almost no alteration in philosophy. As another old Liberal, Ronald Reagan, was wont to say, Liberalism left him.

My adventures with the conservative movement began once my adventures in the pool were over. A distinguished professor of diplomatic history at Indiana, Robert H. Ferrell, had convinced me that I was somehow suited for graduate study in history and so for a while I was holed up in the graduate stacks of a great library, reading old documents and dreaming of an America long gone. Then sometime in the spring of 1966 I looked up from dusty pages to behold an astonishing sight. On a campus where serious scholarship had theretofore coexisted with the collegiate rituals of beer drinking and flirtation, there appeared an expanding crowd of bug-eyed messiahs heralding a New Age wherein war would be passé and the citizenry would convene daily to monitor the government's business, maybe even the world's business. Owing to technology's stupendous advances, workers would have vast stretches of leisure in which to compose poetry or sonatas midst the marijuana fumes. Dope was going to supersede the cocktail. Sex would be for our time what religion had been for the Middle Ages and with the same promise of celestial mysteries. This was the message of what was called in the early 1960s the New Left, a *reductio ad insanum* of Liberalism, and both Liberalism and conservatism roused its hackles. Unfortunately, university faculty members were too ideological to be offended and too agelastic to laugh.

The New Left's message-bearers affected about the same bohemian uniform one would have seen slinking through the shadows of exotic Greenwich Village in the early 1960s if one had been attracted, as I had been, to folk singers and the remnants of the Beat Generation. Greenwich Village's bohemians generally laid claim to a libertarian philosophy, a lyric socialism, and an absorption with artiness that appealed to the imagination of a restless college boy, but only while on a lark. Once through a season or so of neurotic longhaired girls, their guitars, and their e.e. cummings, it was back to a clean, well-lighted place for me.

Now, on college campuses in the mid-1960s, the intellectual heirs to the Greenwich Village flakes suddenly took on a numinous authority that was as unanticipated as would be the abrupt elevation of all campus gardeners to the rank of full professor. These *enragés*, however, were not as entertaining as the Beats and the folk singers. In the words of the historian Alonzo Hamby, they were "the latest manifestation of a tradition of middle-class reformism that periodically had surfaced in American history and that had provided much of the distinctive tone of early-twentieth-century progressivism. Its proponents were highly educated, affluent, moralistic, and alienated from the worlds of business and commerce."[2] Yet in a swift passage of months, from the fall of 1966 through 1967, their influence, somewhat like British Mad Cow disease, spread within academe, contaminating scholarship, social life, and university administration.

By the late 1960s, the New Left and lesser utopians were pulverizing the foundations of Liberal culture. They were but one element in a gigantic assault that was changing America's regnant philosophy, Liberalism, perhaps forever. From Franklin D. Roosevelt to George Bush, America's political leaders have maintained a relaxed consensus on a broad range of middle-class values. Thus Democratic and Republican politicos could golf together without fear of violence. But a growing number of left-wing reformers were so intensely gripped by their sacred vision that the notion of a Loyal Opposition was but a misty abstraction in their restless minds. Within academe and then government they created a crisis for Liberalism. Again, the observant Hamby spied the drift of the decade when he wrote of a "crisis of the spirit for American liberalism and for the country as a whole. While some of the Great Society's academic formulators considered it a series of 'income transfer' programs, they had not presented it as such to Congress, and they evaded debate about the goal of income redistribution. . . . Among welfare recipients there suddenly emerged a sense of entitlement at variance with all past American tradition. Where the New Dealers had stressed the importance of work in exchange for federal benefits, advocates of 'welfare rights' in the 1960s denounced work requirements. Soon such a position was the new orthodoxy of American liberalism."[3] But there was more to the new orthodoxy. There was a sense of apocalypse. "This is our basic conclusion: Our Nation is moving toward two societies, one black, one white—separate and unequal," Otto Kerner's Special Presidential Advisory Committee on Civil Disorders reported.[4] As a *New York Times* report on the findings of an even more dubious commission, William Scranton's Commission on Campus Unrest, reveals, this sense of dire happenings was pervasive, even with the most implausible topics: "Unless it [the division between established society and the new youth culture that generates intensifying violence] is stopped, the nation could disintegrate into near-civil war—'a brutal war of each against all,' the unanimous commission warned in its final report."[5]

Back on campus much of the professoriate was sorely tempted by the delights of this New Age: rock music! tight jeans! tom-cat amour! pills and powders and weeds that spin the room! The impetuous among the faculty might in the dark of the night slip into a Marcusean paradise of wild, libidinous *evoes*, where there could be tragedies: untimely hernias, cardiac arrests while atop the most intellectual cheerleader of the Class of '72, an attack of asthma in the darkened marijuana den as every young face breaks into grins. The student Left was promising to end the War and to uncork the elixir of eternal youth. On every campus, visionary profs were suddenly converted to the New Age. In a matter of months even the vacuous pastime of student government was transformed into another instrument of protest. The left had politicized one more innocuous diversion. On practically every campus, in practically every academic department, almost overnight, politics could not be avoided.

To return to those years of the late 1960s is to enter a soft-focused fantasy combining the perverse, the brutal, and the slightly goofball. Yet to return to them, if ever so fleetingly, is a requirement if we are to understand the conservatism that followed. In the late 1960s the heroic aura that John F. Kennedy had conferred on waging "limited" war against Communist insurgency vanished as our Vietnam interlude grew lurid and grisly. Civil rights evolved from a fond hope for a distant tomorrow into a vexed exigency. Now the culture of the American cosmopolitan cracked, opening itself to all the diversity of the seamiest sections of Amsterdam. The final years of the 1960s spun wildly, and it was within that kaleidoscopic rapture of drugs-liberation-dissent-revolution that *The American Spectator* was hatched.

Convinced that the radicals menaced personal liberty, democratic society, scholarship, and high culture, an unlikely band of theretofore apolitical students began to participate in campus politics at Indiana University. In the fall of 1967 we founded our own campus political party, and I founded a magazine to break the left's monopolistic hold on campus media. That fall, when classes convened, Indiana University had become the first major campus whose student body president was a member of the Students for a Democratic Society, the most popular national student organization of the New Left. The following spring, after a winter of antiradical politicking and of publishing a kind of journalism that shocked the faculty— it being assumed by the profs that only leftist students could be rude—we routed the radicals, making the Indiana student body the first to return student government to the moderate majority.

The report of our victory appeared on the front page of the May 5, 1968 *Chicago Tribune.* Perhaps it is by sheerest chance, but that front page will be of inestimable value to future historians. Embalmed on it are most of the leading monsters of the era. To review it today is to gain a surprisingly accurate sense of the lurid zoology of 1968. Centered on the page was our glorious achievement:

Bloomington, Ind. May 4—A few years back, students who were called into the dean's office said, "What did I do?"

Now they say, "Whom do I appeal this to?"

Robert H. Shaffer, dean of students at Indiana University, believes that statement of attitude sums up what is happening today on college campuses thruout the nation. Parts of it are good, and parts are bad, he believes.

In the last couple of years, I.U. has experienced marches and sit-ins and things such as students demonstrating against chemical companies and booing and jeering Secretary of State Dean Rusk. . . . However, many students there see a change in the image of the school and a possible return to conservatism.

What followed was pure fustian from me, from my compatriots, from our New Left adversaries, and, of course, from the wretched Dean Shaffer. All our sentiments were muddled but none more so than the ejecta of Dean Shaffer's mind, he being the quintessence of the late 1960s university official, always posing as defender of embattled enlightenment, always surreptitiously sniffing the winds in anticipation of the main chance. The May 5 *Chicago Tribune* should have tipped Shaffer off as to the drift of things. Framing our story were the monsters of the unfolding drama. Across the entire top of the front page in bold 150-point type the banner headline roared "BLACK POWER WINS AT N.U." and introduced a news story that began: " 'Black Power' students who had seized Northwestern University's old administration building Friday claimed victory last night in a settlement in which admittedly university officials completely capitulated." The story was to the right of ours. Above us and in the far left-hand column another story began: "Saigon, Viet Nam, May 5 [Sunday]—The Viet Cong shelled Saigon and a dozen other South Vietnamese cities early today and infiltrated small sniper and suicide squads into the capital." To the right of this story was a 22-point headline: "LBJ Wants Viet Talks Speeded Up." And directly next to us was a 26-point headline: "Students Aid McCarthy, RFK," introducing a story which began: "Indianapolis, Ind., May 4— Thousands of student volunteers for both Sen. Robert F. Kennedy of New York and Sen. Eugene J. McCarthy of Minnesota arrived in Indianapolis by chartered buses last night and this morning for two days of campaigning in Indiana's three-man Democratic Presidential primary Tuesday.

"Kennedy's slogan has been: 'On May 7 Indiana can choose the next President of the United States.' "

Here was the spring of 1968 in all its fated agitation. On this garish page the only vestiges from more conventional times were two, a brief report that the ninety-fourth Kentucky Derby had been won by Dancer's

Image; and, across the very top of the page, the notice: "TODAY! COM-PLETE BUTTERFLY DRESS PATTERN. . . . See the Feature Sec-tion." Both make happier reading today than the bulletins from the New Age. Sadly, Indiana did not choose the next president. Sadder still, LBJ's "peace talks" were not "speeded up," and whatever noble goals were being sought by Northwestern's advocates of Black Power they surely resolved nothing, leaving troubled consciences and troubled minds still troubled. Not even the oncoming Viet Cong gained their objective, their patrons to the north eventually taking control of the land that they had died for.

My friends and I did, however, keep our magazine alive, and presently it grew from being an Indiana University, off-campus, antiradical magazine to being the principal magazine of antiradical students at Harvard, the University of Chicago, and the University of California at Berkeley, where we had friends eager to write and distribute an antiradical disturber of the disturbed. Soon the magazine was popping up on other campuses, too. Without ceremony it had become the magazine of antiradical students nationwide.

The final years of the 1960s were years of futile whirl. One day a college boy might repair to his dormitory attired in smart Brooks Brothers hab-erdashery. The next day he might reappear wearing Jesus sandals, bell-bottom trousers, a necklace of cheap beads, hair unkempt, stubble on the chin, and a beatific gaze for a face. Unlovely women were joining nonce organizations such as W.I.T.C.H. (Women's International Terrorist Conspiracy from Hell—and you can say that again!) and discarding their bras.[6]

The war went on. Newer dissident groups formed as the old ones grew angrier or dissolved. Martin Luther King, Jr., was temporarily eclipsed by the Black Panthers, whose specialty was to threaten politicians and police, and then to flare into stupendous dudgeon when the literal-minded cops took their displays of artillery or their bloodcurdling threats seriously and counterattacked. To a 1970 Moratorium Day audience in San Francisco, Black Panther David Hilliard raved, "We will kill Richard Nixon. We will kill any mother-fuckers that stand in the way of our freedom"—and he apparently was surprised when the calaboose door clinked shut on him.[7] The demonstrations and harangues proliferated until May 4, 1970. On that day four college-age demonstrators—not all students—were shot dead during a violent antiwar confrontation with the Ohio National Guard at Kent State University. Shortly afterwards two black students were killed at Jackson State University.

"A widely circulated photograph of a young woman kneeling above the inert bleeding body of Jeffrey Miller captured the stark impotence of death, a blood immersion that haunted this generation of Americans. Mass annihilation hovered almost as a cliché around American children born in the baby boom of World War II." So poetized Peter N. Carroll in his suitably puerile report of the Kent State riot, *It Seemed Like Nothing Happened*. Professor Carroll is, of course, one of the hundreds, perhaps thousands, of charlatans who have made the myths of the 1960s their own especially marketable commodity.[8] A market for maudlin hooey about the decade's radicalism and protest has endured ever since. It is a tasteless joke that history has played on those of us who opposed the radicalism of the era and were, as a matter of fact, more representative of the era's youth than were the radicals. The Kent State tragedy was eventually transformed by peddlers like Carroll into one of those transilient events of American history, supposedly as dramatic in its effect on my generation as Pearl Harbor had been on my parents' generation.

The wretch described by Carroll as a kneeling "young woman" was in fact a fourteen-year-old adolescent and a runaway at that. As for Carroll's lurid claptrap about a "blood immersion" and hovering clichés, the majority of American youth supported the Vietnam War almost to the time of U.S. withdrawal, as did their parents. The public actually sided with the National Guardsmen after the Kent State shootings; and, upon investigating the event, the Justice Department found no grounds for prosecution. Even the New Age idealists were not absorbed with Kent State for long, not that they have been much absorbed with anything for long, save that wonderful person they call "me." In the early 1970s too many other marvels were in the air: new hallucinatory drugs, never-before-available sex acts, mysterious revelatory philosophies from the Orient or Southern California, and dozens of other history-making events, such as assassinations, gigantic protests, and rock concerts.

Kent State was of a piece with a turbulent time. Within hours of the shootings I participated in a television talk show whose guests included the man who snapped that famous photograph, John Filo. The poor fellow was eager to retail the news of the dreadful happenings that he had just witnessed, but his voice was lost in the hubbub raised by a large fat woman whose flaming vision made discussion of Kent State or anything else unfeasible and possibly dangerous. Every time Filo piped up, the amazon—then head of the National Organization for Women—squashed him. She had suffered an inspiration that in those loony times was even more absorbing than Kent State. She believed that there would come a day when women would become equally competitive with men in professional football. She believed that after liberating women from "institutionalized sexism" they would grow to be as big as linebackers, and she wanted another of the show's guests, the speechless National Football League Commissioner Pete Rozelle, to hear the good news.

Of course, the glad and glorious morns of the 1960s could not last. Soon sour humors seeped into New Age culture. Gruesome absorptions were spreading throughout a relatively young and, one would have thought, sanguine society. Its episodic fears of nuclear holocaust were again returning along with episodic fears of ecological catastrophe. Presently mass hypochondria gripped the country, despite the fact that longevity was increasing so rapidly that the real problem facing many Americans was not how to keep themselves alive but how to go gently into that good night, to die "humanely" and with dignity. As the 1970s wore on it became obvious that the participants in the 1960s revels were suffering a colossal hangover. Watergate gave them a jolt of the old excitement, but then they returned to their sour humors.

After the 1960s American intellectual life was to grow grim. The intellectual life of the Republic had not always been grim. In the 1920s it had resembled a gigantic, coast-to-coast café, clamorous with diverse voices and tinkling glasses, Prohibition notwithstanding. During the 1920s and 1930s the intelligentsia's ranks were open to such diverse figures as Irving Babbitt, John Dewey, Max Eastman, T.S. Eliot, Sinclair Lewis, Edmund Wilson, Mencken & Nathan, and Thorstein Veblen. Then the café quieted down. By the 1970s the diversity at the tables gave way to a series of somber recitations: "No Nukes," "Small Is Beautiful," "Get on the Right Side of Revolution," "Nixon!" "Ford?" "The Poor!!!" Now diverse voices were scorned, conformity became more slavish with every year. In Reagan's 1980s the condition actually worsened. In prior times members of the intelligentsia learned from experience and occasionally acknowledged error. After being enchanted by totalitarianism in the 1930s, writers like André Gide, Arthur Koestler, and Malcolm Muggeridge wrote candidly and insightfully of their lapses in judgment. In the 1970s and 1980s almost no American who had once predicted doom for America while praising Fidel Castro, Ho Chi Minh, or Mao Tse-tung, ever recanted. Prominent Europeans recanted, but I can recall no prominent Yankee fan of totalitarianism who ever withdrew his praise of Castro or Mao.

Surely one of the reasons so few Americans recanted was that America is a commercial republic; and, at least for intellectuals, there were profits to be realized in abominating the Republic. One needed nothing more to become a successful sage than an infectious anti-American dithyramb of the sort blubbered by that perpetual graduate student Susan Sontag. In a characteristically pedantic 1966 essay, "What's Happening in America," she sobbed: "America was founded on genocide. . . . It's the whole character structure of modern American man, and his imitators, that needs rehauling. . . . The truth is that Mozart, Pascal, Boolean algebra, Shakespeare, parliamentary government, baroque churches, Newton, the emancipation of women, Kant, Marx, and Balanchine ballets don't redeem what this particular civilization has wrought upon the world. The white race is the cancer of human history. . . . This is a doomed country, it seems to me; I only pray that, when America founders, it doesn't drag the rest of the planet down."[9]

Whatever potent deity this insufferable pinhead prayed to, her entreaties were apparently received quite favorably. The planet has survived magnificently, and Miss Sontag has prospered, too (in 1990 the MacArthur Foundation gave her a five-year grant of $340,000 just to continue thinking). For that matter, almost every other mediocre writer willing to blubber along with Sontag about the horrors of home has prospered too, and so the *Amerikaschmerz* spread to every enlightened province of New Age Liberal culture, to faculty lounges, to think tanks, to health food shops, to tanning salons, to aerobics classes. The morbid tales that dog the American past and present spread from every ecologically correct wine-tasting club to the last surviving Marxist knitting circles. The bawling even issued from the White House once Jimmy Carter had liberated it from the heavy hand of Gerald R. Ford. All these sobs contributed to what I shall in a later chapter define as *Kultursmog*, a culture polluted by the politics of the infantile left and by the conjurings of some terrific mountebanks.

Jimmy Carter may have been but a clever and vacuous Snopes, yet he knew how to seize power in the gloom of 1976. He had taken note of the left intelligentsia's dominance of culture, and so he aped its sham pieties. He became the cornpone hope even of Norman Mailer. Jimmy stumbled. At times he fell. Yet whenever he was in extremis he deftly worked the vaguely leftist crybaby sensibility of the times. A choice example of his lugubrious act came on July 16, 1979, when he stole a tear-stained page from the pinheads to lament America's "paralysis and stagnation and drift." Most Americans were perplexed by this yawp, but the balding, fattening *enfants terribles* of the 1960s were soothed, especially by his idiotic finale: "One of the visitors to Camp David last week put it this way: 'We've got to stop crying and start sweating; stop talking and start walking; stop cursing and start praying.' "[10] If you think I made that up let me direct you to the Carter Papers in the Jimmy Carter Presidential Library, located somewhere in Georgia, if there are Carter Papers.

Now I shall be frank. Through all these years I had a ball. The magazine developed as no other American intellectual review ever has. From an off-campus student sheet it grew to become one of the major intellectual reviews of American conservatism. Because *The American Spectator* commenced operations in the great days of the 1960s youth culture, it might be expected that the hangover of the 1970s would afflict us, too. But as we never fell prey to the hooey of the 1960s, so too we remained immune to the ghastly aftermath that knocked off Abbie Hoffman and so many of our peers. *The American Spectator* might quite properly be catalogued as an artifact of 1960s youth culture, but it is about the only such artifact to have passed through the 1970s without ever undergoing detoxification, incarceration in a drug abuse clinic, Gestalt therapy, a fleecing from an Eastern swami, fundraising harangues from Rennie Davis, or treatment for any of the appalling diseases associated with 1960s scortatory rituals.

Two decades after the fevers of 1968 the giants of that year were in a hell of a shape. Those who had survived were groaning about the vanished glories of faraway days, but I was a happy fellow: I had no police record, my 1960s girlfriend was still with me, and not one of my children had turned me in to the FBI or sought my assassination. Through all these days of leftist melodrama, little children had preceded me throwing flowers.

Not a lot has been written about the antiradical students of the 1960s, although they, not the radicals, typified their generation. Ignored as the born blanks of America's bourgeois masses, many rose to prominence in the Reagan years as members of Congress, of the administration, and of state governments. Others became giants in the world of business. Some merely faded, but others were destined for a large role in American public life. During the campus protests of the Nixon years most of the key anti-radicals at one time or another entered into liaison with our magazine (originally called *The Alternative*) either by writing for it or attending one of our periodic conferences held at Harvard, the University of Chicago, and at Berkeley, where we invited distinguished speakers such as Alexander Bickel of the Yale Law School and Martin Diamond, the Straussian political theorist, to lecture on democracy, dissent, alienation, and other issues then at the heart of 1960s pandemonium. Thus, in this examination of conservatism's rise and subsequent discomforts I hope you will not consider my occasional excursions into autobiography outré or self-indulgent. Conventional chroniclers of the era for some reason are given to portraying the rise of conservatism as one of nature's rare uncaused causes, the consequence of another cursed Invisible Hand, or, perhaps, the result of a moral lapse; but there were actual human participants at work. Many of them filtered in and out of our antiradical cabal; and most thought their activities to be enlightened, moral, and beneficial to the Republic. You can decide for yourself.

In opposing radical protest we were faced with two unusual problems, both of which resurfaced years later in conservatism's time of crack-up. We seemed to lack a tradition to hark back to and we certainly lacked institutional support. Though we represented the views of most young people in that turbulent era—the youth vote was never radical in the 1960s, and at the height of the youth rebellion in 1972, most young people voted for Richard Nixon—we knew of no style available to us for engaging in political discourse, and we had no reliable source of financial support. The radicals frequently came from the Liberal tradition, and they were soon drawing on the well-established Western tradition of left-wing protest. *Pari passu* with Liberalism's slide into the New Age, radical students were aided and abetted by the universities and other bastions of Liberalism where those who survived the 1960s eventually were to gain tenure and the power to bore future generations without fear of reprisals. My colleagues may have been more representative of the American mainstream, but the American mainstream expressed itself politically only on election day. We needed to express ourselves more frequently and in print as well as in debate and in public demonstrations. To do this effectively a political movement needs a style.

Fortunately the American past was not as barren as the American present. With a little scholarly digging we uncovered, a few decades back in the American past, a literary tradition of amused skepticism that conformed to our needs and our sensibilities, to wit, the politically debonair world of the 1920s *American Mercury* and the early *New Yorker*. It was a cast of mind that prized irony, elegance, wit, and accuracy. It was iconoclastic but devoid of the infantile anti-Americanism of the Sontags, the Marxism of the New Left, and the constipated intellectualism of Liberalism's earnest strivers. It was also free of the fussiness of so many traditional conservatives; withal it was combative and amusing.

The style of the 1960s radical was alluring because it promised lewd pleasures and violence. The problem was that those lewd pleasures conduced to decadence. One cannot lead a revolution from any of the eighty positions in the Kamasutra or with a head sozzled by marijuana fumes. The style we adopted was more chaste but offered the compensation of restraining us from transforming ourselves into vegetables. Moreover, a 1920s style of amused skepticism could always expose the sourpuss in the crowd whether it be an old sourpuss such as Garry Wills, who sniffed that we were the kind of writers who thought archaic and unusual words funny, or young sourpusses such as James Wolcott, who in the 1980s dubbed us "Young Farts," by which he meant "a loose clique of wet blankets and party poopers endowed with critical intelligence (they may be stodgy, but they're not stupid) and poised for cultural power."[11]

The tradition we adopted even provided us with a new name when our first name, *The Alternative*, acquired too much the ring of the left-wing counterculture. My first impulse had been to buy the Mencken & Nathan title, *The American Mercury*, which was still doddering around; but publisher Alfred Knopf, the only surviving founder of the *Mercury*, counseled against doing so. Sometime after World War II the *Mercury* had been dragged into the anti-Semitic swamps. Knopf doubted that the bigots' muck could be burned away. I settled on reviving the title of Nathan's 1930s literary magazine, *The American Spectator*, which during its brief life had published such illustrious Americans as Sherwood Anderson, Theodore Dreiser, Eugene O'Neill, and James T. Farrell, who, before typing his last line, appeared in our resurrected *Spectator*.

There was admittedly a whiff of the schoolboy to our early issues, but that is a charge that can be filed against many magazines, not one of which has had the benefit of our defense, namely, we really were schoolboys. Unlike *The New Republic*, *The Nation*, or any of a half-dozen weisenheimer magazines that in recent years have come and gone to the ooohs and amens of the culturati, *The American Spectator* originated as an off-campus college magazine created solely by students. It never had the funding of the young Wall Street heirs and heiresses who bankrolled its left-wing competitors. Nor did establishment journalists lend a hand, thus putting a damper on the proceedings. *The American Spectator* was born wayward and destined to be skeptical.

Yet waywardness and skepticism benefit the writer. Certainly a writer is better served by waywardness and skepticism than by the cynicism and idealism that befool the common writers of our time. The idealist begins life singing, and with surprising regularity he ends life a cynic. He is the sorry fellow who grew to adulthood praising gods who never were, only to end up admonishing against bugaboos equally nil. The skeptic leans towards irony and laughter. America in the 1960s and early 1970s was in

need of a wink and a laugh. It had slogged through sadness and tragedy—
Vietnam, the assassinations of the Kennedys and of Martin Luther King,
Jr., Watergate, and an endless series of absorptions with human squalor.
There was much to weep over, but tears are uncouth. Besides, many of
the same things that make us weep can make us laugh, and laughter is
the superior therapy. Nor does laughter preclude constructive action. My
first impulse as an editor then and now has been to doubt and then to
believe or to believe and then to doubt, but always to doubt. An apostle
became a saint by airing his doubts, men of science have advanced human knowledge by doubting, and there was a time when the capacity to
doubt allowed the pretty girl to save her virginity for a better day . . . or
night.

But by the 1960s the Republic's intellectual purlieus had filled with
ardent believers. It was the culmination of an unhappy trend. After
Mencken & Nathan came waves of reformers in the 1930s and actual
Communists. In the 1940s came the nationalists and internationalists, to
be followed by the existentialists and the modernists. Finally the waves
diminished into the mere ripples of the 1980s, each ripple containing some
new personal improvement zealot. A nation hardly needs libraries when
it has such credulous oafs. And so my colleagues and I fled the imbeciles
of our era for the style of a more stylish time.

Still we needed some sort of institutional support commensurate with
the support radical students received, and we needed an arsenal of ideas
applicable beyond the petty problems of campus life. The rising conservative movement, with its reverence for liberty and reason, supplied us
with values and ideas as well as the modest financial support student groups
need. Equally important, the conservative movement provided superb role
models in William F. Buckley, Jr., Milton Friedman, and, I suppose,
Russell Kirk for the prematurely bald. Coming from an older generation,
they became our counselors and friends, though Milton's first piece of
economic advice to me was useless. In a little office at the University of
Chicago late in the 1960s the distinguished free marketeer warned me that
if the magazine was to live it had to turn a profit. No intellectual review,
however, makes a profit, nor does any other cultural institution, not even
the University of Chicago. Better it would be for me to face the reality of
raising money with the same sort of fundraising campaigns that cover
university deficits than to dream that our magazine would be the first
intellectual review ever to operate profitably. That dream was a fantasy
likely to end in bankruptcy.

At any rate the New Conservatism's devotion to freedom and its unequivocal hostility to the New Left fortified our resolve and put wings to our spirits. But the New Left had provoked hostility on the left too, and from that quarter we got some of our most effective allies. These were the antiradical socialists led by a man who became a major influence on my antiradical compatriots, Professor Sidney Hook, the most competent polemicist of his generation. Sidney taught philosophy at New York University, where he had propounded the ideas of John Dewey, carrying on battles against those whom he perceived as enemies of enlightenment, progress, and democracy. I took a summer class from him in 1969 and left convinced that, though the snobbery of Mencken & Nathan was great fun, liberty, democracy, intelligent debate, and academic excellence as advocated by Hook were to be the fundamental values of *The American Spectator*. On religion Sidney's views were less rooted in Western tradition. He was a confirmed atheist, convinced that his final destination was a compost heap. Reason told him so.

Despite his ardor for combat and the high seriousness of his thought, he was a man of endless generosity and kindliness. He also had a proper capacity for comedy and contributed to some of the most ribald departments of *The American Spectator*, particularly "The Current Wisdom," where with suitable introduction we quote the asininities of the month. Late in his long life and after a pleasant supper with the Irving Kristols, we were exiting through the lobby of the New York Athletic Club. Gesticulating in his usual vigorous manner, Sidney was fondly recalling those battles that had been fought with *The American Spectator* as his ally. Many *American Spectator* writers had been his students and many more were his disciples. A rapture of gratitude for the life he had led overcame him and, swelling with warm memories, the old atheist looked heavenward, palms upturned and exclaimed: "Sometimes I'd like to look up and thank G-G-G— . . . but"—and he shook his old head in amusement—"I can't. The evidence, there's just not the evidence." And off we lurched. Supplied with Yahweh's evidence, what a great rabbi Sidney would have been; but what a great man he already was.

WITH SIDNEY'S COUNSEL, my colleagues and I were destined to wage over two decades of cultural battles against the left and against Liberalism, but it all began in the 1960s with the institutional support of the young conservative movement. Among the conservative writers and pols there were many poseurs, but even among them the issues were serious: freedom, the maintenance of a great civilization against the poisons of totalitarianism from without and of frivolity from within. The conservatives revered the free society and feared that it was passing. Liberalism by the 1960s had become many things: a disturber of the peace; an extinguisher of meaning in words and deeds; a far-flung process of standardization threatening individuality everywhere save in the bedroom and in the hoosegow. The conservatives challenged all this, particularly this process of standardization, both the comparatively gentle standardization at home and the rougher process of standardization practiced abroad in the Soviet bloc. The conservatives also resisted the loss of artistic standards and the rise of nihilism, but always they came back to the defense of personal freedom, particularly economic freedom, against the drabness of collectivist Liberalism.

In the 1960s the conservatives were the true rebels in a rebellious era. Multitudes of protest movements were on the march in the land, but only the conservatives were truly independent of Liberalism. The conservatives wanted to break completely with modern Liberalism's drift into statism. They usually claimed to be representative of the average American. Whether their claim was true or not depended on the issues of the hour, but one point is indisputable: in the provinces of the intellectuals it was the conservatives who were the real underdogs in an era supposedly hospitable to underdogs.

To be a conservative in the 1960s was to stand fast at Valley Forge, the Alamo, the Battle of the Bulge, or at the performance of a Bach oratorio in the faculty lounge at the University of California at Berkeley when scruffy profs wanted to blubber about their favorite Frank Zappa album. Wherever we went amongst the elites of the Republic, we conservatives were heavily outnumbered. Some found this an exhilarating experience. In 1955 William F. Buckley, Jr., had vowed in his first issue of *National Review* to stand athwart history; and he obviously relished his solitary stance, though even Bill was dismayed at times by the Liberals' indignation. I remember in the 1980s, when the Oxford Union invited me to debate the Rev. Jesse Jackson. Bill was all for it, but he worried that I would not be prepared for the trauma of performing in a debating hall surrounded by hostile lungs. I went into immediate training, reviewing Jesse's jingles, developing a few of my own, preparing an instructive fandango full of stirring metaphysical meaning for the assembled students of oratory and taking daily calls of encouragement from Bill. Alas, all efforts were to no avail. The English students caught Jesse double dipping. He was endeavoring to hoodwink both the Oxford Union and the London City Council into paying his lavish expenses and those of his vast retinue, thus giving him a handsome profit. Jesse was canned, and there went my only chance to go up against America's would-be Mussolini, the William Jennings Bryan of the paraverbal.

Surely Bill Buckley must have recognized that conservatives have become accustomed to being underdogs in the cultural wars. Etched sharply into my memory is a debate in which three participants and a hostile upper-crust Manhattan audience had at me for an hour or so, after which one of the debaters, that master of garbagespiel Murray Kempton, charged me with dishonoring Mencken's legacy by being—get this—a "conformist." Think of it, with the entire audience against me, all other debaters onstage in superlative dudgeon over my every expressed thought, Kempton still calls *me* the "conformist"! I reminded Murray that at university debates, at egghead talk shows, wherever intellectuals gathered I was always outnumbered; but to no avail. In the New Age neither words nor simple mathematical computations conveyed meaning.

The conservative movement was not only the Republic's underdog movement, it was also the least celebrated of movements. In the 1960s and early 1970s it received nothing comparable to the publicity attending the antiwar movement, the youth movement, or the gruesome feminist movement. And yet only the conservative movement was to attract enough support from the citizenry to capture the White House. Perhaps I should be a big enough person to let this last point pass unremarked. Perhaps it is mean and uncharacteristically divisive of me to remind the reader that, while the mandarins of the *Kultursmog* celebrated every left-wing movement coming out of the 1960s, only the conservative movement was gaining a national following sufficient to capture the White House in the 1980s. But if this is a petty point let me make a larger one. The daily news that is warmed up and seasoned by the chefs of American journalism is frequently not the significant news of the day. In the decades since the 1960s the journalists have often passed over the truly significant while hyping the trivial, and transmogrifying piffles into towering calamities.

For two decades journalists dwelt extravagantly on every protest movement heaved up by the professional *indignados*. The only news one was likely to read about conservatives was the bad news. The rising conservative tide was completely ignored by the journalists until it washed over them on November 4, 1980, soaking their reporter's pads and ruining their day. One of the unhappy side effects of the journalists' absorption with 1960s protests was that ordinary Americans came to expect infamy and horripilation daily: exposés of FBI break-ins; of terrorist groups; of presidential conniving, cover-ups, and humiliations. Conspiracies were reported in all quarters. Americans came to feel that government scandal and political violence were the staples of modern life. A day without them was a letdown.

One of the unremarked legacies of the 1960s has been the generalized sense among Americans that something dreadful is about to happen somewhere. America's state of fearful expectancy may have expired with the arrival of the 1990s, but before it did it made many Americans easy prey for charlatans with phony tales of horror. Recall if you will the supposedly racially motivated murders of black boys in Atlanta that turned out to be the work of a black man, the supposedly racially motivated assault on Tawana Brawley that turned out to be a fabrication, the imminence of an AIDS epidemic amongst American heterosexuals, California's medfly, and something about "killer bees" migrating, I think, from Acapulco.* Yet the one large event that went pretty much unnoticed was the growing conservative movement that suddenly won the presidency in 1980.

From the 1950s to the election of Ronald Reagan a conservative counterculture was developing. It contained all the elements for the making of a true political culture. It had distinct traditions, values, and roles for each participant. There were conservative philosophers, economists, professors of politics, editors, and polemicists. There were slogans, for instance that flavorous line lifted from the conservative philosopher Eric Voegelin: "Don't let *them* immanatize the eschaton." There was a student cadre developing within organizations such as the Young Americans for Freedom and the Intercollegiate Studies Institute. There were even conservative folk singers, one of whom, Tony Dolan, became an important speechwriter in the Reagan Administration. The conservative students enlivened college life with political seminars, lectures, and debates. They organized rallies, first for Senator Barry Goldwater, later for California's Governor Ronald Reagan and a lengthening list of lesser messiahs, such as Congressmen John Ashbrook and Phil Crane.

Ashbrook and Crane were typical of the movement's early politicians.

---

*And those responsible for maintaining journalistic standards did not seem to care that those standards declined as credulous journalists were exploited. In 1981, after discovering that it had conferred a Pulitzer Prize on a *Washington Post* reporter for a story that was sheer fabrication, the Pulitzer Prize committee withdrew its prize and conferred it on a *Village Voice* journalist whose story was that she had conducted a jail-cell interview with a murderer, the killer of a distinguished civil-rights advocate and congressman. The murderer's message to the journalist was that his dead, hence defenseless, victim had been a voracious homosexual. Presently the Pulitzer Prize committee was notified that no such jail-cell interview ever took place. Some of us insisted that the award be withdrawn yet again, but to no avail. The committee was not *that* interested in standards to embarrass itself twice.

Both embodied the traditional political conservatism of the Midwest. Ashbrook came from a very political generation that had captured control of the Young Republican National Federation in the late 1950s. Crane was from the same generation, but he spent his twenties and early thirties in academe, where he studied the emerging canon of conservative thought and contributed his own philippics to the evolving conservative critique of Liberalism.

Ashbrook entered Congress before Crane and rose to distinction there as a conservative watchdog. When conservatives felt their influence slipping in the Nixon Administration, they tapped him to challenge Nixon's renomination. His candidacy created a temporary split among conservatives, some going with Nixon and power, others with Ashbrook and principle. Ashbrook never fetched more than 10 percent of the electorate in the primaries, and so he went down, but after the Republican national convention he sent those of us who supported him a memento redolent of the movement's heroic state of mind: a photograph of Churchill, misty-eyed, seated in the back of a limousine and waving his V-ictory sign. Below it was printed a famous line from the old man's 1941 speech to the student body at Harrow: "Never give in. Never, never, never, never! Never yield in any way, great or small, except to convictions of honor and good sense. Never yield to force and the apparently overwhelming might of the enemy. . . ."[12] Romantic resistance to overwhelming might was a leitmotif of the movement, many of whose members entertained Churchillian delusions.

Crane was more philosophical than Ashbrook, but in the conservative counterculture the philosophical and the political cohabited comfortably. Crane came from a large family of well-educated conservative Republicans rooted in the Midwest. He earned a Ph.D. in American history at Indiana after completing the program with unusually high academic distinction. Then he became a professor at Bradley University in 1963, and took to a college lecture circuit that then featured active give-and-take between the Liberal status quo and the emerging conservatives. At Indiana University in the 1950s he and other politically active students had founded conservative campus organizations—some political, some intellectual—that still existed when I became politically active a decade later. Without the foundation that Crane built, it is doubtful that our later antiradical movement or our magazine would have been established.

By the late 1960s several campuses became breeding grounds for the conservative counterculture. Yale, with a tradition dating back to Buckley, turned out student activists. The University of Chicago had several departments where conservative scholars turned out high-grade work, and soon wavering Liberals at Harvard's Department of Government contributed to the conservative ferment. Conservative student leaders emerged on these campuses, but it was in the Midwest, at the University of Wisconsin and Indiana University, that conservative student activism became most notable, thanks to the ongoing support of businessmen in each state and to the occasional renegade prof who might pop up even at a great Liberal university without being put to death. On both campuses "underground" conservative magazines sustained antiradical students to the alarm of many faculty members who still worried more about the possible violence of the right than about the real violence of the left. And, incidentally, that violence is frequently forgotten, though it was clearly observable and occasionally murderous. At Indiana University the library suffered arson twice, other buildings were damaged, and professors were harassed. At the University of Wisconsin the Left was responsible for a series of bombings in the late 1960s, the most tragic being the destruction of the Army Mathematics Research Center on August 24, 1970. That bomb killed a post-graduate researcher, 33-year-old Dr. Robert Fassnacht, and destroyed the life's work of five physics professors, along with the Ph.D. theses of two dozen graduate students.[13]

At Indiana we enjoyed the full ambiance of the conservative counterculture. The vigorous campus Left, long in place, and the well-established campus Right bequeathed us by Crane both gained national prominence, making Indiana University a splendid microcosm of the era's ideological struggles. Famed radicals and conservatives visited campus frequently, which increased the excitement. Short of heaving bombs, we conservatives practiced all the arts of political activism then practiced so expertly by left-wing students. We distributed literature, carried protest placards, called in speakers, and threw raucous parties, always with an ideological undercurrent. Leaders of the conservative counterculture followed Crane and the editors of *National Review* to our student-sponsored seminars and debates, keeping morale high and the liquor cabinet empty.

Our headquarters and place of residence was a dilapidated old farmhouse standing shakily on forty hilly acres of eroding Hoosier topsoil. Located a few miles into the hills outside Bloomington, the old ruin was dubbed "The Establishment" by M. Stanton Evans, the conservative stalwart then editing the editorial page of the *Indianapolis News* and energetically representing our side on the campus debating circuit. From The Establishment we kept in touch with the travels of movement luminaries, invited them to Bloomington whenever they were in the area, and raised hell.

The legend grew that we were opulently endowed by the electronics pioneer Sarkes Tarzian, a local tycoon allegedly bent on spreading the capitalist conspiracy—or perhaps by the FBI. Left-wing students were as susceptible to conspiracy theories as the far right—and perhaps it is worth noting that in the 1960s few members of the conservative movement could be fairly described as "far right." Legends aside, for seventy-five dollars a month we got the whole forty acres, complete with a rusting 1952 Chevrolet raised on blocks on the front lawn—all the rustics in the neighborhood had a jalopy on blocks, if only to house their chickens. Owing to my transient interest in folk singers and Greenwich Village, the dump had a distinctly Bohemian character to it, making it all the easier for Liberals in transit to the right to visit us with clear consciences. The Establishment contained no hint of Country Club Republicanism. Even Sidney Hook's colleagues and disciples among the Social Democrats could feel comfortable amid the debris.

There on a hillside in our gray, shingled farmhouse we edited the magazine and battled the rising tide of radical students midst political posters, campaign memorabilia, sagging bookshelves, beer cans, and a disgusting collection of empty prescription bottles left by an earlier tenant, the live-in girlfriend of an Indiana University swimmer. The girl had been a *Playboy* centerfold, and if the labels on the bottles that she left in every closet and beneath every sofa are any indication, she assumed room temperature long ago.

We even indulged in what was in those days a specialty of the left, guerrilla theater. In guerrilla theater, participants, inspired by politics, undertook to comment on controversial issues through drama, usually street drama. It was an excellent way to attract media, for it usually involved some form of violence cloaked in idealism and the media have a weakness for violence—it films well. Leftists could count on enormous media coverage by heaving cream pies at public figures. We tried our hand at such dramatics with the hope of demonstrating to the media their role in encouraging violence; though in keeping with our democratic principles we did not commit violence ourselves.

In 1968 Clark Kerr, then the infamous father of the modern postwar "multiversity," was assaulted during a public address at the IU Auditorium. His assailant was typical of the radical youths of the time. The son of progressive parents, he was an erstwhile honor student now transformed into a crazed primitive by the transient fires of ideology. By hitting poor old Kerr, he flushed whatever his cause was into the headlines; and then he was gone, perhaps to a booby hatch or perhaps only to jail. Eventually he would make some sort of reappearance into polite society but always he will remain bitter. One of the surprises of the 1960s generation is how few of its radicals ever learned to respect normal American life, even though their radicalism almost destroyed them and only the stability of normal American life prevented their irreversible ruin.

On campus our conservative student group annually conducted a full week of debates and lectures featuring conservative guest speakers operating at a high level of intellection, but never did we get the free publicity of the pie-throwing radicals. To demonstrate that violence was the key to leftists' PR success, we staged our own pie ambuscade. During the week in which we brought conservative guest speakers to campus, a Vietnam veteran, then a sophomore at Indiana, posed as "Dr. Rudolph Montague of Columbia University." His audience, composed of students and profs, sat in rapt attention, prayerful at the chance to hear from so famous a prof from so distinguished a university. He did not fail them. Though possessing an indolent and empty mind, our imposter had heard enough of the Liberal cant to satisfy his audience. Gravely he intoned a long, discursive, and almost incomprehensible lecture on "Progressive Solutions to the Urban Crisis." Suddenly another of our conspirators assaulted Montague with a cream pie after shouting thunderously "Montague, you Communist." Our point was made. An apparent act of violence attracted more media than we had ever imagined, but our success was our undoing. The press could find no trace of Dr. Montague, and when Indiana University officials contacted Columbia University to apologize for the atrocity our hoax was exposed. We expected a hush of respect. Instead we were excoriated for wreaking violence that was not violence on a professor who was, by the way, nonexistent. I only wish our imposter had possessed the wit to ask Indiana University for tenure. How could he be denied in that atmosphere?

Despite the uproar, we continued to hold debates and to invite speakers to campus. Reviewing the guest list of the late 1960s and early 1970s, one sees how American politics was evolving. At first our guests were strictly drawn from the conservative movement—Crane, Buckley, *National Review*'s Frank S. Meyer. Around a keg of beer and late into the Indiana night we would gather to discuss the politics of the Vietnam war or of radicalized campuses. Then, as Liberalism's radicalization threatened ever more campuses and publishing houses, our guest list expanded to include Irving Kristol, Nathan Glazer, and an ambitious young writer from the staff of Colorado Senator Gordon Allott, George F. Will. He was one of a spate of very bright young Capitol Hill staffers around in the 1960s, all eager to write for us. The phenomenon died with the passing of radicalism, as did another phenomenon of the late 1960s and early 1970s, an abundance of junior faculty members from great universities who, like Roger Rosenblatt, an assistant professor of English at Harvard, wanted to oppose campus radicals. Roger volunteered to be our first literary editor and after a year went on to the National Endowment for the Humanities, later becoming a distinguished journalist and editor. There was, in the early 1970s, a historic procession underway, as sensible Liberals parted company with radicals. The man who led the procession was Irving Kristol. He became one of the most influential intellectuals of his time.

CHAPTER 4

Travels with Irving
The Wandering Liberals
Find the Right and Do
the Honorable Thing

IRVING KRISTOL'S PROCESSION THROUGH the postwar decades was
steady, serene, upward, ever upward, but peculiar. Admire him though I
do, I still cannot satisfactorily account for his advance through four decades
of intellectual and political strife to the leadership of that faction of American conservatism known as neoconservatism. Initially the neoconservatives were Liberals, but in the late 1960s and 1970s each in his own way
and for his own reasons ditched the left for our side. The conditions that
created neoconservatism were clearly observable. Each individual's evolution followed a splendid logic. But Irving's ascent towards the rank of
neoconservatism's leading eminence remains slightly enigmatic, as an
American's taste for Chinese cuisine is always slightly enigmatic.

This is not to say that there was anything unusual about Irving's larval
period, given his origins in New York City. As with his friends Nat Glazer
and Norman Podhoretz, Irving's was the Horatio Alger formula adopted
for those whose trade is to be the commerce of ideas. Irving began pe-
nuriously, a poor Jewish boy arguing radical politics in the cafeteria of
City College of New York, he and his radical anti-Stalinist pals holding
down Alcove One, his Stalinist adversaries bivouacked in Alcove Two.
Both alcoves are now as fabulous in the minds of the New York intelligentsia as Sartre's table at the Café Flore—grandiosity being a common
affliction among the intelligentsia of our nation's apple. Tell the members
of the New York literary set that the cafeteria of City College has become

a stop on every sightseeing tour and few will realize that a leg is being pulled.

Irving's early socialism was a routine delusion borne passionately by his peers in New York in the 1930s, but so ardent was Irving that upon graduation he rejected officer training so that he might serve in World War II with what he called "the common people." Then, having faced German guns, he returned to face the disquisitional fusillades of the New York intellectuals, an uncommonly combative group whose members have been at each other's throats for years—initially over the real Marx, then the real Freud, and on down to the real Betty Friedan. Obviously theirs is a story of decline. But to return to my point, they have long been quarrelsome. If one really wants to live the life of the intellectual and avoid gastrointestinal disorders, I would advise against residing in New York City. Boca Raton is a nice place and Sun City, too.

After the War Irving became an editor and writer. Yet as year chased year he wrote only short pieces and edited only dour intellectual reviews or books of very limited interest. The books were always somewhat academic, for America's urban intellectuals in the postwar era grew strenuously academic. No more the urbane life of the literary cosmopolitan for them. They moved from Marx to the contemplation of more useful stuff: urban planning, social problems, income distribution amongst the blacks, the Jews, the Aleuts. It became pretty leaden. In fact, as Irving's peers aged they frequently became rather schoolmarmish, whether they remained on the left or moved to the right.

Steadily, as gray accumulated round his temples and the hairline retreated, Irving gained eminence. A full-length book never came, though he abounded with critical ideas. An esoteric vision to mesmerize the dopes never came either. Still Irving's stature grew. Somehow he was invited to address scholarly bodies, though he was no scholar. By the late 1960s he was being invited onto the boards of corporations, though he was no businessman, and, in 1969, he was offered a mysterious teaching chair at New York University, though the only student of his I ever met was a Manhattan real-estate developer who boomed Schopenhauer over Marx. For four tumultuous decades, on Irving came, neither a prophet nor a spellbinder; such progress is commendable, but, still it puzzles me. Some New York intellectuals create a monumental oeuvre and are revered. Others lie there on their analysts' couches and explode, while paying $145 for a forty-five-minute hour. Still others simply fall by the wayside, lost in recondite philosophizing comprehensible only to them and the pigeons on the bench across from them. Irving, on the other hand, proceeded stolidly and uneventfully. His universe of acquaintances steadily broadened to include the intelligentsia, corporate titans, and the President of the United States.

In the early 1970s, President Richard Nixon invited him in to dine and to counsel. Irving's activities now quickened. He never gained the celebrity stature of William F. Buckley, Jr., or of John Kenneth Galbraith. Perhaps he was too studious. At any rate, he would have been ambivalent about such celebrity. He was enormously self-assured, but every now and then one spotted something elusive beneath the self-assurance. I think it was ambivalence. He was kindly but given to fleeting hauteur, wise but at times unexpectedly impatient, and even somewhat eccentric—particularly when it came to career advice: he suggested that I quit graduate school to practice journalism, which was fine. But then he suggested law school, which could have ended in my untimely death from boredom. Why law school? Irving never rid himself of what we might call the ethnic determinism of his generation of New Yorkers. In Irving's youth Irish-Americans became politicians, and in affluent America I would be a better politician if I had a law degree. Young people usually knew enough to file away his career suggestions and forget them.

Irving was an advocate of little magazines; and he left in his wake a string of carelessly begotten ones, all of the highest quality but most rather poorly attended to, like bastard waifs fathered by an insouciant nobleman. Irving's view was that so long as the right people read you your circulation could be negligible. It took me years to recognize the insularity in Irving's character, but surely this quirky view of magazines is an example of it. America keeps changing. Those who are the right people today may be the wrong people tomorrow. The United Kingdom, where in the 1950s Irving edited *Encounter*, may have the same establishment year in and year out, but not America. I believe Irving's London period shaped a part of his mind forever. Back in New York he always kept a fresh stack of English periodicals by his TV chair. His wife was a historian with special interest in the Victorian period. There was a residue of English mannerisms in both of them. In the 1970s when I edited *The Future That Doesn't Work: Social Democracy's Failures in Britain*, a study of socialism's moribundity published by Doubleday, Irving was quick to suggest appropriate British contributors. Though it had been two decades since he had lived there, he had obviously kept up with British life.

There was, then, beneath Irving's cool exterior, a vast amount of ambivalence. He ran hot and cold, but he was always running. In fact, much of the mystery of Irving's advance through the decades may have been dispelled by the man himself when he told his friend Midge Decter, "You have to keep a horse running." From the late 1940s he always had a horse at the track, and so in late 1979 when that most perspicacious of political scientists, James Q. Wilson, dubbed his friend Irving the Godfather of neoconservatism, the title stuck.

Notwithstanding Irving's restless motion, it is unlikely he ever sought to be a leader, at least not very persistently. Among *engagé* intellectuals one frequently encounters those with a glint in the eye and an itch to head a mob. Neither the glint nor the itch was perceptible in Irving. He was New York's version of a man of letters: well read, very intelligent, inveterately polemical, and attuned to cultural politics. Every once in a while one caught a glimpse of his origins—there would sit the urbane editor of intellectual quarterlies, and suddenly a brusque gesture or rude interjection reminded one that here was a cocky guy from Brooklyn who probably could hold his own on the streets of his youth. Now, however, he was a humane but unsentimental Jewish intellectual, a bookish man who often read in front of a TV with the New York Knicks on. Pulled between activism and bookishness, urbanity and pugnacity, Irving with his ambivalence made an unlikely leader for an ideological movement. How, then, does one account for his rise in the practical world of politics or, to be specific, cultural politics? Truth be known, it had something to do with lunch. Irving was a luminous colloquist, particularly at lunch.

To be sure, he was masterful at receptions, too, and at those solemn intellectual conferences where the truths and errors of an issue are masticated into one great cud of irrefutable if ephemeral truth, and where the bright egghead demonstrates his intellectual fitness and availability for yet another conference in the long chain of confabulations that intellectuals have been running since, I suppose, the Renaissance, all paid for by benefactors with a yen for *Kultur*. At these palavers Irving demonstrated star quality.

Even more crucial to an intellectual's prospects than the conference is the lunch. This does not only hold for intellectuals. Lunch is as important to personal advancement today as a proper marriage was in the good old days. Whether Irving recognized the inestimable value of a properly arranged lunch I do not know. I do know that he lunched assiduously with an enormous variety of people, sometimes to prodigious effect. The historic fact is that one day in the winter of 1979 he was having lunch at his favorite restaurant, the Italian Pavilion, blinking his nervous blink, unconsciously patting a curl in his graying, neatly cut hair, his other hand impatiently waving his constant companion—a Kent cigarette. In his dry, somewhat reedy voice he intones his brisk judgments, a slight New York accent shaping his words. Then *Esquire* magazine hits the newsstands, featuring a gigantic spread on neoconservatism. It was in this monumental issue that Jim Wilson referred to Irving as the neoconservatives' Godfather. Instantaneously Irving actually became "the Godfather" of an intellectual movement that was already a decade old. He filled a need, but he did so ambivalently.

My friendship with him began in the turbulence of 1968. Change was in the air. Numerous Liberals were goose-stepping into the New Age. Others hesitated. All the certitudes of the Liberal orthodoxy were being tested and conservatives grew optimistic. The same conservatives who, in the aftermath of the Goldwater defeat, worried that LBJ's agents were tapping their telephones or that their fledgling political organizations were under IRS scrutiny, suddenly imagined themselves to be playing the same transforming role here that the Fabian Socialists once played in Britain. By the sheer force of their ideas American conservatives might soon commandeer American culture. Off in his book-lined apartment on Riverside Drive, Irving rejected the New Age and began to see merit in these conservatives. He was still a Liberal Democrat, but his mind was wandering. This was 1968, a year of wonders.

The passage of time can obscure even the most momentous events but not always; occasionally an event protrudes from the mist, gaining an unforeseen prominence even as it recedes further back into the past. As the 1960s fell back behind the 1970s, the 1968 assassination of Bobby Kennedy took on a poignancy for me that I had not anticipated. On April 24, 1968, I was on stage with the presidential candidate, watching as he cast his spell, mesmerizing a student audience with a new vision of America chastised, of the Third World exalted, of American progressives finally on the right side of world revolution—a term very much in vogue in those days.

It was between 1966 and 1968 that many of the children of America's Liberals became radicalized. The children of the far left went first, then the Liberals' progeny. Nineteen sixty-eight was the moderates' turn. In that year moderate politicians like Bobby Kennedy and thousands of moderate college students transported themselves from normalcy into the New Age. Cashiering the moderation of their pasts, in some cases the conservatism of their pasts, they ingenuously accepted a New Left critique of society that they would theretofore have snickered at. The visions proffered were all New Age Nirvana, but the reality was cracked bones, sirens, and blood drying on the pavement. A disgruntled leftist had assassinated Bobby

Kennedy's brother, John, and soon a Third World leftist would assassinate him, though two of his favorite campaign targets were colonialism and the overweening pride of the West.

With eerie clarity I recall his 1968 appearance before an expectant audience in the vast Indiana University Auditorium. There he stood; and in a striking blue suit, as blue as the bluest sky, he rang out the new wisdom: America had reached too far, the Third World had been kept down too long. In the flat accent of Massachusetts he declaimed: "It is unlikely that whatever the outcome of the war in Vietnam, the dominoes will fall in either direction. . . . Cambodia, under the leadership of Prince Sihanouk, has sought neutrality . . . , but acted strongly and successfully against any internal Communist activity. Laos . . . has held back and even made progress against its domestic Communists, the Pathet Lao. . . . In Africa, the active anti-colonial movements, in Angola and Mozambique, are led by native nationalists, closer to the West than to Communism." Few skeptics were in the audience that day, and in the following years, as the dominoes fell and each of the above countries suffered the totalitarian lash, few New Age Liberals ever acknowledged how tragically wrong they had been.

Twenty years later I came to know Paul Corbin, Adam Walinsky, and other Kennedy aides from the 1960s. They knew their boss. They were clever and patriotic, and they insisted that Bobby Kennedy would have recognized his error had he lived—such, they insisted, was his intelligence and political acuity. Well, his *volte-face* would have been a welcome challenge to the multitudinous delusions New Age Liberals were to bring down on American life, diabolizing the American past and present, while rendering reality always more painful than it need be. By 1968 the New Age Liberals were focusing on another fear that Kennedy harangued that day, "the danger that in seeking universal peace, needlessly fearful of change and disorder, we will in fact embroil ourselves and the world in a whole series of Vietnams." Sixteen years later Jeane Kirkpatrick would identify this species of pietism as the "Blame America First" syndrome, but it all went back to 1968 as the New Age's Demostheneses harangued against a tyrannical West that hardly existed and on behalf of a humane Third World that existed not at all. "The present direction of Soviet society," Bobby Kennedy pronounced, "is toward greater moderation in foreign policy and greater internal freedom." Ah, the New Age circa 1968: all truths untrue, all hopes hopeless, all trust untrustworthy.

Having uttered his last blithe asseveration, the candidate's wiry figure bent out over the students' outstretched hands to touch, to autograph, to sanctify. Here was the glorious embodiment of the era's foremost political illusion, a "New Politics." Finally, he turned from the maelstrom of upturned faces, and, assuming (erroneously) that I was his escort, asked to be taken to his car. I have forgotten what it was that we talked about as I led him through the maze of curtains backstage, perhaps the effect of his speech. It would have been a likely topic, he being a congenital pol in the height of campaign fevers.

At the time I was just a college boy in an adventurous mood, but with the passing of years and still more assassinations, this escapade has taken on a macabre significance for me. Having filled the auditorium with mild exhortations to revolution and mild chastisement of his country, here was Bobby Kennedy dependent on the good will of a young man whose reactionary politics he had just excoriated. (Unbeknownst to Kennedy I was then supporting Governor Ronald Reagan's fledgling presidential campaign.) A few weeks later, dependent again on good will and fair play, Kennedy was gunned down without mercy and by one of the sons of the Third World whose aspirations he had championed. Lost in the clouds of the New Age, Bobby Kennedy and his followers were utterly blind to the dangers they courted, dangers that I fear the keepers of the American record will now hush up. In the early 1990s, as the Cold War wound down, the theoreticians of the peace movement immediately set about rewriting Cold War history, casting it as a hoax brought down on the American taxpayer by our military-industrial complex and casting the Soviet Union as a nation of bunglers dithering in a system bound to collapse under its own weight. Such were the extremes to which the anti-defense protestors would go to deprive the Cold Warriors of their victory.

Outside the Indiana University auditorium that April afternoon I helped Bobby Kennedy into the back seat of his waiting car. He looked up and smiled. I smiled too and dropped onto his lap a Ronald Reagan for President button. His car sped away before I could get his response. Years later his old aide, Corbin, insisted that Kennedy would have had a good laugh. But had Kennedy been told that the comparatively obscure name on that button would go on to become the dominant political figure of the 1980s while the "New Politics" of 1968 subsided into the unhappy past, would he have laughed?

The winds of 1968 that swept Bobby Kennedy leftward buffeted Irving, too. Something was weakening his fellow Liberals' old resolve. No longer were they so capable of resisting those glassy-eyed savants always found floating on the periphery of every Liberal cause. Irving recognized that the utopians were gaining access to the various control centers of American

Liberalism, the universities, the publishing houses, the media. In *The New York Times Magazine* and other Liberal establishment journals where he frequently appeared, he now remonstrated on the limits of government and social engineering. Irving had come to these conclusions because many of his Liberal academic friends, for instance, Nathan Glazer, had found in their research cause to question Liberalism's more grandiose claims. Then, too, the conservatives' critique of Liberalism was beginning to have an effect on him.

Why he began reading the conservatives I do not know. He was, of course, intellectually curious, but another impulse may have been at work. In the 1960s, if one cited the work of a conservative, say Milton Friedman, one was sure to raise a fellow left-wing intellectual's toupee. Irving, being a Liberal long before he became a conservative, always derived a great deal of satisfaction from asking the annoying question, adducing disturbing evidence, positing a mischievous proposition. To be sure, Irving was intellectually curious about the conservative critique and, being a gentleman, he was tolerant, but a deeper element in his Liberal background inspired his early interest in the conservatives.

Liberalism's most deeply held political value—in fact its only steadfastly observed political value—is that item mentioned early in most criminal codes, to wit, the misdemeanor of disturbing the peace. This explains the peculiarity of Liberal tolerance, which is almost never extended across the board but almost always extended to those fantasticos further to the left of Liberalism. Tolerating leftist zanies is tremendously disturbing to ordinary Americans; ipso facto Liberals tolerate them chivalrously and go aflutter over their every wild-eyed scheme. Liberalism has elevated disturbing the peace to the level of a metaphysical imperative. A review of nearly a century of Liberal policy reveals Liberals undertaking many ambitious projects and promoting a multitude of humane values only to revise these projects and values once the bourgeoisie no longer objects. Thus the Liberal tolerates talk of a guaranteed annual income, and if that does not shake up the guy next door the Liberal thumps for the system of taxation favored by the late Mao Tse-tung. The Liberal favored a color-blind society, then black militancy, then quotas. He will support nudity on the beach and, once the bourgeoisie acquiesces to nudity on the beach, he will urge it in the shopping mall or across the street from the old people's retirement home.

Irving tolerated conservatives and grew curious about their critique of Liberalism in part because he recognized that the conservatives were conserving the liberal values enshrined in the Constitution—values most Americans, Irving included, admire. But if I know Irving, he had another, more amusing, motive, to wit, a good word for conservatism was certain to disturb the peace. Irving was an equal opportunity disturber. So faithful to Liberalism's fundamental political value was he that he disturbed fatuous Liberals as well as ordinary Americanos.

Nor was Irving alone in disturbing the Liberal brethren. Within the provinces of Liberalism a critical mass of writers and academics was falling out of sync with Liberalism's contemporary thrust. These discontented intellectuals required a leader who shared their Liberal background and their antipathy for Liberalism's drunken dance into the New Age. After a thousand lunches, a hundred conferences, unnumbered lectures and essays, Irving was the logical leader, just as Jim Wilson asserted. However, neoconservatism's prospects as a political movement would have been more auspicious had its leader been a more single-minded pursuer of power. On the other hand, had Irving been more covetous of power he would have been less representative of the neoconservatives, for as a group they were more given to the pursuit of ideas than to the pursuit of power. They wanted to establish the Truth in each issue they took up. There have been intellectuals who were more interested in power than in truth, for instance Benito Mussolini or—perhaps closer to the American context—George McGovern. Neoconservatives were different. They wanted to get at the Truth; it was a weakness; it was a constant distraction from the great game of politics. And another thing—they were often too acerbic or volatile for political canoodling. They were effective in government service, but that was a consequence of a Liberal past, not a hunger for power. They had been raised as statists, and they knew the tricks of the bureaucratic game.

When I say that neoconservatives were intellectuals, I use the term as Hayek used it, meaning dealers in second-hand ideas. Some were scholars, but most were acting as intellectuals, trafficking in used ideas. Only a minority of the adepts of the 1950s' conservative revival were intellectuals. Others were businessmen and politicians. All were mavericks remote from the centers of American culture. The neoconservatives had prospered at the very center of that culture. They were Liberals, frequently very distinguished Liberals. Many taught at prestige universities—Harvard had an especially active colony of neoconservatives. Others worked at prominent publishing houses, think tanks, and foundations. When Liberalism's adherents were diverted from the modest promises of New Deal Liberalism to New Age Liberalism's *bouleversement* toward pacifism, egalitarianism, personal liberation, introspection, and generalized utopia, skeptical Liberals became alarmed. When they spoke out against the New Age they found themselves being labeled neoconservatives. They had always had a large say in how our culture treated things, but now, usually against their wills, they were being lumped in with conservatives and rendered ever less influential.

Most gamely accepted their fate. They continued to examine New Age Liberalism with the kind of rigor that intellectuals in revolt have always displayed, and with the same gusto. *The Public Interest*, founded by Irving and his amiable factotum Daniel Bell in 1965, became an omnium gatherum for analyses of practically every aspect of American government. Yet the revolt of the neoconservatives from America's increasingly idiotic intellectual mainstream differed from other American intellectual revolts in one important aspect. Earlier dissident intellectuals, for instance those who wrote in *The American Mercury* in the 1920s and in the original *American Spectator* in the 1930s, complained primarily about art, manners, mores, and ideas. To this list of concerns the neoconservatives added public policy, and they stressed it over all else.

In the 1920s, when critics laid siege to their decade's dominant culture their subject was rarely policy, though they at times might fall upon government censorship, loyalty oaths, or Prohibition. By the 1960s, however, government policies had spread so luxuriantly throughout society, entangling so many areas of American life, that the neoconservatives spent more time on policy than on manners, customs, or art. Consequently many of them were not a lot of laughs. Policy is usually a bore for lively spirits, and a large number of neoconservatives were unembellished policy analysts. To publish the best writers of their time, Mencken and Nathan had to endure bores of such colossal cheerlessness as Theodore Dreiser. I had to survive *policy analysts!* I had to ask them to join me for a drink, occasionally even for two drinks and supper! Perhaps these gruesome encounters explain the deep sense of personal identification I have always had with George Jean Nathan's crack, "I drink to make other people interesting." The seriousness of the neoconservatives assisted them in getting to the truth of most of the policy issues of Lyndon Johnson's Great Society. It also made their autopsies of subsequent issues invaluable. But this seriousness was also limiting; had more of them possessed a flicker of joie de vivre they might not have missed the things that were about to elude them in the 1980s. We were approaching a decade abundant with gaudy fools. Policy analysis renders a budget comprehensible, but other matters slip by.

When I first met Irving, nothing slipped by him. It was, as I say, 1968, and the whole decade had made perfect sense to him. He had been reading the Greek philosophers and Edmund Burke ("You can never read too much Burke," he would say).

Through the gauze of time I see him sitting in his office at the publishing house, Basic Books, manuscripts and books on social science or political philosophy scattered about. On the walls hang bits of contemporary art— the kind popular among the New York intelligentsia of the day, say a cold, black and white photograph of a pickle on a stool, the lighting arranged so that a ghostly shadow is cast from what is, after all, only a pickle on a stool. Sunlight beamed through the dirty glass of a window unattended by draperies or blinds, its shaft of light illuminating every speck of dust in the air and making the room uncomfortably warm. In the sunlight of this sparsely furnished room sat Irving, abloom in middle age, kindly and cheerful, brisk and incisively intelligent.

I was there to interview him for our magazine, which was at the time only an off-campus project. By 1968 some of the younger members of the conservative movement were beginning to notice Irving as a potential ally. Most of the older conservatives were wary, but then those of us in conservatism's younger generation had never been diagnosed as mentally ill or suffering from any of the other afflictions that Irving's friends, the Danger-on-the-Right Liberals, laid to the conservative movement (and we shall discuss their charges shortly). It was easier for us to see merit in Irving's skepticism, and to those of us caught in the campus upheavals Irving appeared as a guru. He recognized the pathologies of the era and warned that authority was being drained from American institutions, not merely the authority of the law but the authority of intellect, the authority that distinguishes excellence from poppycock, Beethoven from the nonce lilts of rock and roll. Finally, Irving recognized the drift of domestic politics. In his 1968 interview with me he predicted Liberalism's demise, despite the gallant leaps that it seemed to be taking in all directions. He recognized that it was precisely those leaps that would tear Liberalism apart.

There in his Manhattan office, at the height of New Politics fever, Irving foresaw that future American politics would be "considerably less liberal." "Any kind of militance," he said into my whirring tape recorder, "—especially extralegal activity—on the part of the left in this country will certainly give rise to a corresponding reaction on the part of the public."[1] Over the next decade the left-wing militance spread, and with it conservatism. Presently the conservative movement ousted Liberal Republicans (referred to in the biased argot of the day as "moderate Republicans") from the party's leadership and went on to capture the presidency and even the United States Senate. It was not merely the comeliness of conservative ideas that brought American conservatism from obscurity to power. It was also the "militance" that Irving had remonstrated against a dozen years before, and, to be sure, the infusion of talent that his neoconservatives brought to conservatism once they had finally shaken themselves of their last Liberal bugaboos.

Bear in mind, the migration of these wandering Liberals to neoconservatism took years. It was not a mass conversion, for the neoconservatives were not driven by a religious impulse. They were the least impulsive of the Liberals. Unlike the New Age Liberals who were converted to their newly agitated state by some chiliastic vision orchestrated by a host of Isaiahs, Jeremiahs, and the inimitable Dr. Timothy Leary of Harvard University, the neoconservatives arrived at their position after a careful survey of the changing intellectual terrain, prolonged reading, logical deductions, and a period of personal reassessment during which they abused any conservative friend who happened to be in the area. As I had decided to publish their work in *The American Spectator* I was to take my lumps for over a decade and not only from neoconservatives. My friends, the conservatives, saw the wandering Liberals' arrival at *The American Spectator* as evidence that I was about to "sell out," which to the conservatives meant seeking personal advancement by deserting conservatism.

The conservatives' apprehensions were warranted. William F. Buckley, Jr.'s *National Review* had provided occasions for several well-known opportunists, such as Garry Wills, to advance over the bodies of conservatives whom they had knifed. Many conservatives believed that, once radicalism was out of fashion among Liberals, Irving and his cohort would wander back to Liberalism. Then, too, each neoconservative took so long to flush all the Liberal vapors from the mind that movement conservatives naturally became impatient with their fussiness. Even in 1968, when Irving was sounding so reasonable in his interview with me, he was very rough on conservatives and in such left-of-center environs as *The New Republic*.

It was an election year and the editor of *The New Republic* invited him to draw up the "case" for Hubert Humphrey's presidential candidacy in his June 8, 1968, issue. There Irving wrote: "In these pages, I need not explain why the prospect of electing Mr. Nixon depresses me. Suffice it to say that he appeals to *the wrong majority* to govern the United States in these times—a majority whose dominant temper will be sullenly resentful of the social changes we have been experiencing and impulsively reactionary toward the crises we shall inevitably be enduring," and Irving extolled the "pragmatic liberalism" that "represents the only vital and enduring tradition of American government since 1932."² Who could blame the conservatives for being suspicious of the fellow who composed those lines or, for that matter, about those of us on the right who admired him? At the time Hubert Humphrey might have been too dignified to abandon himself to the frivolities of the New Age (hence Irving's admiration), but for decades he had been among the most intensely ideological Liberals in his party. Lyndon Johnson had chosen him as a running mate in 1964 chiefly to allay left-wing mistrust. Conservatives hated Hubert, and when my new best friend Irving heaved up the above testament they naturally grew uneasy about me.

I, however, had made a calculation. I reckoned that the fissure running through Liberalism, separating the romantic utopians from the practical defenders of the Liberal tradition, was widening beyond repair. The tendency of ideologies to shatter into fragments of extremism is well-documented, and Liberalism was providing more documentation daily. Nineteen sixty-eight was the year of the protesting child; the gun-toting militant; middle-class *enragés* agog with dope, rock, and orgasm; and Irving had no sympathy with those adult Liberals who admired the dissipations of apocalyptic youth. He recognized the radicalism of the times as destructive to the New Deal's Liberal legacy. He was right. Despite the popular vaticinations about how my peers on the left were going to be the salvation of the world, all they were about to achieve was a slight increase in petty crime, the inauguration of a nationwide drug problem, an increase in sexually transmitted diseases, and the crack-up of Liberalism. According to my calculations, that would mean that most wandering Liberals would be transformed into conservatives. Unfortunately, that transformation was going to take a lot longer than I expected.

In the meantime, members of the conservative movement were distressed over the new voices being introduced into the magazine. There were well-known Liberals such as Irving, Pat Moynihan, and Martin Diamond, and there were less well known but equally undependable new voices such as Roger Rosenblatt. The conservatives eventually forgave me for fraternizing with the neoconservatives, but I am not sure they will ever forgive me for another editorial decision I made. In 1970 I chose as my first Washington correspondent an aspiring writer whose independence of mind and prickly manner toward the conservative movement caused acute acidosis on the right: George F. Will.

George had enormous verve for combat and he peppered me with puckish letters suggesting where the magazine might next strike the Liberal behemoth. He also had a lamentable weakness for riling up the conservatives. Eventually George went on to become a well-known writer and television personality, but his delight in stinging the conservatives continues. Today he calls himself a Tory, though in his cocoonery at the *Spectator*, George's column was titled "Letter From a Whig" (and so energetic was he that occasionally he contributed more than one article to an issue). The conservatives' pique gave George colossal pleasure. Two conservatives were particularly neuralgic about George: M. Stanton Evans, the conservative journalist and activist, and *National Review* book editor, Frank S. Meyer. After George's every essay, both would ring me up and burn my ears over one or another of the heresies he had allegedly committed.

It was thrilling to see how George would painstakingly shape an essay to give the conservatives maximum displeasure while advancing positions that fundamentally agreed with them. George had a knack for this sort of writing. It was a wonderful gift. Possibly it issued from that mysterious afflatus spurring the artistry of so many fine writers, malice. Possibly it was George's way of advancing himself in the media. Whatever has motivated George's right-baiting, he has occasionally given himself over to eruptions so intemperate and gratuitous, and so destructive to his reputation for sagacity, that one has to wonder if George is afflicted by what we might call writers' hysteria, wherein the patient temporarily loses control of his literary tools and of his mind. One thinks of the time that George was composing a perfectly plausible column on Vice President George Bush, then the presidential front-runner and the chosen successor of Will's friend, President Ronald Reagan. Suddenly the hysteria gripped George and out came: "Bush's recent New York performance suggests that although the 1988 nomination is his to lose, he has a gift for doing things like that. . . . What Bush said is gibberish, but not just gibberish. It is a lie. . . . the unpleasant sound Bush is emitting as he traipses from one conservative gathering to another is a thin, tinny 'arf'—the sound of a lapdog.'"[3] Doubtless there is art in such outbursts, possibly there is some hidden wisdom, but those of us who like him wish George would maintain his composure.

At least the unpleasantness that I suffered from the conservatives during the neoconservatives' excruciating metamorphosis was confined to a few acidulous telephone calls and letters. My ordeal with the neoconservatives was more protracted and painful, for, if I wanted to publish them, I had to endure the prejudices that emanated from each as he acclimated himself to conservatives. This had not been in my calculations.

In college one is exposed to a vast amount of information that is quite untrue, and it is most unjust that one should have to demonstrate one's mastery of untruths to graduate—one has to go even further to graduate with honors. For those who studied politics in my generation an important source of disinformation was Samuel Lubell's *The Future of American Politics*, a required text in government courses. The book's underlying flaws all derive from the author's hopeless idealism; Lubell believed that politics is a rational act, that voters calculate logically and vote their interests, that at the ballot box selfishness triumphs over puerile sentiment. Thus Lubell believed that lower-income earners would join the Republican party once they had become affluent and suburban. Such romantic reasoning left many Republicans sozzled with false expectations and caused students of political science to leave college full of confidence in democratic man's capacity for self-preservation.

The truth is, however, that out in the neighborhoods, in the precincts, in the university faculty clubs, and in the polling booths, politics is dominated by sentiment and prejudice. Lubell should have studied sports before he studied politics. When a family of Dodgers fans moves from Los Angeles to San Francisco they do not necessarily become Giants fans. Frequently they remain loyal to the Dodgers. When Democrats moved to the suburbs they remained Democrats for years. Some went even further left, but only slowly did any become Republicans. Sentiment and prejudice are powerful restraints on right reason.

Both were to restrain the neoconservatives from making a clean break with Liberalism. Had I known this before getting it into my head that neoconservatives were headed towards alliance with my fellow conservatives, I might have escaped some of the long, painful hours ahead during which in-transit neoconservatives pummelled me with their prejudices against conservatives. All the charges against conservatism that had accumulated in the 1950s and 1960s had to be overcome. Each neoconservative had to work through his deep-seated beliefs that Barry Goldwater and his supporters had disordered minds, that some were hicks and others nostalgic for times faraway and aristocratic. Every neoconservative was aware of the Liberals' Danger-on-the-Right treatises, which argued that the members of the conservative revival admired lynch laws, blue laws, Robber Barons, military rule, racism, monarchy, and the aesthetic theories of the philistine. Only slowly did neoconservatives shed these beliefs. Meanwhile, as every one of them began moving my way, I had to bear with patience hurtful bigotries, first from Irving, who led the move rightward, and then from Nat Glazer and Jeane Kirkpatrick and all the others whom I admired. Not even the European neoconservatives would let up.

The Danger-on-the-Right tracts had been read on the Continent, and for several years such evolving leftwingers as Jean-François Revel and Olivier Todd spoiled my Aprils in Paris. Ever the pensive Frenchman, Revel seemed to shed only one old left-wing prejudice a year. The last to go was his animus against capitalistic acts between consenting adults. It was about 1977 when the erstwhile socialist accepted the free market. At the time I reminded him that thitherto he had derided Milton Friedman's ideas as antiquated. His reply was swift: "Ah, but old ideas have new applications!"

During a conference that *The American Spectator* sponsored at Harvard in 1971, Norman Podhoretz, the editor of *Commentary*, a magazine that had served as an incubator for 1960s radicalism, lulled me into an ambush that is enshrined in my memory as epitomizing all the false charges endured by me so charitably during my missionary years with the wandering Liberals. Norman was now parting company with Liberalism and soon would be a treasured friend, but many of the Liberal prejudices against conservatives still chafed in his mind. On that faraway day he charged me with (a) an infatuation with the police, all police, (b) a dread of smut, (c) an infatuation with the military, all military, (d) a prissy Victorian phobia against sex, (e) an infatuation with money, (f) a fear of status loss, (g) an infatuation with big business, and (h) a propensity to conceal deeply held feelings—all standard tenets of the Danger-on-the-Right Liberals. On this last point Norman had something. As twilight was creeping in, lengthening the shadows of the vast dining hall where he had me trapped, I was indeed concealing at least two deeply held feelings. The first was that Norman, despite his fine intentions, was the prude in the room; and the second was that if I could extricate myself from his sermon promptly I had a better than even chance of having a drink with a terrific co-ed seated next to me and growing visibly restless. Norman was a few minutes into a new topic— an exegesis of the spiritual origins of my hay fever—when we bid him farewell. Victorian scruples restrain me from betraying our ultimate destination.

The layman might be surprised to hear that intellectuals are so irritable, but there it is. Intellectuals of all persuasions are prone to disputes of astounding belligerence and personal enmity. Quite possibly their ferocity derives from their privileged childhoods. Once the budding intellectual begins polishing teacher's apples, he rarely has to fear that his insolence will lead to an incoming smack to the chops. Teacher will protect him. Hence intellectuals are warlike, and we peace-loving Americanos should be grateful that the American intelligentsia rarely has access to weaponry any deadlier than typewriters or word processors, and that few American intellectuals are sufficiently fit to lift these instruments and hurl them at their enemies—some of the lady intellectuals can, but their number is not large. If the intellectuals ever took up arms against each other they might constitute a menace to public safety comparable to the violence laid to the Tonton Macoutes of the Caribbean. In chapter 2, I noted the feuds dividing the conservative movement's libertarians, traditionalists, and anticommunists. Earlier in the present chapter I mentioned the quarrelsomeness of the New York intellectuals. It follows that neoconservatives, too, were disputatious. In the Reagan years their readiness for combat gave them an unattractive reputation for factionalism, and I am afraid the reputation was warranted.

One or two of them became very hard to stick. Think of it. Here were certain latitudinarian members of the conservative movement such as myself trying to pave the way for the neoconservatives' entry into the conservative camp, and we found ourselves set upon by homicidal intellectuals driven by fathomless angers and the bizarre notion that if one had not critically read some illuminatus like Claude Lévi-Strauss one was lost. The most ferocious example of a bilious neoconservative was, of course, the legendary Hilton Kramer, problem child. Hilton was another of those A students who can never quite get over his superior mind or transcend his bad manners. Kramer was the embodiment of the homicidal intellectual, and frankly I wish he had remained on the left. He is not what we Americans call a "nice" person. It is alarming that his movement to the right continues, for if he ever falls under the influence of those conservatives who reverence the Right to Keep and Bear Arms, he could become truly dangerous. Conservatism has not yet had a mass murderer on its side. In point of fact, the most famous assassins in recent American history have been progressives of one sort or another. Hilton armed could blemish our spotless record.

In 1982 he left *The New York Times*, where he had written excellent art criticism, and began a conservative arts monthly, *The New Criterion*. It was stimulating and competently edited, but apparently the satisfactions it afforded him were never sufficient to anesthetize Hilton's intrinsic rage, and so he passed through the 1980s blasting away at all sides. Like an armored personnel carrier lost in war-torn Beirut, he fired at anything that moved. What his view of the good life was I could never divine from his writings or from his public displays of emotion. He had the intellectual's usual white-hot anger, and apparently never enough enemies to quench it. When all his hooey about art and high purpose has been analyzed I believe that experts will agree that he can be dismissed as a malcontent, but do not turn your back on him.

Yet, I digress. Let us return to the neoconservatives and to the causes of their journey to the right. Slow though that journey was it demonstrates a sobering truth. For many intellectuals their political ideas are the product not simply of logic and learning but of outside factors thrust upon them, misadventures and fears, personal conditions, fortuitous phenomena, a wrong number dialed late in the night, a bad bowl of matzo ball soup— history's unwelcome visitations. This was certainly true of the neoconservatives as they wandered towards conservatism. Things were being forced upon them in the 1960s and 1970s, and the workings of their powerful intellects had as little to do with the transformation of their ideas as did the workings of their gall bladders.

Cleopatra's nose changed the course of history, and so did Dr. Marx's pants. Had he possessed a second pair, perhaps of a finer weave, perhaps with a better fit, he might have acquired a different perspective on the rituals of the bourgeoisie and thus forsaken his gripes to become a precursor of Fred the Furrier or T. Boone Pickens. Charles Darwin's theory that mankind evolved from the ape might have been the result of studious observation and deduction; but it is equally plausible that while puzzling over the origins of man Dr. Darwin looked out the window of his study and saw his hairy gardener hanging from a pear tree. Hesto-presto, an idea comes to him! Suddenly the scholarly Dr. Darwin has a theory of man's origins to rival Genesis. To be sure, learned members of the intelligentsia are capable of excogitating their hypotheses from high-flown principles; but material conditions press in even on lofty minds. So do sheer accidents: a hairy gardener, a flawed spouse. Can anyone doubt that Jean-Jacques Rousseau's conceptions of humanity were influenced by the fact, admirably established by Professor Maurice Cranston in his estimable biography, that the French philosopher had taken for his lawful wedded wife an illiterate dimwit? Read *Émile*, his book on educating the young. Doubtless one day M. Rousseau and his pals sat around marveling at Mme. Rousseau's confused attempts to pull on her socks, and *Émile* was half written. Had he left it at that, by the way, it would have been a better book.

So it was with the neoconservatives. Things had been thrust upon them. In the 1960s they had examined the condition of their cities and their campuses only to conclude that all their fellow progressives' suave theories were going haywire. Manhattan had become a dangerous place. In fact, as Daniel Patrick Moynihan, the former neoconservative American ambassador to the UN, was to observe, the world had become "a dangerous place." The welfare state's botches, the Third World's atrocities, the spread of Communist tyranny and holocaust in places like Southeast Asia—all were blunders that bore in on the neoconservatives.

The bloody aftermath of the fall of Southeast Asia demonstrated anew that Carthage's fate remained a possibility for all nations, particularly democratic nations. As the prisons and graveyards of Southeast Asia filled, as cities were renamed for tyrants and villages abandoned, some American Liberals reviewed foreign policy issues with a rigor that had not been in fashion during the early 1970s when airy optimism about Communist intentions sealed Southeast Asia's fate. It was becoming dangerous for small countries to be friendly with the United States, and some Liberals became aware of Israel's perilous predicament, surrounded as it was in a sea of enemies. The realization that another American ally, one that had been particularly close to Liberal hearts in the post-World War II period, could go the way of South Vietnam provoked the neoconservatives to part company with the isolationists and pacifists who arrogated the Liberal banner in the 1960s and 1970s.

Israel's catalytic role in turning many a Liberal into a neoconservative gave birth to the myth that neoconservatives were mostly fearful Zionists alarmed over Israel's fate. In truth many of those who were becoming neoconservatives were not actually Jewish, for instance, Paul Seabury of Berkeley, Edward Banfield and James Q. Wilson of Harvard, and Jeane Kirkpatrick. Nor were they particularly fearful. Many were bold critics of the American scene, convinced that Liberalism was degenerating and ardent to challenge the received wisdom of the herd. Many, such as Banfield and later Kirkpatrick, braved violent protests to lecture on college campuses. A barbarous world was being thrust upon these neoconservatives, and they chose to resist. Irving saw what was afoot and in a celebrated crack defined neoconservatives as "Liberals who have been mugged by reality." That is my point precisely. Times were changing. Reality was being transformed, and its unpleasant features were being thrust upon those who cared deeply about freedom and democracy.

At some point in the middle 1970s something marvelous happened. As neoconservatism's critique of limitless government and New Age utopianism was attracting ever more adherents, the culture opened up and gave this increasingly conservative critique a respectful hearing. Never before in the postwar period had such a phenomenon occurred. Thitherto the merest suggestion that there might be limits to social policy or that an activist foreign policy might be essential for peace was grounds for being exiled from public life or branded a rightist fanatic. Now this point of view was being respectfully debated on campus and in the media. Conservatives and neoconservatives alike were being invited to join such illustrious organizations as the Council on Foreign Relations or to take positions in the Kennedy School's Institute of Politics at Harvard. Such attention came as no surprise to neoconservatives, most of whom had for years been active in the Republic's circles of power. However, to those of us who had been part of the old conservative movement, this attention was a very agreeable surprise. Suddenly the moment was ours. We felt in command. We were the beneficiaries of Liberalism's Crack-Up and of our own hard work. Yet there was another agent for change at work. Never underestimate the vibrations of the *Zeitgeist*.

CHAPTER 5

The *Zeitgeist's* Fair Winds Turn Foul

From Irving to
Betsy Bloomingdale

Usually I take my stand with the empiricists. That which cannot be tested by the senses is barely credible. But if I can see the consequences of some unseen force, well, just possibly that force exists. This is my case for the *Zeitgeist*. The late G.W.F. Hegel, the philosopher most closely associated with the concept, would doubtless sniff at such a succinct elucidation; but, Dr. Hegel, life is short.

Enormous changes have whipsawed American political life since the 1960s. There has been an unprecedented shuffle of ideas and enthusiasms, as the life of an idea or of an enthusiasm grows ever shorter. In 1968 the New Politics was radical; by 1980 the New Politics was conservative. How does one account for it? Consider the *Zeitgeist*, blowing out of the earliest days of our civilization, bringing along bits and pieces of the moral, intellectual, and social debris of history. At some point in the early 1960s it increased its velocity, gusting to hurricane force and changing the Republic's fashions, enthusiasms, celebrities, and desiderata. Never in recent times had it blown with such force. By the end of the Kennedy Administration men no longer bothered to wear hats. Women began lacquering their hair with something called "spray-net."

Think of it! In 1968 the *Zeitgeist* picks up a Eugene McCarthy, gives him a constituency of college youths, and makes him the hope of a generation. Brief months later it drops the poor fish. McCarthy wanders on. He runs for high office again and again, but the *Zeitgeist* blows differently now. It supports different values. The forlorn candidate gets no lift and so decays gently somewhere in the hills of Virginia, writing pleasant poesy and wearing silly hats, anything to snare the recognition of the mob. The mob, alas, is primed for different acts, and poor McCarthy's Children's Crusade of 1968 is an act sealed away in another era. The spirit of the time has moved on.

One's mark in the world is not decided solely by the *Zeitgeist*. Will-power, intelligence, and virtue doubtless play their part; but the *Zeitgeist* cannot be overlooked. Napoleon would have had the mind of a military genius were he born in Corsica in 1769 or in 1949. But owing to the Enlightenment, the dissipation of monarchy, the rise of science, Josephine's tresses, and dozens of other historic developments, the stage was set by the end of the eighteenth century for a conquering Emperor. By 1949 the little Corsican's military bearing and flair for uniforms might suit him for nothing more awesome than a role as doorman at the Ritz. ("*Bonaparte . . .* my bag!") The *Zeitgeist* sets the scene and decides what lines will play.

The *Zeitgeist* is composed of such picayune elements as caprice and such colossal forces as history. It is a current of ideas and sentiments that blows across all the lands of the earth, into our minds and across our hearts. Its velocity varies, but its motion never stops. It explains how a feminist is a sage today; though her sour foresister, living in a prior century and haranguing pretty much the same harangues, might have been nabbed by the local witch patrol and turned into a cinder. It explains why, in a given era, behavior never countenanced before is suddenly the behavior of many, and a thought hitherto unthinkable becomes commonplace, then an embarrassment. The gods of the moment will in time be gods discarded.

Mathematics and science abound with examples of an idea whose time has come, of men developing parallel ideas independently. Towards the end of the seventeenth century and unaware of each other's work, both Gottfried Wilhelm Leibniz and Isaac Newton were working up the fundamental theorem of the calculus.[1] The method of "least squares" now used in geodetic surveying and other mathematical computations was independently discovered late in the eighteenth and early in the nineteenth centuries by Carl Friedrich Gauss and Adrien-Marie Legendre.[2] During World War II there was the parallel development of the jet engine in England and Germany. (The Nigerians also made parallel strides until both Nigerians broke for lunch and never came back.) The *Zeitgeist* explains why a style of music or poetry or thought catches on. The style suits the times. Bach preceded Haydn and then was lost for decades until the learned Mendelssohn retrieved him. Today we think Bach will be heard forever, but surely in time he will again lapse into oblivion. Cézanne followed Monet, but would Cézanne have painted as he did without Monet and would the public have accepted him? Pierre Augustus Fhanan revived the Neoclassical style in Paris in 1924, but who has ever heard of him? Perhaps his time will come, but, well, maybe you are in sympathy with his work. I am not.

By the late 1970s, socialism no longer inflamed the hearts of the ever hopeful. In the United Kingdom Prime Ministers Edward Heath and James Callaghan gave way to Margaret Thatcher, the pristine capitalist. President Jimmy Carter gave way to the ghost of Barry Goldwater. The *Zeitgeist*— the force of ideas and actions long forgotten, the consequence of millions of roads not taken, of many a charmingly turned ankle, and more than a few glissades on the banana peel—opens the way for great men and fools. How it works has never been satisfactorily explained, not by the aforementioned Hegel or by Goethe, Kant or any of the others who have pondered it. But that it does work is demonstrated by thousands of history's abrupt vicissitudes.

The sudden emergence of the neoconservatives represents one such vicissitude. The conservative intellectuals were in point of fact petering out. The conservative revival, aging through the 1950s and the 1960s, came to be called the conservative movement. Its founding theorists, however, began to expire, giving way to political activists such as Phyllis Schlafly and Paul Weyrich. They were effective activists, particularly Schlafly, but for the battle of ideas they were not equipped with armament equal to that of the political intellectual. Conservatism's founding theorists and polemicists had tried to train successors by establishing educational organizations such as the Intercollegiate Studies Institute, an organization founded specifically to do for American intellectual life what the Fabians had done in England. Somehow, it was slow going. Frank S. Meyer and James Burnham, who as editors at *National Review* had inspired closely reasoned thought and political action, passed without successors. Only William F. Buckley, Jr., could be counted on to perform with consistently high intelligence on the national stage into the 1970s. There were no more Meyers or Burnhams to support his act. Mute evidence of the dimming of the conservative movement's intellect could be seen on the masthead of *National Review*, where the dying generation of learned polemicists was replaced by dimmer lights, for the most part writers with no particular credentials beyond a few essays. Rarely did one of them have a learned book to his credit. Academics, particularly economists, continued to spread the free market enlightenment, but they were not agile publicists comparable to Meyer or Burnham. Most did not write particularly well. Their theaters of operations were economics departments and government bureaucracies. But in public forums they were infrequently seen.

Irving Kristol's crowd came to the rescue. They were erudite and extremely intelligent. Perhaps because they had so recently been good Liberals their concerns had more resonance in academe and the media. By comparison the interests of surviving conservative founders such as Russell Kirk seemed mildewed, though Kirk did not seem to care, nor did many other surviving writers from the original conservative movement. With a presidential candidate of their persuasion active nationally and headed for the White House, one would have expected these conservatives to be preparing to wield power on the national stage, but they were oddly somnolent. The neoconservatives were more energetic and, so it seems, more influential. Even an unfriendly critic of neoconservatism, Peter Steinfels, had to admit in 1979 that the neoconservatives' "impact has been immediate and enormous."[3] With the election of Ronald Reagan, conventional Liberals of the Steinfels variety sensed that the neoconservatives were destined for power.

The neoconservatives brought divers talents to conservatism. Their movement included social scientists, literary intellectuals, philosophers, journalists, and the kind of all-purpose political writers that the French call publicists. Furthermore their interests varied. Taken together, however, the neoconservatives' catalogue of concerns included a qualified acceptance of a welfare state; critical approval of the corporation and of Big Labor; qualified respect for social science, which older conservatives generally rejected as humbug; and a devotion to political philosophy that differed from that of older conservatives. The neoconservatives took their political philosophy as it was taught by Leo Strauss and his students, whereas to older conservatives political philosophy was literary, a part of the tapestry of Western civilization. To neoconservatives the ancient philosophers provided guidance for the present. Neoconservatives were animated by a high seriousness and in the battle of ideas a flinty partisanship. In time, some of the neoconservatives, notably Podhoretz and his wife, the indispensable Midge Decter, would revive the movement conservatives' anticommunism and defense of traditional values. The onanism of the New Age disgusted them. Considering the intellectually repressed decade that was to follow, one looks back on the 1970s and sees an opening in the clouds: a brief and unexpected period during which Liberals actually examined themselves and encouraged their critics. I suppose this period of self-examination was a consequence of the excesses of the late 1960s: of the student radicals, of the anti-Vietnam war demonstrations, perhaps even of the Vietnam war (a progressive's war), and the Great Society (a progressive's orgy). Whatever the reason, for a brief but splendid moment criticism of Establishment Liberalism grew luxuriantly throughout all the forums and around all the totems of Liberal culture. The neoconservatives were just the people to launch the critiques. Their views attracted wide and often amiable notice. Sophisticates were fetched by them, for they had one trait that all sophisticates, even bogus sophisticates, relish, to wit, an allegiance to intellect. To every pursuit they applied intellect: to sport, to business, to culture. They were incessant, sempiternal eggheads. Irving applied intellect to watching the New York Knicks. Jeane Kirkpatrick applied it to French cuisine. Ernest van den Haag resorted to it in his pursuit of the fair sex, and Nat Glazer in his meditations on graffiti—and more on that anon.

One spring afternoon I was driving Pat Moynihan through the back hills of Indiana in a very hot Porsche, finely tuned by my favorite mechanic Lorenzo Semeria whose former clients had included the Ferrari racing team and two-time Formula One world champion Jim Clark. Lorenzo was the maestro of metal. He once diagnosed an engine problem of mine from three hundred miles away after asking me to place the telephone receiver beside the revving engine. Of course, he had to be a maestro to postpone premature entry of any of my sorely pressed Porsches into the junk yard. Since the 1970s, conservative writers have had a passion for fast cars, as P. J. O'Rourke documents for all history in his admirable treatise *Republican Party Reptile*. What P. J. elides is that around machines we are all spectacularly klutzy; we need our Lorenzos. Thanks to him on that spring afternoon my 911 was its brawny self, braking, cornering, and accelerating, effortlessly—all to Pat's delight. But what fascinated him was not that the road kept slipping out from under us or that the trees on either side were now a blur. Rather, the former Harvard prof wanted to know where I had *learned* my driving technique. Had I done as his neoconservative colleague, James Q. Wilson, had upon acquiring a similar piece of Stuttgart iron—namely, taken it to Bob Bondurant's grand prix driving school to study driving styles. "But of course, Pat"—how could I tell him that what he adjudged technique would have been more accurately perceived by the cops as the ingredients of a reckless homicide charge?

Such was the studiousness that pervaded the neoconservatives' lives in the 1970s. Their confidence in ideas and in the imperium of intellect inflated them with confidence as they approached the 1980s. However, unbeknownst to them the realms of the intellect were being transformed into grassy and idle pastures for a new kind of intellectual, aggregately defined as the bovine intelligentsia. The *enrages* of the New Left and the 1960s protests were now a decade older. Where once they wore Jesus sandals, hooves had sprouted. The emphasis on "feeling" that emerged in the 1960s was spreading, transforming vast herds of profs and sophisticates into maudlin nincompoops; young Werthers outfitted by L. L. Bean. We, of course, believed that the high seriousness of the neoconservatives would rescue American intellectual life from this appalling bathos. But the winds of the *Zeitgeist* were still blowing, and neoconservatives were in for a letdown that I am not sure they have ever fully understood. History's wheel grinds on; few neoconservatives appreciated how pitiless the process could be.

Always, from the Liberals' first volcanic eruption of indignation against the conservative revival, through their subsequent episodic outbursts, Liberals had repined that "Oh, how America does need an Intelligent Conservatism," wholesomely countervailing Liberalism. That venerable Liberal gogue, Columbia's Lionel Trilling, had reviewed American intellectual history and found only reformers and revolutionaries. He could not find one American of note willing to conserve anything from that great and tireless shredding machine that is known as progress, not James Madison, Henry Adams, Daniel Webster, or A. Lincoln. Where was Intelligent Conservatism to be found in America? Well, for a while in the 1970s Irving and his associates seemed to fill the bill, while maintaining their reputations as respectable intellectuals. Irving still lectured to academics. He was still quoted as an authoritative source on radical excesses and corporate life. By the middle of the Carter years it seemed that thanks to Irving and his band of brains the day all fair-minded Liberals had longed for was finally at hand; America was about to get its circle of Intelligent Conservatives.

All this congeniality towards the neoconservatives was a part of the aforementioned period of Liberal self-examination, but then a terrible revelation spread through the precincts of Liberalism—Irving was not just another of the Approved Conservatives whom the Liberals occasionally and indulgently certified. I have in mind men like Clinton Rossiter and Peter Viereck, who might speak wistfully of certain conservative values while disparaging the conservative revival for its putative radicalism or moments of kinkiness. Irving and his associates had actually completed their intellectual journey. No longer did they hurl Liberal prejudices against conservatives. They had entered into friendship with the conservatives. In fact, many had done an Irving; they had actually become *conservative*.

That was going too far. Suddenly in the early 1980s the aura of intelligence that Liberals had perceived around Irving could be seen no more. The Liberals' period of self-examination was *finito*. Now the neoconservatives suffered the kind of shocking apodiabolosis incurred by so many who stray too close to the conservative camp. By the second Reagan Administration the neoconservatives, many of whom were serving the Administration with distinction, had become even more hateful than movement conservatives. The neoconservatives, after all, were apostates. What is more they had committed the one intellectual offense that among pedestrian minds is intolerable; the neoconservatives had been prematurely right. It wrecked their careers among the bovine intelligentsia. The neoconservatives were right about the nihilism of what they called the adversary culture. They were right about bureaucracy's tendency towards elephantiasis. They were right about Liberal prescriptions for urban problems such as welfare, crime, and drugs. They were right about the excesses of the Great Society, and they were right about the essential good sense of America's middle class. They should have known trouble lay ahead.

Nonetheless, even after the diabolization of the neoconservatives, it was clear that they had changed the terms of political debate from the days when social improvement was always predicated on the activism of government. They had introduced a concern for efficiency in institutions and for personal accountability in individuals. When, in 1968, Edward Banfield brought together much of what composed the neoconservative critique of the Great Society into a monumental analysis of contemporary urban policy, *The Unheavenly City*, academics submerged this scholarly and honorable Harvard prof in vitriol. Yet he and the neoconservatives persevered with their analysis of social problems, and sixteen years later, when Charles Murray published *Losing Ground*, a book whose findings built upon Banfield's, the mob scene that greeted Banfield was not repeated. The critics now felt obliged to mix vitriol with a simulacrum of scholarly analysis, much of which accepted—without acknowledgment—essential elements in both men's arguments, for instance, their conclusion that the elimination of poverty was much more complicated than merely enriching welfare payments. That had been the pert solution prescribed by writers such as John Kenneth Galbraith in years past (and, incidentally, it was still Galbraith's solution in the 1990s), but poverty had persisted despite all the billions expended to eliminate it. In some instances poverty had actually deepened despite increases in government largess. The depressing process could not be ignored forever.

The neoconservatives also changed the terms of debate in the areas of family structure and crime. No longer was Pat Moynihan's warning that welfare threatened black family life dismissed as racist. Nor was there wide resistance to the admonitions of James Q. Wilson and Ernest van den Haag against indulging criminals. As the neoconservative case gained adherents throughout the 1970s, its particulars on matters of economics, sociology, and government became familiar to government bureaucrats and academics. After all, bureaucracy and academe had been the neoconservatives' point of origin. The conservative movement had not been able to cast even a ray of light into these regions. Now the neoconservatives' wisdom shone everywhere with the result that by the late 1970s they had brought their mix of sobered-up Liberalism and conservatism to some of the most influential centers of modern thought.

Yet by the beginning of the 1980s those inhabiting these centers of thought had changed. The bovine intelligentsia were moving in, and woe to intellect. They were plodders and conformists, conversant only with a well masticated cud of 1960s adolescent thought. As long as possible they shied from the neoconservative critique. When denial was no longer feasible they would quietly adopt one or two of the neoconservatives' ideas, say an insight into welfare's encouragement of dependency. But almost never would they acknowledge the origins of these ideas unless their intent was disparagement. In this way—and temporarily—a semblance of bland conservatism came into fashion among the bovine intelligentsia of the 1980s. After all, some of the Great Society's wilder projects were spectacularly coming a cropper. Yet the bovine intelligentsia's conservatism was to be an ephemeral conservatism and one without any conservatives allowed in on the proceedings. It was a typical case of Liberal denial.

On those rare instances when the bovine intelligentsia had no other recourse but to acknowledge the existence of a neoconservative, they simply misrepresented him, depicting him as a ghastly fellow, a scoundrel, an opportunist, a crank, a plutocrat. Of all the behoofed members of the herd who set out to misrepresent the neoconservatives, none was more industrious than Peter Steinfels. Like many Liberals, he viewed the neoconservatives' tergiversation from Liberalism with alarm, and so he dutifully undertook a 336-page effort at damage control, *The Neoconservatives: The Men Who Are Changing America's Politics*. It was not the work of an original mind. It simply applied the old canards of the Danger-on-the-Right propagandists to neoconservatives. For me, it was very entertaining to witness my old antagonists defending themselves against the same invidious prejudices that they had brought down on me not so long before, but that Steinfels could not come up with one original slur was surprising. Three decades had elapsed since Liberals began scowling at the conservatives. Through all those years the Liberals had been white hot, and yet their indignation stimulated no creativity whatsoever. So much for the positive power of passion in politics.

The neoconservative "outlook," Steinfels argued, "preoccupied with certain aspects of American life and blind or complacent toward others, justifies a politics which, should it prevail, threatens to attenuate and diminish the promise of American democracy."[4] Think of it, after all their years spent thumping for Hubert Humphrey and practically every progressive item on the Liberal agenda, Irving and his congenital Liberals were now lumped in with the likes of Richard Weaver and Russell Kirk as enemies of democracy. When the charge had been leveled against Weaver and Kirk it was absurd. When leveled against Irving it was a bore, but there was a supplement to the charge that made it slightly more interesting. Steinfels attempted to claim that neoconservatism was a geriatric condition, associated with tired, aging Liberals incapable of experiencing the bold delights of the New Age. I was in a position to expose these prejudices for the flapdoodle they were. Half the writers in *The American Spectator* were neoconservatives. They harbored an almost embarrassingly idealistic reverence for democracy. Moreover, many were in the springtime of their careers. Thus I invited some to appear in a symposium that would put the kibosh to the many fallacious ideas then circulating about neoconservatism.

Our 1979 symposium entitled "Why Are There Neoconservatives?" adduced fresh evidence of the neoconservatives' genealogical link to Liberalism. It demonstrates that the neoconservatives brought a new spirit of liberality and cosmopolitanism to the conservative camp, and it makes it irrefragably clear that the neoconservative contagion had spread from Irving's generation to Liberal youth. Irving and his pals were neither senile nor alone.

Adam Meyerson, then in his twenties, a former managing editor of *The American Spectator*, and now on the editorial staff of *The Wall Street Journal*, was the most eloquent debunker of Steinfels's balderdash, writing that "neoconservatives are Liberals with a sense of tragedy. We wish it were possible to live without defense budgets, but realize that it is not.

We'd like to campaign for comprehensive national health insurance, but are afraid that its costs would interfere with the achievement of other humanitarian ends. We wish we could call out clearly for the downfall of corrupt despots, but we fear, for example, that what may follow the Shah or Somoza will be even worse." He went on to say that "neoconservatives also have a sense of progress. . . . What excites us about modern times is that the lives of ordinary people in most countries are improving so rapidly. . . . We welcome more than we fear advances in technology."[5] And Elliott Abrams, later to be Assistant Secretary of State for Inter-American Affairs (and an Iran-contra legend), after boasting of his early days as National Chairman of the Campus Americans for Democratic Action and lamenting that contemporary Liberalism was falling into the clutches of the New Left, drew a significant distinction between himself and movement conservatives, stating that he had always stood as a Liberal "in supporting social security, collective-bargaining laws, voting-rights guarantees, and much other such social legislation. It is this that separates neoconservatives from conservatives."[6] Abrams was touching upon an important distinction between conservatives and neoconservatives. The latter frequently came from the family of Big Labor and remained comparatively friendly to labor. The old conservative movement had been hostile to labor; its members revealed an unacknowledged liberality when they allowed these apoplectic Liberals into their camp. Obviously the conservative movement was not as intolerant as its critics had claimed.

Considering the boldness of their thought, the neoconservatives should have felt the noose falling around their necks. Surely they were aware of the bovine intelligentsia's derelictions in favor of mediocrity and conformity. Yet, there was a streak of naivete in the neoconservatives. They admired mind, and could not imagine intellectuals who would put mediocrity and conformity before intellect. They thought they could remain aloof from vulgar politics, and that superior ideas would be recognized and accepted. Such seriousness would prove to be an astigmatism for the neoconservatives throughout the 1980s. As the decade went on, most neoconservatives found themselves proceeding through an ever darker passageway, in what direction they could not say, and when they arrived at the 1990s they were as surprised as everyone else. One of them actually wrote an essay, "The End of History?," with which many of his colleagues, to my surprise, concurred.

The light began to dim for the neoconservatives as early as 1978. Then for the first time I noticed that Irving was missing things. In the summer of that year it was obvious to conservatives with an eye for politics that

Ronald Reagan was headed for the Republican presidential nomination. He deserved the nomination. I remember discussing Reagan's possibilities with Bill Casey over lunch in the spring of 1978 at the Clipper Club high atop Manhattan's Pan Am Building. Casey sized up the situation with a clear sense of its politics. Reagan had proved himself a worthy candidate. By virtue of seniority and demonstrated political acumen, Reagan was first in line for the nomination. Absent a series of pratfalls he deserved the Republican nod. Casey's reasoning was persuasive, and I was glad to do my part for the Reagan campaign. For reasons I did not understand at the time, Irving was not supporting Reagan. When in June of 1978 Governor Reagan's aide, Peter Hannaford, asked me to host a dinner party at which the candidate might be introduced to leading neoconservatives, I flew to New York and put together a soiree at the Union League Club. Irving would not attend the dinner, not even out of curiosity.

At the time I suspected that Irving's disrelish for Reagan came from a residual disdain for the old conservative movement. Hoary prejudices still tumbled out of him at times. Later I concluded that Irving thought the evening would be a waste. He already had his 1980 candidate, a young upstate New York congressman, Jack Kemp. For a decade the momentum had built behind neoconservative ideas. Jack was a proponent of those ideas, and according to the Godfather's calculations he would be sweeping past the old dinosaur, notwithstanding the fact that conservatism firmly controlled the Republican Party and that the old dinosaur was recognized by most Republicans as "Mr. Conservative." I never questioned Irving about his refusal to dine with the future President, but surely it was more than loyalty to Kemp that kept Irving away that night. He was losing touch with the drift of the *Zeitgeist*.

Fortunately, the Podhoretzes and the Glazers resisted Irving's deductions and joined the Reagans in the walnut-panelled fastness of a private dining room. Nat Glazer, shifting characteristically from foot to foot like a be-spectacled jazz man, fell into a highly cerebral discussion of subway graffiti with the former governor. Nat, formerly on the faculty at Berkeley, now on the faculty at Harvard, had recently pondered graffiti's sociological significance in an essay in *The Public Interest*. Reagan followed his elucidations pensively as all good pols should when intent on seduction, and, if I recall correctly, threw in his own observations on fugitive art. Then he laid siege to the Podhoretzes, admiring an essay or two that had been brought to his attention. The drinks flowed, the blarney proliferated, and the Podhoretzes' residue of Liberal haughtiness for Reagan was greatly reduced by the time we exited into the Manhattan night.

Through the evening I had stayed glued to Nancy. What immensities passed between us I cannot now retrieve from memory's dark hole. I do recall that when the room's air conditioning went berserk the gallant within me arose and covered her shivering shoulders with my blazer. In fashion this look of full shoulders and ample sleeves came to be known as the "puffed sleeves look." It became the rage of 1981 once that singularly exquisite designer, Carolina Herrera, drew attention to its beauty. The look was perfect for Nancy, giving her a stately bearing to offset the slight skittishness that occasionally glinted from her large and beautiful eyes. (We have heard *ad nauseam* about the skittishness, why not more about those eyes?) Is it possible that she too noticed the full shoulders, the flowing sleeves, and passed a recommendation on to Carolina? If so, someday history will credit me with having extended the influence of neoconservativism beyond the circles of policy analysts and into a power center that no neoconservative had ever perceived or analyzed, to wit, the province of high couture, wherein at that very moment dwelt some of the geniuses destined to be the giants of American public life in the 1980s.

America had gone through a colonial period, a period of civil war, and a period of industrial revolution. In the first half of the twentieth century it became a world power, ultimately the paramount world power. Now in the 1980s it would enter the charity ball stage of its civilization with the Republic's dress designers becoming respected figures, as our generals were once respected figures, and church leaders, and fat, cigar-chomping senators, and the presidents of Ivy League colleges. In fact, by 1984 Mr. Ralph Lauren of Polo (whatever that might be) had surpassed congressmen and senators and even Billy Graham as a sought-after guest at Washington dinner parties. Such advances by the fashion set, if uninterrupted by plague or cataclysm, could by the twenty-first century make Washington the equivalent of Versailles in the 1780s; and let us put out of mind what happened to Versailles shortly thereafter.

Where was Irving the night we were dining with the next President of the United States? Possibly he was reading an economics text. In the best sense, Irving was a dilettante. When I first met him he was arising with the sun to work through the texts of the ancient Greek philosophers. The result was several years of uncommonly profound political commentary. When Irving had satisfied his interest in political philosophy he moved on to economics, and in the mid-1970s one would see him carrying rare books on economic theory, often new books but sometimes books written in the last century and in the eighteenth century. The result of Irving's economic lucubrations was his advocacy of "supply-side" economics, which, of course, became a major stimulant of the 1980s economy—more on this later. It was Irving's enthusiasm for supply-side economics that conduced him to support the presidential ambitions of Jack Kemp. The economic determinism of Irving's youth perhaps never completely left him; his Trotskyism shed its 1930s skin only to become 1980s Republicanism.

Notwithstanding the ceaseless industry of Irving's mind, I do not believe that he or any neoconservative ever took any notice whatsoever of the "puffed sleeves look." If they did, they never mentioned it to me. After latching onto the theories of supply-side economics, the Godfather and his *capos* would come up with no criticisms of the political culture and no policy suggestions commensurate in heft with those that they had championed in the 1970s, not that supply-side originated with the neo-conservatives. Arthur Laffer, an economics professor, uncorked it, but those neoconservatives of an economic turn of mind proved to be supply-side's most effective popularizers. At *The Wall Street Journal* Jude Wanniski and the resourceful Bob Bartley spun the ideas of supply-side economics into scores of commentaries. Wanniski wrote a splendid economic treatise, *The Way the World Works*, and with a small coterie of others peppered government officials, editorial writers, and pundits with reminders of supply-side's relevance to our economic exigencies.

Early in the 1980s Irving became bored with economics and moved on to foreign policy, but here the results were not so felicitous. Somehow he reached the conclusion that America should withdraw from Europe and embrace the distant Orient. The idea was daring. I think it had something to do with a conception of the evolution of business and markets. Many neoconservatives had from their early days in the fla-fla land of socialism sustained an interest in various dread aspects of capitalism (and various saintly aspects of labor unions). The modern corporation was a particular fascination for them, and as they were true intellectuals their thoughts inclined towards the daring. I believe it was his absorption with the corporation that induced Irving to urge a foreign policy *démarche*. At any rate, the ideas that ensued were flimsy, insouciant about NATO's delicate history, unmindful of the years of diplomatic effort that led to it, of America's intrinsic isolationism, and of the vast disparities between the West, a culture that still thrills to the first three bars of the "Eroica," and the Orient, a culture that goes dreamy over the pentatonic scale played on gongs. Better it would have been for Irving to return to his role as neo-conservatism's Godfather. By the early 1980s the gains of the neoconservative-conservative coalition needed to be defended. In the circles of power we were being elbowed aside by Oscar de la Renta!

As I say, it was not only Irving who missed the significance of the "puffed sleeve look." No neoconservative remarked on it, not even Jeane Kirkpatrick or Midge Decter, both of whom had more bounteous sympathies for life's possibilities than the saturnine, constipated policy analysts whom Irving frequently admired. Consequently it took the neoconservatives half the 1980s before their most percipient minds recognized that aside from a few matters of policy such as supply-side economics, stricter prosecution of criminals, and cost-benefit analysis, the New Politics of the decade was not their politics. The New Politics of the 1960s had embraced the young and the black and the women; it bespoke revolution. The 1980s' New Politics was gayer. It quietly accepted many of the principles of the conservative movement, but the New Politics of the 1980s was dominated by the fashion designers and the interior decorators and the celebrated; it replaced an ardor for revolution with an ardor for charity balls. Irving and his policy analysts could not imagine such a thing, nor were they any good on the dance floor.

One day at the dawn of the Reagan years, when the rays of our triumph still gleamed across the morning skies, I walked Irving back to his Fifty-Third Street office. Not surprisingly, we were returning from lunch; and as we were standing there digesting amiably, and contemplating the gorgeous possibilities that lay ahead, a soundly sozzled little man wobbled along just beneath our noses. It was probably an uncharitable thought on my part, but judging from the squatness of his skull, his wrap-around mouth, the two neat holes that served as a nose, and his watery eyes, it occurred to me that one or more of this anuric little man's immediate relations was probably a frog. Before I could apprise Irving of my speculation I also noticed that the little man crossing beneath the gaze of the editors of two famed Reaganite periodicals was actually one of the most illustrious *litterateurs* of the Old Order. "Do you know who that is?" I tested the Godfather. He was at a loss. By now the little frog in a white wine sauce had passed on. I told Irving that it had just been his honor to view the mortal remains of Truman Capote. "Someday, Irving, after they bury him in the American Pantheon, we shall have to stand in line for hours to see him. If we ever have a Pantheon." Irving sniffed. Capote was a has-been, not worth a laugh. Irving considered café society passé. His brand of high seriousness was ascendant in Washington now. And off we went, Irving to smoke cigarettes and pat his hair in the office above, perhaps while preparing a manuscript about supply-side economics or while making a few calls on behalf of an excellent prospect for chairman of the National Endowment for the Humanities (William Bennett was his candidate); and

I to . . . actually I have forgotten where I went. All I can say for sure is
that I probably gave café society a little more thought. It did not seem to
be adjourning for the Reagan era as Irving seemed to assume. Its inhabitants
were mostly nitwits, who cast left-wing votes while lolling in right-wing
opulence; but what would replace them, supply-side economists quipping
about marginal tax rates in *People* magazine? The local Republican Wom-
en's Club planning charity balls to raise funds for Nicaragua's Contras?
The neoconservatives had no sympathy for the frivolous side of society.
In fact they had little sympathy for society, and they had absolutely zero
entertainment value. That was most unfortunate, for contemporary America is desperate for entertainment.

Once in government neoconservatives were capable bureaucratic op-
erators, but they had little feel for the hand-to-hand aspects of politics—
either on the campaign trail or in the smoke-filled room. They took such
politics for granted even as they took political organizations for granted.
They had grown to maturity in the Liberal culture where institutions were
well established and where the challenge was to advance through hierar-
chies rather than actually to create an institution, neoconservatives had
only a vague idea of how hard their conservative allies had worked to build
the sparse number of organizations that sustained the fledgling movement.
In point of fact, the neoconservatives created few institutions aside from
Irving's small-circulation journals, and if some of us in the conservative
movement had not invited the neoconservatives to join our institutions I
am not certain that they would have sought us out. Whatever the case,
they were invited into the American Enterprise Institute and the Heritage
Foundation. They were invited into our magazines and conferences. Then
with the election of Ronald Reagan, savvy conservative pols such as Bill
Casey, Fred Ikle, and Peter Hannaford placed them in the Administration.
Irving's hour was at hand. Steadily he had risen in the world. He had been
an occasional adviser to President Nixon even before being dubbed the
Godfather. Now his neoconservative allies were in every area of the government. Remembering his influence in the Nixon years, I expected him
to be a major force in the Reagan Administration. Luigi Barzini's judgment
that we faced our moment in history was about to be validated.

Yet hold the champagne; if 1980 proved to be any conservative's moment
in history it proved to be Betsy Bloomingdale's. I wish that in this intimate
memoir I could report on my many illuminating encounters with Mrs.
Bloomingdale; but, alas, I have never met the lady. Her ideas are as remote
from me as those of the Yanomamo Indians of the greater Amazon rain
forest. The anthropologists tell us that the Yanomamo are the most violent

people on earth. I do not know whether Mrs. Bloomingdale has a mean streak. All I do know is that during the 1980s she was very rich and stylish, and her favorite dress designer was, I believe, Chanel–Christian Dior–Christian Lacroix–Emmanuel Ungaro–Saint Laurent. She was destined to spend more time in the Reagan White House than Irving—and so was Emmanuel Ungaro.

Betsy Bloomingdale and the dress designers were not the only figures to preempt the neoconservatives. There was also that curious political type known as the Country Club Republican, or—more respectfully—the Republican pragmatist. Serious minds recognize the great game of politics as a facet of history, infused with ideas and values, and topped off with interludes of precious comedy. The Country Club Republican has little taste for ideas and values. He perceives politics as a Process, a Process for balancing budgets, maintaining national security, setting national agendas, and realizing each goal on the agenda in an orderly manner. (How or why items are placed on the agenda is scarcely his concern.) Aside from the Process, the Country Club Republican sees politics as an opportunity to meet people from other states, and occasionally even other countries, and to wear lime slacks with one's blazer—occasionally the slacks are beige, having whales and little ducks on them. In chill autumn, Country Club Republicans opt for silly plaids beneath their blazers. The neoconservatives did not know what to think of such people, nor, for that matter, did their conservative allies.

Naturally, I too have found them curious. They seem to be creatures of instinct rather than of intellect. Fortunately, their instincts are usually sound as the instincts of a well-bred spaniel are usually sound. They are self-reliant and self-protective. In an elemental way they are conservative, but it is conservatism governed by inertia. In government the Country Club Republicans were very helpful to Ronald Reagan, for they kept the paper flow going, but they were treacherous towards conservatives of both species, for the ideas of these right-wingers riled up the Democrats and frustrated the Process.

The combination of the Country Club Republicans and 1980s New Politics was too much for the Godfather. While neoconservatives served effectively in the State Department and other bureaucracies, they made few appearances on the White House staff, and it was left to Edwin Meese and, briefly, to William Clark to advance conservative interests. Irving made it to the Reagan White House only twice, once for an economics discussion with the President over dinner and once for a luncheon with the President and expressly at my suggestion. I was there too.

On September 22, 1982, we lunched in the cabinet room with the President and his assistant presidents and with representatives from such other conservative publications as *Commentary, National Review,* and *Policy Review.* Over the next few years many conservative ideas became government policy via policy analysts. This was the occasion for the bearers of conservative culture to bring the ideas and values of that culture into the White House and to coalesce as a cultural community. The President walked in with a powerful retinue, Chief of Staff James A. Baker, III, National Security Advisor Clark, Deputy Chief of Staff Michael K. Deaver, Chief Counsel to the President Meese, Director of the Office of Management and Budget, David Stockman, and the Country Club Republicans' secret agent, David R. Gergen, then serving as Director of Communications and Planning. Irving had convinced us that Gergen was a friend. He would help us do with conservative intellectuals what FDR and JFK did with Liberals, to wit, lend presidential prestige to a political culture.

With the midday sun enhaloing his head and shoulders, the President bid me sit across from him in the Vice President's chair, which I took to be a compliment at the time. Even now I think he meant to compliment me, for he said something to the effect of "This is your show." Irving was at my right, for I expected him to take over the proceedings like a proper Godfather. The President's disposition was as sunny as the Rose Garden behind him, though the assistant presidents seated on either side of him did not appear to share his cheerfulness. I thought we were just doing what Irving did so well, having lunch, making a few connections, dropping a few golden nuggets of thought, advancing the conservative counterculture. But the assistant presidents were apprehensive. They sensed that the arrival of these writers portended a full-scale coup.

The plot's origins could be traced back to the afternoon of August 16, 1982. Sleeves rolled up, tie down, I was wrestling ferociously with a passage of quintessential importance to chapter two of what would eventually be called *The Liberal Crack-Up* when a silken voice on the telephone informed me that the President would have a word with me. "President? President of what?" I thought indignantly. My surmising was cut short when the old charmer came on the line, appeasing my irritability as effectively as my nocturnal martini. Literature could be postponed for *les affaires d'etat.* I have always liked Ronald Reagan, and if I never meet another pol like him my reputation as a literary tough will suffer no further damage. He possesses an easy kindliness that evaporates the plentiful reservoirs of contempt that I hold for most pols still upright and a menace to the national treasury.

I remember the first time I set out to get rough with Ron. It was in pursuance of my journalistic duties wherein I always strive to be as much the he-man as Ben Bradlee, though I remain college-educated. Naturally I was driven to the former governor's Pacific Palisades house in a limousine—we journalistic he-men do not disdain the amenities. It was 1978, and I carried a quiver abundant with sharp questions for the potential presidential candidate. They included what at the time were considered the two lethal questions, (a) his advanced age and (b) his tendency towards languor. He seated me on a couch and went off to the back of the house to answer an emergency holler from Nancy. When he returned, he plumped himself down on the couch. Unfortunately, his heavier weight ballooned the couch's ample cushion, tipping me so that I slid smack against him. There I remained, trying to ask the Tough Question while snugly pressed against an apparently oblivious interviewee. Had witnesses been present they would have seen two men in a large room seated side by side on a couch, the older man perfectly at ease discussing his political future, the younger man furtively but vainly trying to inch his way out of the crater the two bodies had created in the couch's cushion.

Ron got off gently then, as he did again that August afternoon when he called from the White House. I had written a column arguing that the White House pragmatists, as they were called, were undercutting his plans for tax cuts and causing a rift within the conservative community. He insisted that a tax increase then being pressed upon him by congressional Democrats would ensure three dollars of congressional budget cuts for every additional tax dollar. He disputed the news stories that the pragmatists were conspiring to enfeeble conservatives and asked how the rift with them could be overcome. It would take six years and publication of Mike Deaver's egregious memoirs before any of the pragmatists would come clean and validate my claim that some on his staff had committed various acts of betrayal. As for the Congress's promises of budget cuts, it never made good on them. We did, however, temporarily end the rift dividing the President from his friends. Our solution was lunch with Irving. Recalling that through a series of informal luncheons with a group of economists the President remained in touch with conservative economic opinion, I advised a similar series of luncheons with conservative editors to keep the President *au courant* with the conservative point of view; and *à la* FDR and JFK, this conservative President would be encouraging the growth of a community of like-minded intellectuals. In this instance his achievement might be even more salutary for he would be assisting a community of like-minded journals—all important elements in the establishment of a conservative political counterculture.

And so on September 22, 1982, I awoke in the Hay Adams Hotel and prepared to lead representatives from *Commentary, National Review, Policy Review,* and *The Public Interest,* into a luncheon with the President. Later we hoped to broaden the group to include *Human Events* and other responsible conservative journals. Irving was our veteran luncher. A decade before, his luncheon companions had included the likes of President Richard Nixon, and so effectively did he lunch in those days that his influence in the Nixon White House spread despite his presidential endorsement of Hubert Humphrey. In fact, when Pat Moynihan left the Nixon White House to become ambassador to India, Irving was in the running to replace Pat as the President's chief advisor on domestic policy. Now Irving would become a White House presence to the benefit of the conservative revolution, or so I believed.

Unfortunately this was not intellectual New York in 1969. This was political Washington in the 1980s, and the Country Club Republicans were on the alert. None believed that we were there merely for lunch or to establish something so vague as an informal relationship with our friend, the President. It was a drive for power, a *coup de main* against them, and the President seemed to be leaning our way! The most insecure of the assistant presidents, which is to say the most inveterate schemers, had been politely telephoning me for a week to reassure me that each was a genuine conservative and a faithful reader of *The American Spectator.* One, Richard Darman, had caught me just as I was leaving the hotel to pledge that he was not only an admirer but also an "intellectual"—yes, an intellectual!— and he assured me that *The Public Interest's* executive editor, Mark Lilla, would vouch for him. "Stop by the office after lunch for coffee," he insisted. Espresso? Cappuccino? What do such intellectuals drink in the early afternoon?

The lunch was very agreeable except when I would accidentally lock eyes with one of these grim assistant presidents. For his part, the President was in fine fettle. I made only one point: "You have won the political campaigns. The intellectual battles have been won too. Your adversaries have no spellbinding dreams or policies left that have not been tried. The terms of political debate have become conservative. No longer do we hear calls to limit economic growth, radically redistribute income, or negotiate with every hostile country. Now is your time to implement the policies of limited government, economic growth, deregulation, and a strong foreign policy. You have the power *and* the ideas." Now that was a thrill! I had lived to deliver a stirring exhortation to the President of the United States in the privacy of his own home, and whilst seated in the very chair in which Vice President Calvin Coolidge had once slept! From the other side of the table five pairs of dilated pupils focused upon my beaming face. Only the President seemed to share my enthusiasm, and in his "gosh-goll-darn-it" demeanor he asked Dave Gergen to schedule a series of these pleasant luncheons. Apparently we were going to have access to the President! The conservative counterculture's future was assured!

Dave came shivering toward me after coffee (shivering is part of his demeanor) and to my amazement blurted out that I probably would be more comfortable dealing with a staff member friendlier to me. Friendlier to me? Irving had assured me that Dave was friendly to all of us conservatives. Actually, Dave had thrown in with the Country Clubbers, and all my talk of Ideas imperiled the Process. He enlisted the overworked but "friendlier" Ed Meese to schedule further meetings and we were lost in Ed's congested briefcase. Our group never met again. The White House had been saved for Betsy and Nancy, the designers and interior decorators and, of course, the Country Club Republicans. As the 1980s passed, the only reliable member of the conservative counterculture on daily duty at 1600 Pennsylvania Avenue was the President, and he was not getting any younger.

We had arrived at the White House too late. The *Zeitgeist* had again picked up velocity. A new arrangement of people, of ideas, of tastes, of fantasies, all beyond the analytical power of neoconservatives, was passing the neoconservatives by.

This is not to say that the left was now in power. Once again it had completely missed the drift of things. Writing as though the neoconservatives were the same threat they had been in 1979, the left's writers assaulted neoconservatives with desperate fury. Their exertions did nothing to advance them, but they did manage to increase the Country Club Republicans' state of alarm over the neoconservatives. It was bad enough that the neoconservatives dwelt on ideas. Now the left's denunciations had made the neoconservatives "controversial," which is to say more damaging to the Process than ever. For a sense of the bitchy, gratuitous tone, savor a column from the May 20–26, 1981, *Village Voice*, by that slavish ideologue of the left, Alexander Cockburn: "What do Norman Podhoretz, Hodding Carter, Saul Bellow, Robert Silvers, Barbara Epstein, James Schlesinger, Arthur Schlesinger, R. Emmett Tyrell [sic], Edward Albee, Martin Peretz, Pat Derian, Stanley Hoffman, William Bundy, and Bayard

Rustin all have in common?" Well, we all signed an advertisement denouncing a Soviet media campaign to discredit the people of Poland. It had been drawn up by the North American Study Center for Polish Affairs and printed in *The New York Times*. Cockburn was not pleased that the plight of the Poles had evoked such unanimity: "Irreproachable cause no doubt, but the forging of an entente between the intellectual factions indicated above" upset him. "I could," he sobbed, "never sign anything to which Emmett Tyrrell or Norman Podhoretz had lent their names."

In the 1980s a curious schizophrenia was spreading through the Republic. There was public gloom over the plight of bankrupt farmers, unemployed toilers from the smokestack industries, urban vagrants sleeping on sidewalk grates and communing alfresco with their mysterious demons. But there was also this happy fascination with Oscar de la Renta and his fellow designers, Mario Buatta and his fellow interior decorators, and with all their clients, the 150 or so nocturnal popinjays who were so minutely observed by those contemporary Tocquevilles, Liz Smith and "Suzy." All were pioneers leading the Republic into its charity ball stage of civilization, an evolution unforeseen by any postwar social scientist at any think tank or university anywhere.

Liz Smith and Suzy wrote gossip columns. They were frequently invited to balls and toney dinners to cover the gory scene. They would circle the tables, clasping their reporter's pads and jotting down—what? Seating arrangements of ingenious conception? A *saumon fumé* portentously left unconsumed? A silk-swathed elbow in a soup bowl? One would think they were covering sports events or wars from the front lines, but what coarse hostess would invite gossip columnists to the party? In years past, persons of quality sought to stay out of the gossip columns. Now many employed press agents to smuggle their names into these columns. The columns were read in every hamlet and metropolis, despite the fact that each gossip column was practically a photocopy of its immediate predecessor, featuring the same social giants, the same designers, the same interior decorators; and all traversing the same geography—usually the Upper East Side of Manhattan, occasionally Southampton, and Nancy Reagan's White House.

These were the wits and the sages of the 1980s. The intellectual roles of Dorothy Parker and the Algonquin Round Table, of Mortimer Adler and Arnold Toynbee were now being filled by Valentino, Scaasi, Oscar, and someone by the name of Jerry Zipkin, whom I once met as he sat smiling from a chintz-clothed chair and giggling like a bag lady. In an era when the media were lamenting the plight of the wretchedly impecunious while simultaneously lionizing the flabbily affluent, the incongruity was hard to take. What did Suzy's readers in Dubuque think they were getting when they read her? Why would any serious citizen care to attend one of these imbecilic parties? The tedium could have been life-threatening. If there was ever a witty line uttered or an amusing escapade undertaken, Suzy never jotted it down. All she recorded was the evening's line-up at the punch bowl, and in a style as tiresome as that of the *Racing Form*.

Yet if the dispatches from the ballroom were devoid of wit or charm they were turgid with authoritative accounts of the ladies' dresses, their proceedings in divorce court, and occasionally eyewitness reports on the decor of various festival rooms. But how many variations on a flower arrangement can there be, how many variations on a piece of women's clothing that—it is a fact—is essentially a large pillow case with openings for the arms and neck?

Perhaps Oscar and this fellow Valentino are geniuses of the first rank, but how many masterpieces do they have in them? Brahms could come up with no more than four symphonies. Shakespeare with or without Bacon wrote only thirty-seven plays. I cannot believe that in the 1980s even the Wolfgang Amadeus Mozart of dress designers ever excogitated more than a dozen evening gowns worthy of note by Suzy and Liz's readers. Yet, many of these geniuses became forces to conjure with, not only among the Manhattan social set but also within circles of political power such as the Reagan White House.

Historians who perform the final autopsies on Liberalism will observe that one reason for its crack-up was that by 1979 it had nothing left to do. It had reformed all that was imaginable to reform. It had disrupted practically every region of American life. It had disturbed all its neighbors and even neighbors in foreign lands. Yet, the 1980s fascination with the decade's New Politics of designers and interior decorators and their grinning clientele suggested that perhaps the Republic itself had nothing serious left to do. All the oaths to relieve the unemployed, the homeless, the freedom fighters here and there were only empty boasts. The real American, whether Democrat or Republican, was lost in reveries of parties and parvenus.

Early in the 1980s, I became convinced that America had moved on from the policy critiques of neoconservatives, and I looked for a sociologist capable of filling the readers of *The American Spectator* in on these new developments. Irving was no help. Fortunately I remembered an inquiry I had received in London at Brown's hotel from a Greek philosopher and Jet Setter who, in the spring of 1981, on the stationery from Aspinall's gambling club, invited me to join him on a drunk. At the time I had prior commitments (in those days London had a lot of drunks), but by 1983 I had read this man's works in various periodicals and recognized him as a seasoned guide eminently capable of leading us through the 1980s. His name was simply Taki. He was a playboy for whom life had begun at 8:00 P.M. every night for the past twenty-five years whether he was at his residence in Athens, Gstaad, Paris, London, or New York. He was a society columnist for London's *Spectator*, and as he was suitably conservative I made him European editor for *The American Spectator*. As I saw it, with the evanescence of Irving's generation, Taki became the true New York intellectual of the 1980s. Moreover, his father's international holdings made him rich enough to survive on *The American Spectator*'s low-calorie honoraria.

Taki was a fabulous figure, as so many Greeks are; or else Henry Miller has badly misled us in that wonderful book, so abundant with his own sharp perceptions and childish ideals, *The Colossus of Maroussi*. In it, Miller chronicles his 1939 Greek idyll with Lawrence Durrell and the Greek raconteur Katsimbalis, who, as portrayed by Miller, is the prototype Taki. Says Miller, "Greeks are an enthusiastic, curious-minded, passionate people. . . . [7] A Greek is alive to the finger-tips; he oozes vitality, he's effervescent, he's ubiquitous in spirit. . . . The Greek . . . is an adventurer: he is reckless and adaptable, he makes friends easily."[8] Katsimbalis and Taki also made enemies, despite their ready reserves of generosity.

The Jet Setter is a migratory animal. It winters in Switzerland; its springs and falls are spent variously in London, Paris, or New York; it summers in Tuscany, the Greek islands, or *tres chic!* St. Moritz and Gstaad. Taki followed the great migratory routes of his species for years, gabbing ceaselessly, drinking, laughing, making love, picking fights, playing polo, tennis, cards. He was proficient at karate and on the ski slopes; and he told fantastic tales. He made friends with his exuberance and his lapses into kindliness, and he made enemies with his utter disregard for conventions and his lapses into cruelty.

He was a fine athlete, an inveterate carouser, a snob who somehow managed to know the *crème de la crème* of international society, some of whom liked him; others sued him for libel. He had a very complicated and explosive code of honor. He lived by it and briefly went to prison because of it, but it defeated me with its melange of Hemingway, Plato, St. Paul, the Samurai, and someone named Porfirio Rubirosa, a playboy who earned Taki's awe when he got himself killed by crashing his Ferrari somewhere in the Bois de Bologne in the early hours of July 6, 1965. At a restaurant on Brompton Road, Taki once regaled me, a British economist, and a political philosopher with his concept of a proper religion. It was a rendering of Christianity filled with pagan images, and as he spoke I saw in his darting brown eyes scenes from the bull ring, ordeals by fire, ancient rites by half naked savages—so much for Taki and religion—he was not a systematic thinker.

Taki would have been a totally dissolute washout by his fortieth year had he not been disciplined by sports, particularly by karate, which he picked up in 1965 along with a black belt; and by writing, which he learned at the hand of Bill Buckley while skiing with Bill in 1970. As a writer he was superb. Tom Wolfe, in *The American Spectator*, praised his exuberance, high style, and daring. Taki had most of the gifts of a fine writer including the capacity to work hard . . . at least at writing.

He had an amazing memory. He told marvelous stories. He had no regard for the truth—once he astonished me during a dinner party by notifying his rather cultured guests that I had been a personal friend of Toscanini—which, owing to Toscanini's age and my youth, was impossible. "No, Taki, the conductor was Fritz Reiner of the Chicago Symphony," I lied. Taki had a good story going. Why ruin it with the facts? For decades people, even polite people, asked Taki for dinner just to hear his stories, most of which put him at the center of the action and all of which were extremely funny. He was well read, intelligent, and the rare Jet Setter who dared to defend genuinely controversial political ideas. Some were very wrong headed, but at least they were ideas. Writing well was almost the only serious theme in his life. Otherwise it was mostly fun, money, parties, fashion, models, and putting down the poseurs. He was the perfect student of the 1980s. He had the mind of a superior gentleman and the emotions of a bum. I liked him immensely, though I suspect he hurt almost as many people as he amused.

This was my sociologist for the decade. He told me who Cheryl Tiegs might be, and the Duke of Beaufort. He actually knew that fellow Zipkin and Liz Smith. Joan Collins, a movie star, had bragged in an autobiography of her affair with him. Furthermore, I could call him at any hour of the day or night for an article—he slept only intermittently.

Together we covered the Grand Prix of Monaco for *Car and Driver* magazine. At the Hotel de Paris *tout le monde* knew him, and, when the hotel's smartly liveried flunkies spied the name Tyrrell on my luggage, we were ceremoniously conducted past the long lines of "beautiful people" waiting to register. (The dopes had mistaken me for a member of the Tyrrell racing family.) A hotel manager personally escorted us to a vast suite overlooking the course, Taki having assured the desk clerk that his famous father had reserved the room well in advance. Alas, Taki had *forgotten* to reserve *any* room, and shortly after our glorious entry we were ignominiously booted from the hotel. Taki caused such disasters frequently. There was a flight across the Atlantic with me in first class and my immensely wealthy friend (again he forgot his reservations!) seated back in steerage among scores of ancient ladies returning from the Holy Land. Several became airsick and his solicitude was boundless. He left the plane at JFK with an old girl hanging on each arm as he carried one of the ladies' pieces of carry-on baggage, an empty bird cage. He was a saint. While we awaited our baggage, he cruelly insulted an astonished parvenu for tastelessness. He was a sinner.

Perhaps his greatest talent was remembering and retelling stories: the time he was suspended from Gstaad's Eagle Club for inciting a food fight that left the British Ambassador coated with cream cakes. After the suspension he and his buddies hired a chopper to spray snow on the club members during a fête. The chopper crashed en route. Minutes later it would have crashed on the club. Then there was the time he believed his friend Gianni Agnelli's facetious report to him of the death of the Greek king. Gullibly he passed the information on to all the Greek shipping magnates, who responded patriotically by sending mounds of funeral wreaths to the royal palace where the king lay near death but not dead yet. Practical jokester that he was, he could convince no one that this too was not his joke. He once broke up a party of royals from three countries by sending a forged letter announcing the imminent arrival of an infamous aristocrat whom not even the royals could endure; and one night he broke into an English neighbor's country home and rearranged the furniture. Unfortunately his neighbor was upstairs, squiffed and copulating adulterously. When the gentleman came down to investigate the racket the rearranged furniture confused him. He thought he was in a strange house, and broke for the countryside where his confusion got worse.

Taki's name terrorized the British and American upper classes, which is one of the reasons, I suspect, that he was eventually picked up at Heathrow airport, an envelope of cocaine boldly protruding from his pocket. I had suspected that he used drugs, but our friend Tom Wolfe counseled me against admonishing Taki. Some writers owe part of their greatness to innocence. Thus they see everything with a fresh eye. This explains part of Tom's art. He feared Taki's feelings would be hurt were I to raise the painful subject of drugs with him. Tom, of course, catches on quickly—hence his unique combination of freshness and skepticism.

Despite all the silliness, Taki's zest for politics impressed even the most exacting political minds. I had introduced him to former President Nixon during one of the old pol's dinners with conservative writers. One morning, many months later, after it was reported in the New York papers that Taki was headed for an English calaboose, President Nixon telephoned me inquiring as to what might console our Greek friend. RN's sympathy was touching. I suggested he send Taki a hacksaw. His stationery would surely get past the guards. Instead RN sent a simple letter of encouragement that, as a matter of fact, did impress the guards. After Taki emerged from the penitentiary he was as rambunctious as ever, but he thought it a great kick now to tease minority groups in his columns, and so I had to part company with his work in our pages. Americans take ethnic jibes more seriously than Europeans. Consequently we lost our sociologist of the 1980s. But by then the decade was about over. On came the era of George Herbert Walker Bush, an era without a road map and with a question hanging over it. Would the conservatives have the ideas and the resourcefulness to consolidate and move beyond tax cuts and anticommunism?

CHAPTER 6

Illusion and Denial
*How the Liberals Vindicated
the Late Anna Freud*

ALL PEOPLES CIVILIZED AND uncivilized spin about themselves a lovely filigree of illusions, some of which endure long after their creators vacate the premises. One night in Rome the economist Antonio Martino showed me such a beguiling artifact. After strong coffees at the Caffè Sant Eustachio, Antonio gunned his Fiat through the swirl of Roman traffic and up the Aventino Hill to an old stone wall where he bid me gaze through the large iron keyhole rusting within its gate. The wall, part of the Piazza dei Cavalieri di Malta, dates back at least to the second half of the eighteenth century. Through its keyhole I spied a dimly illuminated garden path, framed by tall cypresses that arched over it. At the end of that path, there floated in a celestial luminescence the colossal dome of Saint Peter's basilica. Of course, this is an illusion created by the engraver Piranesi and other pious minds intent on demonstrating some tremendous truth now long forgotten. The dome seen floating at the end of this mysterious garden path actually exists far across town in the Vatican, where it crowns Saint Peter's.

America's pietists do not demonstrate their tremendous truths with such elemental props as garden paths and ancient walls arranged on legendary hillsides. America is a hive of technology, and so Americans rely on those great technological hoodwinkers: the camera, the microphone, lights, sound! They create illusions that can be beamed everywhere, into theaters, private homes, on street corners, on billboards, everywhere; and then they are gone, replaced by other illusory ephemera—more lights! more cameras! more sound!

Immediately after the election of Ronald Reagan the bovine intelligentsia and all the inert minds under their spell summoned the mighty engines of illusion to demonstrate two tremendous truths: (a) that Jimmy Carter had not been defeated for his policies but for his ineptitude, and (b) that in 1980 no one was actually elected president. No idols had been disturbed. Every false piety remained in place. Nothing had changed, except that the presidency was now vacant and would remain so until the next presidential election. The gifted Arthur M. Schlesinger, Jr., spoke for the Old Order when he argued that "what the voters repudiated in 1980 was not Liberalism but the miserable result of the conservative economic policies of the last half dozen years."[1] Jack Newfield concurred and added a touching note of exhortation, "We must understand that the main reason Carter was defeated was because he was an incompetent conservative president."[2]

As for Ronald Reagan, well, somehow he was not the duly elected president of the United States. Rather he was but an actor performing a B-grade dramatization of the presidency from what once had been the executive mansion of the government of the United States. Sixteen hundred Pennsylvania Avenue was now a Hollywood set. According to this illusion, America had no national government, only an actor with orange hair broadcasting from the Oval Office. Let him rhapsodize about tax cuts, economic growth, low inflation, and the threat posed by the Soviet military buildup. This group was not buying it. As the years passed and Ronald Reagan presided over the longest period of peacetime growth in American history, with low inflation, high employment, and productivity nearly 30 percent higher than when Jimmy Carter left office, [3] these tenacious skeptics ignored it all. From the day the orange-haired imposter entered the White House the Republic had become, as Felix Rohatyn put it, "a first-rate military power and a second-rate economic power"[4]—all evidence to the contrary notwithstanding. Ronald Reagan, supported by an able staff of writers, directors, and producers, had created one more Hollywood fantasy. What made it all particularly offensive was that Reagan's fantasy had been achieved at taxpayers' expense!

Then, sometime in the fall of 1981, about the time Reagan was calling for $80 billion in additional budget cuts, the skeptics developed another somewhat contradictory illusion. The actor president was now in effect something more than a president. He was a tyrant dedicated to creating homelessness and hunger. Other illusions followed.

With all the technological instruments of deception at their disposal, the critics pervaded the country with the illusion that the Reagan Administration was a camorra of unparalleled corruption, though few Reaganites were ever jailed and none on the common corruption charges that sent scores of congressmen and state officials to the clink during the Reagan years. There was the illusion that the Reagan Administration was provoking the Soviets to new levels of hostility, though the Reagan Administration was advancing towards history's first nuclear arms reduction treaty and pressuring the Soviet Union to withdraw from Afghanistan. There were the sequential illusions that Reagan was popular solely because he was charming and then solely because of "magic," and then—in the Administration's last days—the illusion that Iran-Contra revealed him as a lamentable bungler, though he starred at summitry despite his advanced age and Mikhail S. Gorbachev's undeniable heartiness.

Of all the illusions propounded throughout the Reagan Administration, the most fanciful and enduring was the illusion that the economy was on the verge of collapse. One heard it everywhere, notwithstanding the fact that the American economy was one of the most robust in the world. Martin Anderson was to argue in 1990 that "we do know from official economic statistics that the seven-year period from 1982 to 1989 was the greatest consistent burst of economic activity ever seen in the U.S. In fact, it was the greatest economic expansion the world has ever seen—in any country, at any time. . . . The amount of wealth produced during this seven-year period was stupendous—some $30 trillion worth of goods and services. Again, it was a world record. Never before had so much wealth been produced during a comparable period."[5] Yet if the Administration's critics ever noticed the economic boom they did so only prefatory to warning that ravening inflation was just around the corner or that some other economic calamity was about to befall us. From November 1982 to 1989 the American economy created almost 18.7 million new jobs—more than Europe and Japan combined. And contrary to another popular contemporary fantasy, these jobs were not menial or "dead-end" jobs. From 1982 to 1988 the number of minimum-wage jobs fell by 25 percent while jobs paying $10 or more an hour climbed 67 percent and real per capita disposable income expanded by 14.4 percent.[6] Still the critics remained prolific in spinning their gruesome illusions for the 1980s.

The Liberals' dogged creation of illusions throughout the Reagan years reveals one of the most significant differences between Liberals and conservatives. The Liberals are prodigiously resourceful in the production of comely legends. The conservatives are almost completely impotent in this department; few even know where to hire a storyteller. As we shall see in due course, this difference accounts for many of the conservatives' second-place finishes in political races that they might have won.

Mention to a Liberal one of his embalmed and sanctified heroes, or, better still, one of his many imagined villains, and he will gabble on inveterately according to the party line of the moment. Do the same with a conservative and there is a comparative stillness. Conservatives are not even very long-winded in execrating their enemies, contrary to all the Liberals' myths about conservatives' hate campaigns. It is not that conservatives are restrained by high principle or that their dispositions are mild; many are excellent haters. But, unlike Liberals, most conservatives keep their hates to themselves; they simply are not very communicative. Some are almost nonverbal, for instance, many conservative businessmen.

Thus there were very few conservative writers available to write anything about the President that would undo the era's illusions. At the White House there was not even an interest in such writing. On one occasion an *American Spectator* writer got it into his head to chronicle a week in the President's life *à la* the books that John Hersey and Jim Bishop had written about earlier presidents. I recommended the project to friends in the White House, but neither press spokesman Larry Speakes nor any other White House aide with whom I spoke could even see the point of such a book, much less cooperate with the writer. Former President Richard Nixon assured me that this would change when Pat Buchanan came in as White House communications director. It never did. Shortly after Pat took his new position I suggested that we might revive my writer's interest in chronicling the President's week. Pat discouraged me, saying "That'll never fly in this White House."

Against the exiguous number of friendly books written about the Reagan Administration in the 1980s, the Liberals created a veritable New Age presidential library of books and essays proffering Liberal legends of the Reagan Administration's vast corruption, economic charlatanry, and un-paralleled stupidity in high places. At the end of the Administration some White House aides did write memoirs of the kiss-and-tell variety, but these issued not from the literary impulse but from the old Republican aptitude for commerce. The authors wrote not to communicate ideas or to set the record straight but to acquire a little more loot to hand over to their brokers. Despite all the chatter about Reagan's bringing Hollywood to the banks of the Potomac, there was never an effort to create a Republican Camelot or a *Sunrise at Campobello*. The conservatives' only essay into political drama that I can recall was the creation of a necktie decorated with a very stuffy profile of Adam Smith, the late economist, and that tie, worn so sedulously by Edwin Meese and other Reaganites, had been designed by movement conservatives years before the Reagan Administration.

By contrast, well before Jimmy Carter had vacated the White House, the Liberals had filled a long bookshelf with admiring studies elucidating all the mystery and grandeur of what was both in theory and in practice a clown show. It is a testimonial to the Liberals' literary genius that, despite the unpromising material made available to them, they gamely scripted for Jimmy a first-rate legend to gild his aberrant charms, and they preserved the legend long after Ronald Reagan began demonstrating that the failures of the Carter years did not have to be. In fact, the legend endured even after Jimmy's dreadful memoirs came out, revealing him to be the cheap little ass that he was—always meanly partisan, ever the shifty moralist, *in secula seculorum*: vulgar beyond belief. Carter's autobiography is so ghastly that he who reads it hazards brain damage. Yet in 1982, when the book went out for review, conscientious Liberal reviewers gladly sustained Jimmy's legend: very smart, very honest, very sincere, very Christian, and— get this—very "enigmatic"! Halfway through the Carter Administration that one word had become obbligato to all carriers of The Legend and it endured—enigmatic! Jimmy Carter was the most brazen political dope-fetcher ever to smirk from behind the big desk in the Oval Office. He was a politico as transparent as Lyndon Baines Johnson or the Dean of the Yale Law School, whoever that particular operator might be at any given time. In pursuit of the voters there was no bathos, no boast, no flattery too mortifying for him to utter. Still the fabulists persisted in deluding themselves and their clientele by calling Jimmy enigmatic.

If the life of Ronald Reagan did not inspire conservatives to fashion a proper legend for him, it is unlikely that they will ever immortalize anyone. He came from one of America's most glamorous settings, Hollywood— and from an epic period, the Hollywood of Capra films, of Cooper and Stewart and Wayne. While leading the Screen Actors Guild he had faced down dangerous foes, so dangerous in fact that he was prevailed upon to carry a gun. For nearly thirty years he championed a political cause that left him always the underdog. He first sought the presidency in 1968. Against the odds and an incumbent president he made a valiant fight for it in 1976. In 1980 the sages dismissed him as a has-been, too old for the rigors of the campaign trail. Yet he remained debonair, sparing us all that cloying sentimentalism and self-pity that seemed to be major ingredients of the times. In the end he triumphed. At the age of sixty-nine he took up the greatest challenge of his life, and he did it with style. One final point, his presidency was a success. Despite a would-be assassin's fire, cancer, and the creeping infirmities of old age, Ronald Reagan presided over the most successful presidency certainly since Eisenhower's, and, as I shall argue later, probably since FDR's.

By Washington's standards, Reagan was an intriguing character. He did not partake of the freneticism, the exaggerated drive, the bombastic commitment, the empty agitation and vaporous oratory that characterize most American politicians pursuing their sacred calling. Nonetheless his leadership was stupendously effective, faltering only after his party lost control of the Senate. Reagan was at ease with the world. He was principled, but somehow detached from the squirrelly urgency that has brought down so many of our recent Messiahs. What Robert J. Donovan said of Harry Truman in his 1977 biography could also be said of Reagan: "a buoyant, good-natured, secure individual with a sense of well-being that had carried him through the storms and crises."[7] His most heroic crisis, of course, was brought about by that bullet that just missed his heart. He responded with grace, a series of wisecracks, and courage. Not since Andrew Jackson had a president faced such dangers and survived, and Old Hickory did not weather his ordeals so entertainingly. As has been said of German humor, Old Hickory's public quips were no laughing matter. Had the Liberals been presented with a life similar to the life that Reagan actually led, they would have fashioned it into a box-office hit, perhaps dozens of box-office hits.

Owing to the Liberals' knack for mythopoeia and to the conservatives' curious incapacity in this art form, Americans throughout the Reagan years were simply stuck with the Liberals' illusions, illusions, by the way, that usually had no basis in fact whatsoever. That dome that appears to float at the end of a path on the Aventino Hill may not actually be at the foot of a garden path, but it is a dome and it does exist somewhere. The Reagan Administration's alleged corruption, incompetence, and parlous economy were illusions at variance with the prosperity and peace of the 1980s. Liberals not only ignored reality; they denied it. It almost seemed as though the Republic's reporters and editors actually preferred illusions to the truth. (One envisages the news editor just minutes before Dan Rather is to go on the air reviewing the lead story for the "CBS Evening News": "Perfect! Not one word is accurate. Not one statistic is true or informative. We'll go with it. This is news! The illusions of our time remain intact!") Of course not all writers retailed tendentious falsehoods. Some penetrated the illusory data and spurious analyses to describe the world faithfully. Before his death, Theodore H. White wrote that "the election of 1980 marked the rejection of a whole system of ideas that dominated American life ever since 1960. The basis of all those ideas was high promises to everybody—promises to save the cities, promises to take care of the sick, the old, the universities. By 1980 we had promised ourselves almost to the point of national bankruptcy."[8]

Just so—the correct interpretation of the 1980 election is not that it was a mandate for conservatism, but that it was a renunciation of Liberalism, a Liberalism gone to seed. In chronicling this renunciation along with the subsequent years of growth and relative calm, historians will doubtless want to explain why an entire class of intellectuals socked themselves away in illusions rather than admit the bright rays of reality into their cheerless lives. These historians will benefit from reading Anna Freud's masterwork, *The Ego and the Mechanisms of Defense*. Miss Freud, now deceased, was the daughter of the esteemed Dr. Sigmund Freud of Vienna, Austria, so historians of a progressive cast of mind will need no further introduction. In her book she argues that normal people as well as neurotics, when faced with anxiety-causing situations, frequently practice denial. In its extreme form, psychotic denial amounts to seeing and hearing but refusing to acknowledge what is seen and heard. Miss Freud's findings conform with researches I myself conducted in the early 1980s and published under the now familiar title *The Liberal Crack-Up*.*

In it I noted that certain Americans have practiced denial for years. The peace movement practiced denial after the 1975 fall of South Vietnam, Laos, and Cambodia. That sequence of events unhappily vindicated the "domino theory" first propounded by President Eisenhower and later adopted by supporters of the Vietnam War, who warned that South Vietnam's fall would be followed by the fall of all Southeast Asia. When most of these countries did indeed fall, with one bloody thud after another, you would have thought that at least some antiwar activists would notice the domino theory's tragic validation. But the peace movement and its sympathizers remained silent. They surely saw and heard the fall of these three fated countries, the film clips of the flotillas of boat people, and the film clips of the Cambodian holocaust; but they refused to acknowledge what they saw and heard.

Some even went to the bizarre extreme of arguing that the bloodshed and tyranny following Southeast Asia's fall could be laid to those hawks who had predicted bloodshed and tyranny and had prosecuted the war to

---

*The historian Alonzo Hamby reached similar conclusions in his 1985 study *Liberalism and Its Challengers: FDR to Reagan*, and Senator Edward M. Kennedy of Massachusetts, to his credit, reiterated our conclusions in a March 29, 1985, address at Hofstra University. Then he forgot.

prevent these evils. This was William Shawcross's thesis in a widely celebrated work of deception entitled *Sideshow: Kissinger, Nixon and the Destruction of Cambodia.* Peter Rodman exposed its claptrap in the March 1981 issue of *The American Spectator* and in a devastating exchange with Shawcross in our July 1981 issue, both of which may be found in the archives of your favorite public library. For that matter, the exchange is reprinted in the 1987 paperback edition of *Sideshow*—much to Shawcross's credit.

As for other acts of denial, consider that for many years Americans of an irenic temperament denied the difference between the United States and Dr. Marx's paradise in the Soviet Union. In the 1980s, all New Age Liberals, and even many Liberals in a comparatively unaltered state, denied that the Reagan Administration was presiding over a peaceful and prospering America. They denied the Administration's other successes too, and for a while they even denied that the Reagan presidency existed. Finally, when scholars in the early 1980s posited the thesis that the old Liberal coalition was in a state of crack-up, Liberals again responded with denial.

Think of it, so wild and divided had the Democratic Party become that in 1988 the runner-up for its presidential nomination was the radical mountebank Jesse Jackson. Had a man this radical ever before come so close to the Democratic nomination? Never, yet practically no Liberal acknowledged or bothered to refute the perfectly observable fact that Liberalism was now fragmented among extremists and out of touch with the majority of Americans. This clearly observable phenomenon of Liberal Crack-Up was responded to with a blank face. Miss Freud in her day had only examined a few isolated patients and then only one at a time. Imagine her joy if she had lived to see an entire class of people, many of them otherwise quite healthy and sane, all manifesting acute symptoms of denial. Few researchers in any field have ever had such thunderous confirmation of their theories.

Liberal denial, I am sorry to report, went to such irrational lengths in the 1980s that, after having denied that the presidency of Ronald Reagan existed, many Liberals began to deny that *they* existed. They pretended that no one so sensible as they should be called a Liberal, and in the 1988 presidential campaign they objected indignantly when Vice President George Bush accused Governor Michael Dukakis of "Liberalism"; the charge was a smear, they declared. In the 1980s Liberals began to practice what I have called in earlier scholarship "masked politics." Like guests at a masked ball, they came to politics wearing disguises. They were "environmentalists" or "consumerists" or "feminists" or "peace activists." Some forthrightly admitted to all the various enthusiasms of New Age Liberalism, papering their Volvos from bumper to bumper with the stickers of each glowing cause. However, most New Age Liberals, for reasons I have yet to fathom, restricted their public espousals to one or two enthusiasms. "I am a friend of endangered wetlands and I vote for progressive candidates"—says Specimen A. "I am against the nuclear madness and I am a Democrat"—declares Specimen B. I never met one to admit: "I am a Liberal of contemporary mores; I'm for the whole ball of wax—and the wax is a lot different today than in the time of that comparative moderate FDR. I mean today we're radical and really out to lunch!"

Did the New Age Liberal recognize that he was dissembling in not admitting precisely how thoroughly marinated in ideology he was? During the Reagan years a leitmotif of the Liberals' criticism was that the Reaganites were "ideologues." But surely the Reaganites were no more ideological than their critics, and they were almost certainly less so, as I shall argue in chapter 15. Since the 1960s the Liberals have been inducting ever more desiderata into the national agenda, reorganizing the family, paring back the influence of churches, advancing the influence of educators, and increasing the schools' duties so that they might include sex counseling, psychotherapy, and social engineering of the utmost rigor and ambition. The Reaganites' ideological agenda was for the most part merely composed of negative reactions to these obnoxious innovations. They wanted to lower the Liberals' high taxes. They wanted to return to an earlier consensus on, for instance, abortion or on pornography or on school prayer. In most of these areas, even in the supposedly reactionary 1980s, the Liberals held the Reaganites off.

Whether or not the Liberals recognized how wedded to ideology they were, their disguises completely seduced many Americanos, particularly in the press. Think of Ground Zero Week in the spring of 1982. Its organizers successfully palmed it off as a movement embracing all manner of Americano, from left-wing pacifists to right-wing militarists. Truth be known, Ground Zero was masked politics done to perfection. No conservative participation was likely and none materialized. Yet the press fell under the organizers' spell and reported the event as an All-American demonstration for peace rather than the simple protest of Reagan strategic policy that it was.

During these first fearful days of "the Reagan madness," practically all the marchers in the Ground Zero orgies were New Age Liberals, concealing their orthodoxy behind the mask of your friendly nuclear neurotic. The unhappiness of these New Age Liberals was to intensify as the years passed and Reagan endured. In the best of times those who bear the burden of reform are not very happy people, absorbed as they usually are with the many malfunctioning parts of Utopia. From the 1960s on, however, reformers have become moody to the point of extreme despair. They have discovered, even as they boom the New Age, that Utopia contains more malfunctioning parts than had been anticipated, and nothing they have done has prevented the catastrophe of daily life from growing steadily more catastrophic. Through it all the victimized have grown in number: first blacks, then suburban housewives, then homosexuals, and on until pioneers of the New Age began extending their solicitude to the civil rights of laboratory animals. With all this gloom issuing from so many influential Americans, no wonder a morbidness has spread throughout our public discourse as ordinary citizens have been ceaselessly assaulted with reports of ecological unpleasantness, weird illnesses, economic ruin, homelessness, hunger, and war. In such an atmosphere laughter becomes highly controversial.

CHAPTER 7

Trials with Charlie
The Neos That Failed and
Did the Dishonorable Thing

LAUGHTER DID BECOME CONTROVERSIAL. Yet among those who participated in masked politics in the 1980s there was one group that was having a picnic—the so-called neoliberals, especially the neoliberal journalists. Democrats and Republicans alike celebrated them. The Republicans celebrated them because they seemed to be espousing rudimentary conservative values. The Democrats admired them because, though they did indeed espouse some rudimentary conservative values, they walloped the hell out of conservatives with exquisite derision. Their favorite gambit was to raise up some perfectly unexceptional conservative principle, say the swift and certain punishment of criminals, and then to expose conservatives acting in dereliction of said principle—say conservatives who fail to insist that white collar criminals (perhaps tax evaders or jaywalkers) receive the same strict sentences as bank robbers or serial murderers.

As I take full credit for anticipating the neoconservatives' conversion to conservatism, it is only proper that I admit to being wrong about this later specimen of neopolitico. I assumed, as did such seers as Irving Kristol, that neoliberals would walk the neoconservatives' well-trodden path to conservatism. After all, like the neoconservatives, these neos had no place else to go if they were sincere in their scrupling over Liberal extravagance. Disturbingly, however, they were even more fastidious than the neoconservatives about holding on to their old Danger-on-the-Right prejudices, and their derision of conservatives frequently seemed to go beyond duty's call.

Considering how sectarian and touchy Liberals were becoming, however, I expected the hour was drawing near when New Age Liberals, indignant over the neoliberals' inchoate conservatism, would excommunicate them, and by the early 1980s it seemed that this ex-communication would come sooner rather than later. The neoliberals were getting very chummy with neoconservatives whilst Liberals were growing markedly more intolerant. My own correspondence with neoliberals was growing quite cordial, suggesting some unspoken mutual respect, some affinity, the kind of harmony that perchance exists between Elks living in Cherry Hill, New Jersey, and the Elks of Bangkok.

In keeping with this era of good feelings between neoliberals and conservatives, I was in 1984 invited to the seventieth anniversary dinner of *The New Republic,* the preeminent neoliberal organ. Naturally I accepted, and on the appointed evening headed off to Washington's National Portrait Gallery, full of the expectation that this neoliberal dinner would abound with serious minds and lively intellects all steeled to the defense of democracy and liberty against the terrorists and totalitarians then rampant around the world. Alas, these neos did not live up to expectations. Why they had begun to court conservatives in the early 1980s I cannot fully explain. I suspect they feared that Ronald Reagan's influence on American culture might be as transforming as Franklin Roosevelt's influence had been in the 1930s. They were fearful that history might pass them by. The days when Liberals "sailed against the wind" had ended long before. Now they followed political fashion. Recognizing that political power had passed to conservatism, they wanted an option on it.

All things considered, I had a splendid evening on my night out with the *New Republic* crowd. For a supposedly intellectual review, the magazine had attracted a surprising abundance of Democratic politicians to its party, and there remains a lewd joviality to Democratic politicians even though their intellectual allies incline towards the grisly. Of course, I experienced some perilous moments when prudence and the looming presence of an unforgiving feminist or consumerist bid me fade into the shadows or behind the bulbous paunch of a nearby professor. In those days my work was appearing every Monday morning on the op-ed pages of their *Washington Post,* and occasionally some innocent Liberal reader, unaware of the variety of thought available on that page, would venture a paragraph or two into my column before feeling the blood rush to his cheeks. Others, the devil-may-care types, might occasionally sneak a lascivious peek on purpose. Some might even read an entire column before slashing their wrists. The *Post's* correspondence page frequently crackled with these Liberals' appraisals of my work. "I am appalled . . ." the letters would begin, or "I am outraged . . ."

Needless to say, on my evening with *The New Republic* I did not remind any of the assembled free-thinkers of my irregular views. Instead I listened dutifully for evidence of the neoliberals' reawakened sense of reality. To my regret I heard very little of the serious, erudite conversation then current at similar neoconservative or conservative soirees. In fact, it seemed that all intelligent discourse segued into a numbing sough of self-congratulations; not witty self-congratulations either but the leaden, foreboding kind that can make Washingtonians so dismal even at cocktail time.

Nothing I heard that night suggested that these neoliberals recognized how far Liberalism had strayed from the moderate liberalism of the past. To hear these amnesiacs tell it, Franklin Roosevelt, Harry Truman, and John F. Kennedy were all perfect likenesses of Walter Mondale in 1984 and, I suppose, Jesse Jackson later. Moreover, they were the masters of the unproved hypothesis. Every amelioration in the American condition they laid to the influence of environmentalism, consumerism, or whatever other reform movement they might put to their tendentious purposes. Here then was a pretty complacent bunch. True, its members no longer controlled the political course of the Republic; but they were confident of their dominance of a jejune culture and that was enough. No, save for the slightly higher octane of their hubris, the crowd at *The New Republic's* seventieth birthday celebration was not very different from any other group of Washington partygoers, and there were as many limousines waiting to take the assembled humanitarians home that night as might be found at a fête for Republican fat cats. A pervasive hypocrisy filled the room, putting the laugh to the postprandial speeches about what a hell of a mess the Republic was in, and how these brave reformers had improved American life despite all the objections from the bourgeoisie. Betty Friedan's tirade epitomized the sham of neoliberalism in a particularly memorable way for me.

There she stood, bellowing as we sipped our espresso and longed for home: ". . . have it all . . . come a long way . . . still a long way to go . . . now, feminism's SECOND STAGE!" In the distant future, when America's war between the sexes is looked back on as but another chapter in human folly equal in futility to, say, Prohibition or vegetarianism or Napoleon's invasion of Russia, Miss Friedan's excretions of cant will be wholly incomprehensible. However, to those of us then living through

Betty's heroic revolution we still got the point. It was that, thanks to feminism, the American gal no longer was consigned to Uncle Tom's Cabin. Moreover, through the feminist analysis it had been discovered that women were really men (and men were really what had once been known as ladies). While Betty howled, the assembled swelled. Idealism polluted the room. I looked across the table to exchange smiles with my wife, but to my surprise she was not amused. Rather, she appeared to be in turmoil. Her eyes reminded me of the time she suffered motion sickness in an unsprung New York taxi plunging along on Manhattan's lumpy thoroughfares. When the speakers had subsided and all *The New Republic*'s heroes and heroines had taken their final bows, I hastened to her side. By then she had recovered and was, in fact, just a little pleased.

What had happened was this. As soon as Friedan had piped up about raised consciousness and equality, a venerable Liberal journalist seated at my wife's side began playing pizzicato up her leg, apparently oblivious to Miss Friedan's message. During dinner he had won my wife's admiration by telling her how highly he esteemed me, having followed my "career" from its earliest triumphs. Well, that night he let his interest in my career go too far. My wife might have been faintly pleased, but I know Betty would have been vexed. As for me, well, at least I discovered that not much had changed even in the House of Neoliberalism; and before I could give our Casanova the jolly what-for he was gone.

We left that night with Penn Kemble, who during the 1960s had opted for the most principled and austere form of radicalism. He had been a Social Democrat. Sometime late in the 1960s, Penn had fallen out of favor with the Liberals by opposing violence on campus and favoring effective prosecution of the Vietnam War. He was to suffer their further disapproval in the 1980s by opposing the Sandinistas' dictatorship in Nicaragua and supporting Contra aid. Being a good Liberal in the New Age had become less a matter of adhering to timeless principle and more a matter of conforming to an exacting, if volatile, etiquette. Kemble was not a proper conformist and soon he too would be called a neoconservative.

My hopes for neoliberalism were, then, misplaced. These were not Liberals toughened by Depression, dictatorship, and world war. They were not principled enough to follow Kemble's independent course. These were Liberals coddled in the Me Generation. In exalting themselves above conventional Liberalism, the neoliberals were creating a distinction without difference. They had made their way in the world, teasing the attentions of conservatives and hornswoggling Liberals by ferociously falling on conservatives. Their deficiency was not in the department of intellect but in

the department of character. Succinctly put, they were devoid of honor—
though to speak of honor is, in modern politics, to raise an utterly irrelevant
topic somewhat like discussing chastity at a sex education class or, better
yet, the proper care of your daughter's chastity belt.

Stripped of their pretensions, particularly their insufferable rodomontade, the neoliberals appear to the trained eye as nothing more than ambitious young Liberals bereft of the courage of their convictions and
occasionally bereft of convictions. Their only unshakable belief was the
rather common American belief in one's own stupendous self-worth. Their
favorite word was *me*. Neoliberals wanted all the benefits that Liberalism
offers—the swell media posts, the university appointments, the approval
of polite society—but none of the historic burdens, one of which in the
early 1980s was acknowledging the facts, for instance, recognizing that
Theodore White's aforementioned analysis of the 1980 election had
something to it and that history was about to leave Liberalism at the
gate.

Like a beauty fingered by time, Liberalism had now lost the means to
entrance, but the neoliberals were not quite certain that conservatism had
a sure grip on the future. Thus the neoliberals, too, practiced masked
politics. For them neoliberalism was a mask to be worn until they could
discern whether Liberalism had a future. So artfully did the neoliberals
play both ends of the political spectrum that, as the decade wore on, many
diehard Liberals (Paleo-Liberals, one might say) bloomed with hope that
neoliberalism would rescue them from history's dustbin.

These forever hopeful adherents of the Old Order had been reading
Arthur M. Schlesinger, Jr., and in the bleak years of Reaganism Arthur
reassured them with his theory of historical cycles. Perhaps cheered by the
presence of the neoliberals, perhaps by reading the stars, Arthur at some
point in the 1980s began reminding his readers of Arthur's Marvelous
Cycles. They come and go according to an impartial process first detected
by his father, Arthur M. Schlesinger, Sr., in the 1930s. Tick-tock, tick-
tock; America moves from high-minded Liberalism to a low-minded conservatism and—tick-tock, tick-tock—back again.*

Now Arthur believed that his vast and stupid force was again at work,

---

*Incidentally, surely Arthur does not believe that history, the illuminating study to which he has
devoted so much of his life, is a tale decided by the mechanical action of some huge dead pendulum
hanging from the sky, dumbly swinging back and forth; left-right, left-right. If that be true, then what
is the point of the political activism Arthur so tirelessly advocates? Why would anyone stand for
principle against the imperturbable movement of Arthur's cycles? The wise pol is he who senses the
movement of the cycles and conforms. Arthur's history has no heroes, no rogues, no point.

shoving the Republic into another cycle of Liberal bliss. The diehards of the Old Order spied the neoliberals and identified them as instruments occultly ordained to deliver the Republic from conservatism in the approaching Liberal cycle. Once again, they were wrong.

Recall if you will the sad fate of 1988's crop of Democratic presidential candidates. All save two—Paul Simon and Jesse Jackson—had been proud neoliberals. They were members of what *Newsweek* termed "the most exciting intellectual movement in America."[1] Alas, come the spring primaries of 1988, Americans were snickering at them and dismissing them as "the seven dwarfs." Hopeful Liberals stubbornly stuck by them. The dwarfs' mishaps on the campaign trail would not dissuade them. These Liberal optimists had been tipped off that a Liberal cycle was certain; call it neo if you will.

Hendrik Hertzberg of *The New Republic*, his brain gassed with Schlesinger's ratiocinations, let out a tremendous yell when Governor Michael Dukakis, an early neoliberal, won the Democratic presidential nomination. "Pity George Bush," Hertzberg roared. "Dukakis will be a much more formidable opponent than the Bush people could have imagined. . . . It will not be easy, for example, to depict Dukakis as a tax-raising liberal who thinks the answer to every problem is a government spending program.* It will not be easy to depict him as a cultural radical."[2] Actually, it was. Neoliberalism was not that different from any other sort of 1980s Liberalism and had no special future. It was merely a mask for Liberals of a particularly ambitious and craven sort. Once the voters had caught on, the neoliberal politicians' popularity peaked and they scrambled back to Liberalism. Ending their deception, they reverted to the old Liberal bromides. Not to do so would have cost them even the support of the Liberal diehards.

Thus candidate Richard Gephardt, who in the heyday of neoliberalism had presented himself as an enlightened proponent of free trade, had by Campaign '88 returned to championing protectionism for the labor unions and a dozen other causes dear to the hearts of Liberal interest groups. Massachusetts Governor Dukakis, too, once the White House itch got him, changed from being a brash neoliberal to being a faithful servitor of the Old Order. As the neoliberal governor of Massachusetts in 1983, he

---

*As you will recall from chapter 6's discussion of Liberal denial, by the 1988 presidential election Liberals were even denying they were Liberals and accusing the Bush campaign of smear tactics for associating Governor Dukakis with Liberalism. I hope this explanation of Hertzberg's weird outburst is helpful.

had rejected organized labor's efforts to pass mandatory plant-closing legislation. He was convinced that, as his representative pronounced to the state legislature, "the state's competitive edge would be quite damaged by this bill."[3] In Campaign '88, however, he was back in the Democratic claque applauding national mandatory plant-closing legislation and most of the other desiderata of the Democratic factions. Most of the other neoliberal presidential candidates underwent the same depressing metamorphosis. During their neoliberal phase they had gladly abused some traditional components of the Liberal constituency—usually organized labor—but when it came time to make political choices they chose the safe harbor of traditional Liberalism, spoke out sonorously for government spending plus government taxing, and were recommended to posterity as "the seven dwarfs."

A distinction without a difference, then, that is about all neoliberalism amounted to, and those of us who had harbored such hopes for them should have recognized it. As early as 1984 one of the neoliberals' chief hagiographers, Randall Rothenberg, had admitted as much when he wrote: "there is no statistically significant difference between traditional liberals and neoliberals. On both economic and social issues, their voting records indicate that the two groups are far more liberal than the 'average' Democrat."[4] The best that can now be said about the neoliberals is that they represented a tacit admission that something was fla-fla with conventional Liberalism, but they were neither competent diagnosticians nor competent therapists. Unlike the neoconservatives, who resolutely supported intelligent new theories about society and the limits of government, these neos had no theories and no resolve.

Critical as I am of the Liberalism of the New Age and of those Liberals who would not resist the New Age, I have always willingly admitted that the earlier liberalism of the New Deal had comprehensible and even defensible ideas. What is more, its proponents had the courage to defend them. They believed in the planned society. They believed in Keynesian economics and progressive education. They believed that social problems were susceptible to social reforms. Possibly, as my grandfathers always insisted, these ideas were erroneous and corrupting; but they were at least arguable.

By the 1980s, however, Liberals had been seduced ever further towards the left—that is to say towards the infantile, self-absorbed left of the New Age. Had they been candid, the Liberals of the New Age would have declared themselves socialists, so atrophied was their regard for property rights and so vast had become their vision of state power. They agreed with most of socialism's propositions. They were in open sympathy with socialists all over the world (even violent socialists). Yet not many New Age Liberals ever came right out and called themselves socialists, and for at least one very good reason. As political systems go, socialism was too exacting for the child of the New Age. Socialism required action, decisiveness, resistance to vested interests, the cracking of a few heads every now and then."* It demanded active governance, and the only act of governance that the New Age Liberal was capable of was raising taxes. He believed in taxing the middle class to the utmost reaches of the tolerable, though even here he was tentative. He denoted the middle class as "the rich" and he preferred to tax them surreptitiously through tax bracket creep. To Liberals in the New Age, reality could be fudged. Words, it was presumed, had no consequences beyond their idiotic music and actions were but empty poses. Ideas became vaporous collections of complaints, and so, when it became necessary for the neoliberal to revert to the old Liberal orthodoxy, the tergiversation was easy. In the 1980s Liberals and neoliberals did not truly believe in much of anything other than personal advancement.

Neoliberalism's hollowness was obvious fairly early. In October 1983 the neoliberals held their first and, so far as I know, their last national conference. Gathering in Washington, they proposed to define the precepts and rituals of the neoliberal canon and to plot a glorious future. The ensuing homilies provided ample evidence that the movement was a colossal deceit. Most were uttered *allegretto*, in keeping with the movement's refreshing verve. There was, however, at least one somber voice, that being the voice of Charlie Peters, the new movement's well-known leader. With tedious frequency Charlie compared himself to Don Quixote; and for some reason no neoliberal thought it funny, though possibly none had read *Don Quixote*—the movement was pretty much philistine. At any rate, beyond comparing himself to one of literature's most famous fools, Peters was the slightly unctuous chief cook and bottle washer of *The Washington Monthly*, another neoliberal organ. He was also the conference's convener, and his career was characteristic of that of most neoliberals.

Charlie was a lifelong Liberal who for years had been receiving claptrap

---

*For those who see in socialism only the sweetness of humanitarianism and none of the tough-mindedness that is so often just beneath the sweetness, allow me to suggest a passage from George Bernard Shaw's 1927 letter to the Austrian Socialist Friedrich Adler: "Now we, as Socialists, have nothing to do with liberty. Our message, like Mussolini's, is one of discipline, of service, of ruthless refusal to acknowledge any natural right of competence. We admit no liberty whatever until the daily debt to society is paid by the day's work"—and Shaw was a Socialist with a sense of humor!

accolades for spotting some minor errancies committed in the name of Liberalism. He had become one of Liberal Washington's socially approved scolds, which is to say that though he raised episodic ruckuses he rarely raised one about anything significant. Admittedly, as Liberals are not given to any self-criticism whatsoever, he deserves some token of esteem. His public service was small but not nonexistent. Perhaps a drinking fountain in the Rayburn House Office Building could be named for him. He was a Liberal who did some good, at least temporarily. His complaints may have restrained one or more of the Liberals' fiscally idiotic catapults into the futile. After a while, however, his nitpicking became boring, then unconvincing, and finally one had to adjudge that in its sempiternal totality this niggling was a sham—a pretense for avoiding serious examination of Liberalism's fundamental policy errors.

Neoliberal complaints were usually sufficiently vague to obviate serious debate. Furthermore, they were invariably petty. Think of it! From their larval moments in the early 1970s they fussed over minor points about the bureaucracy, the civil service, Subsection E of paragraph 12 of Section 7 on page 227 of H.R. 133, just below where Mrs. Bottomley spilled her coffee. Meanwhile, the world was roaring and shaking all around them. At the United Nations, Ambassador Daniel Patrick Moynihan—then a neoconservative—rose up to warn that democracy had become so unpopular that it faced extinction. The Soviet Union was engaged in history's largest peacetime military build-up. Its functionaries were at work in over a dozen troubled countries. In the Third World most Western values were disparaged or repudiated. Suddenly the West was under assault from a relatively new kind of warfare, state-sponsored international terrorism, whose practitioners could strike almost anywhere. Through all this tumult, neoliberals such as Charlie Peters only had eyes for a little policy tinkering at home. Crime, drugs, and other social pathologies were making life in America's ghettos markedly more wretched and many of these social pathologies were spreading throughout America. Major shifts were taking place in the nation's economic structure, in its strategic planning, in its relations with the outside world. To all these momentous phenomena, neoliberals responded with banalities, self-congratulations, and the worldview of an accountant.

Peters had watched Irving Kristol gain eminence, and Peters deduced that he too could attract notice by appropriating the prefix neo-. He even got himself christened "Neoliberalism's Godfather." But whereas Kristol had shed an old orthodoxy and assisted in developing a modernized conservatism suitable for contemporary American life, Peters was absorbed solely with minor policy rearrangements and soporific truisms that have been passed around by Liberalism's trained parrots for years: "we live in an interdependent world," "education is an investment in the future," zzzz, zzzz.

As writers are even less responsible for their conduct than politicians, Peters and his journalistic colleagues could utter this sort of sententious bunk endlessly and suffer no ill effects. Thus, long after the neoliberal politicians had dropped their neoliberal masks and returned to Liberalism, the annoying neoliberal writers continued to brag of their superiority over every form of political life known to the Republic.

Peters, for instance, would boast that he favored entrepreneurial businessmen over the old mossback businessmen and "financial traders." That might sound bold and innovative, but it meant that he was hanging on to the conventional Liberals' prejudice against issuing stocks. Government, he thought, should induce investors to invest in "new plants and equipment instead of simply trading old issues, which is what most of the activity on Wall Street is about today." Enslaved still to the old Liberal orthodoxy, Peters had little understanding of markets. Contrary to his stagnant Liberal belief, fresh capital cannot be raised for "new plants and equipment" without free and vigorous markets. Experience demonstrates that government will not invest capital as efficiently as private investors. Perhaps over the short run a true socialist, raising capital through coercion, might invest it wisely but only over the short run; and anyway Peters did not have the heart to opt for socialism. In his finest hour he had premonitions that something was wrong with Liberalism. But, aside from fleeting moments of heroic doubt, Peters and his neoliberals lived comfortably close to the illusions of Liberal orthodoxy. At their famous 1983 conference, an economist by the name of Paul London solemnly advanced the notion that inflation is caused by the public's unwillingness to oppose price increases. No one snickered or corrected him. This was how far the assembled had evolved in their understanding of a problem that had so recently debauched the currency of the United States and at an alarming rate. The neoliberals were all slogans and hollow homilies—all firmly founded on the ideas of yesteryear.[5]

Rather than relying on serious ideas and theories, the neoliberal got by with solemn poses and a schoolboy's sneer at easy targets, that is to say, at older Liberals, organized labor, and a stereotyped conservative who existed for the most part solely in Liberal Danger-on-the-Right folklore. In the crunch, neoliberals were timorous and eager for applause. Their cowardliness contributed to the rapid decline of political debate in the

1980s. They and all other varieties of Liberals simply refused to debate those who disagreed with them. The kind of debates that had once pitted William F. Buckley, Jr., against Gore Vidal or John Kenneth Galbraith were over.

Of the neoliberal politicians, Senator Gary Hart was the most gifted. He was a campaigner of the utmost cunning. Day and night he campaigned, and had it not been for some of his nighttime campaigning in 1988, he would most likely have received that year's Democratic nomination. But the little creep in the back of his head—in others it is called conscience—goaded him into challenging the journalists to investigate his scortatory projects, and unfortunately for him they did. Presently they had him and a cutie barricaded in his very own home, and so this 1980s edition of JFK was laughed out of the race.

Of all the Democratic candidates, only Hart had been sufficiently gifted to address more than one fragment of the Liberal coalition at a time. For our purposes he is worthy of closer examination because he was the epitome of the neoliberal pol, manifesting as he did the neoliberals' stupefying combination of gasconade and spinelessness. Hart was one part intelligence and the rest bluff. There he stood, the exemplary neoliberal of the hour, boasting of his superiority to Liberalism, coyly suggesting a few nuggets of conservative wisdom, but then, well, he needed votes and so in Campaign '88 back to the old Liberal inanities he did go, another neoliberal bereft of courage or convictions.

Hart had sought the presidency before. In 1984 he visited one of the most he-man universities in America, Texas A&M, where in neoliberal fashion he let off a fierce blast against that most conventional of Liberals, Walter Mondale, accusing poor Walter of complicity in the "weak," "inept," and "uncertain" Carter Administration. With Old Glory snapping in the breeze, he bragged: "As President I will not hesitate to use force when vital American interests are threatened." Would he really? In his very next sentence the caveat was filed: "But I will not hazard American lives where our purpose is unclear, our goals are unattainable, or negotiation has been left untried." Those who have performed autopsies on the neoliberal corpse understand how essential this gelatinous condition was to neoliberal rhetoric. Every bold proclamation was quietly accompanied by a suave retraction. In his 1984 campaign Hart even retreated on promising continued military aid to El Salvador's moderate anticommunist government, then being imperiled by Communist guerrillas. In fact, if elected president Hart promised to terminate military aid "immediately," as if doing so were an act of heroism.[6]

The inanity of the neoliberal had been revealed even more vividly during an interview with Hart in the February 28, 1982 *Washington Post*. When asked "to what extent does the United States go to resist the formation of a Marxist government," particularly in the Western hemisphere, Hart haughtily pronounced that the United States must "deal country by country. . . . I don't think we ought to automatically assume that a self-determined Marxist government is something we can't stand." And the lecture continues: "our interest lies in seeing [that] the entire region is not totalitarian or totally anti-American." All right, a modicum of anti-Americanism is permissible, but the line *is* drawn at "totalitarian." So the *Post* asked if Nicaragua is totalitarian. "No, not so far as I know." And Cuba? "It's not a government I'd want to live under; it's certainly not democratic." The *Post's* intrepid interviewer would not be put off. How about identifying a real-life example of totalitarianism somewhere, he asks the Hon. Hart. Hart responds: "Sure. Extremes of the right and the left all over Latin America." "Like?" asks the *Post*. "Paraguay," comes the brave reply. "That would be the right. What about the left?" comes the unwelcome follow-up. "Well, Cuba is not totalitarian and it's not democratic." Now the questioning becomes rigorous: "If Cuba is not a totalitarian government, what is?" "I don't know," responds the neoliberal who had bragged to Bill Moyers in 1980 of his relish for *"outthinking"* his opponents. From this point Hart collapsed into pitiable whimpers. Asked if Cuba is more or less democratic than the Soviet Union or if perhaps it is inaccurate to describe the Soviet Union as totalitarian, the candidate who would someday so boldly address students at Texas A&M hoists the white flag: "totalitarian is probably a word that I should not have used," and with his tail between his legs he bawls that it is futile to use military force to protect American interests "even in our hemisphere."[7]

Neoliberals such as Hart suffered a common Liberal delusion, to wit, that a good intention, earnestly expressed, is a policy. This tendency to confuse good intentions with right policy was memorably chronicled by Richard Vigilante, whom The American Spectator commissioned to report on Peters' 1983 convention. His piece flavorously conveys neoliberalism in all its pomposity and muddled substance. According to Vigilante, the assembled neoliberals were adamant for " 'community, democracy, and prosperity,' no-fault divorce and auto insurance, national service, 'entrepreneurial, creative behavior and management' which represent 'neoliberal ideas in management . . .' "[8] Their creed was then the usual cant with a few crazy tics. The evils that they vowed to destroy were for the most part noncontroversial: "unions that exclude the poor from the job market, unions that raise unemployment among their own members, management executives who pay themselves too much, silly legal technicalities that let criminals off the hook, more law schools, more lawyers, lawsuits, the civil service, weapons that don't work, weapons that cost too much, greedy social security recipients [the Rockefellers and the Mellons are frequently mentioned—RET], greedy tax protesters, the student draft deferment, economic regulation, credentialism, seniority, the adversary system of justice, snobbery, people who put themselves first, and . . . the Bendix merger."[9]

Like other contemporary giants of American public life, the neoliberals were earnest without being, in the French sense, serious—that is: reliable, trustworthy, genuine. They suffered the grandiosity of the New Age, and in their tumescent egotism they assumed that all things were possible for those who spoke in high-flown terms and struck a heroic pose. Their inability to distinguish a good intention from a good policy perhaps explains their hostility toward the Reagan administration. Possibly they thought Ronald Reagan's policies of tax reduction and military rearmament represented his highest ideals. Perhaps they thought conservatives conceived tax reduction as a virtue in itself rather than a means to an end—in this case, economic growth. Thus they watched the Reaganites strive to cut taxes and foresaw the end of the Internal Revenue Service—one of their favorite government institutions. They watched the Reagan Administration increase the military budget and foresaw a never-ending process whereby the Merchants of Death would accumulate ever larger mounds of armaments. In the *mousse à la confusion* of their minds they could not discern that the Reagan Administration's policies were distinct from its objectives and thus that tax reduction and rearmament were actually instrumentalities towards a vigorous economy and towards arms reduction—two goals the Reagan Administration actually accomplished.

But if neoliberalism had much in common with other species of Liberalism, one thing about it was, so far as I have been able to ascertain, unique. Its writers were even more egregious fakers than its politicians, and in the 1980s they proceeded in their hypocrisy long after their pols had retreated to Liberalism's cushy confines. Neoliberal politicians could be held accountable for their blowsy utterances by the electorate. They needed political support at the polls; and, as I have said, in the heat of campaigning most came forward, dropped all pretenses, and fessed up to their essential Liberalism. The neoliberal journalists were never put under similar pressure to retire the humbug.

As has been true of many contemporary journalists, neoliberal journalists have not been required to write accurately or candidly; all that is required of the contemporary journalist is that he do nothing to disrupt the reassuring monotony of the media. The American press has come to be governed by a corporate mentality all its own. Conservatives say it is Liberal prejudice that pervades the media; more accurately it is a corporate mentality that appears Liberal. There is a corporate mentality that stifles many of America's large but aging industries, rendering them staid, unimaginative, and insular. The same conformist mentality stifles American media, most of whose editors and writers, producers, and talking heads dutifully conform to the prevailing mediocrity, leaving the protections of the First Amendment unnecessary. Few American journalists have the wit or the brass to write anything bold or controversial anyway. For the most part they all have the same ideas, affect the same mannerisms, adopt the same moods. They even dress the same: vaguely military attire while in the field, Brooks Brothers facsimiles otherwise.

These are America's gray flannel journalists, and they are as careerist and conformist as Sloan Wilson's 1950s target in *The Man In the Gray Flannel Suit*. Though the neoliberals were a bit more full of themselves than the standard journalist, they usually conformed nicely to each requirement of this corporate mentality. Late in 1987 one of American journalism's rare independent minds, Robert Bartley, editor of *The Wall Street Journal*'s editorial page, asked me to review a slim volume by the neoliberal journalist Michael Kinsley.

Kinsley was to neoliberal journalism what Hart was to neoliberal politicking: an epitome. Dutifully the young and hungry Kinsley had worked his way through the ranks of gray flannel journalism, boasting of his independence while adhering fastidiously to the dictates of the corporate mentality, bending principles and defanging uncomfortable facts while maintaining a vast moral superiority. Like other neoliberals, he set himself up as a snoop and a snot, but he was also a hopeless materialist. He began the 1980s at *The New Republic* coveting thy neighbor's goods and ended the decade at *Time* and on the Cable News Network, coveting thy neighbor's goods. His climb was steady if self-delusory—he thought he was different. In sum, he labored in the conventional Liberal temples, subscribed to the same mysteries, was animated by the same passions—which is to say his spirit was kindled by envy, jealousy, hurt, and the urge to be a superlative nuisance.

His book is a collection of *rechauffé* prose gathered under the characteristically schoolboy title *Curse of the Giant Muffins and Other Washington Maladies*. Curious readers reached for it to discover if this promising neoliberal journalist had lived up to the customary neoliberal boast of having transcended Liberal cant. Kinsley's career had been interesting. He was widely boomed as an agile writer with a flare for the hilarious *aperçu*. He had, indeed, provided some laughs as his career arched towards the heavens, but there was also a disquieting datum. For all his comparative youth, Kinsley had found himself entoiled in a surprising number of bitter personal controversies over how much he was paid, the measly amount of time allotted to him by management at holiday time, and other curiously small-minded concerns. Employers had complained of his ethics: a junket to Lebanon, his choice of manuscripts for publication, his general taste. There was the time when *Harper's*, under his editorship, called Clare Boothe Luce a "courtesan" in a headline. Later the magazine insulted Susan Sontag, the writer, associating her with rock groupies of desperate libido. Kinsley ducked the first controversy by pleading ignorance of courtesan's unsavory meaning. How he got out of the second I do not recall; possibly he said "she looked good to me." Over the years his taste did not improve. During the Bush Administration's attempt to mobilize the nation against drugs, Kinsley, just as he was vacating the editor's chair at *The New Republic*, published a piece in which Jefferson Morley bragged about using a drug called crack. The gravamen of his essay was that it is somehow laughable for politicians and commentators to oppose drugs if they have not used them. It is a complaint that he could apply to the whole criminal code with equal cogency.

Kinsley has always been given to amusing put-downs—a dispensation allowed him in the misogelastic media because he presents himself as a moralist. And that he is, but in strictly contemporary terms. *Curse* reveals him to be absorbed with the minor peccancies of the moment. Nowhere in it or in any of his other work does he demonstrate an acute awareness of our time's great evils. As with Charles Peters and other neoliberals, he seemed only passingly aware of the totalitarian shade that in the mid-1970s had been pulled down over Southeast Asia, the decline of much of the Third World into barbarism, terrorism's manifold dangers and injustices, or the enduring horror of Communism, so rivetingly elucidated once again in 1986 by Armando Valladares's gruesome memoir, *Against All Hope*. As the 1980s went on, Kinsley did not even demonstrate much awareness of the squalor of our slums, but then America's slums never fetched many neoliberals, lost as they were in policy technicalities and the intricacies of high-tech gadgetry.

Yet as time passed Kinsley was increasingly celebrated, and the adjective applied to him with curious inveterateness when *Curse* came out was "smart"—not "intelligent," not "thoughtful," just "smart." Possibly this is because being "smart" is another neoliberal conceit, but if I were Kinsley this term would make me a little uneasy. His work is strangely devoid of many of the marks of a civilized mind. He almost never shows an interest in literature, music, history, philosophy, or any of the lesser arts—for instance, cuisine, fashion, the manners of a gentleman. In brief, he is a philistine. I suspect that it is precisely his uncivilized cast of mind that prompts others to call him smart and leave it at that. They too recognize his uncouthness, though they have been too polite to mention it. Yet Kinsley's narrowness should come as no surprise. As he himself indicates in one of *Curse*'s rare affectionate essays, he once worked for Ralph Nader, a pest after his own heart. In this particular essay, Kinsley emerges as perhaps the most sedulous interpreter of the master's work.

Not surprisingly, Kinsley is absorbed with petty details. Take him to the Louvre, and he will note that the worn stone of the museum's ancient steps constitutes a safety hazard or perhaps that the lighting does not conform with that required in a favorite building code, say that of Newton, Massachusetts. He might also see potential problems with the old building's ventilation system. Pour him a glass of Château Beychevelle. He might wonder that there is no health warning on the label or insist on knowing who paid for the bottle . . . and how much. The planet Earth could be imperiled by pestilence and flames, and Michael Kinsley would insist on making just one more point about New York financier Felix Rohatyn's tax write-offs.

Close examination of his writings in *Curse* and elsewhere reveals that Kinsley, like other neoliberals and despite their pretense to autonomy, is actually a very conventional Liberal. His protests to the contrary are merely another example of a neoliberal pretending to an independence he does not have. True, Kinsley has little reverence for past Liberal pieties. And true, he delights in serving up fearsome drubbings to conservatives as he discourses on the sordidness of their putative motives. But this is just the neoliberal's way of advancing a career. It represents no philosophical break from Liberalism. As a matter of fact, by afflicting both conservatives and Liberals, Kinsley is being true to the sole remaining principle of conventional Liberalism. He is disturbing his neighbor. As I have posited earlier, the one fundamental and immutable political principle of Liberalism is to disturb the peace, and Kinsley has embraced that honored misdemeanor unflinchingly. He has tirelessly disturbed his neighbor, persistently hectoring all the old Liberal bogies: the corporations, the military, the middle class, and occasionally by resorting to the latest conservative analysis. In point of fact, he is a Liberal of the finest mettle. Michael Kinsley served as an Eleanor Roosevelt for the 1980s. Perhaps some day he will marry a President.

However, in reading his accumulated utterances in *Curse*, I became aware that the way in which he afflicts Liberals is different from the way in which he afflicts conservatives. At Liberals he merely sneers, leaving them hurt and bemused as to the substance of his complaints. They should have taken solace in knowing that there is no substance to his complaints. In fact, he does not even pause to offer substance. Consider when he sneers at the Democrats' devotion to Social Security, and to agricultural price supports. Aside from reproving these programs because they "benefit people at least as well off as those who are paying for them," Kinsley goes no deeper. The Liberals have stated their rationale for these programs, but Kinsley simply ignores their rationale. He does not want to challenge them. He does not know enough to challenge them.

What he wants to do is to disturb people. He is not opposing Liberal programs from the point of view of a Friedmanite free marketeer. Milton Friedman's policies would raise all people's incomes. Kinsley, if you follow what passes for a theme in his economics, seems to want to lower everyone's income. Perhaps this is another example of his petty moralism, but do not discard the thought that here again he is delighting in disturbing his neighbors. Surely Kinsley recognizes that lowering the incomes of his fellow Americans is going to annoy them. Remember his disputes with former employers over money. Disturbing people is the height of his idealism. In *Curse* he also takes off against the peace movement by sneering at its melodrama and sense of urgency. Earlier in those sections of *Curse* where he abuses conservatives, he blames them for "helping to spread war fever." Fine, then why does he sneer at the peace movement for suffering the ensuing fever? Because he is a nuisance. For him it is a matter of principle—practically his only principle.

Yet Liberals get off easier than conservatives, which is not to say that he bothers to refute the conservatives' positions either. What he most frequently does with conservatives is misrepresent them. He ignores their most telling arguments. He offers false analogies. He tortures logic. He, unless he is ignorant, lies. For instance, to write as he does in *Curse* that "some conservatives speak almost wistfully of the advantages enjoyed by ruthless totalitarians . . . and medieval religious zealots . . ." is to carry inaccuracy to the point of sheer invention. And it is equally dishonest to write that the Reagan Administration's "greatest moral outrage is reserved for people who acquire some advantage because they are black." When he composed this humbug, had Kinsley forgotten Ronald Reagan's moral denunciation of Communism? Contrary to other inaccurate assertions in *Curse*, "greed" is *not* admired by supply-siders. Neoconservatives do *not* "see socialism everywhere." And when in the 1980s conservatives criticized the left for seeing "moral equivalence" between Washington and Moscow, left-wingers were *not* merely speaking of the equivalence of the two powers' strategic forces as the disingenuous Kinsley claims. Left-wingers were declaring both regimes *morally* equivalent; conservatives were right to object to such a grotesque misstatement.

Kinsley's literary style has had admirers and critics, the former drawn mainly from the serried ranks of the gray-flannel journalists, the latter drawn from the more select ranks where mind meshes with character. Were he alive, Macaulay would doubtless be numbered among Kinsley's critics, at least to judge from his 1830 appraisal of Robert Southey: "In the mind of Mr. Southey reason has no place at all. . . . He does not seem to know what an argument is. He never troubles himself to answer the arguments of his opponents. . . . It has never occurred to him that there is a difference between assertion and demonstration . . . that two contradictory propositions cannot be undeniable truths, that to beg the question, is not to settle it. . . ."[10] George Orwell, too, would be a Kinsley critic; and Orwell's 1940 essay on Britain's dismal intellectual scene suggests where we might have found Kinsley were his pert presence in London when Hitler was menacing the bourgeoisie. (And what a laugh strutting Adolf would be for Kinsley!) Orwell considered the conventional intelligentsia of prewar Britain and excoriated their "general negativism, querulous attitude, their complete lack at all times of any constructive suggestion," and finally their "emotional shallowness." But could Orwell or even the great Macaulay imagine that the little ass whom they were assessing adhered to a public philosophy whose only unchanging and unchangeable moral imperative was playing the role of public nuisance?

And so the neoliberals were mostly opportunists with a few sententious Charlie Peterses along for soap-opera effect. They recognized that something was wrong with Liberalism and perhaps that something was salutary about this thing called conservatism. But they lacked the courage to follow the route so recently taken by the neoconservatives. They had their careers to think about, and after the first two years of the Reagan Administration it was becoming clear that the writer or politician who took the neoconservatives' route was going to have a rough ride.

Nonetheless, this is not to dismiss the neoliberals completely. To be sure, they lacked courage; and those who quietly plagiarized conservative ideas while sneering at conservatives lacked honor, but they had one great gift. They had a nose for the *Zeitgeist*. They were keen to recognize its shift in the early 1980s. Suddenly there were little terrors in the air. Conservatives were *not* being invited into the universities and into the media. The hospitality accorded them in the late 1970s had vanished, as had the intellectual interest. The neoliberals took note of all this and hunkered back to wherever it was that Liberalism might take them: voting rights for trees, Medicaid for house plants. Whatever zany course Liberalism in the New Age might embark upon these neoliberals would follow. Daring was not their strong suit.

CHAPTER 8

Conservatism, R.I.P.
America's Longest-Dying
Political Movement

WELL, PERHAPS THERE IS another reason that the neoliberals did not follow the neoconservatives into conservatism. The neoliberals as a rule have avoided unpleasantness, and there has been an extraordinary amount of unpleasantness associated with being conservative. In fact, from its first stirrings the conservative movement has been the occasion for condolences. Americans generally avoid death as long as they can, and, to hear American pundits' reports on conservatism over the years, it has been a dying movement from the start.

With episodic regularity our gray-flannel journalists have filed reports of conservatism's imminent death, regardless of the patient's condition. Hence, to many bystanders the conservative movement has had as much attraction as a ride in a hearse. Suggestions that Liberalism might be unwell have surfaced in the press only in the aftermath of presidential elections and then only since, say, 1972; but reports of conservatism's demise have been familiar press fare through all the years of conservatism's steady growth.

I hasten to add that the inaccuracy of these reports is not simply the consequence of journalistic ineptitude or dishonesty. Rather it is owing to the nature of American journalism. The corporate mentality of America's gray-flannel journalists makes our political commentary repetitious to the point of monotony. Once a theme gets attached to a subject, that theme is repeated endlessly without regard for its accuracy or even for its piquancy.

Our media might best be conceived of as one gigantic transcontinental echo chamber, resounding with no more than one or two simple and imprecise tunes on any one topic. Years ago the themes that were attached to American conservatism were themes of morbidity and decline, and they stuck. In fact, historians might someday describe conservatism as the Republic's longest-dying political point of view. Whatever conservatism's future might be, it is unlikely to occasion many charming news stories. Too much unpleasantness has already been attached to it.

In chapter 2, I quoted some of the sour notices that accompanied the rise of the movement. Here let me quote some more, my special intention being to demonstrate the movement's years of marginality and the opinion-makers' continually grim assessment of its prospects. When Barry Goldwater wrested the Republican nomination from conventional Republicans in 1964, reviving the Republican party with libertarianism and anticommunism, conservatives came alive with hope. The pundits, however, diagnosed the Goldwater nomination as conservatism's last gasp. The day after the Goldwaterites assured their candidate the Republican nomination in San Francisco, the funeral fugue began. "The nomination of Barry Goldwater for the Presidency is a disaster for the Republican Party," *The New York Times* solemnized, and not just for America but apparently for the world. The *Times* reported the San Francisco diableries as "a blow to the prestige and to the domestic and international interests of the United States"—and that was back in the days when Liberals still believed the United States possessed prestige.[1]

In contrast to Liberalism's disparagement, the Goldwater campaign was actually the catalytic moment for the conservative movement. Many who in subsequent years became the most effective conservative activists were roused to political awareness in 1964's uncommonly ideological campaign. Typical of the young conservative recruits of the era was my colleague Baron Von Kannon—a Midwesterner who enlisted in the Goldwater campaign, read the writings of Russell Kirk, Milton Friedman, and William F. Buckley, Jr., and embarked on a career of activism in the Young Americans for Freedom, the Young Republicans, and the Intercollegiate Studies Institute, all key organizations to the movement. He became the first publisher of *The American Spectator*, a major force at the Heritage Foundation, and in the 1980s an effective fund-raising consultant for the increasing numbers of conservative political organizations.

Many young conservatives summoned to the colors in 1964 followed Von Kannon's course, crowning their careers with the Reagan campaign in 1980. For some reason the Reagan years never hatched such a sizable congeries of philosophically informed conservative activists. I think it has something to do with the decline of intellect that through the 1970s and 1980s attended the spread of higher education throughout the Republic. The droves of bored Ph.D.s coming off the production lines of our third-rate graduate schools, vowing to inculcate personality disorders among college students, have had their effect. Rather than promote a love of learning, the profs promote a hatred of learning among multitudes of young people roosting at those overrated high schools that we presume to call institutions of higher learning. But in the early 1960s higher education occasionally encouraged intelligence, and a prodigious number of young conservatives attracted to the Goldwater campaign became well read in conservative thought.

This is not to say that the Goldwater campaign summoned a particularly large number of activists, but no other event since the end of World War II attracted so many well-versed conservatives so eager to advance conservatism. The young people who came to serve conservatism in the Reagan years had energy but little philosophic foundation. Few had read the works of Hayek or Friedman, Oakeshott or Weaver, or any of the popularizers of these scholars. This proved to be a weakness, but not one the critics remarked on, lost as they were in recycling the same criticisms and death notices that had attended conservatism from its first eruptions years before.

Some would have thought that the rise of Goldwater was a sign of conservatism's health. Instead all the critics could see was death and lunacy. Goldwater himself was adjudged mentally ill by a zany crowd of psychiatrists polled by Ralph Ginzburg, a publisher on the lucrative left now buried by time. And when on November 3, 1964, Lyndon Johnson demolished Goldwater, a fresh spate of obituaries appeared, all following the theme struck by the dean of Washington columnists, James Reston: "Barry Goldwater not only lost the Presidential election yesterday but the conservative cause as well. He has wrecked his party for a long time to come and is not even likely to control the wreckage."[2]

As the intellectuals and the political strategists of the young conservative movement regrouped and planned future subversions, the media's echo chamber again resounded with pessimism. In *The New Republic* Professor Roger H. Marz struck a particularly depressing note: "The anti-Goldwater Republicans now say that the election was a permanent, total repudiation of extremism and that the Republican Party has no future unless it returns to moderate platforms and candidates. . . . In my opinion, the Republicans have no future, even if they take the road back."[3] One could assemble a stout chrestomathy of such bulls throughout the 1960s. No less thoughtful a man than the historian Richard Hofstadter declared that the Goldwater defeat "broke the back" of American conservatives.

M. Stanton Evans, one of the leading conservative pundits of the day, saw things differently. Responding to these death notices, Evans argued that the future of American politics would be with conservatism. In his prescient 1968 book, *The Future of Conservatism*, he observed that inflation, taxation, and statism were provoking the South and the West to rebel against the Great Society and in support of "limited government at home, opposition to the welfare state, augmented firmness toward our enemies abroad."[4] Here was an early explication of the "Southern Strategy" made famous a year later by Kevin Phillips in *The Emerging Republican Majority*; but conservatism's critics continued to doubt.

Throughout the 1960s and into the 1970s, the members of the New Conservatism found themselves being put down as reactionaries, un-American, even as radicals—the unattractive sort of radicals, not 1960s youthful idealists. According to Walter Lippmann, "there is no more unfounded claim than that Barry Goldwater is a conservative. . . . Sen. Goldwater is in fact a radical opponent of conservatism who, under the banner of personal freedom, would compound that moral disorder which is the paramount problem of the modern age. . . . They are not conservatives in the American tradition. . . . Their outlook is neither conservative nor Republican."[5] Yet Evans's judgment and vision proved to be superior to those of his critics; conservatism was growing, and not the rude conservatism over which Lippmann laments.

Conservative scholars were churning out research at such venerable universities as the University of Chicago and Yale University, the former being particularly famous for its free-market economists and political theorists, the latter being equally famous for turning out such gifted polemicists as William F. Buckley, Jr., and, a few years later, Evans. In the 1960s the travel schedules of Buckley and Evans grew increasingly congested with debates, lectures, magazine articles to be filed, books to be written in opposition to the prevailing wisdom. Buckley's *National Review* provided a national forum for conservative thought and a team of proselytizing editors to travel the campus circuit, aiding and abetting growing colonies of conservative student activists. Yet Evans argued in vain when he attempted to notify Liberals of conservatism's growing presence in the land. To the Liberals, conservatism remained at death's door, though as the years wore on Liberalism was not in such good health either, weakened as it was by the factionalism of the youth movement, racial and sexual militants, and other fanatical mountebanks. On into the 1990s the popularity of Liberalism continued to decline within the electorate, undone by Liberalism's own ideological self-indulgence. Yet it was the conservatives' supposedly moribund condition that was reported in the press.

During the early days of the Nixon Administration some of the media's funereal accounts of conservatism abated. Then came Watergate, and though Richard Nixon was no movement conservative and in fact movement conservatives had challenged his 1972 renomination, now the media expected conservatism to pass from human history forever. After all, the conservatives had stood by President Nixon's policy on Vietnam, though his strategy was not their strategy. Then they stood by him as he struggled to stay in office. Soon they found themselves a renewed topic of morbid reflections.

Characteristic was a *Washington Post* column by David Broder, who wrote in early 1975: "The Republican Right is a headless horseman."[6] And Lou Cannon finished a column by lamenting that "the party is caught in a dilemma of decline. People usually join political parties in the hope of accomplishing something, but the Republican Party is in such a state of decay that it is unlikely to attract groups or individuals that want to get their hands on the levers of power. There are so few Republicans left in the country that it remains to be seen whether anyone will walk in through the party's more widely-opened doors."[7] Pundits remained in doubt about conservatism and the Republican party right up to the dawn of the Reagan Revolution. In *Fortune* magazine Everett Carll Ladd, Jr., presented an arresting version of this theme in an article ominously titled "The Unmaking of the Republican Party." Wrote Ladd: "The G.O.P. has been losing adherents since 1960, and these losses have been concentrated among liberal and moderate elements. As a result, the party has become more conservative and has found it harder to generate a broad appeal." Then Ladd quoted a curious observation from a prominent political scientist at the Massachusetts Institute of Technology, Professor Walter Dean Burnham: "The smaller a minority becomes," Burnham believed, "the more likely it is that its extreme tendencies will become overrepresented . . . and then gain more control over the party . . . which causes the party to continue to lose ground."[8]

Once again, as with so many discussions of the evolving conservative movement, Burnham had everything wrong but the facts. "Extreme tendencies" did, in truth, take over the Republican party; and the party was, to be sure, the smaller of the two parties. But the party did not continue to "lose ground." The electorate came to perceive the Republicans as creditable. The majority party turned out to be the party cursed by a growing overrepresentation of "extreme tendencies" and so it was the Democrats who steadily "lost ground." In 1980 the conservatives entered the White House with an ease unanticipated by them and certainly unanticipated by those who had been writing their obituaries for two decades. It was the conservatives' moment in history, but remember the conservatives who won in 1980 had spent years reading their own death notices. Naturally, when they arrived in Washington many were somewhat insecure. Their insecurity in a culture that never really opened to them burdened them with enormous pressures as we shall see.

CHAPTER 9

Conservatism, Allegro con Brio
Out of the Kultursmog
and into the White House

In his last dance of the evening, the oldest man ever to be elected president of the United States has just swirled across the floor of the White House's grand foyer and suavely ascended to the executive quarters overhead. It is one of his first state dinners, and were Professor Walter Dean Burnham in attendance he would be scowling. "Extreme tendencies" are everywhere. For over two decades the media's echo chamber had been reverberating with news of the conservatives' welcome moribundity, but tonight conservatives of all varieties have filled the White House as never before. The guest list included eminences from *two* conservative think tanks; one of the Coors beer barons; California tycoons long associated with "extreme tendencies"; Lt. General Daniel O. Graham, U.S. Army, retired, a Star Wars prophet; Richard Allen, for two decades one of the conservative movement's pre-eminent strategic thinkers; William Simon, formerly Secretary of the Treasury but now a major strategist in the conservative movement; and, all the way from Indiana, the editor of the movement's newest national intellectual review. Unlike his Republican predecessors, Ronald Reagan was not coy about bringing his ideological allies right into the White House to enjoy the usufructs of victory.

It has been a dazzling evening. The guests—craving one last handclasp with him—startle me. After all, our fortieth president has surely had a long day. The pomp and clatter of this state dinner for Australia's Prime Minister Malcolm Fraser has been enough to tire me, and I can always rely on the restorative power of a nocturnal cocktail, even at state dinners. Ronald Reagan does not betake of this "coping mechanism," as the quacks have come to call mere booze. He is but a light tippler, his only known "coping mechanism" being his uxorious attachment to Nancy. Now as he crosses the red carpet to the elevator that launches him and the love of his life homeward, he remains as genial as the morning sun.

His haleness is about to become legendary. It has been but three months since he took a bullet to the chest. In the years ahead he will endure colon cancer, skin cancer, a prostate operation, intermittent hobbling in his right leg, and the anemophilous complaints of America's one-party media. After eight years of governing he will depart the White House, aged 78, with much of the old spring in his step, a 67 percent approval rating, the distinction of being the country's oldest president, and, according to his official biographer Edmund Morris, a chest measurement one and one-half inches greater than it was before the attempt on his life. While recovering he began a weight-training program, and upon retirement he will insist that he has actually put *two* more inches on his chest. Let the historians debate this last matter as they will, it is an unassailable fact that Ronald Reagan became the first president since 1952 to serve two full terms. How would his adversaries account for it?

Ronald Reagan's presence throughout the 1980s drove the eminences of the Old Order to dramatic mood swings of such intensity that I considered it advisable for the Food and Drug Administration to monitor the nation's Perrier supply for traces of LSD—my advice was not taken.

At first the Old Order practiced denial, then hysteria. The spectacle was unforeseen. Presidential administrations had been peacefully coming and going for over two centuries. Many of these changes meant extensive policy revisions. Never before had a whole class of people exhibited prolonged disorders as a consequence of mere presidential transition. An analogy might be the anti-Roosevelt fulminations of some old-fashioned, upper-class conservatives in the 1930s, but they did not constitute an entire class and their reaction was simple pique, not weird psychotic episodes. I myself have provoked numerous outbreaks of *latah*, that unpleasant neurotic condition where a sudden "start" triggers uncontrollable laughter, obscene outbursts—that sort of thing. Innocently I might, perhaps in the lobby of the Guggenheim Museum, mention Ronald Reagan's name, and *whammo*: laughter, obscene oaths, the shakes. There is evidence that, from the election of Ronald Reagan on, there has been an increased incidence amongst the Old Order of Munchausen's syndrome, wherein the afflicted repeatedly admit themselves to hospitals, though they are perfectly healthy. The Old Order greeted the Reagan foreign policy with paranoia, his oratory with nausea, and certain anti-Reagan polemicists, for instance Mr. Garry Wills, endured long periods of *koro*, particularly after White House press conferences. *Koro* remains rare in the western hemisphere, even among members of the Old Order, but in Africa and the Far East where its outbreaks are recurrent, the afflicted will suddenly sense that his male member is shrinking.

Given the Old Order's unstable response to the Reagan years, it is tempting to speculate on how its designated historians might chronicle the 1980s in their official histories of the twentieth century. My view is that, like superstitious landlords who design their buildings omitting a thirteenth floor, the Old Order's historians will write histories of the twentieth century and simply omit the 1980s. The entire decade is too troubling for them. To the parched eminences of the Old Order the decade was a chronological black hole. As it continued, members of the Old Order would sometimes act as though there were no Reagan presidency. At other times they acted as though it were a catastrophic tyranny.

Yet, without catastrophe and with a lengthening list of accomplishments, Reagan governed, cheerfully overcoming all trials, all obloquy, and even the weirdness factor that has haunted recent presidents. Admittedly, the weirdness was there at first. President Johnson had suffered an uncontrollable urge to show a surgical scar in public. Jimmy Carter had been attacked by a ferocious amphibious bunny. Reagan's election was accompanied by a spate of bizarre news stories after some idiot discovered the coincidence that since 1840 all presidents elected at twenty-year intervals had died in office (William Henry Harrison, Abraham Lincoln, James A. Garfield, William McKinley, Warren G. Harding, Franklin D. Roosevelt, and John F. Kennedy). I assume that when Reagan survived his two full terms the credulous dullards who had been fetched by this superstition recognized that Ronald Reagan lived and so cashiered the superstition. The adepts of the Old Order who for eight anxious years lived without catastrophic incident never did smarten up. The national catastrophes they prophesied never took place. Yet their low opinion of Reagan was never revised. Compared to the members of the Old Order, even superstitious minds were more reasonable.

Now, however, we are in attendance at an early Reagan-era state dinner. The party is winding down. Within the official rooms of the White House a sense of expiration spreads over the hundred or so worthies from politics and other walks of life who now grow weary and perhaps a bit embarrassed by the false intimacy each experiences in such grand dinners, a false intimacy that is the burden of great dinners wherever they are held in modern America. The undercurrent of laughter and chatter—punctuated by the thud of an occasional political pronunciamento—abates. The last bottle of Cabernet Sauvignon (Robert Mondavi 1974) has petered out. The entertainment is over, the coffee and cordials flow more slowly. Even the stalwarts of the Marine Band begin to slump in their resplendent red coats. The guests slip away.

None of the presidential residences of any of the other great powers is quite like this, not the Elysée Palace, nor Number 10 Downing Street, and certainly not Buckingham Palace, though the genius of eighteenth-century Frenchmen and Englishmen shape American political behavior to this very day. The ambiance of the White House is unique. Within these old walls has been captured the simplicity of what the Founding Fathers called Republican Virtue, despite the awful fact that America has become the world's leading nation and is capable of nuclear holocaust any day of the week. The White House is not just presidential; it is *American* presidential, and so American informality is always a threat to the pomposity of eagles, braid, brass, and the other paraphernalia of the presidency. Richard Nixon captured something of the warmth of the White House in his last hours on the presidential rack when he called in his cabinet and his White House staff for a final good-bye. "This isn't the biggest house," he said. "Many, and most, in even smaller countries, are much bigger. This isn't the finest house. Many in Europe, particularly, and in China, Asia, have paintings of great, great value, things that we just don't have here and probably will never have until we are 1,000 years old or older.

"But this is the best house. . . . This house has a great heart. . . ."[1]

That is the White House, and touched by the glow of a house with a great heart I nudge my inamorata out the front door into the night, where we are suddenly dwarfed by the gigantic snow-white columns of the north portico, the pillars that support the White House's early–nineteenth century pediment. It is pitch-black beyond the wrought-iron gates of the White House compound, but we two diminutive figures making our way beneath these gigantic pillars are bathed in light and leave monstrous shadows. Soon we shall be in the warm darkness beyond, then into the cool darkness of our Hay-Adams Hotel suite across the street, and without those monstrous shadows. Over coffee the next morning we agree this is indeed the conservatives' moment in history. Last night the guest list included conservatives with a sense of mission, movement conservatives, the same people judged clinically insane and near death these last few decades. They never appeared in such numbers at the Nixon White House or during the Ford interregnum, and so we speculate over the conservative movement's prospects. Our speculations are mostly off the mark.

Though all of us—movement conservatives, neoconservatives, libertarians—had labored mightily against the ponderous stupidities of Jimmy Carter's administration, enthroning as it did so much of the idiocy of 1970s New Age Liberalism, the election of this president, Ronald Reagan—the conservatives' dream candidate—still amazed many conservatives. Frequently in the first year or two of the Reagan presidency, a conservative activist would greet another with some variation of "I can't believe we won." Not that Jimmy Carter was expected to be re-elected in 1980, but almost no pundit made the obvious deduction: to wit, if Carter lost, Ronald Reagan would win. That unwelcome deduction was simply avoided; hence the approach of a Reagan Administration was ignored. Even conservatives were unprepared for his election. Peter Hannaford, reviewing his experience on the 1980 Reagan campaign, writes: "Up to the night before the election, the networks and the major polling organizations had a near consensus that it was 'too close to call.' "[2]

The next day, overwhelmed by the unforeseen landslide, the American press reported the occurrence as a kind of miracle. Both candidates' pollsters had recognized the imminent Republican victory. So an accurate prediction was possible. Yet not one of the professionals of network news made this prediction. Given the Carter Administration's disastrous record, the press's failure to predict his demise is an egregious lapse. The only news-gathering conglomerate I found willing to predict Republican victory was the news network in exile, Richard Nixon. On October 28 over matutinal coffee with me and the publisher of *The American Spectator*, my friend of many pleasant years Ron Burr, the former President predicted both the election of Ronald Reagan and every Senate outcome but two. Now that's news.

The conservatives' amazement over a victory that was inevitable and the media's ignorance are illustrative of an unfortunate condition in American society, to wit, that its high culture, even its mid-culture, is enveloped in a smog. Unfortunately no experts have been called in to examine the condition, for those who create it believe that it is a public good. They are stimulated by its stale aromas and morbid thoughts. It has not occurred to them that this *Kultursmog* might be a public health hazard.

One American for whom the *Kultursmog* proved almost fatal was Judge

Robert Bork, who, upon recovering from the unprecedented ordeal of his Supreme Court confirmation hearings, eloquently described the *smog's* comprehensive contamination. In *The Tempting of America* he writes:

> In the past few decades American institutions have struggled with the temptations of politics. Professions and academic disciplines that once possessed a life and structure of their own have steadily succumbed, in some cases almost entirely, to the belief that nothing matters beyond politically desirable results, however achieved. In this quest, politics invariably tries to dominate another discipline, to capture and use it for politics' own purposes, while the second subject—law, religion, literature, economics, science, journalism, or whatever—struggles to maintain its independence. But retaining a separate identity and integrity becomes increasingly difficult as more and more areas of our culture, including the life of the intellect, perhaps especially the life of the intellect, becomes politicized. It is coming to be denied that anything counts, not logic, not objectivity, not even intellectual honesty, that stands in the way of the 'correct' political outcome.[3]

The "correct" political outcome, I need hardly mention, is that divined by the New Age Liberal, whose incessant politicizing has polluted "the life of the intellect" and much else in American society. Any American aspiring to intellection beyond the level of the sports page or that of country & western *Gemütlichkeit* is going to ascend into an atmosphere rank with the political gasses spewed from universities, policy institutes, protest movements, the media, and all those other grim institutions that serve as the smokestack industries of American culture. As was the case with nineteenth-century German *Kultur*, America's *Kultursmog* has eliminated most forms of intellectual individualism with alarming thoroughness. There was a time when American culture was teeming with diversity and even with heresy. But over the last few decades the atmosphere of American culture has grown stale as the arts, ideas, ethics, and every product of intellect has been tainted with the political vaporings of the New Age. Where once there was the free exchange of thought—at least among the intelligentsia—now there is only *Kultursmog*, through which hardly a breeze of independence is allowed to flow.

The *smog* poisons discussion, lest discussion endanger the "correct political outcome." It contaminates thought. A few perfectly reasonable ideas and urbane sensibilities remain within our *Kultursmog*, but they are the residue of better times. Most new ideas and new sensibilities are essentially political. The politicized atmosphere that they create spreads into every area of intellectual life. It penetrates museums, concert halls, and all other artistic milieus. It encourages the segregation of art into such absurdities as Feminist Art or Homosexual Art. Who knows, perhaps there is Vegetarian Art; and the National Endowment for the Arts might someday endow an exhibition of Lunatic Art, or how about the Quilting of Bedwetters? Wherever the believing Liberal encounters *Kultursmog,* he inhales it with relish, much as the country bumpkin inhales diesel fumes, and to similar effect. The bumpkin sniffs diesel fumes on a country road and is put in mind of the lurid and luscious streets of *the big city* whose air is perfumed by the metropolitan transit; the Liberal sniffs the *Kultursmog* and is put in mind of *progress.* However, the Liberal is not the only American affected by *Kultursmog.* The conservative cannot completely shake it either; and so, though conservatives championed Ronald Reagan's candidacy and believed in his ideas, many could not really accept that their day was at hand.

One of the most corrupting ideas of the *Kultursmog* asserts that there is no place in any recognized phenomenology for conservatives except that House of Horrors that the Liberals take us through so frequently, a waxworks of American history where Klansmen are on display, Know-Nothings, anti-Semites, hicks, and bigots of every variety save the Liberal bigot. This highly inaccurate conception of conservatism causes Liberals to underestimate conservatives and usually to get drubbed by them on those infrequent occasions when they face conservatives in debate. Unfortunately it also convinces many conservatives that they are marginal to American culture.

In the late 1960s, when Irving Kristol and other careful students of American politics noted that the future of American politics might, as Irving put it, be "considerably less liberal,"[4] the conventional Liberals apprehended no change in the air. For them the momentous movements were all still coming from the left. Characteristic of their obliviousness was a 1967 *Time* magazine cover story on William F. Buckley, Jr., concluding with the *Kultursmog's* usual low expectations for conservatism: "Despite the adoption of certain programs that might be considered conservative, the U.S. public is unlikely to swerve from its liberal course no matter how much a solitary Buckley may prod."[5] Irving knew better.

Thirteen years later most Liberals still thought that this fatuous judgment was in effect, and so influential were they within American culture that many conservatives could not but agree. Even at the end of eight years of Reaganism there were conservatives who believed that Liberalism had dominated the Reagan Administration, for instance Ed Crane of the Cato Institute and Howard Phillips of the Conservative Caucus, who actually called Ronald Reagan "a useful idiot."

Just as certain vilified ethnic groups are known to adopt a self-image mirroring the bigot's low estimate of them, some faint-hearted conservatives had adopted the *smog's* judgments of conservatives. Their politicians may have won the presidency and the Senate, forcing the opposition to lean towards conservative positions or perish. Their intellectuals may have vanquished the conventionally-minded advocates of collectivism and rendered the advocates of appeasement dubious. Still, many conservatives could not believe that they were ascendant. Victory was not their custom. They were ill prepared to govern. They were the people of France in the late 1930s, lost in petulance, apprehension, and self-doubt.

Some did overcome their amazement. Grasping the historic change, they saw their opportunity. Ronald Reagan was not just another Republican. He was a product of their self-conscious political movement, which had grown abundant with ideas and useful principles. Reagan had been active with many of the postwar conservative organizations, from the Young Americans for Freedom to the American Conservative Union. He was a subscriber to *The American Spectator, Commentary, Human Events, National Review,* and other conservative publications. His thought contained an ideological component, and he gathered intellectuals as well as politicians around him. Bill Buckley was a close personal friend. He knew Milton Friedman well. Not since Teddy Roosevelt and Woodrow Wilson had an American president come to office who had been so intimate with intellectuals before his coronation. Many of us in the conservative movement had supported Ronald Reagan's presidential ambitions since 1968. I met him during that campaign. After organizing a party of students to greet him at Indianapolis airport, I dined with the candidate at a small dinner at Indianapolis's Meridian Hotel, after which he sent a letter of gratitude, my first communiqué with him.

This Republican, then, was one of us. Unlike Richard Nixon, who was only a moderate conservative, and unlike 1968, when there were few conservative think tanks or journals to support a Republican president, President Reagan was a product of an intellectual movement and at his disposal was an arsenal of journals and think tanks and a formidable grass-roots fund-raising network. The conservatives' think tanks were our alternative to the Liberal universities; they provided the intellectual support: the policy analysts, the writers, the policies. They produced the conservatives' antidote to the *smog*.

The American Enterprise Institute laid much of the intellectual groundwork for the deregulation movement. The Hoover Institution was the most influential center for free-market studies, and it sustained a superb analysis of world Communism. The Center for Strategic and International Studies was a residence for a cross-section of scholars of an activist cast of mind—such as Paul Craig Roberts, Michael Ledeen, and even Zbigniew Brzezinski—to study foreign policy and economic issues. Finally, the Heritage Foundation duly distinguished itself for rapid policy responses to political developments and for fomenting conservative intellectual activism. The American Enterprise Institute was frequently referred to as the Republicans' "Government-in-Exile." It was a haven for former Republican government officials while they awaited their return to power. Hoover had created a resource base with one of the world's largest archives. Heritage was the youngest of the conservative think tanks and by the early 1980s had become a command post for Washington conservatives. These conservative redoubts were relatively new. Until Ronald Reagan no Republican President had ever had access to such massive resources. With all these intellectual assets available and a landslide political victory behind us, it seemed manifest in the early months of the Reagan presidency that this was to be another epochal presidency similar to those of the alphabet presidents, FDR, JFK, and LBJ. For the conservatives their moment in history was moving *allegro con brio.*

Personally my pleasure was tinged by apprehension that all my literary works then in progress might soon be brought to flummox by presidential importunities. Back in 1969, when our magazine was still run out of an Indiana farmhouse and still a college boy's plaything, the Nixon White House often called with theatrical requests for our reactions to various presidential initiatives or speeches, occasionally inviting one of our editors in to meet some low-level White House functionaries with time on their hands. Occasionally there were more useful meetings with Pat Buchanan. He and a singularly generous group of conservative speechwriters, such as Bill Gavin, John Coyne, and later Ben Stein, submitted advice and occasional articles.

Those were great days. The radicals were in full thunder and easy to observe. I recall an evening carousal in Greenwich Village during which I found myself in the company of a girlfriend of Bob Dylan. Far into the evening she pontificated on the numinous marvels of the hallucinogen LSD while I remained loyal to Ballantine Ale. LSD, she believed, was going to create a second Renaissance, and, if properly mixed into the municipal reservoirs of Moscow and Washington, would so improve everyone's mood that the Cold War would end. I believe the lady's name was C.C. What ghastly fate awaited her I never discovered. Though to be able to converse with me after I had a few quarts of ale aboard suggests that she had the talents to become a prosperous shrink. Or did she become a bag lady in the 1980s, a faculty member at the Duke University Department of Women's Theology and Witchcraft, or a fruit-and-nut evangel in some seedy health-food emporium?

And what ever happened to the tubby black fellow who, though a member of the Black Panther party, was elected Indiana University student body president in 1970. I debated him on a television show in the early 1970s and recall how proud he was of the ring he wore on a chain around his neck. The ring was supposedly made from an American bomber that had been shot down in Vietnam. I remember the hurt in his eyes when members of the camera crew reproached him for wearing this contemptible piece of jewelry—it had been a gift from his girlfriend, perhaps the daughter of a godly minister. And then there was Mrs. Emily Harris. So radical was she that eventually she and her nice middle-class husband enlisted in the Symbionese Liberation Army, kidnapped Patty Hearst, and knocked off banks. In the early days of our magazine she was an impeccable member of Bloomington's progressive community, and she easily edged my wife out in the competition to teach in the local public school system. Rumor had it Mrs. Harris believed that the writers around our magazine were armed and dangerous. Her fears were understandable. We had all heard radical profs lecturing on the conspiratorial designs of the contemporary Ku Klux Klan and on various conspiracies engaged in by the American intelligence community. Such profs proliferated in the 1960s and early 1970s, and their fanciful warnings about the American condition sent many credulous left-wing students on ill-advised paths leading to the cal-aboose or to the drug rehabilitation center.

Possibly the fair Emily had also learned of my personal involvement with the hellish Vice President Spiro T. Agnew, whose telephone call to my Indiana farmhouse one autumnal afternoon woke me from a pleasant slumber, induced by my seasonal confrontation with hay fever, Mother Nature's darker side. One afternoon in 1972 he called three times. Twice my secretary, suspecting him to be a crank caller hostile to my siesta, slammed down the phone (no crank calls for her!). When Agnew's secretary finally got through, he came on the line and asked me to become one of his speechwriters. I was polite, but, looking across the endless fields of Hoosier pollen, I had to turn him down; the literary life was more to my liking and so was Indiana. I did, however, agree to become a White House consultant, which became the cause of embarrassment on my resumé. The abbreviation for consultant on my White House paycheck was misinterpreted by some klutz on my staff to mean "White House Counsel" and for some time my resumé listed me as having held the same White House rank as Bob Haldeman and John Ehrlichman. It was not until around the time of the conviction of White House counsels Haldeman and Ehrlichman that we corrected the botch.

The scandal of Watergate thrust many conservatives into the glooms. Most had defended Richard Nixon long after such a defense was politically clever, which was typical, considering conservatives' proclivity for getting aboard history's death wagons. For my part, I watched the doomed White House in astonishment. Through most of the Nixon Administration the White House was in truth a heavily-defended fortress against protesters; but by the last year of the regime the White House took on the atmosphere of a bunker in time of war, the President's nicely tailored aides loyally defending the "old man" against the scraggly leftists and nicely-tailored Liberals all intent on bringing down the elected government of the United States despite tensions in Europe and the Middle East and open warfare in Southeast Asia. I recall the President's most valiant defender, Pat Buchanan, suffering through painful bouts of arthritis, his desk top cluttered with rows of aspirin bottles, his crutches at the ready in anticipation of another debilitating attack. Buchanan recognized that the Democrats were "out to get" Nixon. I doubted that the Democrats would really drive Nixon out.

Anyone familiar with politics knows and expects a pol to cover his gluteus maximus. Surely none of the Democrats wailing about morality in government would have acted differently from Nixon, though they might have more adroitly covered up the idiotic break-in. In politics there are the formal rules and the informal rules. The formal rules are all very ethical. The informal rules include such stuff as covering up a political aide's blunders. Practically every White House since that of FDR had covered up its blunders and deceits, and some of those cover-ups obnubilated misdeeds far more serious than a tenuous association with lulus such as Gordon Liddy—think of LBJ's Bobby Baker or the irregularities of the 1960 presidential election. What surprised me about Watergate was that the Democrats suddenly held the informal rules of government up as impeachable offenses. The eventual consequence of this sudden change in the informal rules was the paralysis of the presidency of the United States and the enslavement of all the Southeast Asian states we had fought so long to protect.

At any rate, as a consultant to Vice President Agnew I made frequent flights aboard Air Force Two. He was, contrary to contemporary accounts, an interesting man, for he had a fine sense of the absurd and abundant curiosity. He relished giving those he called the "radic-libs" a hot foot in each speech, just for fun, which is not to say that he did not believe that these radicals were destroying important American institutions, such as higher education, the courts, and government in general. In his last days I composed some fortissimo tirades for him, emphasizing ethical statecraft. These, my Machiavellian instincts told me, would ensure the quick elevation of my boss to the presidency once Nixon vamoosed. That not one of my testimonials to the ethical conduct of government was ever used perplexed me. Then out of the blue my would-be president resigned, pleading *nolo contendere*. That ended my days as a Machiavel forever; back to literature.

As I say, all the distractions during the Nixon years gave me premonitions that this time around my literary life would be stunted by the impertinences of politics; close friends were entering the administration. Eventually, two score or more *American Spectator* associates and writers were called to the colors by President Reagan. The maturing of *The American Spectator* towards adulthood had transformed us from the college magazine that we were when Nixon–Agnew had us on the White House Rolodex. Images of Arthur Schlesinger's fate during the Kennedy years made an unwelcome appearance in my mind's eye. Would I become the Reaganites' Schlesinger, resorted to for felicitous quotations, for learned anecdotes lifted from scholarly histories, for liaisons with the intelligentsia? Would I have to go all the way, my every reference to a Reagan becoming a servile panegyric, my every visit to a Reagan party placing me in imminent peril of a dunking in the pool? That was the sort of treatment that Camelot accorded poor Schlesinger.

Mere days after the election the calls from the embryonic government began to come in. The Administration was conscripting large numbers of conservative activists, but also intellectuals, more intellectuals than any Republican administration had ever beheld, perhaps even more than prior Democratic administrations. Ken Adelman, Martin Anderson, William Bennett, Jeane Kirkpatrick, and dozens more names left the table of contents pages of the intellectual and scholarly reviews as their owners answered the call to government service. Never before had conservative academics and writers played such a role in Republican politics, and as Speaker of the House Tip O'Neill's former aide, Christopher Matthews, later noted in his book *Hardball*, this migration gave the Administration enormous strength, for it now abounded with ideas and with those who understood how to use ideas.

Dr. Fred Iklé, a scholarly foreign policy adviser to the Reagan campaign who would soon be Under Secretary of Defense for Policy, was one of the first to ask me for the names of fellow *American Spectator* writers, and he suggested that I allow my name to be considered for Chairman of the Board of Directors of Public Broadcasting. Only devotion to my art restrained me. Bill Casey also sought enlistments from the magazine. I urged him during the campaign to take a look at one of the most capable young neoconservatives, Elliott Abrams. For years Casey had worked with Leo Cherne at the International Rescue Committee, an organization formed in the 1930s to protect intellectuals from tyranny. Thus he was familiar with the role that writers play in politics. Casey was comfortable with intellectuals and thoroughly capable of being one himself, if only he could collect the *Sitzfleisch*.

One evening just before the inauguration he strode into a small party at my Hay-Adams suite to pick up my list of recommendations. To the astonishment of such seasoned polemicists as Adelman, John Lehman, Suzi Garment, and Tom Bethell, Bill plumped his vast frame down among us and opened a Coors. This was to be an Administration characterized by its critics as obtuse toward the life of the mind, but that evening the talk turned to postwar history, to Arthur Koestler, Hannah Arendt, Whittaker Chambers, and other Cold War writers. It is not often that a Cabinet appointee from either party has been able to hold his own on such topics. But Casey was an old man with a young man's imagination. He was the rare man who, full of age and honors and ready for retirement, had yet to begin the most illustrious chapter of a long life. Ronald Reagan had a similar last chapter and Winston Churchill, but not many more. For the next six years Casey was to bring all the truths and legends of the Cold War to bear on a set of policies that eventually remade the West's relationship with the Communist world. Most of those who drank Coors with Bill that night were soon aboard the Reagan Administration.

Unbeknownst to them, however, the *Zeitgeist* was shifting even as we entered our moment in history. The *smog*, that gloomy cloud over American life embracing political ideas at its core and artistic ideas out on its gauzy peripheries, reacted badly to the change taking place in Washington. The inhabitors of the *smog* wanted no part of us. Troubled by the political change in the land, the *Kultursmog* detached itself from the politics of the country. Those who breathed it broke off all debate with conservative critics. The little terrors intimidating the neoliberals were quite real, and even some Reaganites began to flinch. By the early 1980s ideological discourse was no longer a two-way debate. The voices of the *smog* would no longer engage conservative critics, nor did they any longer find a Buckley amusing. Liberalism had lost control of the Republic's politics, owing to the democratic process; it was not going to hazard losing control of the Republic's ideas. And so, in the forums of thought, conservative intellectuals steadily lost influence. Their work was simply ignored, and even in the White House their presence grew "controversial."

At some point in the spring of 1981 I got a call from Peter Rusthoven, associate counsel to the president. If ever there was a fellow who could say "I got my job through *The American Spectator*" it was Peter. While at Harvard Law School he had written our public policy column at the recommendation of Professor Pat Moynihan, then an unofficial *Spectator* adviser. A Hoosier by birth, Peter took his law degree back to Indianapolis, where he practiced the forensic arts and continued writing a very competent series of pieces on public policy for us. Reagan's adviser on the 1980 campaign, Peter Hannaford, read them and commissioned a memo from Rusthoven that became a prominent ingredient in the Republican presidential nominee's acceptance speech. Eventually Rusthoven joined the office of White House Counsel Fred Fielding, and now my former *Spectator* colleague was on the telephone.

He asked that I cease and desist from claiming the President as a reader of the magazine. In the magazine's house advertisement, which listed famous subscribers, we regularly reproduced a photograph of Ronald Reagan's old address label from his Pacific Palisades residence. There were, Rusthoven said, complaints from the public. The ad was neither illegal nor in dubious taste, but some in the White House wanted to avoid controversy over the President's conservative ties. I acceded, but here I was allowing low prejudice to marginalize Ronald Reagan's conservative friends. The *Washington Post* had just described *The American Spectator* as Washington's new "in" magazine, but some in the White House wanted us out. I was innocent enough to go along, but once the fainthearted in the White House had distanced the Administration from us, what other magazine would authoritatively defend the Reagan Administration when it deserved defending?

The President, with unanticipated dexterity, was moving a select number of conservative ideas up his agenda and into policy, but frequently his staff was out of sympathy with his work. Even some of his old California colleagues were quickly contaminated by their new environs. Washington is not New York or Chicago. Rather it is more like the prairie cities of the great Midwest. It is Omaha or Indianapolis, albeit more abundant with lawyers and lobbyists, all of whom are overpaid, and with an elite that is not Republican. There were many members of the Reagan Administration who felt very insecure working in an Omaha of Eastern Seaboard Liberals. Of all the insecure Reaganites, he who quavered most violently in these strange environs was Michael Deaver, the President's personal slave. That surprised me.

I had met him in the mid-1970s. During a lecture tour in California, I stopped off at the home of a Reagan aide and made the social blunder of discoursing in Deaver's presence on the inestimable value of Pat Moynihan's Family Assistance Plan. Deaver was shocked. The Moynihan plan sought to lure the able-bodied off welfare permanently by rewarding the working poor with benefits that would make work more desirable. I cannot recall Deaver's objections other than that they were admirably reactionary without any of those disconcerting curlicues of high policy analysis that frequently adorned the neoconservatives' public policy bulls. It goes without saying that I was profoundly relieved when he joined the 1980 Reagan campaign. In fact, at Hannaford's suggestion, I gladly leapt to Deaver's defense when, during the Republican primaries, he was temporarily shunted aside.

Well, that was a mistake. True, in the microscopic area of his cerebrum that he reserved for personal philosophy, Deaver was probably splendidly reactionary; but he was not a principled reactionary, for he had no political principles. A political factotum charged with sniffing the currents of the time and putting them to his boss's purposes, he became a disaster for conservatives. In sniffing, he was all nose and no brain. His nose went to work in Georgetown and Martha's Vineyard and paid little serious attention to the changed currents of contemporary American politics.

His pathetic attempt at a memoir echoes with artless boasts about the sophisticated figure Deaver cut among all the latter-day Madame de Staels of the Vineyard. The poor sap even boasts of having restrained the boss's conservative impulses and of segregating the President from his baleful conservative pals. Possibly Deaver exaggerates his influence, but after his departure to private life White House speechwriters did tell me that they had been cautioned against making any reference to conservative intellectuals in presidential speeches. Now that is not very farsighted for a conservative president who presumably wants to influence the present and the future.

Upon hearing the speechwriters' complaints I decided to mention them to the President. As luck would have it my opportunity came during a private meeting in the Oval Office, precisely six years to the day and hour that an assassin had tried to do him in. Worse still, the Iran-Contra scandal was then blowing through the press with hurricane force. Engaging the President's attention was hopeless. One of the charges in the air in those vexed days was that the President was not sufficiently in touch with the daily details of government—a prudent position to take in my view; brief years before, the nation had witnessed Jimmy Carter nearly destroy his government by treating the presidency as though it were a four-year oral examination on governmental administration. But the President's advisors had cowed him into assuming the role of someone he was not, to wit, the Master of Detail (and Bungler of Strategy). To appease the critics of the Iran-Contra deal, Ronald Reagan's aides tried to transform one of the finest political leaders in recent American history (more on this anon) into a whiz kid, and so there I sat with a very tired Ronald Reagan whose mental software kept kicking in long, boring, nigh unto inscrutable renditions of current governmental statistics on all aspects of policy regardless of my question or state of consciousness.

It was bizarre. All the details were for his assistants to know. He had governed masterfully by concentrating only on the grand themes of his government, and here the little fellows around him had turned him temporarily into an idiot savant. Hence, the facts tumbled forth. When I referred to Iran-Contra as a "scandal," he groaned and objected to the use of the word. And when I mentioned the speechwriters' complaint that they were banned from quoting conservatives in speeches, he doubted that such a ban existed. For some reason Ronald Reagan never would admit that aides on his staff were disloyal. Back in the fall of 1981 when he had called me, inquiring about the origins of conservative impatience, he showed the same reluctance. Then I told him that the conservatives suspected that the so-called pragmatists on his staff were undercutting his tax policies. The President would have none of it, and I will always wonder how he received the admission in Deaver's memoir that the conservatives were right. Moreover, how did the President receive the news of Deaver's and Mrs. Reagan's infatuation with the Martha's Vineyard *literati*, all of whom abhorred the Reagan Administration?

In his nauseating little tome Deaver relates his enthusiasm for the playwright Lillian Hellman and the novelist William Styron, two ritualistic leftists and, in the case of Hellman, a Stalinist. As artists, both were passé; but their warped vision of politics would not even countenance a moderate Democrat, to say nothing of Ronald Reagan. If Deaver ever read a page of either writer's work it was just before crashing into deep sleep, still somehow he got the idea that both were social peaks worth climbing toward. As he climbed he brought traces of the *smog* into the Reagan White House. The *smog* may have sealed itself off from the conservatives, but here again we see that the conservatives could not seal themselves off from the *smog*. What kind of man was Mike Deaver? Well, does it tell you anything that he concludes his tale of social triumph among the Hellmans and the Styrons thus: "Sometimes I think we need more artistic people in government service. They are often eccentric, but their virtue is that, unlike generals, they want to blow up only themselves."[6] Revolve that in your mind.

CHAPTER 10

Guicciardini's Kind of Guy
The Real Reagan

THE CASE AGAINST RONALD Reagan was stated early in the presidential campaign and remained essentially unchanged through all the days of his presidency. Generally smog corrodes, but *Kultursmog* has usually acted as a preservative. It has preserved more inaccurate ideas then any religion ever heard of, or any cult.

At the outset the complaints were essentially that Ronald Reagan was warlike and a sworn enemy of anyone beneath the tax brackets of Beverly Hills. *Also he was a boob.* Later as relations with the Soviets became more amicable than at any time since World War II, and as a period of unparalleled economic growth dragged on, these earlier complaints melded into that continuo of dark murmurings that composed the *concerto grosso* of political commentary through most of the Reagan years. New complaints were added: he was a liar (Iran-Contra!), a poor manager (Iran-Contra!), superstitious. *Also he was STILL a boob.* Today, in the cool, clear air of post-Reagan America, a review of all these complaints reveals several unpleasant truths about Reagan's critics: they were uneducable bigots, resistant to the rules of evidence, to empirical observation, and to logical deduction. They were subject to flashes of grandiosity and surprisingly dependent on the intellectual instruction of the far left, notwithstanding their protests to the contrary.

The indictment framed by the resident savants of that most influential institution of the American *smog, The New York Times,* remained in effect for years, magisterially aloof from reality, surviving even into Reagan's retirement. As the economy prospered, as democracy spread, as international tensions relaxed, the inhabitants of the *smog* made only slight revisions in their case against Reagan, demonstrating their aforesaid bigotry, their incapacity for objective thought, and their ferocious partisanship. For a review of their indictment, begin with August 25, 1980, when Anthony Lewis began collecting the charges. Reagan, he wrote, "seems likely to accelerate the nuclear arms race. He might strain the relationship with Peking to the point to where the Chinese would reconsider their attitudes toward the Soviets."[1] On September 7, colleague Tom Wicker added another durable charge. A Reagan Administration "threatens a heightened arms race and a retreat from hard-won liberal achievements."[2] As Americans prepared to vote, a *Times* editorial summarized the case issuing through the *Kultursmog:* "Ronald Reagan is easily caricatured as a bellicose ideologue, ready to roll back the clock on all social welfare. . . . He seems genuinely to believe that the vain pursuit of arms superiority will bring the Russians begging to the bargaining table. . . . Too often, Ronald Reagan's clarity and robustness sound more like bluster, bravado and refusal to recognize that America is no longer, if it ever was, king of the world."[3]

Ten months into the Administration the bill of indictment had been completed, and John B. Oakes duly retailed it in the November 1, 1981, issue of the marmoreal *Times.* According to Oakes, the Reagan Administration was "a harshly reactionary revolution. . . . President Reagan has substituted a mindless militarism for a foreign policy. . . . Much of it will be dissipated in the self-defeating spiral of an open-ended nuclear-arms race that poses a greater threat to our own internal and external security than all the Communist propaganda that ever emanated from Moscow. Already the cost of Reagan's policies is devastating to our country in economic strength. . . . On the domestic front, needed budget-cutting has devolved into shameful budget-gutting. It affects the health, the safety, and the well-being of every American. Combined with skewed tax reductions favoring the rich, it has turned the war against poverty into a war against the poor."[4]

For eight years this doleful *concerto grosso* groaned on in lugubrious F minor; and when the stock market swooned on October 19, 1987, the virtuosi played their familiar themes with renewed ardor; Lewis (in the

Times!): "The age of Reagan is over now, no matter what happens"[5]; Robert Reich (in the *Times*, again, same day, same page!): "The binge is over"[6]; John Kenneth Galbraith (in *Newsweek!*): "This debacle marks the last chapter of Reaganomics."[7] Right up to the end the inhabitants of *Kultursmog* beheld Reagan and groaned; columnist Pete Hamill: "Now we will have to pay for Reagan's party, learning to live as the world's leading debtor nation. We will have to acknowledge the waning of our economic power, as the true engine of the world shifts to Tokyo and the rest of Asia. The mayhem of the drug gangs will get worse. The ghastly army of the homeless will recruit many more troops. And Reagan will live out his days, surrounded by the California rich. . . ."[8]; *Time:* "Reagan's bread-and-circuses strategy will mar his place in history."[9]

Enough, enough, in fine and in sum, the Reagan Administration brought no cheer to the *Kultursmog's* organs of commentary, all of which remained affixed like parasites to that lumbering, oafish dinosaur, the American left. Despite the evanescence of left-wing thought almost everywhere else in the world, most of America's organs of commentary remained fastened upon the wisdom of an increasingly irrelevant point of view. Thus Anthony Lewis's position on the Reagan Administration was probably fixed forever after *The Nation's* 1981 asseveration that "The signs are as clear as they could be that we are about to have a government that will hide a regressive and repressive domestic policy behind an aggressive and adventurous foreign policy."[10] A decade later Ronald Reagan was sunning himself in retirement, but neither Lewis nor *The Nation* showed any sign of revising their assessment. Reagan's eight-year term was over, but Lewis's lifetime appointment to the op-ed pages continued in venerable ignorance.

One of the little-noted truths of twentieth century American politics is that it possesses what the poet Blake might call a fearful symmetry, to wit: our far left suffers many of the same fears as our far right. The left-wing ideologues of the 1980s suffered terrors markedly similar to those suffered by right-wing ideologues in the 1930s. Both inveighed against what they perceived as a repressive government in Washington; both feared projecting American power abroad. The 1980s left adopted the Boland Amendment, restricting the president from foreign entanglements; the 1930s right fashioned neutrality acts, which President Franklin D. Roosevelt had to maneuver around to assist the British against the Nazis and to prepare America for the inevitable.

Yet, similarities between the 1930s and the 1980s do not end with similarities between each period's ideologues. Blasphemous as the thought might be, similarities between the decades' two dominant political figures stand out. The presidencies of FDR and Ronald Reagan were both epochal. The Roosevelt presidency broke with America's tradition of isolationism. The Reagan presidency broke with the post-Vietnam period of neo-isolationism, or at least foreign policy inertness.

After a decade of enduring the infantile charges against Ronald Reagan I find it bracing to reflect on the similarities between Reagan and the man his critics so loyally admire, FDR. Through guile and willfulness, FDR moved the United States into a period of internationalism that rescued the world from what was shaping up as a very rough patch. He defeated fascism and established foreign policy precedents that enabled his successors to conduct the Cold War effectively into the 1970s.

Reagan arrived after Roosevelt's Democratic successors had grown visibly weary of that Cold War. In the Carter Administration Soviet influence spread practically unopposed. In one year, 1979, the Soviets or their henchmen moved into Afghanistan, Cambodia, Grenada, and Nicaragua; the Shah fell and Iran became virulently anti-American. By the end of the Carter Administration oil shortages, inflation, and terror against U.S. citizens combined with numerous geopolitical debacles to bring American prestige to its lowest level in the postwar period. In the foreign ministries of our allies, friends beheld the Carter foreign policy and shook their heads, and in the United Nations the Third World wildly anathematized Imperial Washington. In response, Ronald Reagan strengthened the military, waged Cold War anew, reversed Soviet gains, and tranquilized the Third World. As his Administration drew to a close it appeared that the Cold War too was finally ending. Soviet expansionism having been unhorsed by Yankee resolve. Eastern Europe on the brink of liberation. A forty-year American policy of resistance to Marxism-Leninism was vindicated.

The presidencies of FDR and Reagan also shared the peculiarity of being epochal in domestic policy. It is the rarest of presidents who can lay claim to having had a substantial impact on *both* domestic and foreign policy. President James K. Polk left a large mark through his mastery of foreign affairs but made no large imprint on domestic policy. President Andrew Jackson left a larger mark—so large in fact that the aging James Madison feared his colleagues' safeguards against unrestrained government were being abandoned. But Old Hickory's influence was restricted to domestic politics; he left no comparable mark on foreign policy. FDR and Reagan, however, were epochal in both theaters of political drama.

Domestically, Roosevelt inaugurated an era of collectivism in which enormous powers thitherto adjudged injurious to our Constitutional balance were arrogated by the federal government. Elected representatives adopted a conception of government that was to dominate Washington for decades, though it was clearly at variance with the conception of limited government advanced by the Founding Fathers. As James Q. Wilson has written, no longer did the elected representative come to Washington restrained by a sense that there were things the genius of American government barred him from doing. Eager-beaver New Dealers gnawed away at the time-honored conventions, destroying what Wilson calls a "legitimacy barrrier."[11] Consequently federal action no longer had to be defended first and foremost on the grounds that the Constitution allowed it but only on the grounds that it would achieve some good effect. Eventually the doctrines of delegation of powers and of states' rights withered until by 1980 legislators felt almost completely unrestrained by Constitutional inhibition. No longer did they come to Washington believing that there were things they could not do; rather they arrived in town believing that there was almost no Constitutional barrier to the reforms they might undertake and that the politician of genius devises ever more government services for the electorate, say: hot lunches for school children, a national corps of certified babysitters, an Air Force Three for Congress's grandees. By the late 1970s the conventional eleemosynary pol was hard pressed to find new spending packages for the grateful taxpayer. His predecessors had left no human need, in fact almost no human velleity, unsubsidized. Worse still, the grateful taxpayers were catching on as to who was picking up the bill for the pols' generosity, and the old style of political action was in danger.

Ronald Reagan inaugurated an era in which the citizenry moved away from accepting the government as a leveler of society, a manager of the economy, and the source of wealth. In the early 1980s Americans began to favor entrepreneurship and to view government as superfluous to the creation of wealth, perhaps even an impediment to it. Astonishingly, this faith in entrepreneurship spread throughout the world, even into those dreary lands where faith in the planned economy and socialism had paralyzed history. By the end of the Reagan Administration even Russians and Chinese were curious about the mysteries of Rotary and the Chamber of Commerce. This sudden resurgence in entrepreneurship had been totally unforeseen by any thinker in the West from any political perspective. The economics championed by Ronald Reagan in America and by Margaret Thatcher in Britain and vindicated by experience surely deserves some credit for the entrepreneurial epidemic of the 1980s. Admittedly, at home Reagan could not make good on his promise to cut government, but he did slow its rate of growth, reducing the federal bite into the gross national product from 24.3 percent in fiscal year 1983 to the 20 percent range.

Thus, Ronald Reagan and FDR share the unusual accomplishment of having auspicated new eras in American history. Both scoffed at the Old Orders they replaced, though note that the Old Order Reagan replaced was *not* the New Deal. That was another false alarm set off by 1980s Liberals. Reagan's adversaries were not New Deal Liberals but rather the illegitimate descendants of New Dealers, New Age Liberals. The New Deal was statist and more egalitarian than libertarian, but it was not utopian and did still strive for measurable goals: jobs, collective bargaining, a higher standard of living. The New Age Liberals were utopians with goals that were purely subjective. They promised those who *felt* victimized by society a *sense* of "empowerment," of well-being, of equality, of fulfillment— nothing that could be verified. Measurable goals were kaput. In point of fact, most of the American electorate whom Ronald Reagan had to address in the 1980s no longer thought of the New Deal as a political issue. It was history, having receded into the past and become a thing to be learned about by schoolchildren, not to be debated by contemporary politicians. Liberals in 1980 could publicly laud the New Deal, but no Republican, not even a movement conservative Republican, was likely to campaign against the New Deal.

The only New Deal policy that remained prominent and controversial in the 1980s was Social Security, now frowzy with unfunded programs that surely FDR himself would have questioned. When in the spring of 1982 Ronald Reagan, prompted by David Stockman's mania for budget cuts, suggested cuts in Social Security, the Democrats fell on him and he never tampered with it again. Had he declared war on the New Deal he would have suffered similarly.

The New Deal was not in danger in 1980. It was as much a part of the American polity as the Bill of Rights. Moreover, in the 1980s America's problems were different from the problems it faced in the 1930s with sudden deflation, widespread bank failures, and a 25 percent unemployment rate. Now the Reagan Administration had to confront a foreign policy in collapse, stagflation, and statist excesses bred of the chaotic 1960s and 1970s. History was moving swiftly, leaving the Liberals fighting yesteryear's battles, defending a romanticized and fantastical New Deal (suspiciously redolent of the New Age) against conservatives who had other things on their minds, things many Liberals apparently did not understand. In a *Kultursmog* of their own creation, they were truly befogged.

But let us extend our discussion of the similarities between FDR and

Ronald Reagan. What does one make of the fact that even their critics' complaints were similar? Both were esteemed lightweights by their peers. Both were adjudged impressionable and disparaged as poor managers. Both were derided for their unusual origins: aristocratic Hyde Park for FDR; Hollywood, home of America's modern aristocracy, for RR. Neither man could ever quite shake the irony of these roots. Roosevelt and Reagan were both acclaimed for their skills in the oratorical art, and then accused of dissimulation. Finally, despite their critics, both were enormously popular at the polls and effective in government. Such are the mysteries of democratic anthropology.

In *Landslide*, a book reverberating with the standard complaints against Reagan, the authors Jane Mayer and Doyle McManus sum up the critics' gruesome assessment in the last year of the Reagan presidency. Reagan was a "bungling leader," presiding over a disorganized White House. By spending an unconscionable amount of time in his pajamas, he demonstrated that he was "out of touch" with the world and "strangely susceptible to the wiles of both his staff and his wife. Far from being a sophisticated manager, he rarely demanded accountability from subordinates."[12] Think of it! Here America was, safe and sound and at the end of a presidency that was without doubt the most successful since that of Dwight D. Eisenhower (another successful president perceived by his critics as a doddering old fool), and the authors can only offer these disparaging judgments. Reagan, the lightweight! Out of his depth in the large affairs of the age! Reagan, the boob!

Truth be known, such complaints hounded FDR too. Walter Lippmann witnessed Governor Roosevelt's 1932 presidential campaign and was filled with premonitions. "I am now satisfied," Lippmann wrote Newton Baker, an old Democratic warhorse, ". . . that he just doesn't happen to have a very good mind, that he never really comes to grips with a problem which has any large dimensions. . . . He has never thought much, or understood much, about the great subjects which must concern the next President."[13] And Lippmann was not the only critic of FDR to utter criticisms that later could be applied to Ronald Reagan. Consider Oliver Wendell Holmes's patronizing estimate of FDR, imparted to the young New Dealer Thomas G. Corcoran: "He has a second class intellect but a first class temperament."[14] For his part, Lippmann continued to depict Roosevelt in terms that conjure up the *smog's* official portrait of Reagan five decades later. "A kind of amiable school boy," Lippmann had written, and in a January 1932 column the illustrious progressive elaborated: "a highly impressionable person without a firm grasp of public affairs . . . a pleasant man, who without any important qualifications for the office, would very much like to be President."[15] Later, Alice Roosevelt Longworth derided Roosevelt and his wife in terms reminiscent of those used years later to deride Reagan and his wife by Mrs. Longworth's leading successor, Gore Vidal. Proclaimed the long-nailed Alice: ". . . two-thirds mush and one-third Eleanor."[16]

As I have said, the critics usually admired these men's powers in the pulpit. Both had mastered the medium of their day, the mellifluous Roosevelt on radio, the genial Reagan on television. What was often overlooked is that both men took a hand in the editing and even the writing of their speeches. So perhaps they were not such thorough boobs—or is it that it does not take all that much intellect to edit and write? Both were accused of manipulating the press; but FDR did it best, and therefore he had a more profound and enduring effect on the press. He took greater pains to bring the press to his point of view. He mixed with select members of the journalistic corps, massaging them suavely. He rewarded friendly journalists and shut his critics out in the cold.

Here again we see a Liberal outshining a conservative in the art of communicating. Roosevelt worked the press with a facility that Reagan and his aides could not equal or even understand. True, by Reagan's time the press had changed. It was now more adversarial. The corporate mentality of its gray flanneled reporters was more conformist and impenetrable. But aside from staging spectacular photo opportunities, Reagan did not involve himself with the media much. Whereas Roosevelt attended to its vanities and genuine needs, Reagan was generally aloof from the press. In his memoir, former White House spokesman Larry Speakes asserts that there were a half-dozen of us who were the President's favorite columnists. Not one that I know of got the personal attention FDR laid out to his favorite journalists, or the leaks. Certainly I received no leaks. Instead we met for chats, and in Reagan's last summer at the White House, he and two hundred or so of his closest security men came to my house for dinner. But our friendship was based on shared political values, never on the business of journalism. The cosseting and leaking that Roosevelt—and, for that matter, Kennedy and Johnson—indulged in with their favorite journalists was simply unknown to Reagan.

The charge that Ronald Reagan manipulated the press is an exaggeration, as, incidentally, is the claim that he was "the Great Communicator." Without a prepared text Reagan frequently became groggy and disjunctive. He gained esteem as a communicator because his message was a great message suited for the needs of the time. Without a text, however, he was scarcely more eloquent than the next pol, unless he had previously focused intensely on an idea.

I recall an interview I attended during the 1984 election. He invited a few of us in to the White House library for drinks, which was not all that frequent an occurrence with him. I was feeling very much at ease seated with three frequent *American Spectator* writers, Fred Barnes, Pat Buchanan, and Warren Brookes. Along with us was David Broder, looking suitably solemn. Liberalism is supposed to be the happy, positive persuasion; but here was another happy, positive Liberal with a four-year Reagan-induced frown. Soon it would be an eight-year frown. After that it would be a Bush-induced frown. That is a long time to frown. When the White House bartender asked for David's order I listened to hear if he was having warm buttermilk, but no, he had cold fruit juice.

After drinks were poured the President answered questions in his usual way, fumbling, slipping into grammatically impossible sentences, framing brief bursts of eloquence with lapses into bewildering aposiopeses. Only when he got to abortion and arms control did the Great Communicator stir from within. These were issues he cared deeply about, and even in a private conversation he was at pains to convey his carefully thought out conclusions. He had wanted arms reductions with the Soviets for years, but now he sensed that conditions for his kind of an agreement were improving. And when he warmed to a subject he had focused on, it was not just his voice or face that advanced his argument; it was his whole body. He really was an actor.

As we were leaving the library, Barnes asked him about a recent movie he had seen in the White House viewing room, *Red Dawn*. Cocking his head, the President began an amiable criticism of Hollywood nudity that we had heard before and would hear again. What was most memorable and instructive was his demonstration of how one of his directors, Ernst Lubitsch, had conveyed the essence of a love scene by filming nothing more than a pair of hands hanging a "Do Not Disturb" sign on a hotel-room door. With his own hands Reagan demonstrated the scene from the movie. All eyes were on his face, but had the writers looked at his hands they would have noticed the hands had come alive with liquid motions. These were the hands of an accomplished actor. In that instant we were given another explanation for why Ronald Reagan was in the White House at that hour. All politicians are actors, but only a politician of the first rank can act like that.

For some reason it disturbs a certain kind of person to be reminded of the many similarities between FDR and Reagan. They will protest that one of these presidents was virtuous while the other was a louse, that one knew what was what but the other was a boob. Yet, partisanship aside, the similarities are there. Perhaps this is so because FDR was the political hero of Reagan's youth. Reagan cast his first presidential ballot for Roosevelt and continued to vote for him in 1936, 1940, and 1944. In those days Reagan was a Liberal, or as he later testified "a near-hopeless hemophiliac liberal."[17] Why would anyone doubt that the youthful Reagan studied and learned from the political colossus of his time? Then too, the studio he worked for in the thirties was saturated with the ethos of FDR. Jack Warner of Warner Brothers supported FDR. At his studio the issues FDR advocated—his stand against the Nazis and for collectivism—became important ingredients in movies. As historian Steven Vaughn has observed in his study of Reagan's Hollywood years, the Warner Brothers studio was in Reagan's day alive with debates over America's role in the world and over Hollywood's mission in shaping that role. Vaughn argues that Reagan's political sensibility was shaped by these debates. Then, as Reagan has said so many times, with the passage of time Liberalism changed, not Reagan. He found himself abandoned and he settled on the right. Indeed he could be numbered among the first neoconservatives.

Of course, there are other reasons for the similarities between FDR and RR. Both men are very American: sunny, practical, sparked by idealism. Though ideologues heave up ingenious intellectual charts to divide Americans into ideological camps, in point of fact there are more similarities among us than differences. We have all been raised on the same Constitution and responded to the same values. The historian David Donald notes that even in so bitter a dispute as the Civil War, Northerners and Southerners acted as "mirror images" of each other on such fundamental questions as financing the war, fighting it, carrying out its diplomacy, writing laws, and conducting government.[18] And so it is with contemporary politics. Americans, whether Liberal or conservative, bring to politics the same moralism, pragmatism, and dispensations from fatalism. Roosevelt and Reagan are Americans. Centuries of enduring hostilities that divide, say, Italians do not divide these two Americans. Yanks, whether they be named Roosevelt or Reagan, have talked of a rendezvous with history and a city on a hill throughout our brief history. These are traditional American images, reaching back to the time of the Puritans. Yet the most profound and illuminating reason for the similarities between FDR and RR is that they shared the same gift for governance, a gift that was completely beyond the ken of the critics and so these benighted carpers fashioned another complaint against Roosevelt and Reagan, namely, that they were inferior managers.

Against Reagan the charges were "detachment" and "laziness." He was insouciant to his government's leaks, turf battles, and general centrifugal confusion. The critics pointed to the repeated clashes between Secretary of State George Shultz and Secretary of Defense Caspar Weinberger. They noted that when he was secretary of state, Alexander Haig was engaged on all fronts, perhaps most fiercely with United Nations Ambassador Jeane Kirkpatrick. In the Administration's early years the so-called troika of James Baker, Michael Deaver, and Edwin Meese was an arabesque of intrigue. This sort of managerial bickering existed in FDR's White House too, and his critics were quick to pounce. As with the Reagan Administration, the Roosevelt White House shook with conflicts among such top Roosevelt lieutenants as Harry Hopkins, Harold Ickes, and Hugh Johnson, and so the critics fell on Roosevelt.

Reflecting, sourly, on FDR's style of management, the devout New Dealer Rexford G. Tugwell would write many years later:

> Roosevelt emerged so slowly from immaturity and grasped so belatedly the commitments of progressive policy that he was forced to function, down to his latest grave decisions, in a confusion he could not afford to share with anyone. The disparity between the talent for political planning . . . and downright incompetence in statesmanlike generalization is very well illustrated by Roosevelt. The gloss on it is very misleading—the charm, the adroitness, the rationalizations! But the shiny surface cannot conceal the boyish alarm, the floundering, and the justification after mistakes. . . . But the masquerade of confident competence was necessary. If the American people had seen behind the mask, their nation might have gone to pieces from sheer collective fright several times in the Roosevelt era. Once, in an illuminated instance, Roosevelt found a way to reassure even many of those close watchers who had penetrated the disguise. He was, Roosevelt said, acting as "quarterback."[19]

The Gipper, perhaps? Less melodramatically and more recently Richard Tanner Johnson has explained that Roosevelt "granted overlapping delegations of authority. This aggravated the strife within his staff. . . . his system encountered more difficulty in coping with the requirements for clear priorities and orderly administration that were called for during the war."[20]

Eventually the Roosevelt style of managed strife was sanitized of all traces of opprobrium by the keepers of the Roosevelt legend. Sometime in the 1960s Corcoran was still at it, polishing his old boss's legend, when he told Arthur Schlesinger that: "One of FDR's greatest strengths was a certain detachment from the details of his administration. He did not try to run everything himself, but gave his people their head. Sometimes he was criticized for letting them go off too much on their own. . . ."[21] Is it possible that Reagan, too, knew what he was about when he let his people "go off too much on their own"? If so, there appeared no Corcorans to laud the wisdom of their boss's "detachment."

Here again we see the Liberals' peerless artistry in rescuing one of their heroes from the critics and transforming him into a god. FDR's friends for the most part held to Corcoran's interpretation of FDR's management prowess rather than to Tugwell's revelations; and they held to it so artfully that when in the 1970s Professor Johnson analyzed Roosevelt's White House he benignly termed it "Roosevelt's Feuding Fraternity."[22] There were no conservative mythmakers to rescue Ronald Reagan from his critics, and so Jane Mayer and Doyle McManus could without challenge present his "Feuding Fraternity" thus: "In Reagan's permissive White House, policymaking was literally up for grabs; proximity to the President was tantamount to power itself."[23] Strip Reagan of his knee-jerk critics, however, and Roosevelt of his mythmakers and their "detached" managerial style stands out as a stupendous political strength. Both men were superb maneuverers of men, for both had exquisite political instincts.

What the critics scowled upon as Reagan's detached managerial style was, as fact would have it, a talent quite beyond the critics' commonplace perspective, a talent not seen in such abundance since Roosevelt, a talent so rare and elusive that, even when Dr. New Deal flaunted it, many of the political cognoscenti of his time could not apprehend it. They believed that they were witnessing the flaccidities of a pampered country squire utterly out of his depth at the White House. The talent so difficult for the critics to perceive is *timing*, in the cases of Roosevelt and Reagan the political timing of master politicians. Roosevelt was indeed a pampered country squire, even as Reagan was a pampered Hollywood star. Perhaps one needs this sort of exemption from the harum-scarum of ordinary life to develop political timing. Certainly the quality demands some insulation from the fears and foibles of fainthearted lieutenants. Whether possessed by an elected president, a hereditary monarch, or an animal control officer on the first rung upward towards the Dayton, Ohio, Mayoral Palace, timing is the element that separates the political virtuosi from the also-rans.

That shrewd and sagacious Renaissance statesman Francesco Guicciardini spotted it when he served as Florence's ambassador to the court of King Ferdinand V of Aragon in the sixteenth century. In a celebrated meditation on political judgment he related that when King Ferdinand, "a most powerful and prudent prince . . . wished to embark on some new enterprise or take a decision of great importance, [he] often proceeded in such a way that before his intentions were known, the whole court and nation already desired it, and cried out—the King should do this—so that on announcing his decision when it was already approved and demanded, he enjoyed incredible support. . . ." "Do not rush wildly at things," Guicciardini concludes, "do not precipitate them, wait for them to mature in their own season." And more, "when you are in a difficult position or dealing with troublesome affairs, let time run on and delay as long as you can, for time may bring inspiration or release you from your difficulty."[24] Closer to home and nearer in time, an American statesman and philosopher of the first water arrived at a similar conclusion; though Calvin Coolidge's formulation was more svelte: ". . . never go out to meet trouble," our thirtieth president admonished. "If you will just sit still, nine cases out of ten someone will intercept it before it reaches you."[25]

While critics groaned about Reagan's disengagement from daily decision making, about turf battles and about the concomitant leaks of his Administration, the clever dog was usually "sitting still," not "going out to meet trouble," waiting for things to "mature in their own season." His timing was not infallible. Now and then he missed volupt opportunities. Now and then impatience drove him to imprudence. Nonetheless a rare sense of timing and adherence to a few useful principles assisted Reagan in becoming the most successful president since FDR.

Like FDR, Reagan rerouted the course of American government in both domestic policy and foreign affairs without losing the support of the electorate. Harry Truman continued FDR's internationalism in peacetime but made no dashing breakthroughs domestically. Ike charmed the electorate but attempted nothing daring. JFK was murdered before presenting himself to the electorate for a second judgment or undertaking substantial policy changes. LBJ moved impetuously on all fronts and came to ruin. Nixon came to worse ruin. Ford was shown the door without even serving a full term, and Carter—well, we have said quite enough about his infelicities.

After all this presidential carnage there arrived at 1600 Pennsylvania Ave. one of the most unlikely presidents of modern times: a former movie star, a card-carrying member of the conservative movement. He retired eight years later having set his countrymen off on new and uncharted waters. My case is, then, that Ronald Reagan was the most successful president since FDR. He revised the direction of American government in both domestic policy and in foreign affairs. Then he retired—voluntarily. Upon retiring, he bequeathed a new conception of the presidency to George Bush, one different from the one he snatched from Jimmy Carter, a conception of the presidency that actually worked.

CHAPTER 11

The Triumphs of Ronald Reagan
American Conservatism Makes Its Mark

THE POLITICAL SCIENTIST RICHARD Neustadt argues that the presidency is a weak institution. Aaron Wildavsky, also a practitioner of that magisterial science, argues that we live in an era whose ideas and institutions are corrosive to almost any kind of leadership. Thus the heir to General Washington, if he wishes to retire on his own terms, must not attempt too many high-flying acts of statecraft. Ronald Reagan never did. That is the new conception of the presidency that he bequeathed to his successor. Reagan delivered oratory that was lofty and provocative; and whilst the oratory was debated the old orator proceeded prudently. He advanced only a few policies, but those policies radically reshaped domestic politics and the West's relations with the Soviet Union.

His major policies were to cut taxes and to rebuild the military. In addition, he wished to squelch inflation and move from a strategy of Mutually Assured Destruction to one of Strategic Defense. He wanted to advance beyond Strategic Arms Limitation Talks (SALT) to Strategic Arms Reduction Talks (START)—an idea of Reagan's since 1976, according to Martin Anderson.[1] The insolent Third World voices haranguing the United States from the United Nations were to be quieted, and, finally, the new president hoped to influence the Imperial Judiciary towards restraint. On this last matter, the President's biographer, Lou Cannon, states that he "won the war to remake the federal judiciary and, to a large degree, the high court itself." Cannon observes that Reagan "was able to appoint more federal judges than any president in history and a higher percentage of the judiciary than any president except Franklin Roosevelt."[2] How profound a change these appointments portend for the Republic only time will reveal, but they could prove to be his most enduring accomplishment. Cannon goes on to quote Reaganite Terry Eastland's boast that "Reagan's success lies not simply in quantity but quality."

Reagan never set himself up as an intellectual and moral superman. Hence when he erred or misstated a point the White House did not quake, nor did the media reverberate with shocking reports of sudden presidential decline as it did when earlier self-proclaimed colossi faltered. In line with Sr. Guicciardini's advice, he did not "rush out wildly" on a dozen policy fronts at once. He risked fewer failures and was less exposed to adversaries' recriminations. Reagan received the delicate and puissant benefits that flow to the leader who is always underestimated. Moreover, when this Republican conservative was pressed into defending one of his conservative programs he had access to well-researched conservative positions, developed over decades and made all the more credible by New Age Liberalism's late-1970s humiliations.

As Reagan's achievements accumulated, his bewildered critics were driven to explaining his successes as the consequence of "charm," then of "magic." No American president in the history of the Republic was ever so closely associated with the supernatural as Ronald Reagan and what makes this so amazing is that those who associated him with heavenly powers were his critics, very few of whom had ever acknowledged a supernatural order before. Reagan, however, had a way of causing his critics to say the damnedest things. At any rate, if the fluttering of heavenly wings did in fact account for Reagan's successes, the magic settled on him only after much heavy sledding during the Administration's early years. At the outset of his presidency the new president had no help from the heavens. His early approval rating bumped along at a mere 43 percent compared with Nixon's early ratings of 56 percent, Johnson's 67 percent, and Kennedy's 72 percent. Even Carter achieved 46 percent, and Bush at the end of his first year hit 79 percent.[3] Unlike his predecessors, Reagan did not let the early polls panic him. He refrained from lurching towards some gimcrack expedient. Rather, he coolly persisted in advancing his primary agenda: the military buildup, tax cuts, death to inflation. When the economy revived, his popularity climbed. I am a Christian and a pious man, but I do not believe the explanation for Reagan's success is to be found in the realms of "charm" or "magic." I believe that Reagan was a success because his policies worked. Admittedly he pushed hard for only a few, but they were momentous and he shoved them forward with clearly observable resolve and command.

Those who argue that Reagan was "detached" and irresolute usually have in mind policies that Reagan did not reckon important or policies that he rated politically unfeasible at the moment. Certainly Reagan suffered lapses of all kinds during eight years in office, but his resolve and command were demonstrable from the outset.

His first policy initiative, the one which laid him low in the polls, put the lie to the charge that he was insouciant or wavering. Before any other undertaking he had to wipe out the double-digit inflation that, since Carter, had blighted every corner of the economy, and he did.

The critics scoff that it was actually Federal Reserve Chairman Paul Volcker, a Carter appointee, who scotched inflation. Yet the Federal Reserve cannot for long hold out against a President's wishes, and as William Greider demonstrates in his chronicle of Volcker's administration, *Secrets of the Temple*, Volcker did not have to. Reagan fully supported Volcker even when therapy against inflation brought on the 1981–82 recession and such a high rate of unemployment (10.8 percent) that we all began planning the president's retirement party. In 1983, when certain Republicans and Democrats opposed reappointing Volcker, Reagan ignored the opposition and gave Volcker a second term. No other president in recent years has persisted so tenaciously against inflation. Certainly Carter did not; he fiddled with price and credit controls. And as for crediting Carter with choosing Volcker, the choice was an afterthought. Having appointed Federal Reserve Chairman G. William Miller his secretary of the treasury, Carter had a vacancy to fill. Volcker was not even Carter's first choice. He was the financial community's choice. Carter acquiesced to Wall Street.

Reagan's remodeled presidency, whether the product of his instinct or intellect, cashiered the lumbering presidential style of his immediate predecessors and blended the office to suit the requirements of the 1980s, an era Wildavsky astutely perceives as corrosive to leadership. He may not have returned the presidency to the pinnacle of power that it achieved in Roosevelt's day, but there is little to suggest that anyone could have or that there was broad demand for such a restoration. Reagan's presidency was effective. Despite the critics' charges, he knew better than to wear himself out in the minutiae that had exhausted such troubled predecessors as Lyndon Johnson, Richard Nixon, and Jimmy Carter, who memorized policy papers like a child prodigy, patrolled the halls of the Old Executive Office Building for shameful television sets, and monitored the White House tennis courts. That last presidential initiative actually became a vexed issue at the poor wretch's April 30, 1979, press conference! History has a pitiless memory.

Kultursmog's sozzled victims, such as Jane Mayer and Doyle McManus, inspected Reagan's record and saw only the "bungling" of a chief executive "out of touch." In fact, Reagan kept his presidency very much on course, as he demonstrated so admirably in pursuing inflation. Unlike his predecessors, Reagan's presidency did not blow up over major policy blunders or wear itself out on numerous unnecessary projects. He had a technique for governing. Following the wisdom of a Florentine sage and a Yankee statesman, Reagan let things "mature in their own season." His *metier* was to wait, let favorable opinion form behind him, and then prudently advance selected policies.

Reagan's long-time aides, Martin Anderson and Peter Hannaford, have explained Reagan's decision-making method as one that relegates the pedestrian work to staff. The political scientist Wildavsky has explicated how effectively it worked. From his early days as governor of California, Reagan would charge his staff with bringing him options. If they did not bring him enough options he would ask for more.* Then when the time was at hand he would make his decision: "Among the many criticisms raised about Reagan," Wildavsky writes, "there is one especially relevant to him as a strategist: he is allegedly run by his staff. My observations are different. From his days as governor of California onward, Ronald Reagan, following his own understanding of how he might best use his talents, has deliberately structured his staff so that he would (1) make the critical choices; and (2) save his time."⁴ Martin Anderson insists that "over the years [Reagan] made all the key decisions on the economic strategies he finally embraced."⁵

Those who accused Reagan of being unduly detached from policymaking were frequently people who had matured during the tumultuous years of his predecessors. They either assumed that the unhappy fates of Johnson, Nixon, Ford, and Carter were the norm for American presidents, or perhaps they simply could not acknowledge a successful conservative presi-

---

*Martin Anderson explains the vacuousness of the Reagan memoirs by noting that when Reagan oversaw their writing he was elderly and unassisted by seasoned aides who might have jogged his memory and sparked his ideas.

dent. But the record is clear that Ronald Reagan was a success and that he pushed resolutely for policies once he deemed them feasible.

Despite the opposition of business and economists, Reagan steadfastly pressed for tax cuts. He thwarted Office of Management and Budget director David Stockman's schemes to tie tax cuts to budget cuts. He recognized, as King Ferdinand of Aragon might have, that the nation favored tax relief. Against both peace demonstrators and budget balancers he relentlessly pursued his military buildup. The peace movement was noisy, but beyond the din the people favored a strong military. True, his speeches reflect an opposition to abortion, support for school prayer, and for other pieces of social legislation dear to many social conservatives; but Reagan recognized that the political support was not there, and so he proceeded as would Guicciardini's long-deceased exemplar. Neither the whole court nor the nation desired this social legislation, and so Reagan made do with oratory, awaiting the day when the public might clamor for each piece of legislation. That is the model of leadership Reagan followed. It was a question of political timing.

To be sure, towards the end of his administration Reagan made some reckless moves, but this was not because he was remote from the affairs of his government. Rather, owing to pressures generated from abroad and to his party's loss of its working majority in the Senate, he became too deeply and personally involved. There followed then his worst failures in office. Impatient with negotiations to free American journalist Nicholas Daniloff from illegal Soviet imprisonment, Reagan precipitated a prisoner exchange between the innocent journalist and the convicted Soviet spy Gennadi Zakharov. The Russians scored. They got back their spy and Reagan lost prestige throughout the world. The Russians were going to have to release Daniloff anyway to keep their European "peace offensive" alive. Reagan should have remained patient and steadfast. Similarly, by becoming too absorbed with the condition of American hostages in Lebanon, Reagan embarked on another reckless course, ending this time in the Iran-Contra affair, a debacle foreordained by the fact that the scheme depended on the trustworthiness of a sworn enemy, Iran. And finally, there was Reagan's ill-timed attempt to unhorse Manuel Noriega in Panama. Again he had allowed himself to be dragged into a reckless decision. Yet his sense of timing was not completely gone. Deaf to his critics, he held out for the INF treaty, the first superpower compact to eliminate an entire class of nuclear weapons and to provide for on-site verification.

As a rule, however, Reagan moved adroitly in foreign policy and domestic policy. When the old man at last laid down his presidential scepter and headed west, unbowed by years or labors, still astonishingly erect and aglow, with no mobs harassing him and pressed upon solely by the disgruntled reactionaries of the Old Order, the nation he left behind was at peace and happily embarked on a course beyond Cold War. Let the Old Order murmur against him, his policies had changed America. No one could say for a certitude where the world was heading, only that it too had changed. The members of the Old Order have depicted John F. Kennedy as a presidential colossus though his tenure was brief and his legislative achievements modest. Now they want us to believe that during the eight years that Ronald Reagan resided in the White House he was no more responsible for the historic course of events that accompanied his Administration than the White House hair stylist. Well, I object.

Domestically, by effecting across-the-board tax cuts and later tax reform, Reagan set in motion the longest peacetime period of economic growth in American history. In addition, by resisting David Stockman and the budget-balancers, Reagan forced the electorate to choose between the Republicans' tax cuts and the Democrats' ingenious spending programs. The electorate preferred the Republicans. The Democrats were reduced to bawling about the plight of unpopular social welfare policies and to advocating the same policies that had once made Republicans such Typhoid Marys with the electorate, to wit, balancing the budget with higher taxes. Walter Mondale had never before borne the grim message that government spending had to be paid for by higher taxes, but the wily Reagan forced Mondale to sound like a 1930s Republican and in 1984 to lose like one.

He also forced the Democrats to lie. Contrary to their charges that Reagan decimated social welfare spending in the 1980s, these outlays rose to their highest levels. Reagan may have wanted to reduce the size of government, but all he managed was to reduce its *rate* of growth, which the visionaries amongst the Democrats seemed to believe could be accelerated out into the farthest reaches of mathematical theory. As for the unpleasant topic of budget deficits: though worrisome, they never warranted the Democrats' hysterics. In fact, as Warren Brookes pointed out in a 1988 review of the Reagan economy, the "nation's total deficit (at all levels combined) this last year was less than $108 billion, or about 2.4 percent of GNP—well below most of the major nations of the world."[6] By forcing the Democrats to urge higher taxes Reagan had exposed a truth never before acknowledged by them, that is: when it comes to picking up the check for government programs, it is the beneficiaries of these programs who have to foot the bill.

Until Reagan cut taxes, Democrats had endeared themselves to the electorate by presenting the federal government as a cornucopia of programs and generous spending, all of which were paid for surreptitiously by inflation and tricky tax increases. The tax increases were grafted onto the economy so that the government could quietly reach deeper into the taxpayers' pockets without seeking their consent. Reagan's tax cuts stabilized federal taxes at the postwar level of a little over 19 percent of GNP; and had he not acted, the combination of social security tax increases and tax bracket creep would have increased federal taxation's bite on GNP to record levels.[7] The Reagan tax cuts had the added benefit of changing the way the American people viewed government and bringing them to a better understanding of the source of wealth. The prosperous aftermath of the Reagan tax cuts demonstrated that, contrary to the Liberals' belief that government creates wealth, government taxation is an impediment to the creation of wealth and to the citizenry's security. Finally, with his tax cuts in place, President Reagan could use the federal deficit to shape the congressional agenda and to increase his influence with the bureaucracy. By limiting the funds available, the modern president gained influence over his bureaucrats and his opponents on Capitol Hill, who could not simultaneously bewail the deficit and call for more spending.

In foreign policy Reagan came to office with the American people riven by discord and anxiety over America's diplomatic moves and strategic policy. By the time he left, the vast majority of Americans were comfortable with Washington's strategic policy. The peace movement could no longer prey on the anxieties of average Americans. Career peace protesters faced a shaky future. By adhering to but a few crucial programs, Reagan had moved beyond arms limitation to actual arms reduction.

In the 1970s the American Cold War consensus frayed badly. There was a huge Soviet military buildup underway and the balance of power between the superpowers was tipping in the Soviets' favor for the first time since the beginning of the Cold War. More nations became Soviet clients during the 1970s than during any other postwar decade: Afghanistan, Angola, Cambodia, Ethiopia, Grenada, Laos, Mozambique, Nicaragua, South Vietnam, and South Yemen. Reagan's assiduous rebuilding of America's military and intelligence capabilities and his rhetorical challenge to the Soviets reversed the direction of Soviet advances in the world. His bold use of American strength in Afghanistan, Angola, Grenada, parts of

Central America, and Libya forced aggressors to weigh their use of force more cautiously. His single-minded pursuit of an arms buildup beyond the Soviets' means and his decision to proceed with the Strategic Defense Initiative, despite the yelps of his critics at home or the Soviets abroad, confronted the Kremlin with America's legendary capacity for the production of high-quality weaponry—a capacity, incidentally, that was the difference between defeat and victory for America's allies in two world wars. Soon, the Soviets faced ethnic and democratic movements whose vitality might also have derived from another of Reagan's decisions, a still secret decision to let Bill Casey's CIA penetrate the Soviets' closed society with a plethora of literature about democracy and capitalism. It was all too much for the jerry-built Soviet system. The Brezhnev Doctrine was set aside, and soon serious arms negotiations commenced between Moscow and Washington.

In arms control negotiations Reagan refused to concede to Soviet demands, impassively endured Soviet walkouts, and insisted on the intrusive verification of all arms control agreements. His singular recognition that Mutually Assured Destruction (MAD) was a dangerous gamble best balanced by a Strategic Defense Initiative (SDI) and his military expansion program, particularly his policy of building towards a 600-ship navy, put global pressure on the overextended Soviets, ultimately bringing Mikhail Gorbachev to negotiate on Reagan's terms. In Washington on December 8, 1987, Gorbachev and Reagan signed the superpowers' first agreement ever calling for a reduction in nuclear arsenals. Commentators began to speculate that the Cold War was ending but few gave Reagan credit for the achievement. So intense was the *Kultursmog's* propaganda against him that by the 1990s his achievements were being obscured as sophists stepped forward, explaining the Soviets' collapse with claptrap and half-truths, the most popular being that "internal contradictions" brought the Soviet Union low.[8] Someday, surely, historians will retrieve the truth.

In esteeming Ronald Reagan's achievement, I stand with former Prime Minister Margaret Thatcher who, on March 8, 1991, in a Washington speech declared:

> In the decade of the '80s, Western values were placed in the crucible and they emerged with greater purity and strength. So much of the credit goes to President Reagan. Of him it can be said, as [nineteenth-century British Prime Minister George] Canning said of Pitt, he was the "pilot that weathered the storm."

> The world owes him an enormous debt and it saddens me that

there are some who refuse to acknowledge his achievements. For the whole world changed:

The Cold War was won without a shot being fired.

Eastern Europe regained its freedom; its people elected democratic governments and they announced their intention to leave the Warsaw Pact.

The Berlin Wall came down, and Germany was reunified within NATO; she and Japan, the vanquished nations in the Second World War, prospered mightily and ironically became the creditors in the new world of peace.

A weakened Soviet Union was compelled by the West's economic and military competition to reform itself; a new, more realistic and clearsighted leadership came to the top.

Glasnost was launched, perestroika was started and we saw the beginnings of democratic politics.

As the Soviet Union abandoned its revolutionary role in the world, the United Nations became a more effective forum for active diplomacy.

And the United States once again became the pre-eminent power in the world.[9]

During all these stupendous achievements the critics of Ronald Reagan were simply socked away in the *Kultursmog*. Their final judgments of Reagan were as inaccurate as their earlier indictments. Return with me to *The New York Times*, in the last summer of the Reagan presidency, and there we find the venerable James Reston sawing away at the same *concerto grosso* with which he began the decade. As the old president was preparing himself for retirement and his successor George Bush was finishing off the Democrats' third straight sacrifice in the bull ring of presidential politics, Reston's tune remained: "Reagan's easy optimism, his amiable incompetence, his tolerance of dubs and sleaze, his cronyism, his preoccupation with stars, his indifference to facts and convenient forgetfulness."[10]

Sometimes a point of view simply petrifies in time. It is no longer capable of discernment or of any fresh cognition whatsoever. Confronted with a new script and a new cast of characters, the scribes of the Old Order can summon up only familiar images from an unchanging past. In the summer of 1988 Reston reviews the impressive record of the fortieth president of the United States and from the time capsule that is his mind hauls up a dusty image of Warren Gamaliel Harding. Well, that is how Reston saw

Ronald Reagan, and there is no point in arguing with senescence. By 1988 the pious Liberal was lost to the present moment, his mind darkened in *Kultursmog.*

Ronald Reagan was not a perfect president. He was not even the perfect prosopopeia of another imperfect president, Franklin Roosevelt. Roosevelt had suavely shaped his place in history. Reagan never even tried. Roosevelt won the hearts of the intellectuals. He charmed the working press while lambasting their bosses, sixty percent of whom were Republicans. He played favorites, building them up and otherwise manipulating the press with the effect that at the time of his death the press had moved from being pro-Republican to being very nearly pro-Democrat. Reagan made almost no effort to influence the intellectuals or to shape the press. He provided soundbites and photo opportunities. If anything, when Reagan left office the intellectuals and the press were even more anti-Republican than when he arrived.

Reagan made other mistakes, perhaps the most serious of which allowed Reston and his friends to preserve and to bedizen their myth that the Reagan Administration tolerated inordinate "sleaze." Ronald Reagan rarely stood by his colleagues when they were under attack for "ethics" violations, most of which were trumped up or selectively applied and few of which ever led to indictments, to say nothing of convictions. The passage of the blowsy 1978 Ethics in Government Act, requiring hundreds, perhaps thousands, of government appointees to detail their incomes, assets, and liabilities had opened to unscrupulous political opponents and to journalists new opportunities to attribute the appearance of scandal on innocent citizens. The partisan pols and journalists could now complain of "the appearance of impropriety," and thereby create a furor capable of driving an innocent person from office.

Over a hundred Reagan appointees suffered through these bogus scandals, and thus was the myth of sleaze created. Scores of innocent political appointees were driven from office in disgrace, though few were ever even indicted. So grave did the problem become that in the spring of 1988 *The Wall Street Journal* editorialized: ". . . one of the tragedies of the Reagan administration has been the devastation of so many people and so many careers: Richard Allen, Al Haig, Anne Burford, Jim Watt, Ray Donovan, Bill Clark, Thomas Reed, Jim Beggs, Bud McFarlane, Bob Bork, John Poindexter, Ollie North. . . . Many of them of course made mistakes, and some of them have found themselves in jobs over their heads. But . . . the Reagan administration never lifted a finger to defend or protect them."[11]

As for convictions in a court of law, the Administration did rather better than the Democrats or Congress. Consider these facts. From 1980 to 1988, a period of the utmost scrutiny, only fifteen of Reagan's several thousand appointees were indicted, seven were convicted and two had their convictions overturned. During the same period, of the 535 members of Congress, fifteen members were indicted, thirteen convicted, and another eighteen would have been investigated had there then been a provision for independent counsels.[12] Or recollect that within one family on the 1984 Democratic presidential ticket the percentage of members indicted or convicted of crime was vastly higher than the crime record in either the United States Congress or the Reagan White House.

Aside from occasional retorts in defense of an embattled aide, Reagan rarely organized their defense. I believe it is fair to say that more careers were wrecked during Reagan's successful presidency than during any other presidency in American history except for that of Jefferson Davis, a presidency whose infractions are well documented. Whether Reagan's refusal to come to the defense of all those aides being lynched by the 1978 Ethics Act was a consequence of his chosen style of leadership or of some flaw in character, it was a mistake. As a consequence, the sleaze charge will haunt his administration for years. It is a mark of his Administration's receding morale and low sense of loyalty that former Reagan aides have written more kiss-and-tell memoirs than those serving in any other Administration in American history. Those morbific little books will weigh heavily upon Ronald Reagan's place in history.

Another criticism leveled at Ronald Reagan is that he failed to seek a mandate in 1984. Rather than campaign on issues helpful to his conservative program, such as deregulation, tax reform, Contra aid, and a presidential line-item veto, Reagan allowed Michael Deaver and the image beauticians to make the 1984 race a hollow popularity contest. As a consequence, he entered his second term with no clear mandate and over the next two years could not forcefully advance the political agenda of the Administration. There was drift at the White House, conducing to the great political setback of 1986, the Republican loss of the Senate. By not forthrightly debating national issues after 1984, Reagan allowed his opponents an influence over that debate incommensurate with their support among the electorate. For instance, his opponents could dominate the debate over Contra aid, filling American minds with phantasmagorias of another Vietnam. Once the Democrats had regained the Senate they put pressure on the president, throwing off his timing and tempting him into the reckless measures that blemish his last years.

This is the line of criticism advanced by such paragons of the conservative movement as Paul Weyrich, and it has merit. During his 1984 presidential debates the President at times sounded as though he were trying to surpass Mondale as a compassionate sentimentalist. He should, indeed, have confronted his Democratic opponent with the failures of Democratic policy and the incoherence of supporting Afghan resistance fighters eight thousand miles away while failing to support the increasingly effective Contras eight hundred miles south of our border. That he did not might well have been a huge error, or perhaps the old master recognized that the people simply were not ready to support the remaining items on his agenda.

Many conservatives came to the conclusion that by 1984 the old President's strength was ebbing. Bill Buckley told me he noticed a marked diminution in his friend's vigor as early as the late 1970s. The President's advanced age prompted some conservatives, for instance, Richard Viguerie and Howard Phillips, to exaggerate the missteps of his second Administration. They speculated that by 1980 his time had passed. For a real Reagan Revolution, they believed that Reagan should have become president four years earlier. The year 1976, they fantasticated, was their real moment in history. Perhaps, but each turn of history's wheel brings us different opportunities for success and for failure. The New Age Liberals had to discredit themselves in the 1970s before Reagan could have a free hand. By the 1980s the old man was, in fact, weaker; but his enemies were bankrupts in disgrace, and even an aging Ronald Reagan was more robust than many men a decade younger and happily retired.

The criticism that Reagan could have achieved more had he become President earlier brings to mind the Swiss historian Jacob Burckhardt's essay "On Fortune and Misfortune in History." There Burckhardt writes: "From time to time a great event, ardently desired, does not take place because some future time will fulfill it in greater perfection."[13] In the Thirty Years' War, Germany twice was on the verge of being united, by Wallenstein in 1629 and by Gustavus Adolphus in 1631, but in both cases the result would have been a Germany inferior to Bismarck's opus. The new Saint Peter's envisaged by Pope Nicholas V would have been an ugly runt compared to the Saint Peter's eventually created by Bramante and Michelangelo. As Burckhardt sees it, even the Dark Ages have merit. Burckhardt admits that in those bleak centuries some of the great art of antiquity was lost forever, but he argues that: "It may be, too, that those great works of art had to perish in order that later art might create in freedom. For instance, if, in the fifteenth century, vast numbers of well-preserved Greek sculptures and paintings had been discovered, Leonardo,

Raphael, Titian, and Correggio would not have done their work . . . in their own way."[14] The conservatism that a younger Ronald Reagan might have launched from the White House in the late 1970s would have been up against a Liberalism as yet free of disgrace and with plenty of fight left in it. His achievement might not have matched his achievement in the 1980s.

One evening over dinner at my home outside Washington, a man who sought ever so diplomatically to have his achievement accurately presented to the American people remarked that his friend Ronald Reagan was a curiously solitary man. Despite his warmth and good cheer, Reagan was always a man strangely alone. Sometimes it was just an aura enveloping a superb storyteller with a world-famous face. Sometimes he actually was alone, as when he sat across from Mikhail Gorbachev in Reykjavik and made daring proposals. Where were his old aides from California, the sharp-eyed conservatives, Bill Clark and Marty Anderson?

Seated at my table that evening, rumpled and gruff but incisive as usual, CIA director Casey spoke of the shifting cast of characters around his boss. There were those like himself who wanted to wage the Cold War to a successful conclusion. (Though on that May Day evening in 1986, Bill was pessimistic about the prospects of peacefully ending the Cold War: he feared events were moving toward the same tragic denouement that he had witnessed in the 1930s.) And there were the younger Country Club Republicans who padded happily through the corridors of the Old Executive Office Building, numb to all the history being made there, sometimes by great figures, sometimes even by ignoramuses. Casey did not approve of the Country Clubbers, and he felt that Mrs. Reagan—"little Nancy," as he called her—had too much influence in government. For six years he and like-minded colleagues such as Jeane Kirkpatrick, Bill Clark, and Cap Weinberger, had labored to reinforce the President's best impulses, but now the lightweights around the boss were multiplying as Casey's colleagues retired. He feared that too many mediocrities were joining the White House staff, and his fears were justified.

Solitude had been Reagan's style as it had been Roosevelt's style: different factions, maneuvering around the president, presenting him with different options. Casey played his part in the game well, but when he and his faction began to be slowed by age, the Reagan style needed fresh replacements and not many competent young conservatives were around.

Perhaps it is the natural condition of a great leader to be always alone, but Reagan's method of decision-making heightened the perception of Reagan's solitude. The critics could mistake his remoteness for the passivity of a Hollywood actor awaiting the arrival of a script rather than the condition of a leader waiting for his policy options, but then they were always wrong about Reagan. It almost seemed they wanted to be wrong. Martin Anderson, reflecting on his boss's solitary style of governance, notes that, working through staff in the governor's mansion in California, Reagan quite on his own adopted what years later would be called supply-side economics. With the same prescience, he thought up a policy of strategic arms *reduction* talks to replace strategic arms limitations talks. Well, this solitary style was fine when his aides were competent, but in the last two years of his presidency the competent aides fell away. Some were forced from office. Some retired willingly. Some died.

In the end the old President was left alone with the second-rate: mediocrities at the National Security Council, in the office of his chief of staff, in his liaison office for Capitol Hill. Surrounded by mediocrities, up against Democratic majorities in both houses of Congress, and aging steadily, the old President's last two years were certain to be hard. Yet even in these rough waters he confounded his critics by performing exquisitely at two summits with Mikhail Gorbachev, maintaining aid for anticommunist forces in all areas of regional conflict, signing the historic INF treaty, handing the presidency over to his vice president (the first such succession since Andrew Jackson handed the presidency over to Martin Van Buren), and retiring with the highest approval rating ever for a retiring president. During these last years the conservatives' grumbles intensified, but consider the show that the old President had put on for them.

In January 1981 an old man already finished with one active life entered the White House to begin another. Winston Churchill did not become prime minister until he was sixty-five. Ronald Reagan was four years older when he became president. All that fortified him were a few political principles favoring limited government and opposition to communism. Eight years later he retired a very old man, and much of the world beyond the *Kultursmog* had accepted his principles. Had Ronald Reagan died in 1979 he would have died a political failure, but then Lincoln would have been remembered as a failure too had he died or been defeated for reelection in 1864.[15] For Lincoln, such was the turn of events over the next six months that, by his assassination the following April, Lincoln would be numbered among the great democratic leaders of world history.

A man's time for greatness often arrives unannounced. In youth life stretches out before us as a roadway of endless sunshine and boundless possibilities. Somewhere, however, in early middle age one becomes aware not only that there is the road ahead but that there is also a lengthening road behind. No longer is life merely a neat decade or two of school days and graduations, youthful ceremonies and summertime idylls. Now behind the person of middle years there stretches a corridor of memories. For the great man the corridor is furnished with rich mementos of great events, of the historic acquaintances, of the rogues who almost knocked him off, and of the loves, some more dangerous than the rogues.

When Ronald Reagan strode into the White House he had already passed through a longer corridor of memories than any American president. It might not have been as grandly furnished as that stretching behind Ike at his inauguration, or Washington or Jefferson, but it had its splendid mementos. On its walls hung tapestries and oils from his tenure in Hollywood and six terms as president of the Screen Actors Guild. Those were the days when he actually had to carry a gun for protection against Communist union goons. At one point the mementos become political, a portrait of him delivering his 1964 nationally televised speech for the doomed Barry Goldwater and then many snapshots of him with Republican notables. As the years pass, the notables grow in importance; some are foreign dignitaries. Soon the mementos are all from politics. He is a leading political spokesman for embryonic conservatism. He becomes governor of California. He takes a stand against 1960s radicals and "Big Spenders." He serves on federal commissions. He travels. Stretching along the corridor

behind him as he enters the White House in 1980 are souvenirs from two failed presidential campaigns in 1968 and 1976, but finally there is 1980. As he passes through the next eight years more mementos will be added depicting him with world figures on momentous occasions. Soon each niche will fill with portraits and busts of his great contemporaries. But these contemporaries are dying off. Casey dies. Clare Boothe Luce is gone. In the end he is almost the last of his generation to wield power, but he goes on surrounded at times by lesser men. On into the late 1980s Ronald Reagan proceeded, changing the politics of America. To the critics he remained a boob, and a few dim conservatives concurred.

CHAPTER 12

The Conservative Crack-Up
Conservatism's Solitary Vice

Two years or so after the old president's retirement, I began visiting with him again. His body was finally yielding to age, but beneath the apparent guilelessness the master pol was still at work. One evening he unveiled a new anecdote for Norman Podhoretz, Bob Bartley, *The New York Times*'s A. M. Rosenthal, and me, anterior to delivering an after-dinner speech in the elegant ambiance of *Forbes* magazine's dining room. Noting that the story was perhaps too scabrous for inclusion in his speech, the ex-President tried it out on us. It was a good story about a brutal encounter with Soviet thugs during one of his presidential visits to Moscow. When he finally rose to the rostrum, an hour or so later, his delivery was rocky. At first he relied heavily on a prepared text. Almost a third of the way into his speech, however, he got a second wind; off he soared, rarely reverting to his text, charming his audience, timing his lines exquisitely. As he approached his peroration the eighty-year-old crooner's little team of speechwriters at work somewhere in the back of his mind decided that they had properly tailored his earlier anecdote so that it would not disturb the digestion of his listeners, and out it came. The old master had been experimenting with us, and now he used the story of the Moscow toughs to give his speech a smashing finale.

Obviously he could still wow a crowd, but friends knew that in retirement he was troubled. The American military, armed with weaponry that never would have been developed without his support, was making America, in the words of Conrad Black, writing in the London *Sunday Telegraph*, "more pre-eminent than any single power has been, except for during the brief post-war vacuum created by the crushing of the Axis and the exhaustion of America's principal allies." Nonetheless, Reagan's critics were still at it, splitting the air with shrieks that America was in decline and that Reagan the boob was responsible. Speaking for Europeans, who were then observing America's prowess at work all over the globe, Black noted that the retired President's critics had reality precisely upside down. Reagan had ensured the transcendence of American power; moreover, "American productivity and wealth per capita are 130 percent and 150 percent of German and Japanese levels. The U.S. GNP is twice that of Japan and Germany combined. Ronald Reagan is the leader who brought the United States to this pinnacle as the world's only superpower." In celebration of Reagan's birthday, Black, a distinguished publishing magnate, went on to adjudge Reagan "one of the most important and successful presidents and one of the most formidable political leaders in U.S. history."[1] But back home all Reagan heard was the rumbling from the *Kultursmog*. It got him down.

What had gone wrong? Another European had the answer. "At the end of the day," observed the extremely perceptive Ambrose Evans-Pritchard, "Ronald Reagan's policies are still being judged according to the criteria of his adversaries. He won the hearts but not the minds of America, and it is impossible to consolidate the conservative ascendancy without both."[2]

Conservatives and neoconservatives across the country throughout the 1970s were, indeed, establishing a community of transmittable values, symbols, and principles. They had developed their own journals, think tanks, and student organizations, all ventilating the ideas of conservative protest. In the mid-1980s one Gregg Easterbrook peered down from the *Kultursmog* and in the pages of *The Atlantic* made an amazed observation that accurately testified to the achievements of the conservative counterculture:

As recently as 1950 Lionel Trilling could proclaim, as if it were incontestable, that American conservatives had no ideas, only "irritable mental gestures." Today, though many conservatives remain irritable, ideas they possess in abundance. Conservative thinking has not only claimed the presidency; it has spread throughout our political and intellectual life and stands poised to become the dominant strain in American public policy. While the political ascent of conservatism has taken place in full public view, the intellectual transformation has for the most part occurred behind the scenes, in a network of think tanks whose efforts have been influential to an extent that only now, five years after President Reagan's election, begins to be clear. Conservative think tanks and similar organizations have flourished since the mid-1970s.[3]

Unfortunately, something was wrong. Throughout the 1980s the conservative movement's dream candidate effectively governed America. Conservative values revived, especially the values of entrepreneurship and pride of country. Yet the conservative counterculture faltered, so much so that by the late 1980s its sputterings evoked fears that conservatives could remain forever outside the mainstream of American culture or perhaps even go the way of American history's fringe groups, say the Townsendites. Founded in California by Dr. Francis E. Townsend, the Townsendite movement in the 1930s summoned thousands of elderly Americans to its conception of government, particularly its plan for an old-age revolving pension fund, and then it vanished. At its height it was influential even among New Dealers, some of whom were smitten by the Townsendite gospel. The movement, however, made a few points and abruptly died, whereupon it was quietly interred in the American cemetery for xenomorphic causes. It has remained there ever since with no promise of resurrection.

The conservative movement had a lot more influence with the presidential administration of its time. Yet, as the conservatives' favorite president was preparing for retirement, their movement was breaking down into a poorly organized congeries of believers, some of whom felt their moment in history had come and gone. Others still held out for one more reform to perfect the Reagan revolution. There were senior conservatives who were willing and happy to bask in their glory. Others were irritable, suspicious of George Bush, withal angered by the state of the nation. Comparing them with the Naderites, who survived the 1980s with their gripes institutionalized into "public interest" mafias haunting all corners of American life, one might well wonder which is going to have a deeper influence on the Republic, the members of the postwar conservative movement or the followers of misogelastic Ralph—that human handkerchief whose sole mission on earth has been to collect all manner of bacterium, virus, and every other sort of human complaint that might assist him in shutting down the free society. The Reagan Administration bequeathed to Americans a renewed enthusiasm for limited government and entrepreneurship, but it left few institutions behind to sustain that enthusiasm. Ralph embedded Naderism's carping litigiousness into American society with his "public interest" pests everywhere. Could Ralph's influence outdistance Ron's?

To mark precisely when the conservative movement began to lose definition and purpose is an unpleasant task for me. I have settled on the Bork hearings as a watershed. Perhaps cold-eyed historians will disagree, but certainly some time in the late 1980s the movement's rigor and resolve began to dissipate. As a political movement it had grown heavy with fundraisers working scams and with many of the movement's leaders ensconced in plush Washington offices far from the grass roots—two points astutely made towards the end of the Reagan Administration by the conservative activist Amy Moritz in *Policy Review*.[4]

Sometime in the mid-1980s the conservatives developed another unexpected problem, philosophical illiteracy or semi-illiteracy. Few of those who came to Washington to participate in the great days of Reaganism were very well versed in conservatism. Truth be known, many turned out to be wholly ignorant of the ideas and the writings of the movement's founders. Luigi Barzini used to complain that because all British gentlemen adhered to "six ideas," the most salient of which was forbearance, it took an excruciatingly long time to decide whether the Brit sitting before him was intelligent or a dullard. By the mid-1980s I was frequently having similar experiences with young conservatives. Most were college educated, which meant that they had acquired a set of manners that—*à la* an English gentleman—allowed them to pass for being intelligent. Yet many were not.

Throughout the 1980s a steady parade of dolts arrived in Washington vacantly intoning the principal beliefs of conservatism while taking positions in government or in the growing profusion of fly-by-night organizations that *soi-disant* conservatives were accumulating along the Potomac. By the time the dolts were found out, they had acquired too much clout to be dismissed. Where once a Frank Meyer or a John Ashbrook might have stood, there now stood Kevin Phillips or, worse still, Howard Phillips, people without a clue as to the purpose or substance of conservatism. In *The New Season: A Spectator's Guide to the 1988 Election*, George Will postulates that conservatism became intellectually fashionable—hence on came the charlatans and simple dopes, all mouthing the conservative canon so dulcetly and confidently but with no more understanding than a parrot intoning the United States Bill of Rights in Japanese. Eventually we came to know them generically as the Stupid Conservatives, and they were an impediment to establishing a cultural alternative to the Liberals.

Yet if George is right that conservatism became fashionable, how do we explain the *Kultursmog*'s sudden hostility to conservatives? It is a demonstrable fact that by the mid-1980s those conservatives who had formerly been invited as occasional guests on network television and in the forums under Liberal control were being quietly suppressed. Moreover, among the intelligentsia the migration of Liberals to neoconservatism slowed dramatically, the only notable migrants being the journalist Lally Weymouth and a handful of disaffected 1960s radicals led by former *Ramparts* editors David Horowitz and Peter Collier.

To grow as a political movement, the conservatives needed fresh recruits who knew something about the conservative point of view and about politics. Instead they got Betsy Bloomingdale and Lillian Hellman's fan Mike Deaver in the White House. Then among the rank and file they got recruits who were either not all that fresh, as in the case of supply-siders, or fundamentalist Christians, who had little in common with the more political members of the conservative movement. While conservatism was spreading among ordinary Americans, sophisticates were turning their hearts against it.

Even George Will drew back, staking out a prickly conservatism guaranteed to protect him from the embarrassment of having allies to defend or obligations to principles that might prove inconvenient. He flayed supply-side economics, endorsed tax increases, took an almost sensual pleasure in mocking the conservatives' scruples against big government, and proffered bouquets to select Liberals while falling on almost any conservative in trouble. Towards the end of the first Reagan Administration he even wrote me to protest being referred to in *The American Spectator*'s advertisements as a contributor:

Dear Bob:

Considering that it has been something like a decade since I have written for the *American Spectator*, and it may be that long before I do so again, I think it would be in the interest of honest advertising for you not to include my name in your advertisements as someone your subscribers are apt to read.

Sincerely,
George

I responded with my usual good will, reminding him of a splendid piece of his that we had published not *ten* years before but *two*. And I expressed the hope that he would appear in our pages again soon. If George was right that conservatism was in fashion he, nonetheless, was taking no chances. Aside from accumulating Stupid Conservatives, con artists, and ingrates, what the hell was going on?

Throughout the 1980s the country was indeed politically conservative. Yet just above the heads of the electorate there brooded the gloomy, befouling vapors of *Kultursmog*. It affected the intelligentsia as injuriously as the sedimentary air of Mexico City affects life in that great metropolis. For a decade it remained gray and cheerless. Down below, the capitalist engines were kept shiny and efficient. The generals and admirals placed their orders for fresh troops and new, improved weaponry. In the White House and in the federal judiciary Reaganites pressed back the outstretched arms of the Nanny State. From Washington, the American foreign policy became forceful again. But overhead the clouds were grim and portentous. Doubtless George sensed danger to his person much the same way that the neoliberals sensed danger to theirs. He abandoned himself to abusing George Bush in personal terms, calling the next president a has-been, a liar, and a lapdog. That cut him off from the White House, where he could have offered some sound counsel.

A bizarre artificiality came to characterize the political commentary of the late 1980s, for which the neoliberals can claim a large responsibility. Nothing they said was ever quite accurate. They were diligent deponents of the slightly true but mainly false. Thus political commentary resounded with hackneyed falsehoods: Bush, the dirty campaigner; the Soviet Union, a casualty of its "internal contradictions"; America, abundant with racism. As for the neoliberals' philosophical development, it remained pathetically retarded. Having moved away from New Age Liberalism, they remained far short of any comprehensible conservatism or of any other semblance of systematic thought. By 1984 their political metamorphosis ceased completely. Soon the whole neoliberal movement put one in mind of nothing so much as a commune of transsexuals who, halfway through their surgical refurbishment, had a change of heart, but too late. And so they huddled there together, neither male nor female—a little sad, and a little absurd. However, their free-floating malice and their lack of principle offered them some compensations. They had become confirmed nihilists, and nihilism is very alluring to American sophisticates.

This I learned from personal experience. When in the late 1970s I wrote *Public Nuisances*, blithely abominating national figures on all sides, the most unexpected people became my fans. I was treasured for walloping Nixonians and Kennedyites alike. My left-of-center fans openly admired a writer who, it seemed to them, believed in nothing and belittled everything. Unfortunately, I did not deserve their high regard, and five years later, when *The Liberal Crack-Up* revealed traces of conscience, some of my old fans felt betrayed. Well, what can I tell you? I have never been a moral idiot.

Among the 1980s' conforming Liberals there ruled a sameness that grew slightly weird as the sameness of a personal-growth cult grows slightly weird. Woe to the daring soul who might carelessly utter an unconventional idea in 1986. There you are, sitting among victims of the *smog* at, say, a meeting of the local Chicken Pox Support Group, and suddenly, in an impish moment, you speak your mind: "Frankly chums, by my lights, Tulsa beats the socks off Paris for night life any time of year"; or, "If you think blacks have it tough in America or that our wetlands are in bad shape, try being an Ibo in the wetlands of Nigeria, or for that matter in the drylands"; or "At least Reagan has been good for the economy and East–West relations."

Slip-ups like that could lead to immediate excommunication, which as the 1980s lengthened, few Liberals would hazard. Seven years into the Age of Reagan, Victor Gold, the fiercely independent conservative writer, had it right when he wrote: ". . . the leading social indicators—education, the arts, the media— . . . remain preponderantly liberal, purveying a cultural *Zeitgeist* that brings even a conservative President to pay obeisance to liberal sacred cows and shibboleths"[5] and then Gold directed his readers' to the appalling spectacle of President Reagan standing on the south lawn of the White House hand in hand with fellow Americans who at that instant were under the pleasant delusion that they formed a transcontinental chain of Americans the better to . . . to what? What the hell *did* President Reagan think was being accomplished with this puerile demonstration? The hand-holders believed that they were being somehow instrumental in alleviating African hunger, but surely Ronald Reagan saw reality more clearly, did he not? The mysteries and rituals that the *Kultursmog* was bringing down on us had come a long way from the days when New Dealers merely spoke of jobs, adequate wages, and collective bargaining. The *Kultursmog* brooding above was always a menace capable of tainting the judgments of ordinary Americans down below. Even Ronald Reagan was in danger.

To understand the conservatives' predicament during the Reagan years one must accept two premises: (a) so politicized had American culture become that it was no longer the open-minded culture of an effervescing republic but rather something repressive and grim—call it *Kultursmog*; and (b) the conservatives could not influence it, escape it, or establish a competitive culture of their own. By the 1980s American culture was being dispensed by an oligarchy that held forth in a *smog* of bias and pusillanimous conformity, utterly resistant to fresh air.

Back in the 1930s, when the New Deal arrived in Washington, there was no *Kultursmog*. There was only culture. It was broad and diverse, and it was relatively hospitable to new currents of thought. Historians tell us that the New Deal went through phases during which different governmental approaches were emphasized. They compute two and sometimes three New Deals. Whatever the correct figure, essentially the New Dealer was a progressive of a collectivist or of a social-engineering cast of mind. Frequently the New Dealer was a cosmopolitan inclined towards high culture. Not surprisingly, then, by the mid-1930s the arts, the universities, and the media were beginning to reflect the themes of the Roosevelt Administration.

During the Reagan Administration no such cross-pollination of political ideas from the White House into the culture took place. The conservative movement that brought Ronald Reagan to the White House was a political movement. As with the New Deal, however, it had cultural and intellectual values that could have found their way into America's dominant culture. From philosophy to economics to political science, even to journalism, American conservatism had developed a particular point of view. Its sophisticates had a perfectly sensible perspective towards the arts, as can be seen in back issues of *The New Criterion* and other journals. Nevertheless, even at the end of the Reagan Revolution the only signs of Reaganism in the arts, the universities, and the media were grotesque caricatures, burning effigies, whoops of derision, and wails of alarm.

In a very significant way the conservatives had failed. They had neither expanded their own political culture to rival the *Kultursmog* nor had they breathed any of their ideas and values into it, unless the crude 1980s materialism of the Yuppies can be palmed off as American conservatism. The Liberal Crack-Up was caused by acts of extravagance; the Conservative Crack-Up was brought on by acts of omission. Even as the Liberal was brought down by too much imagination, the conservative was laid low by too little. In explicating the *Liberal Crack-Up* it was not difficult for me to demonstrate the Liberals' excesses. Quoting them did the trick. Furthermore, all their extravagances were duly confirmed in the public record sedulously maintained by the great dailies of the Republic. Proving the folly inherent in acts of omission, however, is a more precarious project. The great dailies cannot contain reports of deeds not done. What is needed is proof that had the conservatives taken action or acted more imaginatively they would have been effective. Unfortunately, no such copper-bottom proof can ever be adduced in criticizing omissions. All that I can summon to bolster my point is common sense and Clio. Luckily, the history of our great Republic is abundant with instructive instances of presidential regimes influencing American culture and profiting handsomely thereby.

With the election of Franklin Roosevelt, the nascent New Dealers marched forth from their political subculture, from *The New Republic*, *The Nation*, various universities, and Wall Street. They entered the government, of course, but they also seeped into the culture. For instance, the playwright Robert E. Sherwood brought broad New Deal themes to the stage with such plays as *The Petrified Forest* (1934), *Idiot's Delight* (1936), and *There Shall Be No Night* (1940). Sherwood won a Pulitzer Prize for his 1936 play, and he was not the only artist to excel with themes redolent of New Deal enthusiasms. The poet Archibald MacLeish grew steadily as a cultural figure in the 1930s, winning a Pulitzer Prize for his narrative poem *Conquistador*. Composers such as Aaron Copland and Virgil Thomson gained stature and frequently composed music reflecting popular themes of New Deal lore.* Finally, just to ensure a fresh crop of MacLeishes, Sherwoods, Coplands, and Thomsons in the years ahead, Harry Hopkins thought up the WPA's Federal Arts Project, its Federal Theater Project, and its Federal Writers Project—all for bankrolling the creators of culture during hard times.

Throughout the Roosevelt years creators of culture, such as Sherwood and MacLeish, crossed into politics and government with a frequency impossible even to imagine during the Reagan years. The art world of the 1980s would not allow it; the Reaganites would not attempt it. The playwright Sherwood not only wrote plays but also some of FDR's most effective speeches. He further served as a special assistant to the Secretary of the Navy. Over objections that MacLeish was not a trained librarian, the poet was made Librarian of Congress. From 1944 to 1945 he served as Assistant Secretary of State, though he was not a diplomat. Three years after the death of Roosevelt, Sherwood won another Pulitzer Prize for his efforts in

---

*Thomson actually composed music for documentary films celebrating New Deal projects: *The River* and *The Plough that Broke the Plains*.

hagiography, *Roosevelt and Hopkins: An Intimate History*. It is a finely written tale of the relationship between two instinctive Machiavels, as all students of the New Deal have discovered, and some of it is even true. No such migrations occurred during the Reagan years, despite the abundance of writers and thinkers in the Reagan Administration.

My point is not that the New Deal's penetration of American culture was conspiratorial. No secret agents were necessary. There was an aristocratic ethos to the New Deal beguiling to the culturati, and the New Dealers recognized the usefulness of beguiled culturati. Two decades later another Democratic Administration had a similar synergy with American culture. In 1960 the aristocratic ethos of the New Frontier caught the culturati's eye. Very astutely, the Kennedys hailed Harvard, and Harvard responded. Down to the Potomac trundled the historian Arthur Schlesinger, Jr., eager to procure patriotic composers, writers, scholars and other public servants. The culturati responded gratefully to the presidential summons. Over fifty writers, painters, and composers were invited to the inauguration. "What a joy," exulted John Steinbeck, "that literacy is no longer *prima facie* evidence of treason." Archibald MacLeish conveyed his appreciation to President Kennedy upon hearing his inaugural address on an "uncertain short-wave set" whilst holed up with fellow exiles of conscience in that Caribbean hellhole, St. Lucia: "It left me proud and hopeful to be an American—something I have not felt for almost twenty years. I owe you and send you my deepest gratitude." (The culturati *do* get lathered up, don't they?)

Soon Pablo Casals was performing in the White House and Hollywood was transforming the Kennedy legend into art. * At the home of Attorney General Robert Kennedy, the Kennedys held egghead soirees, which came to be known as the Hickory Hill Seminars. Such luminaries as the philosopher A. J. Ayer and the historian David Donald would be invited in to discuss their specialties with high-ranking New Frontiersmen and their spouses. In an inspired move the Administration pilfered Professor John Kenneth Galbraith from the Harvard Department of Economics to be ambassador to India. Presumably Professor Galbraith would not mind being

---

*All these facts are drawn from Arthur Schlesinger's mellow *A Thousand Days* (pp. 729–732), where the reader will also find this curious sentence: "Perhaps only a President who was at the same time seen as a war hero, a Roman Catholic, a tough politician and a *film star* [emphasis added] could have infected the nation with so gay and disturbing a spirit" (p. 729). But JFK was not a film star, and when a film star did become president his Hollywood background was inveterately jeered at by Arthur and his ilk.

posted in that dusty land of haggard poor and serene bureaucrats. The highly regulated and grimly impoverished economy of India seemed to be precisely what Galbraith had in mind for America. New Frontier speechwriter Richard Goodwin forsook rhetoric to become a policymaker in the State Department. Doubtless there were other examples of the culturati moving into policy-making and back into culture.

Unfortunately, the experience of two successful presidencies in the realm of cultural politics taught the Republicans nothing at all. In the Reagan years even such competent and urbane presidential speechwriters as Josh Gilder were kept locked up in the writers' pen. No conservative literary figure was invited to any position whatsoever in government, not Tom Wolfe nor Walker Percy nor even the popular novelist Tom Clancy. In fact, not even William F. Buckley, Jr., played much of a role in the Reagan Administration. While his good friend was president, Buckley's political stature and influence actually diminished. Even Richard Nixon, though less ideological, had a better record for bringing in the literary types, and he made Buckley one of his delegates to the United Nations.

This is not to say that the Reagan Administration was anti-intellectual. It probably brought more intellectuals aboard than the Kennedy Administration, but for the most part these were not the kind of intellectuals who have much of an interest in affecting culture. Most of the Reagan Administration intellectuals were neither literary nor artistic. They were narrow. They were conservative policy intellectuals, people who bring high intellect to bear on one or two areas of policy, after which the mind wanders. Beyond say, Strategic Defense or Marginal Tax Rates, a policy intellectual's interests might well be indistinguishable from those of a shoe salesman. And occasionally the shoe salesman has a more subtle mind. The New Deal might have had a few policy intellectuals around—Wilbur Cohen and M. L. Wilson come to mind—but most New Dealers had broader interests and a grander conception of politics than the typical policy intellectual of the Reagan era. They knew that policy is but one course in the buffet of a political culture. FDR's Tugwells, Hopkinses and Ickeses were, by comparison with most of Reagan's policy intellectuals, Renaissance men—albeit with a Tammanyite touch.

They affixed themselves to politics and to culture and revised both where they could. They understood that politics is more than a set of policies. In democracy it is the promotion of a culture, a web of principles, sympathies, manners, all the fruits of intellect. In the hands of New Dealers, politics was also a cast of heroes and villains. The New Deal's heroes were humanitarians. They were public-spirited and patriotic. They were Good Samaritans with brains. The villains were Republicans, middle-class yokels, enemies of progress. The heroes included intellectuals of boldness, reason, iconoclasm. The heroes had broad sympathies. They were in favor of everything. All they opposed were their villains, which is to say anyone critical of them.

The comedian Lenny Bruce's remark on Liberals applies, of course, to New Dealers: The Liberals can understand everything but people who don't understand them. That may not make them good dinner companions, but it makes them ferocious political adversaries. The New Dealer was an instinctive reformer, confident and avid to bring his therapies to every facet of American life. He was a political prodigy and three decades later the New Frontiersman was his rightful heir. The Reaganites could have learned much from both on how to build a political culture.

It has now been several decades since the New Deal Liberals put the finishing touches on their mythic history of themselves. Every schoolchild is familiar with it: Liberalism is for progress, freedom, defense of the little guy; conservatism is for the opposite. Liberal heroes are well known: Upton Sinclair, Clarence Darrow, Dr. Albert Schweitzer, Albert Einstein, all Kennedys, some Roosevelts, Jesus Christ, Mahatma Gandhi, Ludwig van Beethoven—in fact, practically all the great thinkers and artists from world history have been to some degree a part of the Liberal mythology. The conservatives are Robber Barons, racists, squirrelly military officers, Senator Joseph McCarthy, drunk drivers, cigarette smokers, all the stoopnagels of the West and all criminals not of the Robin Hood variety. Conservatism throughout the prosperous and humane 1980s would make no revision in the Liberal legends.

There is something about the mind or perhaps the glandular structure of the American Liberal that makes him fervently political and *engagé* on behalf of practically every belief, every ghost, and every goblin of the Liberal political culture. The American conservative by comparison is always politically less energetic. He really does not much care about the Liberal mythology or about setting up his own myths. If he is politically active he is almost always active over a narrower range of issues than his Liberal equivalent. Moreover, he is almost always a bit mystified as to what purpose is served by myth-makers or, for that matter, by any bearer of culture. This is unfortunate.

Modern politics is, as mentioned before, increasingly a battle over ideas, and it takes intellectuals of broad intellectual background to champion political ideas. Policy intellectuals are not sufficient. In the 1980s the American people made it clear what they wanted—to wit, peace and prosperity, plus some personal security in their communities. Reagan had the ideas to satisfy the yearnings of modern politics but not enough broadly-based intellectuals to advance his political culture. Not that the conservative movement and the neoconservative movement lacked the necessary intellectuals, but a stone-headed element in the conservative movement and among the Country Club Republicans never understood the value of these minds. Elliott Abrams, William Bennett, John Lehman, Richard Perle, Martin Anderson, Bill Casey, and Jeane Kirkpatrick, and scores of others advanced a wide range of conservative ideas within the Reagan Administration. They did not content themselves with but one or two policies. They advanced conservative culture. Unfortunately, a critical mass of conservatives and Republicans remained benighted as to the value of such minds.

Kirkpatrick's work in *Commentary*, particularly her essay "Dictatorships and Double Standards,"[6] attracted Ronald Reagan's eye. He hired her, and with her came a notably successful policy that quieted the carping from the Third World and inspired a policy to resist Marxism-Leninism. Yet *Commentary* was never again resorted to as a valuable asset for the Republicans. Never again was it cited by the President or sought out for its ideas or for intellects that might be useful to the Administration. The Republican Machiavels had no particular interest in it, despite its proven value as an arsenal of ideas and a training ground for intellectuals potent in the execution of modern politics. After eight years of Reaganism, *Commentary* was no more a part of American intellectual life than when the Administration began; possibly its influence had diminished.

Certainly it is true that in the 1980s the *Kultursmog* sealed itself off from the conservative movement, but many members of the movement exhibited neither the energy nor the resourcefulness to penetrate the *smog* or to create an alternative culture. As for the conservative policy intellectuals, in modern democratic politics one has to represent more than just one policy or one interest to be an enduring political force. One has to promote a political culture.

Basically the explanation for the conservatives' failure at cultural politics is to be found in the conservative temperament, in the kind of people who become conservative political activists, in their usual habitat in American society (business), and in the wellspring of their financial and cultural support (again the business community). I shall discuss all these matters in the next chapter, but let me emphasize my belief that most of the conservatives' failures begin with their temperament.

In a 1964 essay, "Notes Towards an Empirical Definition of Conservatism," William F. Buckley, Jr., writes: "I have . . . sometimes wondered whether I am myself a true conservative. I feel I qualify spiritually and philosophically; but temperamentally I am not of the breed, and so I need to ask myself, among so many other things, how much it matters how one is temperamentally."[7] Well, Bill, as you must know, temperament is to politics what gin is to a martini. It matters. The true American conservative does not have Bill Buckley's temperament, and that is why few conservatives have been as effective as Bill in public life.

The true conservative is private, whether he is an American or a European. As the British political philosopher Michael Oakeshott asseverates, conservatives "prefer the familiar to the unknown . . . the actual to the possible. . . ."[8] They trust in conventions. They prefer the private and personal to the public. Their interest is in family, in private pursuits, in community. Bill Buckley has lived his entire life onstage, beginning at the age of six when he addressed a peremptory missive to the King of England demanding that the British Empire repay its World War I debt to us. Most conservatives are not like him. They may be roused to public deeds by some policy deemed necessary for their way of life or, in time of national danger, by their innate patriotism. Otherwise they stay close by the hearth.

Returning to England after his disillusioning adventure with the left in the Spanish Civil War, George Orwell betrays the powerful pull of the conservative temperament even on him. In a poetic reverie towards the end of *Homage to Catalonia*, the flinty Orwell reveals the conservative temperament's comforts and its dangers. With the perfidies of Republican Spain behind him and staid London coming into view, Orwell writes of "the huge peaceful wilderness of outer London, the barges on the miry river, the familiar streets, the posters telling of cricket matches and Royal weddings, the men in bowler hats, the pigeons in Trafalgar Square, the red buses, the blue policemen—all sleeping the deep, deep sleep of England, from which I sometimes fear that we shall never wake till we are jerked out of it by the roar of bombs."[9] Those red buses and blue policemen; over here, our skyscrapers and amber waves of grain—these unchanging, reassuring moorings of a pleasant, psychologically satisfying life; they restrain the conservative from hamming it up pursuant to some vast and disastrous abstraction *à la* the Liberal. The grand reformist politics of recent decades are not much to the conservative's liking. When such politics conduce to the atrocities of Pol Pot or the absurdities of the politically correct college campus, the conservative's hands are clean. The danger is that the conservative never will leap to political action or, when he does, his leap is amateurish and mediocre and late.

CHAPTER 13

The Crack-Up Continues
The Conservative Counterculture
Against the Odds and Oddities

WHEN WE ENDEAVOR TO explain the behavior of people in groups we perforce resort to generalizations, even at the risk of being set upon by nitpickers. We say the Frenchwoman's natural sense of style makes Paris the fashion center that it is; and up pops some obstructionist pointing to Mlle. de la Motte as she clumps down the Champs Elysées in galoshes, her lovely head swaddled in a babushka. Or some other insufferable ass makes a rather big thing of the fact that the lady across the room at the Café du Dome is cleaning her teeth with a toothpick *après déjeuner* (and the teeth are no longer in her mouth but on the plate in front of her!). Nonetheless, generalizations are necessary.

Social science has proved, at least to the satisfaction of social scientists, that human conduct and, indeed, even whole civilizations can be reduced to data derived from a series of experiments performed on laboratory animals—usually rats. But even the social scientist can only speak in generalizations when he elucidates the failures and triumphs of humans in groups. Thus as I endeavor to explain why it is that conservatives failed to create a potent political culture sufficient to the needs of the 1980s, I shall tender generalizations; let the chips fall where they may.

Generally speaking, the Achilles heel of the conservative has been his temperament. As mentioned a few paragraphs back, conservatives are too much given to the private, the familiar, conventions unexamined and unchallenged. They are only slowly roused to public life. It is not that

212

they are selfish. No data of which I am aware suggest that conservatives are less generous with their time or treasure than Liberals. The American Enterprise Institute's useful old quarterly *Public Opinion* polled Americans throughout the 1970s, finding a broad commonality among them despite the fact that some claimed to be Liberal and others conservative. However, when one analyzes conservative and Liberal leaders, one notes a stark difference. Liberals relish the public life and long for public controversy; not many conservatives do. They tend to keep to themselves and eschew controversy. Robert Novak, who by the 1990s had become the preeminent sage of conservative journalists, reviewing his three decades on the Washington scene, laments the conservatives' indifference to "collegiality." It is foreign to their temperament.

It is my thesis, arrived at after careful study and unanticipated grief, that conservatives are usually temperamentally ill-suited for political life. Their moment in history caught them unprepared. Some did indeed have the temperament to go public, for instance, William F. Buckley, Jr., but not many. The typical conservatives yearn for home and hearth. Problems beyond their narrow line of vision trouble them not. They derive deep satisfaction from the familiar unchanging fixtures of their country; Orwell's red buses and blue policemen; America's stars and stripes fluttering everywhere, its Gilbert Stuart portraits of George Washington in every school. Of course, the catalogue of America's unchanging fixtures is smaller than Britain's, for in America the reformers' zeal is less restrained by a long and cumbrous past. Here reformers are freer to stir up settled ways; and there are gangs of capitalists to aid and abet the tumult. But those familiar fixtures that do endure on the American landscape are important to the citizenry, particularly to the conservative citizenry. They reassure the conservatives' uneasy minds. They conspire to induce the sleep that so alarmed Orwell as the foundries of the Ruhr fired up to produce Hitler's weaponry.

Conservatives want to be left alone. They enjoy their sleep. I suspect that the American Liberals would never have met quite so relentless a conservative challenge in the 1970s or languished so pathetically in the 1980s had they been more restrained with their reforms. For twenty years, however, and with growing wantonness, they injected their rude beliefs into ever more areas where conservatives had assumed things were settled: family relations, school curriculums, community relations, commerce. Neighborhoods were tampered with, parents' relations with their children were revised, porn was legalized, throw-away bottles were proscribed. Intrusive reforms were imposed from above in ways that alarmed the conservative mind.

When reformers changed the mailboxes from the old olive drab to irenic blue they were playing with fire. Doubtless they had their high-flown reasons for exchanging the red of our fire trucks for chartreuse or whatever color it is that they deemed an improvement in the 1970s. Unfortunately for the Old Order this meddlesomeness roused the slumbering conservatives to Civic Action. Most of these Liberal reforms were as irrelevant to human progress as was the bustle to women's suffrage, but the imposition of so many of them so suddenly made conservatives sufficiently restive to enter politics . . . at least temporarily. Few of the aroused conservatives were true Machiavels or even fluent baby kissers; but the Liberals had passed beyond the boundary line of the tolerable, often with nostrums that were palpably idiotic. When the gods sent down a political maestro, Ronald W. Reagan, the game was up. He had been fully trained in the Liberal political praxis; and, of equal importance, he had developed a near total immunity to the Liberals' numerous inanities and false pieties.

Of all the conservative organizations, one of the oldest is the National Rifle Association. Its longevity demonstrates my case that conservatives have to be provoked to politics, otherwise their temperamental disposition keeps them at home and off the soapbox. For over a century the NRA has held together against those reformers who threaten their right to keep and bear arms. NRA members are mossbacks of the most obstinate variety, but politically they have long been more than a match for reformers. They represent the epitome of the conservative temperament. The vast majority are law-abiding citizens who have grown up with a gun over the fireplace or slung from a rack on the family pickup. The gun is emblematic of their sense of America, of the frontier, of the individualistic ethos of their country, of home. The gun is to a member of the NRA what a pint of Guinness is to an Irishman or olive oil to a Roman. The satisfactions experienced by Orwell's Englishman when he sights those red buses and blue policemen are the same as the satisfactions experienced by an NRA member when he spots the gunrack of an armed pickup truck. I learned all this from personal experience, and guns are as unappealing to me as chatty waiters or the Mormon missionary who knocks on the door at 8:00 A.M.

On April 2, 1981, I was scheduled to speak at the national headquarters of the NRA. As the fates would have it, some crazed moviegoer had shot the President three days earlier. Well, a gentleman keeps his word, and I decided to go ahead with my lecture. After all, the President was on the mend and heaving off some pretty amusing jokes. At the appointed hour I arrived serenely at the main entrance of the NRA's Washington headquarters to find that the President's shooting was being used by demonstrators as a pretext for renewing their timeless call for a ban on the private ownership of guns. By the same reasoning they might have called for a ban on Hollywood movies (to which I, for one, would have given full support). These were the kind of protesters who from the 1960s on have lived from one cause to the next, all vaguely left-wing and exigent. The day before they could easily have been protesting the sale of infant formula at the American headquarters of Nestle S.A. The next day they might have scheduled a demonstration against the tobacco industry or the bourbon barons or a new athlete's foot ointment now out of synch with some esoteric immensity of progressive thought. Today it was the gun that had to go— though not because the demonstrators had any especial affection for Ronald Reagan. So here they were, posters bobbing in the air, mouths wide open like the vast and darkened entrance of a cave; yet no bats or winged serpents flew out, only idiot slogans. Into the building I scudded, intent on avoiding all physical contact with these bilious cranks.

Within the citadel I discovered that the members of the NRA were not weirdos fixated in the Freudian mode on gunbarrels and phallic shotgun cartridges. Rather they were upright citizens, deeply attached to their community, their country, its history, and to all the rights and rituals of the Constitution—the foremost of which to them was the "right to keep and bear arms." They were not monomaniacs. Many were history buffs, given to learned eruptions on such topics as Frederick Jackson Turner's "frontier hypothesis" with its cogent explanation of American resourcefulness, ingenuity, and individualism. (This particularly pleased me, for I, too, admire Turner's work for its explication of the unique spark in American character.) They had political philosophies and an elaborate set of ideas relating to American self-reliance and opposition to tyranny. I lectured on current politics, and discovered during subsequent questioning that the audience was composed of intelligent persons drawn from many different walks of life, even academe. Their politics inclined towards the libertarian, but with a jolt of patriotism steeped in backwoods and Great Plains lore. In brief, these were effective conservatives aroused by a threat to the way they lived back home. However, were the reformers to lie low for a while with their anti-gun campaigns, I suspect that even the NRA would not endure. Yet for some reason, gun ownership irks reforming Liberals, and so the NRA will remain robust. Had the Liberals not come a cropper in the 1970s and had they remained potent in the 1980s the conservatives would still be on their toes, and talk of a Conservative Crack-Up would be most unnecessary.

A fine example of the conservative temperament, its assets and short-comings, is the founder and keeper of the conservatives' foremost publishing house, Henry Regnery. Scion of an eminent old conservative family from Chicago, Henry has always been exceptionally civilized, decent, well-educated, and well-heeled—which was fortunate, for no conservative publishing house has ever remained alive without regular infusions of outside cash. Henry had the cash, and in the 1950s and 1960s he spent a bundle publishing the seminal works of the conservative movement. But Henry has been a very private man. In keeping with his cultivation, he is a cellist; in keeping with his temperament, he has played mostly in private. It would be as unthinkable for Henry to perform in the way Bill Buckley performed with the Phoenix Symphony as it would be for him to go to his office riding a unicycle.

For decades Henry has maintained a modest country retreat near the Indiana-Michigan border at the foot of Lake Michigan. There his writers have been welcome to sit by the cozy fireplace or under the fruit trees in the orchard and discuss ideas of large public import. Such a coterie of writers, were they not so conservative, would surely have come to Washington when a practitioner of their ideas became president—but not Henry's friends. In their books Henry and his scholarly associates developed many of the ideas that Ronald Reagan was about to bring to power, but they did not join him in Washington. This was pretty much by choice. Men like Regnery have public concerns but, unlike Liberals, they do not yearn for public life.

In the 1960s it was fashionable to claim that the conservatives were "extremists" or even "radical." Some undoubtedly were, for instance those who would politicize the Supreme Court or castrate it because of a season of unwelcome judgments; or those who wanted to bring down the Central Intelligence Agency because they thought it insufficiently hostile towards Communism. But the conservatives have for over a decade now had control of the federal government with all its concomitant police powers, and it grows daily more obvious that their true weakness is neither extremism nor radicalism but a disrelish for the sempiternal exhibitionism of politics. The ordinary conservative would rather stay home in Chicago, Illinois, or Intercourse, Pennsylvania (zip code 17534 for the curious), or wherever his roots might be. He wants to be left alone, and this temperamental trait encourages a second impediment against the practice of politics. The conservative inclines towards parochialism.

The conservative's inclination is to acquire worldly possessions and then to purr. By contrast, the ordinary New Age Liberal is given to yelling, to organizing ad hoc committees, to joining in protests! He is political, out-going, and *outraged*. His life is an ongoing complaint against reality. When his temperature is at 98.6 he demands reform. As his temperature rises he shouts for revolution, thence for Utopia. The conservative has com-plaints, too, but it is difficult for him to sustain them—at least in public. He finds reality bearable, at times even enjoyable. Only rarely is he brought to political fermentation. Usually he keeps to himself; he has little stomach for that one act so crucial to political action, to wit: reaching out.

The fate of the religious right in the 1990s exemplifies this deficiency. Liberalism's encroachments into areas that religiously-minded Americans had theretofore considered settled roused them to political action. Hopeful conservatives and apprehensive Liberals alike assumed that the rising re-ligious right would be another building block in the conservative coalition. By the late 1980s, however, the major organizations of the religious right were dissolving as their leaders returned to their local communities. The religious right had not reached out to other conservative groups. Then the conservative temperament took hold and these newly-aroused conservatives went home. Even the most effective group in the religious right, the Moral Majority, was unable to reach out and integrate with the national con-servative movement. Hence it withered.

Occasionally in the 1980s I did some television with the Moral Majority's Archbishop, the Rev. Jerry Falwell. He was a gifted TV performer. On Ted Koppel's "Nightline," sometime in the 1980s, Falwell faced the Rev. Jesse Jackson in a widely ballyhooed nationwide debate. Falwell was sen-sational, quick, charming, a powerful room fan against the Rev. Jackson's infantile vaporings. That night, had one been asked to predict which of the two television performers might last longest in public life, the sensible observer would have picked Falwell and envisaged him living out his years as a Rev. Billy Graham, a national symbol, but with political significance. One could imagine the cheap hustler, Jackson, abruptly slipping into oblivion, vanquished by some scandal, perhaps financial, or possibly the consequence of one of his forays into ethnic-baiting.

After all, Falwell's allies were then at the highest level of American government. Even the President admired him. And Falwell had a good sense of politics; when all the smart money was betting against Vice Pres-ident George Bush's succeeding to the presidency, Falwell had the acuity to cast his lot with Bush. Yet by the decade's end, Falwell was in political retirement in Lynchburg, Virginia, and his adversary from that far-off nocturnal debate was the frontrunner for the 1992 Democratic presidential nomination. The political game had burned the Rev. Falwell badly. His supporters at the local level were deserting him for local causes. The Rev. Jackson never had the resources that were available to Falwell, but he loved the game of politics. In fact, it was his favorite game. That is the difference between an American of the left and an American of the right: one is devoted to politics; one is not.

The conservatives' parochialism and attendant ineptitude at coalition-building tripped them up during the Reagan years. Adam Meyerson, the coolly thoughtful editor of the Heritage Foundation's quarterly, *Policy Review*, has reviewed the conservatives' performance during the 1980s and concluded that on narrow issues they were bulldogs, for instance, in pursuing the defense buildup, tax cuts, and badgering for an anticommunist Central American policy. His point is well taken; against ceaseless drizzle from the *Kultursmog* the conservatives endured, but only on isolated issues. They could not advance the whole range of issues representative of a fertile political culture. The conservatives failed to forge a commonality of interests among the single-issue groups they embraced, and thus what political culture they had established in the 1970s remained in suspended animation. Parochialism inhibited them from reaching out to others and building coalitions.

For over two decades I have been a member of the conservative movement—by choice! In rewinding the tapes of memory and reviewing the film, I see hundreds of perplexing incidents in which individual conservatives botched some elementary political task, a Philadelphia Society meeting at which some nebbish is allowed to harangue neoconservatism, a neoconservative enclave in which some popinjay is allowed to patronize libertarians, a Young Americans for Freedom convention that blows up as some libertarian fanatic salutes the New Left, the emergence of a prodigy unwilling to cooperate with anyone and convinced that he has talents exalting him over all others, in the Reagan and Bush years a government commission blundering along unassisted by either philosophical rigor or savoir-faire. Studious analysis suggests that the conservatives' problems as a rule are the natural consequence of parochialism, a parochialism foreordained by temperament.

Conservatives are going to have to confront these weaknesses if they are to endure. When roused to political life the typical conservative arrives with a panacea—occasionally two panaceas—for the Republic's problems: Supply-Side Economics! Traditional Family Values! The Eternal Verities! Economic Education! Beyond his one or two wonder cures, he loses interest. Furthermore, he can envisage only one or two ways to get his solutions across to fellow Americans: Seminars! Position Papers! Political

Action Caucuses! Little Magazines! The Newsletter (at the most exorbitant price imaginable)! The testimonial dinner! Those conservatives who do not totally share one's panacea or *modus operandi* are left out in the cold, bereft of sympathy or support.

Owing to the parochialism of so many conservatives, they never quite succeeded in creating a political culture comparable to the Liberals' political culture. In America, New Age Liberalism is our culture or *Kultur*. There is no alternative. From the fantasy of *Hair* to the Hollywood fantasies of Oliver Stone, New Age Liberalism has served up its sentimental pifflings and all Americans partake or decorously take their leave. In school books the heroes are all the familiar Liberal characters, Gandhi, Dr. King; the wretches and dopes are the conservatives, dour Coolidge, antidemocratic Alexander Hamilton, Nixon! Seemly sentiments are attached to the enlightened left; ignoble sentiments are presumed to be the baggage of the bourgeoisie. All sentient Americans recognize the indoctrination from the *Kultursmog*, but the conservatives do little to thwart it.

In the fall of 1986 I brought my case for a conservative counterculture to Bill Buckley, convinced that its reach had to be extended. Over dinner with Bill and his *National Review* colleagues, at his elegant Upper East Side maisonette (once the home of United Nations secretary-general Dag Hammarskjold), I urged that they return to the practice of *National Review*'s early days when, in its pages and on the speakers' circuit, the editors dutifully circulated the ideas of all sensible conservatives abroad in the land. I suggested that we redouble our efforts to include all reasonable conservative points of view in the pages of our magazines and amplify the findings of our think tanks lest we abet the *Kultursmog* in blocking out conservatism. Over cigars and brandy, Bill demurred. He was satisfied with the world. A personal friend was president of the United States. All the colleagues there that night had become—by Bill's reckoning—major figures. He pointed to Joe Sobran as an example.

Then Bill asked, "What would you have us do?" Well, I am a modest man, not given to lecturing one of the founding fathers of any movement, but the smugness at the table was dismaying. I recalled in the quiet of my mind the allegations then circulating that *National Review* had become sterile. Yet, rather than give offense, I simply reiterated the need for strengthening the conservative political culture or—more precisely—counterculture. My proposal, based on my earliest perceptions of the conservative movement back in the days when it was in fighting trim, was for conservative institutions to "take an interest in each other's work." It was a proposal of modest dimensions, but Bill's response was instantaneous.

Uttered with the kind of hauteur through which some intellectuals hope to demonstrate unimpeachable integrity, he pronounced: "That would be boring." Bill would never want to hurt a friend, and so later he wrote me a kind letter stating that it had been many years since he was "much inclined as an activist." He was not about to become one again. Thus spoke one of the most public of conservatives, a founder of the Conservative Party of New York and a sponsor of the Young Americans for Freedom, a Conservative Party candidate for mayor of New York, the head of the conservatives' rebel movement beginning four decades earlier as a Yale undergraduate. Even the most public of conservatives can only take so much of the political life.

In order to maintain a political culture, there must be writers, editors, philosophers, politicians, a rank and file, and all manner of other fish and fowl. For years Bill Buckley played a half dozen or so of these roles. That was not a healthy exemplar for younger conservatives. It encouraged amateurism and egomania. Bill could play the jack of all trades, but lesser minds could not. After 1980, what role differentiation had existed broke down completely as mobs of ill-educated conservatives arrived in Washington to live vicarious lives as activists and members of the governing party.

In the 1980s, the tendency of conservative activists to see themselves as ideological handymen, capable in any role, broke down the conservative counterculture. The YAF leader saw himself as a combination of political leader, *philosophe*, grand strategist, fund-raiser, and political prophet. Others had the same problem accepting a distinct role in a political culture. That youthful prodigy conjured up a few paragraphs back was no flight of imagination. Such wild ones were forever setting up redundant organizations, costly to funders and without long-range value. Consequently, there were many dilettantes, few of whom respected the genuine achievement of a real writer or a real political strategist. Such megalomaniacs found it hard to stick to their own area of endeavor, become skilled in it, and defer to the expertise of others in other areas.

In Washington it was not unusual for the head of a think tank to also pose as a political adviser or a debater, or even to have syndicated columns appear in his name though others wrote them for him and he might never even read them. When I brought *The American Spectator* to Washington in the mid-1980s, my colleagues and I were astonished, not once but repeatedly, to have conservatives inquire as to "who writes Tyrrell's stuff." Some did not even believe I wrote my column. Few Washington figures write their own prose, I know, but surely most writers do. At the end of this decade, so vague had the Washington conservatives become about the nature of a political culture that they could not recognize the difference between a writer and a politician, an editor and the head of a think tank. On at least one occasion conservative hacks offered to write my columns, much as they wrote speeches and columns for other conservative giants. Now here were real greenhorns. They could not imagine a writer who relishes writing—almost above all else.

Certainly the conservatives' proclivity for narrowness also had something to do with their past. For years they had seen themselves as outsiders, as members of a losing party shunted aside by the *Kultur,* the government, the whole onrush of history. Their theorists, such as Richard Weaver and Albert Jay Nock, confirmed their premonitions that they were on history's losing side; and so they developed a siege mentality and a weakness for sectarianism. Moreover, as the neoconservative philosopher Michael Novak would remark, many were cranky to begin with. Anyone bold enough to take on an establishment, whether in academe or in journalism or wherever, is apt to be. Like Ambrose Silk in Evelyn Waugh's *Put Out More Flags,* many conservatives perceived themselves as being surrounded by enemies; and, truth be known, they loved it. Some would rather make enemies than friends, or even allies. Coalition-building was not to their liking.

In American politics the conservative movement was decidedly *nouveau.* As I shall argue at the end of this book, the conservative movement began in the 1950s by taking great pains to distance itself from the New Deal. Thus it may have appeared more of a grotesque than it was, for by the 1970s conservatism had evolved into nothing more esoteric than a movement advancing the genius of the American Constitution as conceived at the founding. Yet if the essential values of the conservative movement were not particularly new, those active in the movement were. This, too, explains their inability to create a political culture to rival or to deodorize America's *Kultursmog.* With the few spectacular exceptions of a Mellon or a Pew, the conservative domain has been the province of Americans of new wealth and new political awareness. Contrary to the popular wisdom, it is not conservatism but Liberalism that is embraced by old wealth, upper-class snobs, and the institutions of the American Establishment.

Financial support for the New Conservatism of the 1950s came, not surprisingly, from American businessmen, usually recently successful businessmen. In his memoirs, Barry Goldwater shows that the financial support for his presidential campaign was almost wholly drawn from the business sector known for its "rugged individualism." These self-made businessmen remain the chief source of support for conservatism, but rarely do they do anything to correct the conservatives' tendency towards narrowness, for frequently these businessmen are themselves quite narrow. In fact, most are temperamentally ill-disposed towards political action.

It is the rare businessman who relishes politics. Those who do are usually people of superior intellect and character. Most businessmen, even those with high-grade minds and good character, either stay out of politics or play the game half-heartedly. Politics is a nuisance to them. Some, of course, feel impelled to play the political game to preserve a monopoly or subsidy. Yet, for most businessmen, politics comes second, and if they are golfers not even second. They perceive politics as vaguely repellent and nonsensical. After all, the political player usually advances by manipulating subjective phenomena for which few businessmen have any patience. Businessmen are usually under the same curse as the athlete or the scientist; they have to meet objective standards: sales, costs, profits. Intellectuals take such things *cum grano salis*, but the corporate titan who ignores them becomes a corporate bankrupt.

Irving Kristol writes that businessmen "are quite properly pragmatic in their business affairs and are naturally inclined to believe that such pragmatism is sufficient for the conduct of public affairs as well." Kristol goes on to remark that pragmatism in politics "is needed to adapt an ideology to current, particular circumstances. But it is not a substitute for a political ideology."[1] Few businessmen enter politics with an ideology developed beyond the evolutionary stage of an amoeba; one or two ideas, a vague set of prejudices, and a civics lesson learned long ago are about all one can expect from a tycoon breaking into politics. The businessman entering politics does so usually as a conscious act of menopause. He has prospered in commerce and so he changes his life and enters upon public service.

But to make a lasting mark politically, one must have a system of ideas and only a businessman of superior intellect can have acquired political ideas and business success simultaneously. His Liberal opponents, however, usually come replete with ideas—albeit very perverse ideas. And they campaign for their ideas with a ferocity that even the fiercest tycoon rarely possesses—after all, the Liberal is a moralist. As Irving notes, in politics the pragmatic businessman usually seeks compromise, and while he does, the ferocious reformer boldly raises the ante. Reformers generally come from the professional classes and affect a suave cosmopolitanism; the businessman is narrower in experience and in attitude. His interests are specific; the reformer's are universal. What businessmen brought to the conservative movement was money and occasionally a few ideas about commerce or tax policy. Otherwise they reinforced the conservatives' narrowness and disrelish for politics.

It is perfectly understandable that the businessman should be impatient with politics. He has always dealt in palpable things: widgets, Florida swamp lands, a device for removing dog excrement from the pavement with dignity. To him all problems are subject to practical considerations and to a bottom line. However, politics, as mentioned in chapter 3, is mostly a matter of hot air and seduction. It is best pursued at a leisurely pace, with background music and other charming distractions, most of which are as mystifying to the businessman as the reformer's sudden kidney punch.

I remember when Lewis Lehrman left business for politics after great success at creating the Rite Aid Corporation. He arrived with an ideology, for he is a reflective man of superior intellect. The atmospherics of politics defeated him for years. I am not sure that he ever did fully grasp the nature of media; and as for those elements of political stage management that he did finally understand, he did not like them. The cocktail parties, the media events, the PR razzle-dazzle annoyed him. After a decade of noble service to the cause and after almost knocking off Mario Cuomo in a brassy campaign for the governorship of New York, he repaired to the more dependable world of investment banking and financial counseling, glad to be free of the irregular ways of politics.

The businessman is not totally helpless politically. In the short run some do very well. Their conventions are spit and polish and no danger to public health. Their campaigns are organizational masterpieces, frequently resonant with compelling messages and fetching jingles. In office the businessman can be an administrative marvel, certainly by comparison with many dreamy-eyed Liberals of the New Age. But without a deep historic sense of politics, without a broad range of values, ideological components, and a sympathy for the seductive side of the political game, the businessman creates no political community. He leaves no political culture. Irving compares the businessman's performance in governmental politics with his performance in another political jungle, academe. The vast majority of university trustees are businessmen who "loyally spend time and energy raising money to finance . . . left-wing humanities and social science departments, 'women's studies' programs that are candid proselytizers for lesbianism, programs in 'safe sex' that promote homosexuality, 'environmental studies' that are, at bottom, anti-capitalist propaganda, and other such activities of which they surely disapprove."[2]

Fortunately there have been among the conservatives' supporters a few

Medicis and some foundations of an independent disposition—not as many as the Liberals fear; in fact, not as many as the Liberals control, but enough to fund the makings of a conservative political culture. These little gold mines funded the scholars, the think tanks, the publications, the journalists, and, when legally feasible, the politics of the conservative counterculture. But in the 1980s their number did not grow commensurate with the needs of their movement in history. Though many, perhaps most, American businessmen are conservative, they are insufficiently political to fund the conservative movement, even when that movement is defending business. In fact, owing to their many unpleasant experiences with intellectuals and owing to the infrequency with which a businessman can give a surly intellectual a condign smack, my guess is that businessmen take some pleasure in being niggardly towards the intellectuals of the conservative movement. These are the only intellectuals a businessman ever gets an opportunity to punish. By the late 1980s the conservative movement was woefully underfunded. Cut off from universities, from the largest foundations, from government (as a matter of principle), from all the financial sources that bankroll the unprofitable institutions of the *Kultursmog*, the conservative movement needed more support, but the business community only rarely responded. Life had not equipped businessmen for cultural politics.

Some businessmen recognize this. When I filed my early premonitions of a coming conservative crack-up in a *Wall Street Journal* essay, "A Conservative Crack-Up?"[3] I promptly received a call from one of the handful of broad-minded businessmen numbered among the conservatives' Medicis, Randolph Richardson. For decades Richardson had advanced the conservative counterculture, but, he complained, he had rarely been able to interest other businessmen in his long-range commitment to funding the movement. His conclusion was that too few were capable of "grasping those ideas of a highly academic nature" that are often at the core of modern ideological politics. That is my conclusion also.

The successful businessman's day is long and arduous. He has little time for reflection. He deals in tangibles. His appetite for ideas rarely includes ideas incapable of producing that which is tangible. This explains why the conservative businessman serving as a trustee at a great university is so depressingly ineffectual. He sees the university in terms of cash flow, sports facilities, and classrooms. The ideas that are disseminated inside of those classrooms are no more perceptible to him than x-rays.

Former Secretary of the Treasury William Simon is another of the handful of businessmen who have kept the conservative movement afloat.

In a prescient book *A Time For Truth*, he urged businessmen in the late 1970s "to funnel desperately needed funds to scholars, social scientists, writers and journalists who understand the relationship between political and economic liberty and whose work will supplement and inspire and enhance the understanding and the work of others still to come."[4] "Supplement"! "Inspire"! "Enhance"!—Here is a businessman summoning fellow businessmen not just to contribute to a conservative political campaign but to fund a conservative counterculture that might challenge the *Kultursmog*. By the 1990s, despite a decade of political success, the conservatives in the business community had yet to respond. They remained, for the most part, narrowly absorbed with the bottom line, tangible things, the short run. The long, languorous pursuit of politics was beyond their patience.

Concomitant with the conservatives' inability to enlarge their political counterculture was their inability to create a conservative communications network, a media of their own. This was a critical failure. In modern politics a communications network spreads the word and creates some of the personal ties required for a community. In fact, it demonstrates the existence of a community and echoes the conversation of the community for all to hear. Essential to such a communications network are periodicals, national newspapers, occasional books, and the sounds and images of television—"And the word was made videotape," goes the modern notion of incarnation, "and dwelt amongst us." Without video and newsprint the conservatives were in trouble. Unassisted by their own national newspapers, periodicals, television and radio networks, they were dependent on the professional services of their adversaries to present them and their issues to the public.

Since the early days of the conservative movement, conservatives have complained of the raw deal they get from the one-party media, which almost always presents the conservatives unflatteringly, attired in baggy pants and floppy hats, looking buffoonish and at times clinically insane. Truth be known, however, the conservatives have done very little to create a two-party media. For one splendid moment in the early 1970s the Coors family came close to establishing a viable alternative to network news with TVN, a nightly news package subscribed to by nearly forty independent stations and an occasional affiliate station. Unfortunately, in 1975 a combination of technological and economic problems finished TVN off. Had satellite technology been available at the outset and had a bit more money been available to the Coors corporation, TVN might have succeeded where Cable News Network was soon to succeed. "We have a tendency to have think tanks and institutions and organizations to disseminate the true faith," conservative presidential candidate Jack Kemp repined in 1987, "but we're lacking the means of popularizing our ideas."[5] What is still more regrettable, some very conservative businessmen own the "means of popularizing our ideas." As with academe, so with their control of media—businessmen are less interested in the ideas being presented than in the bottom line.

So accustomed to our one-party media have Americans become, they assume that the media in all the other Western countries are like ours: a vast national echo chamber, reverberating a single point of view. This is not the case. The French, German, and Italian media are all more diverse than ours. And consider Europe's English-speaking media. In the United Kingdom, where Margaret Thatcher's era began even before Ronald Reagan's, a healthy Tory journalistic establishment has for years functioned as competently and influentially as its left-wing counterpart. In London the *Times*, the *Telegraph*, half the down-market papers, and a range of intellectual reviews, such as London's *Spectator*, *Encounter*, and the *Salisbury Review*, have been soundly conservative. Consequently, conservative views are discussed more accurately and fairly in the United Kingdom than in the United States, and the British are spared the colossal monotony of America's echo chamber.

There is a vitality to British journalism that is unknown in the land of the First Amendment. Different perspectives are widely disseminated in the United Kingdom, and few British journalists bear the absurd burden of pretending to political insouciance to avoid being charged with flawed objectivity. Most British journalists have long been out of the closet about their biases, and many have still maintained a tolerable objectivity. Moreover, the British audience knows what it is getting from its journalists. Writers for, say, the *Guardian* admit to being on the left and expect that their readers know, too. They do not maintain the self-deceit of the American who claims to be politically virginal but somehow an expert on politics. This kind of tortured poseur produces tedious work. No wonder the market for American journalism does not grow. By comparison the British press is today livelier, more engaging, more serious, and fecund with new enterprises.

When I began reading the British press in the late 1960s, despite the pervasiveness of British statism I was surprised to find a prestigious conservative journalistic establishment abounding with students of free-market economics and even libertarianism. Many of its members were open advocates of the free market and deeply steeped in the conservativism of the British political philosopher Michael Oakeshott. What is more, the members of the Tory press were not segregated into a tiny Tory ghetto on the fringes of British cultural life. It is indicative of the segregation on this side of the Atlantic and of the bias of the American media that when a distinguished Tory journalist comes to work here he slips into the same oblivion as his American-born counterparts. When John O'Sullivan leaves prestigious positions in the London press, as he periodically does, to work for conservative publications here, he enters a black hole. Few American Liberals have any idea who he is. Even when he worked for Rupert Murdoch's *New York Post*, he was invisible. Only when he returned to London to edit the editorial and op-ed pages of the august *Times* did he receive his identity once again as a prominent journalist. I take this as but more evidence of the wide-ranging pollution of America's politicized *Kultur*, or would my critics tell me that British journalists just do not measure up?

The only way to account for the existence of a two-party media in the United Kingdom and a one-party media here is by comparing the two countries' conservatisms. British conservatism has broader interests, based on a longer history and on an alliance between the British middle class and prominent sectors of the British aristocracy. The aristocracy has, until recent years, owned most of the media. In his phlegmatic grandeur, the lordly proprietor of a British paper expects it to defend all the historic values—social, political, religious—that his family has acquired down through the centuries. A compromise has been struck between these aristocrats and members of the Tory middle class. His Lordship's values are defended by the editorial department, whose members are also free to defend their rude belief in free enterprise. When the *Daily Telegraph*'s editorial page was under the deputy editorship of a keen student of market economics, Colin Welch, I doubt the proprietor, Lord Hartwell, was a burning enthusiast for Milton Friedman's forests of dollar signs. In fact, a recent book about Lord Hartwell, *The House the Berrys Built: Inside the Telegraph 1928–1986*, makes it quite clear that the poor fellow was a fargone Keynesian. But, taking his tea on the fifth floor of his Fleet Street office and patting his chelonian girth, this heir to a family institution dating back to the 1850s could take satisfaction that the defense of his conservative values was clattering off the presses below. Profits were not his only objective.

American businessmen in this comparatively young commerical republic compose our equivalent of an aristocratic class, but their interests are limited. Their values are for the most part drawn from modern conservatism. Unfortunately, when the parochialism of conservatism is narrowed even more by the exigencies of the bottom line, the conservative businessman appears even more unimaginative than other conservatives. Even when they own media properties, conservative businessmen seldom attend to any matter other than improving profits. When Thomas Murphy, the head of Capital Cities Corporation, took over the American Broadcasting Company, I uncorked the champagne. Here was an intelligent, sensible conservative, a friend and long-time business associate of that pillar of Reaganism, Bill Casey. Surely Murphy would cut his network's Liberal bias with a shot or two of conservatism. Alas, he left his Liberal newsrooms to the tedious business of reverberating the views of the one-party media.

Or take the case of Walter Annenberg. Returning from his stint as ambassador to the Court of St. James's, he decided to pitch a few pennies from his vast fortune into an attack on the *Kultursmog*. He began to set up a periodical like the *American Spectator* under a different name and format, a biweekly titled *American Views*—an intellectual review similiar to those he found in London. He brought in a fine editor and rerouted some of the best conservative writers into his pages. The higher rates he could pay to his writers made me and other conservative editors fear that we would be abandoned as both our writers and readers swarmed to *American Views*. I think it took two years, but eventually Annenberg lost interest. After blowing several million he folded his right-minded endeavor and returned to that perverse bourgeois custom of bequeathing great wealth to those who oppose its creation—that is to say, to institutions awash in the *Kultursmog*. Never again did he show any interest in the creation of a two-party media or in William Simon's salutary vision of a conservative counterculture.

Newspapers, periodicals, broadcast networks—all are at the heart of a political culture. They give it definition. They display and develop its leading figures and its ideas. They inform its members and its enemies. They reflect the hum and hoopla of its intellectual life. No conservative businessman or group of businessmen managed to set up a national conservative newspaper during the Reagan decade, and very few ever supported the conservative journals. It took Oriental adepts of a Korean evangelist to do that. Yet somehow they found an editor of cosmopolitan learning, keen journalistic instinct, and sound conservative principles, Arnaud de Borchgrave, to take over their paper, and by the late 1980s the *Washington Times* was a worthy competitor to any Liberal paper in the country. Further, it offered an accurate reflection of the conservative counterculture.

The Washington Times's front page reveals the conservative mindset as vividly as *The Washington Post*'s reveals the Liberal mindset. Possibly the crafty Orientals established it so that matutinally they might compare the caprices of both minds*: the conservative mind, dominant in presidential politics, and the Liberal mind, dominant in the *Kultursmog*. Both front pages are as demonstrative as a human face. The conservatives' alarm over national security is reflected in a front-page March 8, 1990, *Washington Times* report on chemical weapons being produced in Libya. That morning's *Post* exiles the story to page A18 and instead runs a front-page report on the prospects of the Mount Graham red squirrel—which, I need not tell you, are distressing. On March 21 the *Washington Times's* lead stories report that a conservative Democrat is prescribing conservatism to cure the ills of his party, Communist China is returning to Leninist orthodoxy, and President Bush frets over the fate of Lithuania. In the *Post* the story of the conservative Democrat is on page B4, the Bush story is on page A17, and there is no China story at all. Rather there is a vexed report on our urban homeless—picture provided.

Quite obviously, conservatives will give a more accurate account of themselves than will Liberals, who of necessity adjudge them low-grade. Yet adequate numbers of conservative investors could not be mustered to sustain a *Washington Times*. Before its predecessor, *The Washington Star*, died, Alexander Haig and a half dozen other prominent Republicans made a nationwide effort to turn up proper conservative buyers, but in vain. When *US News & World Report* was up for sale, a Liberal, Mortimer Zuckerman, snapped it up without notable competition from conservatives; and *US News* had theretofore been relatively conservative. When *The New York Daily News* went up for sale, no conservative bought it, but rather a British socialist, Robert Maxwell. In London, the conservative *Spectator* never turns a profit. What it does do is carry on the conversation of British Tories and add diversity to Britain's public discourse. Consequently, a long line of eager proprietors is always standing by to absorb *la gloire* and the loss. Obviously, there is no such tradition here. Thus, there is little in the way of conservative media.

Through the 1970s and 1980s the only major representative of the American media to reflect consistently the conservative point of view was *The Wall Street Journal's* editorial page. It did so with style and enormous vitality. The *Journal's* news pages usually followed other major media in responding to the same Liberal concerns and with the same Liberal sentiments, but the editorial page was different. It attempted to introduce into

---

*Let's face it, by the late 1980s it made little sense for Liberals to propound the antiquated stuff they thumped for and the conservative agenda, too, contained passé items, on which more in chapter 15.

the media's echo chamber a few unfamiliar tunes. Its pages composed an accurate reflection of conservative intellect in all its strengths and, unfortunately, in at least one of its weaknesses—for culture got short shrift.

The *Journal's* great editorial page editor, Bob Bartley, opened his pages to the most distinguished of conservatism's policy intellectuals. On behalf of the conservatives' conception of a proper domestic and foreign policy, Bartley waged brilliant intellectual struggle, and with an incomparable sense of fair play, always dutifully allowing the left its reply and frequently installing the most adept left-wing and Liberal polemicists as regular columnists. But when it came to culture, Bartley was less concerned. Sometimes his reviewers scrutinized a movie or a book from a conservative point of view, but not regularly, and occasionally quite bashfully. There is no one perspective on art, and there is nothing wrong with a conservative intellectual forum consciously presenting the conservative perspective on an art. But many conservatives, particularly those immersed in policy, do not see the arts as influencing political issues or government policies. Yet the politics of artists and creative writers have had significant political consequences. Think of Delacroix or Picasso or Pablo Casals or consider such diverse writers as Dickens and Steinbeck. That as intelligent a conservative forum as the *Journal's* editorial page was not as consistent in reviewing culture from a conservative perspective as public policy is but another example of conservatives failing to maintain a conservative counterculture.

As for the Liberals, they recognize the importance of ideas and of art to politics. Whether, as media moguls, they make money or lose money, they are enthusiastic promoters of their media, for they value the ideas being boomed. After the manner of English aristocrats, left-wing tycoons such as Arthur L. Carter and Leonard Stern have kept unprofitable publications for the sheer pleasure of defending their peeves and obsessions. Conservative businessmen take their peeves home with them. Liberals buy a magazine or a newspaper and so the American press has drifted away from conservatives. One of the most left-wing of Carter's publications, *The Nation*, began as a Republican organ. Founded in 1865 for educated Republicans, it once sounded like this: "No man in America . . . has any right to anything which he has not honestly earned, or which the lawful owner has not thought proper to give him."[6] Under the control of Mr. Carter—who, let us remember, has amassed much wealth—it now dispenses precisely the opposite point of view. Damn the Liberals for bias in media if you will, but what conservative businessman would buy a Liberal journal and put it in the hands of conservative writers? Simply stated,

Liberals care more than do conservatives about maintaining media. For many years the Sulzburgers have been in a position to cheapen *The New York Times* and hugely increase profits. Instead they have maintained the bureaus and the extensive staff needed to maintain it as one of the world's great newspapers. I know of no conservative family in America willing to emulate them. If *The Washington Times* is ever deserted by its Korean supporters, neither a very wealthy businessman nor a consortium of businessmen will be found to support it.

In America, Liberals dominate media because they care more about them than do conservatives. For a certitude, Liberal bigotry has excluded conservative journalists from access and honors. In fact, as conservatives became more successful in politics during the 1980s, their commentators were less frequently invited into the Liberal media. Writers such as Buckley and James J. Kilpatrick were living through an era when their views were finally being vindicated, but, notwithstanding years of distinguished journalism, their achievements were not going to be acknowledged by any of the eminentos up there aloof and sputtering in the *Kultursmog*—certainly not by the members of the Pulitzer Prize committee. A grotesque transformation was taking place. As the conservatives' policy desiderata were validated by experience, conservative pundits were being ignored or replaced by commentators who had been in error for years, and quite thunderously in error.

Still, conservatives cannot confer all the blame for the media's monotony and bigotry on Liberals. Surely more energetic efforts could have been expended by the conservatives' leaders to purchase a communications system or to build one. No such efforts were made and, as the 1980s lengthened, the theretofore cheerful disposition of conservatives began to sour. Many were actually losing interest in each other's work, a condition deplored by Erwin Glikes, who as a brilliant editor at Basic Books, Simon & Schuster, and later at the Free Press, published many early conservative works and remembered the camaraderie of a decade before when his writers actively and with clear consciences promoted their comrades' ideas. Glikes saw this happy condition change as conservatives were embittered by the pursuit of political power and prestige. In some, so much bitterness welled up that even in public they could not restrain themselves. At a conference hosted by *The Nation*, the irascible Hilton Kramer, after lamenting the exclusion of conservatives from media, was asked by the neoliberal Michael Kinsley how to account for the presence of some of us in *The Washington Post*. "Bad taste," this political genius replied.

Kramer's bile was still the exception; most conservatives simply followed the conservative impulse towards privacy: many now had jobs in government, which they pursued to the exclusion of much else. Ultimately, Liberals were prevailing in media and in culture for the same reasons they were so competent at politics: they loved hamming it up. The conservatives were wallflowers. Considering the difference between each group's performance in media, the insightful Aaron Wildavsky writes that Liberals are "far more likely to initiate stories about themselves or their activities, to feel comfortable with media representatives." Liberals, according to data Wildavsky cites, spend more time with journalists, and Liberal politicians are masterful leakers.[7]

Doubtless we all have startling tales to tell of conservative infelicity with the media. My own favorite is very personal, involving as it did a personal friendship that extended back to graduate school when Dan Quayle and I were members of an informal conservative supper club in Indianapolis, the Beer & Pizza Marching Society. From those days on Dan and I were friendly acquaintances. Never did a harsh word pass between us. He was one of the handsomest men in American politics and, though not the most energetic, certainly not the most stupid. As Vice President he has on occasion displayed intellect and leadership, and there have been those other occasions in which a curious artlessness brought him to foozle.

The occasion I remember best came during an interview for *The Wall Street Journal* conducted by *The American Spectator*'s long-time Washington correspondent, Tom Bethell. All the conservatives' maladroitness in politics and in media Dan crammed into this stark blunder. Bethell rattled off a list of conservative magazines, asking the Vice President if he read any. No, Dan said, he did not; and he insinuated an utterly gratuitous jibe against each, the most memorable for me being his sally against *The American Spectator*. "It's hard to get through *The American Spectator*," he complained. Actually, Dan was an occasional reader of the magazine. A short while later, when another journalist, Fred Barnes, asked him how he had chosen Carnes Lord to be his national security adviser, he replied that he had become acquainted with Lord's work by reading him in *The American Spectator*, where I assume he also had come into contact with his chief speechwriter, Joe Shattan (hired after I recommended him to Dan) and his chief of staff, Bill Kristol, an *American Spectator* colleague since he was sixteen! Dan compounded his botch, to the amazement of Bethell, by going on to sing rapturously of *The New Republic*—which he might have had trouble getting through, too; it had recently declared him a "moron." ("Can journalists keep writing indefinitely that Dan Quayle is a moron," writes *TNR*, "just because he is one?"[8])

The conservative publications Dan had dismissed were about the only places where he could expect to be treated fairly. I thought they deserved better. Thus, in a cover article, *The American Spectator* ridiculed Dan as we might have ridiculed any politician who singled us out for unwarranted disparagement, and presently I got another lesson regarding conservatives' confusion over media. Our criticism of Quayle provoked eighty-six readers to cancel their subscriptions, and usually with an explanation that was as ridiculous as it was revealing. It was these readers' balmy deduction that *The American Spectator* had lampooned Quayle so as to ingratiate itself to Liberals. So low were their expectations regarding journalists that they believed that even conservative journalists would bash Vice President Quayle to court Liberal favor, rather than in response to his obvious insult.

I have sought to explain the conservatives' maladroitness in politics, in media, and in sustaining a conservative counterculture sufficient to the demands of a moment in history, by pointing to the deficiencies of the conservative temperament, its yearning for privacy and its proclivity for parochialism. Even seasoned conservative leaders often entertain only a narrow range of interests: Supply Side! Our Judeo-Christian Heritage! Black Tie Fund Raising Banquets! As the Liberals march by, their placards waving, their slogans disturbing the peace, a boycott planned, a demonstration underway, the conservative heads off for a day at the beach, a session with his stamp collection, a garage sale.

After the election of Ronald Reagan, the conservatives moved to Washington hesitantly. Even I waited several years before abandoning the 100 percent American charms of southern Indiana, and it was with regret that I left. As a conservative I had grown accustomed to the rhythms of home; the customs; the fragrances of the seasons; the familiar faces, all more lined and battered as the years slipped by but withal sources of reassurance against the terror of contemporary life's rapid and arbitrary change.

While the movers were carrying the last of my belongings from my Bloomington home into their trucks for the drive to Washington, I found myself with nothing to do and so wandered over to the Indiana University handball courts, where for twenty years my partners and I had ended the day by focusing on the angles and the hops of a hard little ball. Norman Mailer once wrote me that Cus D'Amato, the great boxing trainer, believed that the only athlete transformable into a fighter was a handball player. The handball player coordinates the movement of his feet with the movement of his hands. He faces his opponent alone, assisted solely by his technique, his conditioning, and his character. But of course handball players exchange swats not against each other's bodies but against a wholly impersonal ball until one player puts the ball out of his opponent's reach. It is the perfect sport.

The courts were empty, and so I went over to the pool for a final glimpse into the watery classroom of perhaps my best teacher. Twenty-five years earlier, Doc tried to turn me into one of the scores of world champions he was training, or perhaps into one of the eight gold medalists who swam on his 1964 Olympic team. (Two of the remaining three gold medals in swimming were won by Australians he had trained.) Did he have hopes that I might become one of the twelve gold medalists on the 1976 Olympic team that he coached? (That year his team won twelve out of a possible thirteen Olympic golds.) I entered the empty balcony where banners and team portraits testified in the silence to one coach's six NCAA championships and twenty-three Big Ten championships. His record will bear repeating for years to come.

To my surprise I found myself looking down on the solitary figure of Doc himself pattering along the pool deck. A few years before he had further engauded his resumé by becoming the oldest person to swim the English Channel, but now Doc's health was failing. Years had passed since he was the dashing middle-aged impresario of Olympians and world record holders. Now he was a solitary old man, stooping under an archaic terry cloth robe that was twenty years out of fashion in the sports world (no sleek jogging suits for him!). Feebly he was preparing to post the day's workout. Several weeks before, when I told him of my impending move, he had imparted this advice: avoid women who might break up a marriage, and avoid the limelight—that last injunction from one of the world's most famous coaches! For a quarter of a century the old man had given me and several hundred other borderline jerks his best. Now I suspected that he, at the end of his career, might be in the glooms like many profs caught in life's twilight. Thinking back on the rascals he had tutored he might have begun to doubt the value of a life spent with ungrateful youth. Looking down on him from the balcony, I wanted Doc to know that he had left me with something more enduring than fading memories of glory; but all I could summon was: "Doc, I'm leaving for Washington"—long, painful pause—"and, Doc, I'll remember your advice." Slowly the old master of the natatorium peered up into the dark heights and responded emphatically: "And, Bobby, don't forget what I said about fame." The erstwhile Liberal was now the *complete* conservative; public acclaim made him apprehensive. But I was not moving to Washington for fame or lipstick on the collar. I proposed to live as my friends Luigi Barzini and Malcolm Muggeridge had lived: within earshot of a great nation's follies. Ronald Reagan had

had five years to pacify the region, and so I feared things might be peaceful to the point of boredom. Luck was with me; I arrived about the time the Iran-Contra imbroglio ignited.

Once again a popularly elected president felt his throne being pulled out from under him by the loyal opposition and the press. The conservatives could do little to help. In fact, I found their condition dismaying. Just as Amy Moritz was to report in the Spring 1988 issue of the Heritage Foundation's quarterly, *Policy Review*, few of the conservative political activists had maintained contact with the grass roots. It was from the grass roots in 1964 that they had mounted their first national campaign, overthrowing the East Coast Liberals' dominance of the Republican party. Now the heirs and assigns of that great campaign were entoiled with the minutiae of Washington politics. Years before, Ralph Nader's nuisances had circulated through Washington and fanned out across America, setting up their *soi disant* public-interest offices and spreading 1970s puritanism throughout the Union. Now the only conservative equivalents were various conservative public-interest legal foundations and some state-level think tanks that proposed to bring a free-market perspective to bear on local policy formation—for instance, the superb Wisconsin Policy Research Institute. Otherwise, the conservatives were either in government, exhausting themselves on policy development, or they were holed up in Beltway organizations, many of which were decidedly dubious, doling out questionable advice on politicking in the Reagan era and indulging in an astonishing range of mass mailings for God, country, and profit.

Some conservatives in government had been tremendously effective. From the original conservative movement, Bill Casey, Secretary of the Navy John Lehman, and Under Secretary for Policy at the Pentagon Fred Iklé doggedly advanced the Reagan agenda. At a lower level, conservatives such as Tom Pauken and Don Devine injected Reaganism into the bureaucracy. Then there were the neoconservatives, who had had the advantage of maturing in America's most political culture, Liberalism. Unfortunately, many conservatives proved themselves to be as unsuited to politics as a member of an anti-cruelty society is unsuited to, say, bear baiting. Most of the fuddy-duddies who came to be referred to as paleo-conservatives were notable flops in the Reagan Administration. Government was not for them—at least not the government of the United States, at least not in this century.

Most of the paleos were thoroughly dominated by the conservative temperament, so much so that they were prisoners of their private musings. A government fit for their participation would be one suspended somewhere in the vapors of yesteryear, far away in old Europe in a time when government ministers wore powdered wigs, tucked dainty handkerchiefs up silken sleeves, and walked with elegant walking sticks. Yet many of the paleos were hopeless incompetents, and frankly I cannot see them as effective politicos even in the baroque world of their dreams. Were they to don powdered wigs, my guess is that the powder would make them sneeze. The walking sticks would keep getting caught between their legs. They would insist on wearing their monocles in an offended king's presence or on smoking their water pipes in the court's nonsmoking section. In the early days of the Reagan Administration, when a paleo of some academic distinction failed to get a prized presidential appointment, he called a distinguished conservative at the Heritage Foundation who had opposed him and challenged the amazed man to a duel. I shall mention no names, but had the duel come off, the paleo-conservative in question might well have blasted a hole in his silk slipper.

When I took up with the conservative movement in the 1960s I noticed these quaint figures tottering around, boasting of their arcane insights and of the esoteric tracts they read. Some of the tracts were illuminating, but others were perfectly balmy. For years I wondered about those who read them and prescribed them so ardently. Were they geniuses? They claimed an enormous appetite for intellect, but many of the things that they got most intensely intellectual about were not for me: the history of the briar pipe, the source of Winston Churchill's bow ties, books by someone by the name of Tolkien, science fiction. The political challenges of the 1980s answered my questions about them. Many were simply not very bright and those who were had no political judgment. The dim ones among them were like dim ones everywhere in modern America. They had been educated beyond their means, and, adrift in their hollow pedantry, they could neither recognize superior intelligence nor their own limitations. These poor fish composed the reactionary wing of the conservative movement that was so frequently pointed to by supposedly alarmed Liberals. They amounted to a very small percentage of the early conservatives and that percentage steadily diminished as the movement grew. There never was any reason for the Liberals' alarm. The reactionaries never could drag us back into another century, not even when aided by one of Professor Schlesinger's mad cyclical swings.

In the 1980s the reactionaries proved that they will never serve in any governmental capacity or play any political role at the center of power. Not one distinguished himself in the Reagan Administration. Worse, in the last years of the Administration the fuddy-duddies agitated themselves

into a pathetic row with the neoconservatives, claiming that the neoconservatives had muscled them aside in government and in the conservative
foundations. It did not occur to them that the neoconservatives had won
distinction by their superior performance and, incidentally, were now
indistinguishable from all other competent conservatives. In the low-down
custom of the age, the fuddy-duddies pointed to superior performance and
alleged foul play. The best case the fuddy-duddies could make against the
neoconservatives was that they were prickly characters, which they were.
But they were not conspirators.

Ernest van den Haag, who for four decades argued the intelligent conservative position on all issues and with a flashing analytical blade, had
the fuddy-duddies in mind when, in the late 1980s, he decried the inert
minds and doctrinaire pronouncements of a certain kind of conservative
who inherits a conservative disposition from his family and follows the
conservative agenda on most matters without ever examining its positions
or even articulating them clearly. For them, conservatism is a set of lapidary
prejudices that alienate them from Liberals but give them not a clue as
to what comes next. When confronted with political conflict, these conservatives utter a few yelps of outrage and withdraw into a delusory world
of bucolic settings, fog-shrouded castles, ghosts, goblins, and Don Quix-
otes.

By the late 1980s this was the world of Russell Kirk, one of the early
members of the conservative movement. In the 1950s Henry Regnery
published Kirk's poetic evocation of conservatism from Burke to Eliot, *The
Conservative Mind*, and Kirk became one of the most celebrated conservative heralds, a major figure in the pages of *National Review*, a campus
lecturer, a guru to conservative youth. But the indelicate moments of
public life did not appeal to him. The tug of the conservative temperament
pulled him home to the world of the paleoconservatives, where many other
fuddy-duddies took refuge once it was clear that politics in the Reagan era
was beyond them. At home in his rural Michigan manor, Piety Hill, Kirk
actually had begun holding seances of some sort. There he would sit,
telling ghost stories as fellow fuddy-duddies listened intently. Think of it!
One of the founding intellectuals of the conservative movement spent the
last days of the Reagan Administration telling ghost stories to pinheads
who grumbled that they had been cut out of government by a neoconservative cabal!

There were other problem cases observable among the conservatives
when I arrived in Washington. There were the fly-by-night conservative
organizations that had sprung up, duplicating the work of older established

groups or undertaking frivolous projects that were as essential to a political movement as a handlebar mustache is to a playboy. In keeping with their flinty dispositions, conservatives have a tendency for falling out with their colleagues and for working only in organizations under their own control. Hence, by the late 1980s, organizations multiplied to promote the Supply Side! Our Judeo-Christian Heritage! The Black Tie Fund-Raising Banquet! Even so, the financial base for all these activities expanded only slowly, causing a strain on resources and increased enmity among would-be conservative leaders.

Worse than the proliferation of superfluous organizations was the proliferation of charlatans and ignoramuses. At some point in the 1980s some of us, who for a decade or two had been adhering to the precepts of conservatism's older generation and who now were entering middle age, felt premonitions that something in the movement was going haywire. We had learned from the older generation and were now turning out policies and books of our own, but around 1985 the realization crept in that our mentors were not playing the role of leaders. There was a hierarchy of conservatives, but it was not acting as a hierarchy. It was not assaying the younger conservatives' work. It was not pointing to new areas for conservative endeavor. It failed to recognize the charlatans among the younger conservatives and the bright fellows among the dolts.

Unbeknownst to those of us who were their juniors by a couple of decades, conservative leaders such as Bill Buckley and Irving Kristol had arrived at 1980 fatigued and, I suspect, a little nonplussed by the presidential election. Neither had pursued being a political or cultural leader with the sort of persistence necessary to anneal a leader. They had enormous influence, but they were ambivalent about using it. For decades they had been repeating the same ideas. Suddenly the ideas were being adopted by ordinary Americans; but the intelligentsia, befogged in the *Kultursmog*, would not budge. The experience, for men so devoted to reason as Irving and Bill, must have been exasperating. Shortly after arriving in Washington I began convening a series of dinners to bring together sensible journalists to analyze and laugh off our politicos' revels. We held the dinners at a superb French restaurant, La Brasserie, not far from the pols' favored forums on Capitol Hill, the very same restaurant where the Hon. Edward Kennedy had held scortatory trysts *à table*. At one of our first meetings Irving reviewed the stubborn condition of the *Kultursmog*. For over half a decade now the *smog* had polluted the Republic while picking up not a trace of the political philosophy reigning at 1600 Pennsylvania Avenue. "I don't know what to do about it," lamented the Godfather, who thitherto had always had a brisk answer for every problem.

It was a sad moment, but a revealing one. In part the conservatives' problem in the 1980s was generational. Leaders like Irving, now in their sixties, were tired. They had devised conservative ideas and made them popular. They had done it without the assistance of an older generation, and they had very little idea of how to work with the generations following them. Had they been active in business or in sport they might have understood the importance of building future leadership, but no older generation had cultivated them and they had no idea how to cultivate a younger generation. They did not understand the need to confer authority on a new generation of forty-year-old leaders, and the forty-year-olds—being conservative and thus depressingly respectful of their elders—were not sufficiently brutal to slay them and wrest that authority.

And so the conservative hierarchy did not act like a hierarchy. It did not cultivate new leaders. It did not admonish the newly conservative camp-followers to study conservative ideas. It did not scotch the proliferation of fly-by-night organizations that were draining off the movement's precious funds. Finally, the conservative hierarchy did not elevate the accomplished activists above the charlatans. Each of these failures demonstrated again the conservatives' central failure, to wit, they had failed to establish a political culture sufficient to their moment in history. The conservative counterculture remained small, its leaders remained overworked and reluctant to act politically. When Lt. Col. Oliver North, halfway through the Reagan Revolution, sought conservative support for the Administration's Central American policy, the conservative movement lacked the recognizable leadership to direct him to that support. Consequently he fell into the hands of the charlatans, principally a Mr. Carl "Spitz" Channell, another of those ephemeral 1980s conservatives who rose without a trace and prospered handsomely. As *The Washington Times* was to report, Channell raised about $10 million for the Nicaraguan resistance in 1985 and 1986. Less than half ever reached the resistance.[9] The rest of the loot went to operating expenses and salaries. There were others like Channell coming to Washington in the 1980s, but the conservative leaders who had decades of experience with the movement did not bother to separate such phonies from the movement's bona fide members.

With the deaths of Bill Casey and Clare Luce I came to realize that a great generation of conservatives was expiring. These were public figures who had a sense of drama, history, and vision. This was Ronald Reagan's generation (and Luigi Barzini's, too, for that matter), but in the late 1980s

its members were fading fast; so too were many in the generation immediately under them. The conservatives in their early sixties were fading
prematurely. They had been fighting the battle of ideas for forty years.
They were gray with weariness. Many, for instance Bill Buckley, had spent
their entire adult lives as political outsiders. Bill could never serve as a
Bernard Baruch or a Clark Clifford for Ronald Reagan or George Bush.
Perhaps Irving could play the role of a Clifford temporarily. At least during
his Liberal phase he had been an insider, but Irving could never stifle for
long the intellectual's impulse to play *provocateur*. No real Godfather
ever had as much fun as Irving. True Godfathers have heavy responsibilities.

There was a need for vigor from a conservative faction within government, but by the late 1980s conditions were all wrong. New leaders were
needed, but there was no way for them to emerge. The sixty-year-olds
were not about to hand over their scepters. The media was not an open
forum wherein the rising conservatives could achieve distinction. With
established leaders worn out and no new leaders asserting themselves, new
undertakings were doomed, as the confirmation of Judge Robert Bork was
doomed. A favorite conservative refrain of the 1980s was "conservatives
never retrieve their wounded." By the end of the 1980s that petulant refrain
began to make me wonder, "Why is it that there are always so many
conservative wounded? Why do conservatives wait for a colleague to
come upon hard times to offer help?" My answer is the conservative
temperament. Things have to be far gone for conservatives to be aroused
to action.

In the spring of 1990 the conservative movement's great debating society,
the Philadelphia Society, had its twenty-sixth annual national meeting. Its
theme, "The Trouble with the Academy," could have been discussed at
any of its previous meetings and probably had been. The speakers echoed
with sonorities we had been hearing for years. As a matter of fact, most
of the speakers had been featured speakers for years. Moreover, despite the
fact that the 1980s was their decade, few of these conservatives had gained
public distinction even in the government of their dream candidate. It was
as though the 1980s had never taken place. We can all understand the
Liberals sleepwalking through this uninviting decade. But how had conservatives managed to? Reagan was their man. Worse still, the aforementioned sour dissatisfaction was spreading unabated through conservative
ranks. This sourness was no friend to the political impulse. With George
Bush in the White House it was time to consolidate conservative gains,
to build lasting conservative institutions in Washington, to see to it that

the think tanks and conservative journals were funded and staffed so that they might endure. Why were the conservatives so morose and reluctant to fortify lasting conservative institutions in the Liberals' redoubt? My answer is that they had missed the great drama of the era. They lacked imagination, and was it Einstein who observed that imagination is more important than knowledge?

CHAPTER 14

The Conservatives' Missing Link

A Muggeridge, a Buckley, or Blank

O<small>F ALL THE ARTS</small> the one most essential to politics is prose. Certainly music has its place in politics and poetry and even design. *Au fond*, however, the politician needs words. When those great gusts of hot air explode from his lungs they must send forth words, or at least familiar noises, lest his audience think him an ass. Without words the politician cannot obfuscate, exaggerate, ingratiate, or let fly a vagrant and totally unanticipated statement of truth.

Perhaps there are exceptions; there have been political campaigns in which the less said the better. The late Warren Harding's 1920 campaign comes to mind. History remembers it as The Front Porch Campaign. The Republican party's wise coves listened to their candidate's bloviations and in an instant recognized that they had to stash the dunce in his Marion, Ohio, home, remote from reporters and almost all human contact. Let the cameras take a few shots of his swarthy winsomeness, but do not let the microphones capture those puerilely potted thoughts.

And there have been other historic political campaigns when all the Machiavels needed was to establish a mood: In a Gilded Age, nominate smiling fat people with glistening bald heads rather than wizened, constipated little fellows; in other times run generals or pediatricians—who cares what is said? But usually a political movement has to have skillful narrators to dramatize the movement's ideas and personalities and to tell the world the great story of the movement's trials and triumphs.

Admittedly, music has its place in politics, but only to stir the heart. Some romantics will argue to the contrary, claiming that music is a universal language. Truth be known, music is no more capable of conveying complex ideas than is Northern Italian cooking or Scandinavian furniture. When the nineteenth century composer Robert Schumann composed music he was a master, but he was a dinkelspiel when he confided to his diary in 1832 that "it is precisely from music that philosophers could learn that it is possible to utter the greatest profundities in the world with an apparent air of trifling youthful frivolity."[1] Well, how would Herr Schumann employ his orchestra to convey with "trifling youthful frivolity" any of the political ideas of the 1980s about taxes or geopolitics? By my calculation all four of Schumann's great symphonies convey about as many complicated ideas as might be conveyed by the violinist Itzhak Perlman blowing his nose. I have listened to great orchestras perform Schumann's *Rhenish* Symphony a hundred times. Always it stirs my heart, but I have perceived no more complicated ideas in it than in the tweeting of my neighbor's canary. The claim that music constitutes a universal language is equally nonsensical. Were Mr. Perlman to appear with the New York Philharmonic performing Jones's Concerto for Lone Gargler he might move the soul of every college professor in the audience. Readers of *The New York Review of Books* would be in tears. Most members of the Modern Language Association would become crazed fans of the genius Jones. But the rest of the audience would surely know they had been had.

A facility with words is as essential to a political culture as it is to any social undertaking. Stories must be told, slogans devised, legends promulgated. Yet in researching the early years of the conservative movement I came across an amazing and intriguing datum. Seated round the campfires, planning the great revolt against Liberalism, there were economists, philosophers, businessmen, politicos, and even a few social scientists. Possibly there was a gastroenterologist and a showgirl, but there was only one distinguished writer. That was John Dos Passos. No poet, playwright, or novelist of distinction was sufficiently ideological or political to commit to *National Review* or *Modern Age* or any of the political organizations of the nascent conservative movement. Not that there were not plenty of distinguished writers in the Republic addressing conservative themes. William Faulkner was at work, as were the poets Robert Frost and Wallace Stevens, but of the serious litterateurs only Dos Passos became active in the conservative movement.

The absence of a literary sensibility among the conservatives abetted their proclivity for narrowness, for it shut them off from imagination and the capacity to dramatize ideas and personalities. To be sure, an economist of Milton Friedman's intellect is likely to have an active imagination, but even an imaginative man like Milton would have to spend years channeling his imagination away from chill economic statistics and towards prose and oratory were he to become as politically effective as, say, Senator Eugene McCarthy. Equipped with very few assets beyond an urge to power and a gift for words, McCarthy launched a successful challenge to an incumbent president. In his 1968 presidential campaign he demonstrated what Adlai Stevenson and other political songsters had demonstrated before, to wit, that a literary sensibility can vastly assist the pol in his need to communicate.

By the 1980s, awareness was spreading that the literary types were beginning to appear on the right. It was often said that our columnists were wittier and more eloquent than those career Liberals of cloying sentiment, clownish moralism, and, well, slovenly argumentation. As Gregg Easterbrook put it in *The Atlantic*, "Today conservative commentators have their liberal counterparts outgunned by a wide margin."[2] In our magazines and books, conservative writing was becoming superior. Yet during earlier decades the conservatives had only a few truly literary figures around to transform their rituals and ordeals into an alluring literature of epic tales, fine lines, and slogans. The early conservative movement lacked a literary component. *

They had few Muggeridges. Along with Luigi Barzini, the writer with whom I felt most in sympathy in the years after the founding of *The American Spectator* was the Englishman Malcolm Muggeridge. His celebrity in America by the early 1990s has pretty much vanished, but from the 1950s to the early 1980s Malcolm was a protean presence, attracting applause from both ends of the American political spectrum for his witty and elegant sallies against . . . well, the drift of things.

Malcolm was an inveterate critic of modernity, with little good to say

---

*The parched condition of the literary art amongst conservatives was widely recognized in decades past. When asked why he employed so many left-wing writers in the early days of *Time* magazine, Henry Luce supposedly replied, "For some goddam reason Republicans can't write." Cited in *The American Spectator*, July 1989, p.18.

about the past, or, come to think of it, the future. Malcolm was a merry devastator. He was a frequent guest on late-night talk shows, where in the 1950s and 1960s the civilized banter of a superior wit was not *malum prohibitum* as it seems to be nowadays. He appeared in many of the most venerated intellectual forums, such as that great cultural hope of the late 1960s and early 1970s, *The New York Review of Books*; and when his memoirs were published in the 1970s his fame reached the heights.

As reminiscences, they were exquisitely reticent about the old rogue's escapades, but their poetic sweep of the 1930s and 1940s absorbingly conveyed the spirit of the age. What is more, Malcolm was an enthusiastic debunker of the high and mighty. John Kenneth Galbraith reviewed the memoirs on the front page of *The New York Times Book Review*, pronouncing them "wonderful" and the work of a "true master of the craft," the craft being iconoclasm.[3] They were a superb read, in part because, as Richard Ingrams later wrote in London's *Sunday Telegraph*, "One of the extraordinary things about his [Malcolm's] life is that, without apparently meaning to, he has been around at all the truly important events in this century and met almost all of the important individuals. . . ."[4] Then too, Malcolm was a stupendous writer, esteemed by Tom Wolfe as being, along with Mencken and Orwell, one of the three great fashioners of English prose in this century. Luigi's diet consisted of readings from biography, history, philosophy, and politics. Malcolm's relied much more heavily on literature and politics. His prose reached the upper rungs of art.

For years I avoided Malcolm, suspecting him, as I had once suspected Luigi, of being too fashionable to be worth knowing. But in early 1975 a piece about him by William Nolte and another by K. E. Grubbs, Jr. appeared in *The American Spectator*, thus auspicating a correspondence between us, thence a hilarious visit in London and a fast friendship. Malcolm radiated enormous personal warmth, a hilarious sense of the absurd, cosmopolitan views, imagination, charm, and a singular dexterity with words. ("Muggeridge was a man," his hostile critic Noel Annan wrote, "who could charm birds off trees.")[5] He was one of the funniest men of the century, and both on this side of the Atlantic and on the other we spent much time together walking the streets of New York or London, gabbing and laughing, popping in on television studios where he was a star, or on college campuses, where the smiles and embraces he reserved for the coeds were warm even after he supposedly banked his libidinal fires with zealous Christianity. In England he introduced me to an older generation of writers and public figures (the generation Annan calls "Our Age") then edging offstage for retirement. Over here I published some of his last works and introduced him to my political friends, along with the few young writers whom he still wanted to meet, most notably Tom Wolfe.

Once in Washington, at a time when the ornate Sans Souci was the premier luncheonette among Washington giants, I had him as my guest. As a joke I arranged a choice table for him and his wife, Kitty, at the very center of the restaurant. I knew they would create a stir. At the appointed hour they paraded in, dressed in their customary bohemian garb of out-at-the-elbow sweaters, dark and tattered pants for Malcolm and skirt for Kitty, a peasant cap on Malcolm, gray hair askew for Kitty. The Sans Souci regulars were agape; the tourists felt cheated—hoping for a Kennedy sighting, they had to settle for a couple of street people. The Muggeridges cackled uproariously, joshing about the place's tony French affectations, dramatically eschewing the lushly sauced viands for stark naked salads (they were now vegetarians, teetotalers, opponents of sexual license, in fine, 180 degrees from their yesteryears), and in general having a grand old time by twitting the solemn oafs seated all around them.

Next to prayer and rereading aloud their favorite authors—Cervantes, Blake, Dr. Johnson—the comic put-on was their favorite pastime; and so as we left the restaurant they got into a comedy routine about the need to purchase typewriters immediately. "You can never have too many type-writers," counseled Kitty; and off to a nearby store we went to pester the salesman with nonsensical questions about Gutenberg, typewriters, and his personal Artistic Process. Then Malcolm bought yet another portable typewriter. In a raucous humor we went on to Brooks Brothers. I needed a dress shirt, and Kitty raised eyebrows by lecturing the increasingly annoyed salesman in her high British accent that "a red shirt is more appropriate for *Baub.*" The spectacle of a seventy-five-year-old hippie going from counter to counter in Brooks Brothers to secure for me a "red shirt" caused bewilderment within the sober ranks of the Brooks Brothers sales staff, whose personnel were perhaps well trained for encounters with besotted congressmen and pompous generals. Against the Muggeridges, however, they were helpless. Wherever they went, Malcolm and Kitty had enormous fun, or so it seemed.

Malcolm was the consummate writer, having published novels, plays, and superb journalism; but his dark little secret was that politics fetched him, despite the wonders he achieved in lampooning it. Politics and power were two of his favorite targets for reproach, but he often derided most wantonly that which lured him most compulsively. In the mid-1930s, though he was pretty much a nonentity, he thought of standing for Parliament and not as a Labourite, which his politics suggested, but as a Tory. He dropped the idea when his maiden speech to a Conservative rally left many unmoved and some bewildered. Though Malcolm suavely disguised his true longings, his friends surely recognized that all the things he abominated—power, politics, egotism, materialism, carnality—were uncommonly strong temptations for him. He was, as they say, a man of contradictions.

Consequently he had immense energy. When we walked he moved at a terrific speed, all the while pumping his hands, cocking his head, laughing, at times howling—and what a thrill it was to make *him* laugh! However, when at home on the Sussex countryside, seated behind the thick walls and beneath the low ceilings of his ancient cottage, he would slow down into a tempo of beatific *adagio*. The cottage had once been the peasant lodging of a twelfth-century Cistercian abbey, the ruins of which can still be seen a mile or so away across the valley floor. Beneath huge beams hewn from thousand-year-old oaks, Malcolm would sit rocking with laughter as he ridiculed all the respectable figures of the world, many of whom he had known, some of whom had been his friends.

We talked often on transatlantic telephone calls, and a ninety-minute train ride from London's Charing Cross station to his stop at Robertsbridge was always the first order of business on every trip to London. The villages we passed through as our train advanced through the greenery of Kent towards Sussex and Robertsbridge—Battle, Tunbridge Wells—all were rich with literary lore. Malcolm and Kitty had lived most of their six and more decades among literary bohemians, weekdays often being spent in London, weekends here in this quiet countryside. Wherever they were in the 1930s and 1940s, Malcolm and his friends had pursued booze and lechery, wordplay and witticism. In the American conservative movement such creatures were almost unheard of.

Malcolm was an instinctive nonconformist who had married into a family of rich socialist nonconformists. Kitty was the niece of Beatrice Webb, who with her husband Sidney had been a leading progenitor of Fabian socialism. Malcolm and Kitty dawdled with socialism and even Communism, but both morbid preoccupations were too restrictive and humorless for them. They returned from their brief journalistic stint in Stalin's Russia to become the first English leftists to snitch on the Noble Experiment. It cost Malcolm dearly. Yet he survived the ostracism of the left. Malcolm could alight upon the most disturbing truths and utter the most abusive taunts. Somehow he actually grew in stature. Every time he wrote a line he ran the welcome risk of detonating a controversy. Nonetheless he survived—though a row he provoked over the merits of the royal family ended forever any chance he had of knighthood.

By the time we became friends, he had drifted from hedonism slightly flavored with mysticism to a Muggeridgean Christianity. Along with the symbols of his earlier enthusiasms he now adorned his cottage with the symbols of the Gospel. His pictures of Don Quixote and the Webbs now were accompanied by gargoyles, crucifixes, and Biblical passages that he had been quoting for decades—even when, in keeping with an earlier *Zeitgeist*, he had been a pagan, thence an agnostic. Now he had sworn off his legendary binges and his amorous trysts to espouse a theatrical Christianity. He had gone abstemious on his old friends, many of whom muttered that his piety was hypocritical, occasioned by the corrosion in old age of certain choice glands and favored organs.

Getting a drink while visiting him presented problems. Privately, he would tell you that he had sworn off booze only in the hope of preserving his literary talent. Still, whenever I suggested we visit a pub in the nearby village I would get the strong impression that he suspected me of being on the brink of alcoholism. As for his conversion, there was a logic to it; all his life he had resorted to the usual palliatives for the furies in his soul. When earthly potions failed, he looked heavenward. What is so suspicious about that? I decided the conversion was legitimate, notwithstanding the ardent concern he still reserved for the fair sex. It was reassuring to know that some of the old passion was still on tap.

His eyes, beneath heavy brows, were crystalline blue, and sparkled. His hair, retreating steadily from his wide forehead and providing a thin thatch across the massive dome of his head, was snow-white. He had a thick, rounded nose, big and fleshy ears, and a wrap-around mouth from which resonated a drawling, exquisitely accented English, an accent that was his own invention. It was subject to much comment. Was it upper class? Not really. Was it the accent of a don? No Englishman ever quite explained it to me, but all noticed it. The skin on his face seemed thick, browned from gardening, creased across the forehead and at the corners of his mouth and eyes from legendary bouts of despair, laughter, and insomnia. Little pebbles of brown discoloration and minute toadstools called polyps gave the face still more memorable qualities.

It was a friendly face, but the insomnia suggested a troubled interior. Evelyn Waugh's insomnia was at least partially linked to the cataracts of champagne and whiskey that flowed across his tonsils daily, beginning about noon. Malcolm suffered even when on the wagon, even after he put his soul in order according to the Christian manual of good conduct.

When he was your houseguest, there was no need of preparing a guest bed. He rarely slept. In 1978, when he stayed with me in Indiana, he would be the last to turn in and by 4:30 A.M. he would be up and at prayer. By then he had become a kind of joyous monk (St. Mugg, as the literary critic Hugh Kenner called him), but apparently his torment remained. His daughter-in-law Anne believed it stemmed from guilt over all those whom he had hurt during the years: the pols and writers whom he gaily besnickered, the abandoned loves, his family. He had four children and a wife. Doubtless he loved them as deeply as he claimed, but in all the years of drifting in and out of work he often wore the responsibility of fatherhood lightly. Again, he was a true bohemian.

The one thing he always took with the utmost seriousness was his prose. He was at great pains to write well, and he was oddly diffident about his talent. He needed constant reassurance, which I suppose explains his womanizing.

During a lecture stop on a college campus in the late 1970s the two of us were crammed into a car so tightly packed with coeds that breasts and bottoms, arms and legs were thrust upon us at every angle. We were threaded together like spaghetti on a plate, and I suffered a Revelation. Whispering into Malcolm's ear I told him that it must be the comic nature of copulation that had inspired the old jokester's famed carnality. He loved buffoonery and what could be funnier than sex, its preludes and its codes— the two-backed creature writhing! The look I got from him was sly. Had I stumbled on one of the hidden truths of his life? Looking back on it now, I think not. Malcolm pursued women for simple reassurance, particularly the reassurance one receives during those wonderful early stages of an affair when one's newfound friend rattles on about all one's finest qualities—real or faked. Malcolm, however, needed constant reminders of these finest qualities; and so on to the next pretty fount of easy flattery and to the next. Coming as he did from the lower classes of so class-conscious a society as Britain's and spending so much time among the snootiest classes, Malcolm doubtless had been stung frequently by the petty affronts of snots.

He emerged in the early 1950s as a celebrity intellectual, a performing egghead, much the way William F. Buckley, Jr., was about to emerge in America. He became editor of the English humor magazine *Punch*, the first to be chosen from outside the *Punch* staff in 112 years. He was also the magazine's most controversial editor, ridiculing the BBC, the Soviet Union, the English Establishment. During the war he had served in British intelligence. Afterwards his influence at the Congress for Cultural Freedom and, in the early days, at the British periodical *Encounter* betrayed traces of continuing contact with MI6, which is amusing given the old boy's many admirers on the American left. My guess is that Malcolm continued doing consulting work for Her Majesty's spooks into the 1960s, which, given his irreverence, cynicism, and Rabelaisian proclivities, is more amusing still and a credit to the British secret service. Aside from Bill Buckley, who worked for the CIA for nine months in Mexico City at the beginning of the 1950s, the only American intelligence operative with a sense of humor whom I knew was Bill Casey (and in the 1990s Bob Gates). Not only was Bill Casey witty in conversation and in flummoxing Congress, but early in his tenure at the Central Intelligence Agency he had his staff in terror while he toyed with the idea of being photographed reading *The American Spectator* for a "Who Reads *The American Spectator*" ad. The Brits have a noble tradition of enlisting literary types in their intelligence service. One thinks of Malcolm, Waugh, and Somerset Maugham. Why the tradition does not exist over here I do not know. Gore Vidal is my idea of the perfect spy—in fact, let the rumor begin that Vidal in Italy was always a CIA operative!

Is it merely coincidental that Malcolm Muggeridge and Bill Buckley became public figures at about the same time? I think not. Both men had an uncanny capacity for reading the *Zeitgeist* and for surviving thereby. Their ascendancy here and in Britain reinforces my point that the literary imagination is an important ingredient for a political movement. In America, Bill, though his constituency was never large nor particularly powerful, figured out how to get the principles of modern conservatism into public view. Anterior to the Reagan presidency and for over two decades, Bill Buckley, rather than any elected politician, was America's Mr. Conservative, and inasmuch as one man can advance a political point of view, Bill did. At the grass roots, Liberalism was losing favor. A disposition towards conservatism was spreading. But it was the literary man, Buckley, who repeatedly rendered academic principle and dull policy lively and alluring to the public. No conservative economist, political scientist, or philosopher managed to do for conservatism what Bill did. He made conservatism intellectually respectable, at least to those who were not hopeless bigots. He shared with Malcolm that facility that prosaic minds can never acquire, imagination. In the fall of 1980 on Bill's television show, "Firing Line," Malcolm explained imagination as Blake has conceptualized it, "seeing into the *meaning* of things rather than seeing things."[6] Imagination helps one make connections that are not readily apparent. It is a boon to men of action.

As writers, both Bill and Malcolm were extremely productive, issuing a steady flow of books, novels, plays, memoirs, and journalism all spiced with sarcasm, humor, metaphor and all the other attributes of a high literary sensibility. Both had a marvelous sense of theater. They became successful television personalities, for they were superb at dramatics and dramatizing their issues. The most valuable of their talents, however, was their knack for selecting some current from the *Zeitgeist* and riding it to popularity, though always they were completely out of sympathy with the *Zeitgeist*'s general thrust. Of course, they shared other talents. Both spoke in accents foreign to their countrymen. Both had an unscotchable sense of fun, a high intelligence, and inclinations towards mysticism and religion. Not surprisingly, they were great friends, and Malcolm became an effective popularizer over here of the non-traditional strains of American conservatism.

Their intuition for the *Zeitgeist* and flair for drama were the primary reasons they were so effective politically. Malcolm dramatized anticommunism and Christianity, once he was finally bitten by the churchly bug. He also dramatized lesser ideas peculiar to his own whimsical self, ideas about the imagination being engaged in a ceaseless confrontation with will, virtue issuing from the former and vice from the latter. It was lovely stuff even if its theology had things upside down. Bill dramatized anticommunism and Christianity too, but he was more conventionally ideological. Malcolm dramatized a portion of the American conservative agenda; Bill dramatized all of it. He even made gray policy matters interesting.

With his sense of theater and his gift for rhetoric, Bill gained a huge presence in American cultural life, though most of our keepers of culture resisted him. Malcolm at first was a welcome figure in the *Kultursmog*, owing to his early apparent nihilism. Then his piety won him exile. At any rate, neither here nor in Britain did Malcolm interest himself in policy. Bill did, and, as I have said, his witty advocacy of the works of economists and political scientists made conservatism intellectually respectable.

Bill and Malcolm's capacities for dramatics are then a consequence of their fertile imaginations and their aptitude for hamming it up. They have been in their way artists, abounding with words and twinkling visions. Neither has been hesitant to engaud his persona by employing extravagant mannerisms and words and by telling a good story. Each has been tremendously absorbed with his own journey through the world. Bill has written volumes about his life in politics, on the celebrity circuit, on the high seas, on the ski slopes. Malcolm produced similar work in the first person singular, though the voice was usually different. Yes, both have struck a world-weary pose, but Malcolm became more forlorn and romantic. Typically he wrote in his 1968 *Apologia pro vita sua*: "The first thing I remember about the world—and I pray it may be the last—is that I was a stranger in it. This feeling . . . provides the only thread of consistency that I can detect in my life."[7]

I have never satisfactorily understood these men's genius for hitching a ride on the *Zeitgeist*. I have known them both well, but I cannot say I understand this aptitude. Malcolm was at best a pariah at the beginning of the 1950s, at worst an unknown. Somehow he rode the *Zeitgeist* to fame, notwithstanding his many unfashionable views. Both men have been partly anachronisms, partly neophiliacs. There were things about them that were as contemporary as the latest New York City social pathology and things that were from a faraway age. I could never understand the mix. There was Malcolm living his last years quietly in Robertsbridge, exalted in Christian bliss, but on his walls, in his bookshelves, in his old clothes and elegantly intoned observations the careful observer could detect traces of what in their time had been the very latest fashions in intellectual and political thought.

Most likely these men's sense of the *Zeitgeist* was intuitive, their exploitations of it being as unconscious as a heavyweight champion's instinct for delivering the knock-out blow, which is not to say that they were unaware of the *Zeitgeist's* workings. In "Boring for England" Malcolm wrote "the collectivity expect those set in authority over them to manifest, in a recognizable manner, the *Zeitgeist* to which they belong. Otherwise they get rid of them."[8] Once he got the hang of it, he could be relied upon to manifest at least one element of the *Zeitgeist* each season and occasionally more. It took old age to get rid of him. He died in Sussex at eighty-seven—at least two decades after he had announced his readiness to become an angel.

Consider how Malcolm worked the *Zeitgeist* from the early 1950s. Beginning then, his *Weltschmerz* snagged hundreds of thousands, perhaps millions, of postwar sophisticates lost in feigned blubberings, and when he took to espousing Christianity it had agreeable modern whiffs of perversity and Kierkegaard to it. His world-weariness and revelations of despair and suicide put him in the best of modern literary company, as did his sardonic denunciations of science and his espousal of the gently irritational. He was widely perceived as being anti-American, which never hurt a Western intellectual in those days when America led the world in resisting totalitarians. In truth, the great Republic amused him, and he had many friendly thoughts about America and many American friends. In the pinch he always took the side of seriousness. He staunchly supported the Cold War. That having been said, he knew that the Zeitgeist would support jokes at America's expense and so he lifted from Georges Clemenceau the line about America being "the only case of a people who'd become decadent without ever going through the stage of being civilized."[9] And he recognized the modern Zeitgeist's hankering for the kind of piquant observation whose power to pique is insured by its simple perversity and essential error. With measured regularity Malcolm distributed such obviously false but eminently quotable observations as: "War, like lust, is exciting but not interesting."[10] Contemporary cosmopolitans love stuff like that even if it means ignoring the huge popularity of war novels and memoirs, the vast market for military history and for military biography. Perhaps in another bon mot Malcolm has explained why so many people spend money on the uninteresting.

Yet it was not only Bill and Malcolm's touch for the Zeitgeist that kept them popular. They had a stupendous sense of fun. Malcolm could always evoke a laugh. He was born with deep resources of humor. When he heard that the American government had shipped pigs from an atomic test site to a laboratory for study he wrote: "They were all receiving blood transfusions and vitamins in air-conditioned pens. A press handout answering criticism of humane societies that it was cruel to submit animals to atomic explosions contained the delightful phrase: 'They have not died in vain.' I suggested there should be a tomb to the unknown pig on which visiting statesmen might lay a handful of acorns."[11] According to his biographer, Ian Hunter, Malcolm referred to Secretary of State John Foster Dulles as "Dull, duller, dulles," to Prime Minister Harold Macmillan as "Macmothballs," to Premier Nikita Khrushchev as "one of nature's blimps—a blimpsky," and of Prime Minister Anthony Eden he wrote: "he bored for England." Then there was Malcolm's riotous review of a book on erotica, Eros Denied, by one of those moronic sex crusaders, one Wayland Young. Pleading embarrassment over the book's rough language, Malcolm proposed to use variations of the author's name as euphemisms for penis, vagina, and the scortatory verb. "Thus," he elucidated, "to illustrate the usage, one might say: 'Inserting his Young (m) in her Young (f) he Waylanded her good and proper.' "[12] Unfortunately, midst all the fun, Malcolm also made the earlier alluded to asseverations on the monarchy. He made them in The Saturday Evening Post, and the subsequent furor among his countrymen included death threats. For months his career seemed to be on the verge of ruin, and his chances for a life peerage were gone. Malcolm was what the British call a controversialist, and he relished the role.

Laughter was the *Taffelmusik* accompanying the small dinner parties that he gave in the cottage at Robertsbridge, where the chief subject of discussion was usually gossip. Even after becoming one of England's most famous Christians, he adored gossip, especially gossip revolving around fornication. There in the old cottage, which for me was happily haunted by figures from his roguish past and lined with books and memorabilia from his controversial exchanges, the journeys afar, the glamour days on BBC television, St. Mugg would abominate those who still got under his skin: his old friend Graham Greene, the Webbs, Stalin, and, of course, D.H. Lawrence, whom he ridiculed with tireless delight, frequently reading the most ludicrous passages of *Lady Chatterley's Lover* for our general derision. We parted company on Jimmy Carter, whose born-again marvels bamboozled even him, and on Margaret Thatcher—"the old fool," he cackled. But always he wanted the very latest news on Bill Buckley, of whom he was very fond. Bill fascinated him even if Bill was good for very little gossip of the salacious sort.

Before Mrs. Thatcher revived the British economy in the 1980s, Malcolm's England put me in mind of a vast attic above an old mansion containing the dust-covered heirlooms of better days. Its personages were usually spent forces, men and women more notable for illustrious pasts than for glowing futures, cultured gentlemen and ladies now gone to seed in the frayed finery of an imperial yesterday. They talked of the War, of the welfare state, of the empire so recently divested, and of writers now dead. All the century's great reforms had already swept their passé land, and now they droned on in the twilight as the great reforms moved on to America: sexual revolution! disarmament! socialized medicine! food fads! Christianity without tears or, better, without Christians! Doubtless my sense of postwar England as a dusty abandoned loft was shaped in part by Malcolm's elegiac humor. The underlying theme of all Malcolm's gossip and most of his writing was that England was finished and the West was, too. It was a theme that wore well in the *Zeitgeist*.

At some point, however, I began to have misgivings. Malcolm's grim predictions never arrived on time or, for that matter, at all. As a false prophet he ranked about even with such environmentalists as Dr. Paul Ehrlich, failed prophet of worldwide famines and other such calamities as yet to arrive. Every time I visited Robertsbridge I left high in anticipation of imminent catastrophe for the West, but no catastrophe ensued. As the disappointments accumulated, I began to feel used. Still, Malcolm went right along prophesying doom. His hearing weakened. His eyesight dimmed. The woeful predictions grew tedious. I lost patience. As Malcolm and Kitty were dear friends and we shared so many beliefs and enthusiasms, I shall lay my final disquietude with them not to the failed prophecies but rather to another matter, the fare of Kitty's kitchen. All the tea we consumed, all the vegetarian menus and the fruits and nuts—this menu, which they inherited from the Webbs, left the visitor in constant need of a toilet. That is no way to live.

I remember one of my last visits to Robertsbridge. Kitty prepared the vegetables and the nuts and I brought along my own Scotch. That night the Muggeridge's guests included their lifelong friends, Lord and Lady Longford, heads of one of England's best-known literary families. Lord Longford was a socialist, famous for his Catholic piety, progressive causes, and dottiness. In the course of dinner their otherworldly claptrap got to me. Enough—I denied that The End was near and notified the Longfords that the West would survive because of the Founding Fathers' insight that "a free society molds a more self-reliant citizen, a citizen superior to the drones of the socialist society." "Good Heavens!" erupted Lady Longford as though an emergency were upon us, "I'd *heard* there were Americans like you." But Kitty came to my defense: "I agree," said Beatrice Webb's niece, "with *Baub.*" She had become another neoconservative.

Such moments of aristocratic disdain can be discomfiting for the Yank abroad, particularly in England, where we can be lured into an unwarranted sense of familiarity—beguiled once again by our common heritage and language. Frequently the unwary Americano will find himself set upon by a vaguely leftist interrogation that, if he responds as anticipated, will transmogrify him into the cowboy philistine of anti-American myth. I discovered an escape from this sort of trap during a temporarily painful luncheon at the London home of my friends, the Tory scholars Bill and Shirley Letwin. At no extra cost to my readers, I pass it on.

The novelist Kingsley Amis was there, along with John O'Sullivan and the learned and ebullient Professor Kenneth Minogue of the London School of Economics. All are politically simpatico and the last two have been unfailingly bright performers on the pages of The American Spectator. Thus the occasion should have been pleasant. Unfortunately we were visited by the dark presence of the founder of British logical positivism, the elfin Professor A. J. Ayer, or Freddie, as he was known informally. During pre-dinner drinks his playful inquiries regarding my *Weltanschauung* were rapidly making it apparent that the venerable philosopher planned to nourish his abundant ego by nibbling on me. Moreover, either after the manner of the logical positivist or the congenital smart aleck, he was not going to advance any counter-argument to my positions. He would only tender questions, then smirk. Freddie was a very vain fellow but also quite winning. Moreover, he was immensely learned, and for those who did not recognize this he would ceremoniously allow as how he had written "ninety-two" books. At dinner parties he seemed to sound this note on the half-hour.

When Shirley seated us facing each other at the end of her elegant dinner table, I feared the ordeal was going to be long and inescapable. The loaded questions began immediately. Then, out of the blue, I experienced the same sudden rush of Yankee ingenuity that saved our boys from the redcoats at the First Battle of Trenton. As the smoke cleared from his first volley of inane queries, I drew myself up over a lovely *oeuf en gelée* and announced: "*Professor*, I have an admission to make. Yours is one of those British accents that I simply cannot fathom, not even when you speak slowly," and I looked away. I had him. Affecting disappointment, he responded: "Oh dear, you shall miss a lot today." My turn: "*Professor*, I shall read one of your books," and again I looked away. Gamely he manages a counterpunch: "I have written ninety-two books." By now his tone is pathetic and so the *coup de grace*. "*Professor*" (and here I advise a tone of ominous impatience), "I said I shall read *one* of your books." The cad is undone. I continued to ignore his impenetrable accent until he mustered one final inquiry: "How," he bleated, "will you choose the book?" "*Professor*" (fix your eyes on your plate or on the ceiling directly above you), "there is always some otherwise useless graduate student around. I shall hire him to read your stuff and then send me the book most characteristic of your thought. I shall read the first and last chapters." That was the end of Prof. Ayer, and the lunch turned out to be great fun. If you follow this tactic the next time you are victimized by a pest, your encounter will be equally enjoyable. A useful variation on this ploy is to tell your pursuer that you are deaf.

Curiously, despite his hilarious talk and the charms of the Sussex countryside, I always left Malcolm's home with a little claw of sadness at work somewhere within me. "A little bit of heaven" is how Tom Wolfe described Malcolm's aerie after we visited the Muggeridges together with Tom's incomparable wife, Sheila (also *The American Spectator*'s art advisor), and in my mind I still see us walking single-file up the spine of a very steep hill, Malcolm in the lead, laughing, next Tom in his white linen suit, a white felt homburg on top, next me, and finally Kitty bringing up the rear with Sheila and the daughter of one of Malcolm's old friends, "Sister Fifi," she was called. She wore a wild religious habit with an immense conical headdress. In her youth she had been a showgirl. For once Wolfe's attire was not the most conspicuous as we made our promenade over the ancient hills and fields once crossed by Roman legions and Celtic kings, Norman knights and Cistercian monks; and now us, modern creatures who might by the next morning be 35,000 feet above ground on a commercial jet halfway around the world.

I suspect that the reason I felt the sadness during visits to Malcolm's domain was his growing enfeeblement and his poetically contrived Christianity. Its otherworldliness was beyond my means. I relish the things of this world and have had the good fortune never to experience the squalor of worldly pleasures in the way Malcolm had, to his enduring anguish. The boozing, the bordellos, the infidelities had left him, deep down, quite sick of himself, and that too made me sad. I suspect his mania for laughter was another attempt to escape the doubts he had about himself. But the doubts remained; hence the insomnia from which he could never escape until the last sleep.

I have had the good fortune of untroubled sleep most of my adult life, and as for sin, my experiences have been different from those of Malcolm and certainly from those of Bill. Bill has been too busy for sin and possibly too virtuous. As for Malcolm's boozing-and-whoring-and-redemption, that life has always had its appeal, but only as an abstraction. Hypochondria bars me from sustained contact with the lurid delights of Malcolm's past. Only once did I visit a house of ill repute; but, whether from virtue or a prevenient sense that health conditions had not been maintained, I exited the joint virginal, unflawed by virus or bacteria, and with a good story—judge for yourself.

I have never knowingly entered a brothel in my life save once in Terre Haute, Indiana, at Christmastime, and then I was thrown out for touching the chicken. It happened this way. During Christmas break in my junior year of college I was finishing off a seminar paper before returning home for the holiday. One evening two friends stopped by to announce the good news that one was going to elope the next day with his preternaturally ugly girl friend. They wanted me to solemnize this important event by taking in the whorehouses of Terre Haute with them. They had even brought some cheap wine to make the fifty-mile drive more pleasant. Brothels as a site for coitus did not then appeal to me on several counts. I am careful about how I spend my money. I am shy and do not make new friends easily. As mentioned above, I am a hypochondriac. And there are questions of morality—I believe it is immoral to exchange bodily fluids (to use

The New York Times' coinage from the early days of AIDS) without the requisite affection and tax breaks. Yet my friends were in need, and I was bored.

Terre Haute was the Pigale of Southern Indiana, and so we had no trouble finding the red light district; it covered most of the town. (I believe the authorities have now replaced it with a university.) Once in the right neighborhood we only had to walk the dark streets for a block or so before sin found us. Ghostly old frame houses stood but a foot or two from the sidewalk. Soon, from behind a dimly lit screen in a window at shoulder height, painted lips whispered lewd enticements. Instantly my comrades clambered onto the porch and through the front door. In the vestibule, where pale pink wallpaper peeled from dirty crumbling plaster, a naked light bulb dangled above our heads, casting grotesque illuminations on us and three ebony working girls in black ballet outfits and wigs.

They immediately began their bargainings. My friends were eager and paid a high price. Soon they were gone and I was left with my scruples and a very temperamental lady of delights who also happened to be about the age of my grandmother—though not as nice. Coitus was now completely out of the question. I tried to be polite. But I am afraid that I couched the reasons for my purity in terms that were somewhat unfamiliar at a whorehouse. The highbrow in me came out. While this elderly black lady spoke in earthy dialect of her special talents I am afraid my protests sounded didactic, perhaps rather haughty. Of a sudden she either adjudged me homosexual or a nut and briskly departed to her quarters. I like to think she went off to read a good book. I know grandmother would have.

Now I was free to browse. The old house was beginning to creak in lascivious rhythms. Groans and sighs sounded as I meandered down a narrow hall towards the back of the house. At the end of the hall I found a kitchen where an ancient black cook stood staring pensively into a pan of greasy chicken parts. We were then living through the great days of the civil rights struggle, and I was properly gung-ho for black emancipation. Thus I attempted to strike up a hearty conversation. Unfortunately the chef was not much given to hearty talk or, for that matter, any talk at all beyond an occasional wary grunt. He did tell me that he had cooked in whorehouses since the 1920s, but that was all. Possibly the lady to whose unemployment I had just contributed was a friend. I tried another line of conversation, and another. Like so many young white men of the time, I was earnest to show my goodwill to blacks, and when simple conversation failed I decided to compliment the chef on his chicken. Alas, I went too far. Though I only meant to point to a particularly inviting wing, the old man abruptly determined that I was about to grasp the morsel, and he bellowed fiercely. "Git yo filthy hand away from dat," he warned, pretty much putting the kibosh on our friendship. I nervously withdrew into the street, feeling like a dog. That night I may have protected my health and my virtue, but I had failed miserably in advancing racial understanding— perhaps another time and under more wholesome circumstances.

Now if Bill Buckley ever visited a whorehouse, it is one of the few personal experiences he has yet to record. He once revealed to us in his syndicated column that he brings a tube of hemorrhoid ointment along when he travels. And he has revealed other indelicacies, but thus far no firsthand accounts from the whorehouse. Bill is that rare American conservative who relishes being a public man. He is a writer with a grand literary style, abundant imagination, a sense of theater, and a vision of life as a swell story. Not surprisingly, he is one of the most interesting of the conservative movement's founding fathers. He has also been the hardest working, the funniest, the wittiest, and about the most successful. In his biography of Bill, John B. Judis writes: "It is impossible to understand American conservatism without understanding Bill Buckley's extraordinary life."[13] Judis is accurate, and imagine the vigor American conservatism would have had if it had contained two Buckleys, or three!

Philip Guedalla, in his classic 1931 biography, *The Duke,* disinters Wellington's advice to Lady Shelley on the education of her son: "There is nothing like never having an idle moment." Bill Buckley would doubtless agree. Knowing him as I have for a quarter of a century, I cannot envisage his ever having an idle moment, and sometimes I wonder not how but why. Why no lazy weeks spent at the beach? Why can he not simply listen to a recording of Bach? Why does he have to play him?

Just as Malcolm's favorite subject was often Malcolm, Bill's favorite subject has frequently been Bill, and he has crocheted an elaborate persona for his readers. First there are his principles, an unusual web of Nockian individualism, dogmatic free market imperatives, and a Roman Catholicism of rare piety, albeit shorn of all those Papal phobias against commerce that have been the economic stumbling block of Catholic countries. But, ever the dramatist, Bill has apprised us of the more personal inclinations of his personality: his dread of writing (though he writes ceaselessly), his avidity for sophisticated gadgetry (the more advanced the better), his skiing, sailing, painting, disrelish for introspection, absolute horror of boredom, and his need for limousines stretched beyond normal dimensions.

Yes, indeed, the Duke of Wellington is Bill's kind of guy, though I doubt that even the hero of the Peninsular War could keep up with him.

Could the Duke compose a syndicated column in the back of a limousine filled with chattering friends? I saw Bill do it en route to Frank Meyer's funeral in Woodstock, New York. I have seen him leap from a noisy dinner table to pound out passages of a Bach partita on a nearby piano lest he be captured by his lifelong curse, boredom. Is it fear of boredom or a superabundance of energy that drives him to deliver annually some one hundred lectures? He founded the fortnightly *National Review,* and edited it for thirty-five years until stepping aside in the fall of 1990. He hosts a television show, carries on a far-flung correspondence, and whilst on his yearly skiing vacation in Switzerland extrudes a novel. Those of a psychoanalytical persuasion doubtless have some ironclad explanation as to why some men so abhor idleness. I only know that Bill does, and in large part thanks to Bill's energy, conservatism has for four decades grown intellectually more prominent. Judis's point is well taken.

Bill landed on the national stage in the early 1950s at about the same time that Malcolm became a figure in England. For the next two decades, by some freak of nature and technology, intellectuals were liable for celebrity status. Bill was sufficiently resourceful to stretch his tenure in the spotlight into the 1990s. He adapted to changing times; through all these years he was a virtuoso lecturer, a stupendous controversialist, and probably the best debater in America. He is an eccentric and an anachronism but he always manages something contemporary to say.

The act began at Yale, where in the late 1940s he rattled the campus with radical conservative proposals voiced from the editorship of *The Yale Daily News.* In the autumn of 1951 he attracted national attention when he further abused Yale with a best-selling critique of it, *God and Man at Yale.* Four years later he founded the first national magazine of resurgent conservatism, *National Review.* With it he united the three intellectual tributaries contributing to the New Conservatism and jolted the Liberals with a mix of erudition and *ad hominem* hilarity vacant from American journalism since the days of Mencken and Nathan. Throughout the 1950s, reinforced by his wealthy and equally political family, he assisted in the founding of most of the essential organizations of the conservative movement. But it was his urbane telegenic third-party campaign for mayor of New York in 1965 that launched him as an enduring national figure. In 1966 he began a weekly television show on which he was so brutally combative that Liberal guests greeted the invitation to face him with the eagerness of a bull entering the arena. Fame now befell him. One could not walk through an airport with him without encountering autograph seekers. The words he so fluently spouted became a torrent: printed words,

lectured words, a debater's words, televised words. His books include treatises, anthologies, novels, and chronicles of his adventures at sea, under
the sea, and on almost every manner of stage.

There is a large spotlight atop the security camera covering the door of
Bill's Upper East Side maisonette. As I have a small *pied-à terre* around
the corner, I pass it frequently. On weeknights it usually burns into the
early morn. Where is Bill? Is he flying in from lectures, debates, and
television shows outside the city, or are the maids preparing for his flight
out tomorrow while he graces one of the charity events that his prodigious
wife, Pat, tirelessly orchestrates from New York or from her elegant estate
in Connecticut? Bill has for decades lived his life at thirty thousand feet,
coming and going. Once, while I was arranging a debate for him at Indiana
University, his indefatigable English secretary, Frances Bronson, exclaimed: *"Be-ill* is the busiest man in America." I did not ask for the
statistics. She was close enough. Bill's frenetic life goes on and on; *the
schedule* is its theme. *The schedule* and the brilliance of his mind have
conspired to make him a *Time* magazine cover story, the subject of a "60
Minutes" portrait, a regular in *People* and other personality sheets. Yet,
aside from an Emmy awarded his television program back in 1968, he has
never been honored with a significant professional award.

At some point, perhaps as early as the 1970s, critics began to charge
that Bill's work had declined, *the schedule* having forced him, as they put
it, to "spread himself too thin." Here the critics missed the point. Bill was
merely keeping up with the times, or more precisely, descending with the
times. Whatever that faculty is that keeps Bill attuned to the *Zeitgeist*,
once again it saved him from obscurity. In the 1980s he fell in with the
fashion set, attended charity balls, and devised special events such as sailing
the oceans and offering video cassettes of the adventure. Then he devised
airborne tours on the Concorde.

Yet, if *the schedule* is not responsible for the metamorphosis of his work,
it took its revenge on him physically and with a curious abruptness. The
mind remained luminous. The voice remained the great Stradivarius of
American political commentary, its grand orotund fullness giving way at
the desired moment to a hiccup of playful laughter or a reedy intonation
of malice or perhaps sorrow—Bill is a consummate thespian. The hands,
too, resisted the exactions of *the schedule*. They remained remarkable
hands, elegant, aristocratic, but hands whose muscle tone and bulging
veins testify to the intensity with which he has hammered his keyboards:
typewriters, word processors, pianos, clavichords, harpsichords. His posture, too, has escaped the consequences of *the schedule*, though it is not

the posture one learns in finishing school. Behind the microphone he still arches his back, stands on tiptoe, slouches, suddenly drives his hand into his back right pocket—how many he has torn out only his tailor could know.

But it is the face that has changed. The blue eyes still dart about beneath the most expressive eyebrows since Mussolini's. The grin still pulls the corners of his mouth up and back into the neighborhood of his ears, revealing teeth that look as though they have been sharpened with a file. But the well-cut features, the boyish—as the phrase has it—good looks that accompanied him through middle age departed at his seventh decade. *The schedule* with its concomitant pills—some for sleep, some for alertness—triumphed over the flesh, and the flesh got no assistance from healthful exercise. Bill's idea of exercise continued the rarely noticed theme that inheres through many of Bill's undertakings, namely, mortification of the flesh. At any rate, upon his sixtieth birthday Bill suddenly grayed. His hair grayed. His face grayed, and a slight bloatedness came upon it. Overnight he was no longer the *enfant terrible* but the aging patrician— save for one momentous detail.

As with Malcolm, the spark of the eternal boy continued to animate Bill's mind, his controversies, and his laughter. The combination of boyishness and sophistication, plus the romantic image of being the lone paladin of freedom, made him an extremely appealing model for two decades of young conservatives, perhaps three. He encouraged them to be bookish, combative, and extremely industrious. That is the good side. The bad side is that a twenty-four-year-old with baroque manners aping the opulent lifestyle of William F. Buckley, Jr., and speaking in a weird English accent, is a little hard to take. Every time one of these popinjays would enter a public room they seemed to be listening for applause and the rumble of timpani.

Very few of the young conservatives who attempted to follow Bill's path into journalism ever made it. After a point, a writer has to adopt his own style. The epigones of WFB rarely did, and conservatism needed more competent writers, not more vacuous poseurs. Bill could have deflated some of this pomposity and developed a future generation of conservative writers and leaders. For some reason he failed. Of course, Irving Kristol failed too. One of the causes of the Conservative Crack-Up has been the failure of the most prominent conservative leaders from the 1970s to develop understudies. Successful businesses do this. So do successful athletic teams. Irving was more successful at developing conservative talent than Bill, and Norman Podhoretz, who never claimed to be anything but a writer and an editor, developed more conservative writers of heft at *Commentary* than either Irving or Bill.

Since Bill's earliest years, when his father encouraged him at the dinner table, Bill has been a performer. In debate, in journalism, in all his endeavors, Bill puts on a swell show. He takes an almost sensuous pleasure in words and, at his best, writes with a taut syntax that is extremely effective in polemical exercises. He thrives in the public light. The conservative temperament has rarely burdened him.

Under his editorship, *National Review* was capable of high seriousness and low comedy, a style that was to influence subsequent waves of conservative journalism. Michael Oakeshott's philosophical quiddities might appear in one issue and another might feature sheer high jinks. For instance, in 1967 the *Review* mocked the impudence of the syndicated columnist Drew Pearson by setting up a "National Committee to Horsewhip Drew Pearson," and four years later the *Review* perpetrated its greatest heuristic escapade. Midst all the melodrama attendant on the publication of Daniel Ellsberg's filched Pentagon Papers, *National Review* published its own faked Pentagon Papers without tipping off the media as to the documents' bogus nature. When media analysts could detect nothing amiss in *National Review*'s forgeries, the magazine's point was made: any knowledgeable student of military matters would have known the contents of Ellsberg's stolen goods. The feigned horror over the Pentagon Papers' military contingency plans from the antiwar crowd was demonstrable farce. This lesson was unfortunately lost on those in the media whom Bill had duped, and, when let in on his prank, the media's potentates condemned him more furiously than they condemned the thief Ellsberg. * Humor was Bill's elixir, and he and his charming sister, Priscilla, the magazine's managing editor, would urge humor on startled young conservatives much the way a schoolmarm might urge proper nutrition. Unlike the prim journals of Liberalism, laughs resounded through the pages of *National Review*. So dispendious was Bill's wit that a whole anthology of it was published in 1970, *Quotations from Chairman Bill*, containing such delicacies as, "One must bear in mind that the expansion of federal activity is a form of eating for politicians."[14]

Bill's exploits fascinated most members of the conservative movement,

---

*A perverse response from authorities that always reminds me of the perverse response of those Indiana University officials who called us bullyboys, notwithstanding the fact that our assault on "Dr. Rudolph Montague" was a voluntary piece of theater to demonstrate the political use of violence by 1960s radicals.

though jealous murmurs did emit from some who, weighed down by the conservative temperament, disapproved of Bill's proclivity for glamour and—worst of all—his proclivity for going it alone, independent of the movement. Here again is an example of the conservative temperament's deficiencies, for these two qualities contributed strongly to Bill's appeal, particularly among students. Bill recognized his appeal among students and dutiously courted the campus. Whatever campus he might be lecturing on, he was always game for a nightcap.

He visited Bloomington frequently, leaving us with blood vessels scorched from the firewater we had taken aboard. Once we partied into the early morn only to be awakened a few hours later by a call from Indianapolis: During our revels I had commissioned an article from Bill. While I slept he wrote, and now he was ready to dictate from the airport. Bill's generosity was as boundless as his energy. Upon being told at the last minute that the evening's dinner party was for my wife's birthday, he rushed to the music section of a nearby department store and arrived at my home with *twenty* long-playing records. Before accompanying me to Yale, where for a change *I* was the speaker, he thought of the cost that our student hosts might incur to keep our dinner properly vinous and scooped up a dozen bottles of superb claret from his wine cellar—it pleased the students and doubtless made my speech a happier occasion. He was generous in serious matters, too. When his old CIA associate Howard Hunt was prosecuted for Watergate-related indiscretions, Bill, out of his own pocket, paid Hunt's legal fees. When Bob Bauman, formerly a conservative congressman, came on hard times, Bill assisted his search for employment projects and provided a $20,000 loan for Bauman's wife.

Bill's religion was the mainspring for all his most important beliefs. His relentless anticommunism, his individualism, his sense of virtue, all sprang from his Catholicism with, admittedly, a little help from his ego—a noticeable difference between Bill and Malcolm was that Bill seemed to champion egotism, while Malcolm indulged it furtively. Yet if religion and self-assurance explain the most important data on Bill's resumé, questions do linger. His relationship with the political movement that he sired has remained elusive. One minute he is wowing the hard core with the conservative party line, say, on education vouchers, and then he is off recommending liberal Republicans such as William Scranton and Nelson Rockefeller for the Nixon Cabinet—this after suggesting that Nixon select that paradigmatic Liberal, John Gardner, as his 1968 running mate! To the conservative faithful these men were arsenic! Bill parted company with the conservatives on other matters, too: on the Panama Canal Treaty, on the legalization of drugs, on making Martin Luther King's birthday equivalent to those of Abraham Lincoln and George Washington. In the late 1960s Bill became, as his Boswell put it, "the man whom liberals loved to hate."[15] Consequently he achieved tenure in chic society, and by the late 1970s, carried traces of *Kultursmog* wherever he went. His occasional infidelities towards the conservative canon might be explained by his independent mind, but what of his proclivity for continually gushing over certain left-wing prodigies who rarely reciprocated? Bill advanced these people into public life far more successfully than he advanced conservatives. How do we explain the talent hunts Bill undertook for Liberalism? Was it his exposure to the *smog* or something more? I do not know.

Bill made himself a battleground. He was such an attractive man that fans and friends naturally vied for his preferment and friendship. That was to be expected. Less comprehensible were the other conflicts he submerged himself in: the conflict between his conservative principles and the fashions of the *Kultursmog*, between his Catholicism and his apolaustic life-style, and between the duties of a conservative publicist and those of a gentleman. As a gentleman, Bill was unfailingly loyal to a wide assortment of friends, many of whom were obviously incompatible. Many conservatives found his loyalty to such nonconservatives as John Kenneth Galbraith and the left-wing Congressman Allard Lowenstein hard to take, but Bill's loyalties persisted. The one loyalty that exacted the greatest toll on him was his loyalty to Richard Nixon during Watergate. He stuck by Nixon all the way into the fall of 1973. The experience left Bill permanently disappointed in Nixon and perhaps somewhat stunned by the brutality of politics.

During his long public life Bill has gone through several phases. In the 1950s he made his debut as a radical conservative. With the rigor of a revolutionary he rejected the dominant Liberalism and took his stand with the emerging conservatism. So pristine was his conservatism that he believed atheism and socialism rendered one unfit to teach at Yale and presumably on other faculties. He refused to support the re-election of Dwight Eisenhower in 1956. He boasted that *National Review* must stand "athwart history yelling 'Stop!' " Times change, however, and so did Bill. Moderation crept into the conservative movement; and the more moderate voices at *National Review*, most notably those of James Burnham and Whittaker Chambers, coaxed Bill by 1964 to, as Judis puts it, "mediate between the ideal and the prudential."[16] Now his radical phase gave way to a political phase. Bill, who had opposed Nixon in 1960, supported him in 1968. In his radical phase he had unified conservatives, but in the

1960s he began purging those whom he considered too extreme: members of the John Birch Society, the bigots of the Liberty Lobby, and the followers of Ayn Rand. Bill's third-party campaign for mayor of New York only whetted his appetite for practical politics, and the growing menace of the American left moved Bill to ally with those old Liberals soon to be called neoconservatives. By 1968 Bill was an active supporter of Richard Nixon.

I cannot recall ever hearing Bill speak ill of a friend except in the late 1970s when I brought up the name of my new drinking buddy, Richard Milhous Nixon. About the time Nixon's memoirs appeared we became friends. We drank coffee together, buckets of coffee—so much coffee in fact that after many a session he would very chivalrously ask: "Would you like to use the facilities?" Well, Bill pronounced my new drinking buddy "boring." Knowing Bill's abhorrence of boredom, it was a pretty strong verdict. Bill's disappointment in Nixon had endured an entire decade. Judis is in error when he says that Bill ended his political phase in 1975 because he was developing a "pessimistic view of conservative prospects."[17] These were promising times for us. What with the tergiversations of the neoconservatives and the goofball ascendancy of Jimmy Carter, our prospects had never been brighter. No, two things moved Bill away from active participation in politics: his disappointment with Nixon and his sense that the *Zeitgeist* was ushering in new tastes.

In the mid-1970s, when less gifted conservatives sensed nothing particularly new in the air, Bill's antennae were at work. The *Zeitgeist* was on the move again. Society was in motion. Its old shapes were losing definition. The world of intellect was merging with anti-intellect, high art with low taste, the university with the junior college. The *Zeitgeist* was howling outside his window, and Bill was adjusting to the shapeless dilettantism ahead. Soon came the reports of his crossing the Atlantic in his yacht. Bill recognized that an audience was forming for such derring-do. Bill wrote more about yachting and produced his first spy novel. In 1975 he dropped plans for a weighty tome on politics. He was in tune with the times.

To appreciate the magnitude of change that Bill was undergoing, one has to recognize precisely how very political he had become in his political phase. By 1968 he had forsaken his conservative radicalism and actively counseled the Nixon campaign. He was encouraging men like Frank Shakespeare, Nixon's future head of the United States Information Agency, to adjourn their philosophical scruples and join the campaign. Then through all the ideological backsliding of the Nixon years Bill stood by

Nixon. In point of fact, Bill came to be more of a fixture in the Nixon Administration than he would become in the administration of his close personal friend Ronald Reagan. Bill even held minor posts for Nixon, serving on an advisory commission of the United States Information Agency and as a public delegate to the United Nations—one of his predecessors was Eleanor Roosevelt.

Bill could have with justification called RN many things, but he had known him well enough to know that RN was never "boring." I got to know RN in 1978 during his exile in San Clemente, not that I wanted to. A mutual friend on his staff, Ken Khachigian, hoodwinked me into it; and so one morning I was ushered into the ex-president's library for coffee: there the scoundrel sat, slouched in a reading chair that appeared to be floating on a circular pond of books and papers discarded beneath it. RN, with a pipe at his side and reading glasses, looked like a fellow editor. Was this a set-up? If so, his makeup artist should have been shot. I shall never forget my first close-up glimpse at that famous face. Cartoonists had been too, too charitable. The face appalled. It did not have creases; it had ravines, gullies, dried creek beds. The jowls hung. Eyebrows sprouted wildly. The skin was raw and peeling. The voice was strong, but there was fluid in his throat, the consequence, perhaps, of a recent cold. We talked for two hours about history, politics, and related books. He asked me to come by again in the afternoon. Reluctantly I agreed. We have been friends ever since.

The character of an interesting man is often like a crystal, sometimes like a diamond. Different facets are drawn out by different conditions—a change of lighting, a shifted position, the colors nearby. The RN I saw was bookish, reflective, fleetingly religious. As with his friend Henry Kissinger, different aspects of his personality entered and exited abruptly, occasionally without warning. Henry over breakfast can move from ebullience to melancholy to ponderous seriousness, all before his coffee has cooled. Perhaps in conversation with these men I have been somewhat the failure, but never did I evoke Henry's conspiratorial side or RN's squirreliness. With me, RN expiated over history, sports, and, less frequently, social problems. Culture occasionally seeped in, but politics was always the main course. He was equally absorbed with the nuts and bolts of daily politicking and with the great sweep of political events worldwide. He was one part county chairman, one part Bismarck.

Some are political animals by instinct and chemistry. Obviously RN was not. Whereas Ronald Reagan's political instincts were congenital, RN's came from studious application, and he learned the game well. One afternoon late in 1978, seated at the great desk in Casa Pacifica, from which he had so often addressed the nation when this was the Western White House, and with the ocean glittering behind him through a spacious picture window, he declared the Carter presidency doomed. "He is," rumbled the man whose own presidency had been doomed like no other, "too proud to learn from his mistakes." A year or so later, he was again ahead of the pack in predicting the election of Ronald Reagan who, he noted, had the virtue of being underestimated and a "toughness" that "will surprise his critics."

RN was usually serious but capable of wry observation. He always struck me as very much the American of his generation, seeing the world as he did in clearly defined terms rather than in the vaporous, happy fantasies of later generations. He liked writers, and I was pleased to bring him together with them. I remember a dinner at his New York townhouse with that energetic French journalist, Patrick Wajsman, and several Americans, among them George Gilder. RN had an excellent Chinese cook and superb Bordeaux. Inspired, perhaps, by Wajsman's presence, he compared recent vintages with each year's political events here and in France. When he arrived at 1968, the year of his election, he was surprisingly vague about the grape, whose quality was not high. When asked to account for it, he hesitated and then dolefully observed that 1968 was the year of de Gaulle's fall. On another occasion late in 1979, following his book tour in Europe, I rounded up twenty young journalists and historians to join him in his suite at the Waldorf Towers. It was the first time I saw him undertake a performance for which he was to become renowned in his years as elder statesman. He gave us a guided tour of the world's trouble spots, commenting on them as they related to Western interests.

For years RN actually got stronger as he grew older. From the time I first met him, on into the 1980s, the appalling face steadily returned to the health of the face that once had filled our TV screens from the Oval Office. Slowly I came to realize that the face I had first seen in San Clemente was the face of unconcealable suffering. As Watergate receded into the past, the therapy of writing books proved to be cosmetic surgery for RN.

Come on, Bill, RN was not boring. He predicted the 1980 presidential and senatorial races with amazing precision. In the late 1970s he predicted a Soviet collapse if we pursued an arms race. In light of all the history he had contributed to, he would have had to be a mummy to bore. I asked him once why the Watergate had been burgled. He slumped, looked wistful: "That's *the* question," he said. Was he really at a loss or did he know, had he once known? The only glimmer I ever caught of the RN that prowled through Liberal nightmares came while we were riding along the East River Drive in the back of his ancient armored limousine. He was silently peering out on a bleak expanse of the river. We were on the last laps of the 1980 election. Republicans were in a sweat over reports of an impending hostage swap between Jimmy Carter and the Ayatollah. *

At any rate, on the eve of the 1980 election Carter was obviously pursuing a deal. It was in the headlines, and I naturally asked RN what he would do were he president. "Cut a deal," he replied impassively. I objected, and sought further explanation. An impatient RN turned to me and repeated: "You cut a deal," and looking back towards the river he added ". . . and then you screw 'em." When I asked how, the former president's impatience enlarged into exasperation: "There are a million ways to screw 'em," he said. "Tell them the deal is tied up on Capitol Hill. Tell them the material is lost in the pipeline."

At the height of Bill's political phase he beheld dreams of the presidency. He entertained the idea of mounting a Conservative Party campaign in 1970 for Robert Kennedy's old Senate seat, and using the Senate as a springboard to the presidency. Then Watergate dampened Bill's political ardor. In 1975, Judis tells us, Bill resolved to write a novel, sail his sailboat across the Atlantic, and perform Bach on his harpsichord with a professional orchestra. His political phase was history. His Phase III had arrived. Blessed as he was with a gift for self-dramatization, he was assured of a handsome place in the golden age of celebrity then taking shape. Bill was once again in sync with the times. His fellow media intellectuals would soon wilt, only to be replaced by the vacuous posturing egos of the 1980s. Somehow Bill got the drift and brought with him more substance than Betsy Bloomingdale or any of the era's other eminentoes.

In retrospect, I believe that Bill had a greater aptitude for reading the Zeitgeist than Malcolm. I say that because the Zeitgeist is harder to follow in America than in Europe. Its currents are more erratic here. Contrary to the received wisdom, the Old World is a much more stolid place than the new. Cultural residue from a thousand years of history still slow the

---

*Though his scheme failed, Carter planned to release $150 million worth of military equipment previously purchased by Iran in exchange for the release of our diplomats. In the future, Carter would gloss over this scheme and, in an interview with David Frost during the Iran-Contra furor, Carter actually denied that he could ever participate in such a foul deed as trading arms for hostages as in Iran-Contra. By then, however, his arms-for-hostages plan had been well documented, most notably by Gary Sick, formerly of Carter's National Security Council.

Europeans' rush towards progress. Here, we wear our history lightly. Not even so magnificent a culture as that of the Founding Fathers is very visible beyond the purlieus of Colonial Williamsburg.

Though claiming to abhor the times, Bill remained timely, hence his different phases, all neatly paralleling the times. In the 1950s his anti-communism made him a voice in the land, and his antagonism to atheism, collectivism, and secularism amplified the voice. In the 1960s, when romanticism and iconoclasm came into season, he again clicked. He managed that thespian masterpiece that always fetches the *Weltschmerz* crowd; he conveyed the sense that deep within him he carried a Hidden Wound. Well maybe he did, and maybe he did not. He broke with just enough conventions to suit the age: finding merit in rock singers, calling for the decriminalization of marijuana, appropriating a properly sensitive murderer to champion—a criminal who, like the criminal Norman Mailer would later champion, promptly returned to barbarism once released from the hoosegow. The 1960s were also a time when intellectuals affected not just intelligence but "brilliance." The image came to Bill easily; he was jarringly intelligent—inanity could bring a quick and devastating riposte from Bill. Finally, Bill was capable of easy dilettantism, which was also a feature of the 1960s.

With the 1970s came further alterations in the *Zeitgeist*, but Bill's antennae picked them up. He hesitated not at all to welcome the arrival of the neoconservatives and his hospitality was sincere. However, as the neoconservatives groaned on with their customary high intellections, Bill sensed—whether consciously or instinctively, I know not—the emerging tastes of the times: the celebrity mania, an absorption with mere personality over serious issues. Staged events, gossip, and the worst outburst of hype in world history—all were coming into season. With Bill's capacity for dramatics he was a natural for this new era. The era of "designer" lines was upon us, and soon Bill was putting his famous name on novels, "sailing books," and documentaries celebrating his multifaceted tastes. He made special appearances in unlikely places, such as TV comedies. It was an ambitious renovation, but it was required. At the outset of his public life the issues had been profound: totalitarianism on the march, nuclear de-terrence, Negro rights, states' rights, the welfare state. Steadily the issues became punier. By the late 1970s the tastemakers of American society were absorbed mostly with nonsensical enthusiasms, bogus fears, and var-iations on a theme of onanism. Bill had to adjust.

In the 1950s and 1960s, when the ideological debates were sharply defined, he was sharply defined. He was a radical conservative, then a more flexible conservative. When celebrity intellectuals had their run, Bill was the conservative in the pack, running with the likes of James Baldwin, John Kenneth Galbraith, Norman Mailer, and Gore Vidal. When in the 1980s the Liberals almost completely broke off communications with conservative polemicists, Bill recognized a trend. Serious debate was over. Staged events were obbligato. And so in sailboats he covered more water than the late Vasco da Gama, and then came the books and the videos. He hit the charitable ball circuit and became a fixture in the gossip columns. In the fall of 1986 he launched a new brand of peanut butter, P.B., "the first peanut butter for grown-ups," at a fête at Tavern on the Green, inviting such eminences of the age as Shana Alexander, Bill Blass, Patricia Kennedy Lawford, and Estee Lauder. In 1989 *The New York Times* announced that, for $39,000 a seat, "about 100 people will fly around the globe, trying to set speed records on a Concorde with William F. Buckley, Jr., the political commentator, author and television host."[18] He wrote a children's book, explored the remains of the *Titanic* in a diving bell, and played Bach with the Phoenix Symphony Orchestra.

The biography that Judis wrote about Bill chronicles the life of one of the post-World War II era's greatest conservatives. It can also be read as a chronicle of decades of changing tastes. In his book, Judis, a man of the left, laments that Bill's celebrity inhibited him from writing the serious books on political theory that were in him and chides Bill for mellowing. Surely Judis cries the crocodile's tears. When in recent years did Liberals admire combative conservatives, and had Bill written serious books of political theory would Judis have written his biography?

American conservatives had all the theoretical treatises they needed. Now they were in need of dramatics, the kind of dramatics supplied best by writers driven by imagination and eloquence, humor and panache. Those were some of Bill's foremost strengths, and he became a commanding figure. Moreover, he conferred élan on a movement in need of it. Perhaps Bill was not the writer that Malcolm was, but he was a far grander figure. That by the 1990s he had not won a single professional award for his superior journalism other than that lone Emmy is a testimonial to the *Kultursmog*'s adamantine bigotry. After all, Bill's vision of the world had been vindicated. Sitting with him in his New York study late in the afternoon in the summer of 1990, I asked him what he thought were his greatest attainments. Dressed in black tie and sipping white wine, he savored recent events and declared "acceptance that the Soviet experiment is genetically flawed, the true values of civilization being antithetical to Marxism" and "acceptance throughout the world of the inferiority of socialism." We talked a bit further and off he went into the night to deliver a lecture somewhere downtown. By then the President of the United States had pronounced Bill "perhaps the most influential journalist and intellectual in our era." Yet from the *Kultursmog* had come not a peep. Not even a guffaw.[19]

CHAPTER 15

Beyond the Twin Crack-Ups
A New Politics for the 1990s

I HAVE A THEORY about Bill Buckley's relentless humor. It is born of despair. About the only other eminence in the American conservative movement twinkling with a literary imagination was Clare Boothe Luce and she too had a humor born of despair. Both were devout Catholics, sozzled in luxury and power, and, perforce, a little sad. Of course, the humor of most modern intellectuals is usually driven by despair, the Liberal's despair—think of Galbraith—being brought on by mankind's untutorable stupidity; the conservative Christian's—think of Bill and Clare—being brought on by the imperfectibility of man. Even many libertarians despair over the prospects of freedom in our modern, congested, easily regimented world. Consequently, most of the laughs issuing from the politically charged intellectuals are just a bit pitiable, as a drunk's successive pops are pitiable.

There was one great conservative whose humor was more genuine and less premeditated: Ronald Reagan. The jokes he told were those of a profoundly happy man, and forget not that no less an intellect than the late Dr. Aristotle began his *Nicomachean Ethics* with the asseveration that life's highest goal is happiness. He who is successful in the quest of it, says the Greek, has become a *megalopsychos* or a great-souled man. Ronald

273

Reagan may be a boob in the eyes of his critics, but quite obviously he is Aristotle's kind of guy. Some see the world as it is and sob. Others see it as it is and make their desperate jokes. Reagan, whether from an inborn disposition or from philosophical calculation, was like the boy in one of his favorite jokes. When faced with a room full of horse manure he was certain that somewhere in that room there had to be a pony.

The world changed stupendously when he was at its center. In the summer of 1976 the passage of time and Gerald R. Ford's political genius appeared to have ended Reagan's pursuit of the presidency forever. Presently, however, the idiot whirl that since the late 1960s had been touching down everywhere in Western life began to spin even faster. Industries failed. Inflation singed the dollars in our pocketbooks. And there were sudden innovations in barbarism. The mass murderers and serial killers who came to the fore from the 1960s on were joined by a new species of modern maniac, the product tamperer, the louse who renders products sold to innocent shoppers lethal. By the 1970s, with the advent of state-sponsored terrorism, the innocent were in danger throughout the civilized world: in European capitals where bombs were set by furtive desperados, on cruise ships, at airport ticket counters, on commercial jets, some of which were blasted from the sky by supposedly civilized powers. Cults sprang up, and occasionally their leaders were accorded respectful hearings from elected officials. Suicides increased, particularly public suicides; and in a place called Jonestown, cult and suicide combined, leaving over 900 cultists dead from Kool-Aid mixed with Marxism.

Coming to maturity in the 1960s and acting as spectator to all the demented whirl of the next two decades, I came to view the world as a series of tentative arrangements, all subject to the erasures of the next gang of reformers. To hear the infantile Marxists tell it on talk shows and in best sellers, the expropriation of inordinate wealth was imminent; America's elites were doomed. Yet, the thought occurred, what would become of the capacious suburban homes from which these youthful revolutionaries had emerged, and what of their country clubs? Would the clubhouses be turned into reeducation centers for the elites? Would several poor families be lodged in each suburban manse? America did not have enough poor families. Could we import them from the Third World? What about all the traditions being so rudely discarded in the 1970s? They were being replaced with Nothing. Could a society exist without traditions? And how many psychotherapists would be necessary to minister to a country unattended by any traditions whatsoever?

Some writers relished the whirl and prescribed that it be permanent.

Others warned against it. Malcolm Muggeridge sensed lunacy in the air. Pat Moynihan, with the wisdom that came so easily to him in the 1970s, remonstrated against a worldwide retreat from the humane values of the West, most notably democracy. Only libertarians such as Milton Friedman seemed cheerful. Capitalism was infra dig everywhere, but Milton trusted to man's good sense. Meanwhile the prestige of the United States sank steadily. Never during all the contretemps of the Cold War had the Great Republic been so widely appraised as mediocre and passé.

The whirl was not confined to America. I remember being in Rome during the mad spring of 1978 when the Italian Prime Minister, Aldo Moro, was kidnapped and shot by a band of ideological zanies next to whom the Nazis, the Fascists, and Stalin's Communists all appeared as suave philosophes. One morning, alone, I sought escape from the whirl by slipping into the Vatican. Perhaps a walk among the gigantic columns of the Bernini colonnade might transport me at least temporarily into a saner time, say, the sixteenth century when Caravaggio was amuck but prolific with things of beauty, or the seventeenth century when Gesualdo was a peril to his wives but abundant with song. All that was missing in those far-off days was air conditioning and mouthwash and, of course, a proper division between church and state.

After coffee and the morning paper I drove up the via della Concilia- zione, with Saint Peter's looming gray and familiar before me. Across the stones of the Piazza San Pietro, great schools of Christians swam hurriedly, pausing occasionally to peer up at the saints whose statues stand atop Bernini's colonnade and the great basilica. A school of Poles followed their bespectacled young tour guide down the steps of the great cathedral. Amer- icans paused for a group picture. Other nationalities drifted this way and that across the lumpy stones. The cops were everywhere, as were vendors and freelance guides and some sooty pigeons.

Alas, I had not escaped the whirl. Amid the familiar flambeau of Swiss Guards, Italian *polizia*, *gelati*-mongers, scurrying nuns, and strutting priests, something unanticipated had been added, a gray multitude of shabby and misshapen people. Even the old center of Christendom was accessible to the whirl. In fact, the bedlamites were about as plentiful here as back in Berkeley, California! Some looked crazed, others merely dirty, tired, and ugly—being down and out in the twentieth century loses its charm after a decade or so. On a bench next to a bored *carabiniere* sat a fat, greasy man in his early thirties wearing only a T-shirt, a pink diaper, and a baby's bonnet, suitably enlarged for the fleshy melon that was his head. The statement he was making eluded me, but there were plenty of other creeps there that day with equally esoteric messages. There was a grimy man in the military garb of a jungle revolutionary, a demented lady with a bird in an old wooden cage. Cadging change were blank-faced hippies, usually a male with a female, usually barefooted and always sallow; both looking at once childish and terribly old.

Hoping to see no more lunatics, I entered the great basilica. The schools of tourists swam more slowly here, lost in reverence for each object of sacred art, Michelangelo's Pièta, now protected by a transparent barrier from the hammer blows of demented artists, the baroque statue of Saint Peter, his right foot worn by centuries of tactile pilgrims, Bernini's bronze canopy held up above the main altar by gigantic spiraling columns. A group of German bumpkins standing by the main altar began singing some unauthorized religious serenade. Their voices were heavenly, though the scene they presented was bizarre and the bizarrerie increased when, unnoticed by the blasé guards, a huge bearded man with gray flowing hair stepped carefully over the barrier cord around the main altar, ascended its steps, and, with head bowed, knelt on one knee. Guards scrambled up the steps. Very courteously and *very* cautiously, they coaxed him down the steps, then simply released the idiot, who, with books under his left arm, strode grandiosely the length of the church. The guards shrugged and walked off, but not me. I kept an eye on this magnifico, who upon reaching the basilica's entrance wheeled, faced the main altar and shouted in elegant English, "Ladies and gentlemen." Then in thunderous German, his right arm in the air, he gave a brief and it seemed to me ill-tempered harangue—though, since Hitler, most German sounds ill-tempered to me. Finally, and with colossal solemnity, he strode into the sunlight and across the piazza, chin thrust out, his gaze ever forward, back, I suspect, to the gas station whence he came. The tourists scattered before him. He could have passed for a university professor.

I headed for the Vatican Museums, and that was my second mistake of the morning. They are perhaps the world's most cluttered, and once in the place I could not find my way out. For hours I was tripping over noseless Roman busts left in corridors or leering gargoyles leaning against walls or triptychs, or sarcophagi filled with God knows what. Obviously the pope never throws anything away. When I finally got to the Sistine Chapel I was in mild panic, and the ceiling-gazers looked as weird as the serenaders back in Saint Peter's. Of a sudden I got the morning's first good idea, a scheme for prison reform that some day might make me as famous with this orb's idealists as Albert Schweitzer or Jane Fonda. Those psychotics stalking the streets of America might very humanely be vacuumed up by two American resources now sadly underutilized, our museums and cathedrals. In Europe, according to my researches, the riffraff are easily lured into these places. They seem to like them, and in secular America the cathedrals, at least, have plenty of empty space. If the scheme worked, the government could build more museums and places of worship, for the voluntary incarceration of our fellow rabble. Of course, during the Reagan-Bush ascendancy the desperate conditions of the late 1970s have mollified considerably, and so perhaps my idea for penal reform is passé.

Yes, the world changed stupendously when Ronald Reagan was at its center, and as I look back I am struck by the conservatives' industriousness during his early presidency and during the wild decade prior to it. With an amazingly high energy level and the utmost perseverance the conservatives expanded their upstart movement, devising policies for limited *but effective* government and fashioning arguments against the agents of whirl. Their intellectuals wrote incisive polemics for a growing arsenal of journals and think tanks. Their politicians attracted a national constituency.

All the organizing, the writing, and the bustle did not seem unusual. In politics during the 1970s and early 1980s, prodigious quantities of calories were being burned everywhere as radicals labored to slam the New Age down on us, and as Liberals vainly pumped life into a New Deal, a New Frontier, a Great Society—they lived even then in the past; a past whose legends they vicariously lived, all reforming lawyers and judges being Clarence Darrows and Felix Frankfurters, all pols being FDRs or JFKs, all eggheads being epigones of dozens of now defunct *beaux ideals.* Moderates burned the most calories, for in all the bustle of the era it took enormous energy to ascertain which side was winning and thus which policies to adopt. Through it all the conservatives fashioned their movement, and in 1980 their moment in history arrived.

Today the politicking has slowed down. The bustle that I knew in days of yore appears anomalous, certainly for conservatives. As mentioned in earlier chapters, without the reformers' mischief threatening them, conservatives lapse into dormancy. Accompanying the whirl of the 1960s and 1970s were swarms of reformers. Their excesses aroused a conservative response. Then the reformers were routed; the combination of their own foolish excesses and the conservatives' stout-hearted opposition sent them packing. Unfortunately, their retreat withered the conservatives' resolve. Now the conservatives experienced a crack-up of their own as some became Messiahs, others became single-issue careerists, and others intellectual isolates of one sort or another.

Conservatism's counterculture grew hardly at all in the 1980s and eventually became totally isolated from the *Kultursmog*. When it came time to muster support for the Bork nomination, the conservatives lacked the voices in the culture to shape the debate or the multitudes of activists to shake Capitol Hill. In the late 1980s, conservatives could win presidential elections, and they will continue to. Yet as long as they cannot gain a significant say in the general *Kultur*, either by admittance to it or by expanding their own counterculture, their role in American society will be secondary. They will forever be on the defensive against issues shaped by the *Kultur*. Even their presidents will be kept on the defensive, at least in domestic matters.

Too much has always been made of doctrinal differences separating members of the conservative movement. As I shall elaborate on presently, the issues on which conservatives differ are so rarefied that they may never become issues of national controversy and, whether they do or not, conservatives have more binding them together than dividing them. What caused the Conservative Crack-Up was not an overactive political gland but the conservative's deep disrelish for politics. By the late 1980s, many conservatives simply ditched politics and went home.

The political zoologist speaks of the Liberal impulse and with good reason. We see its manifestations everywhere: reforms heaved up; reforms abominated, thence reforms reformed; protests and boycotts in bucolic Bull Snort, Georgia; wars fought against poverty, against war, against smoking in public places, against fur coats. Is there a comparable conservative impulse? No. In fact at times there is no pulse at all. Conservatism is not the opposite of Liberalism. It is not of the same genus or species. If this comes as a revelation, remember that the march of science abounds with unanticipated discoveries. Scientists have found that the tomato is not a vegetable but a fruit, the dolphin is not a fish but a mammal, the koala bear is not a bear but a marsupial and the brain of a teenager is not a brain but a gland. Conservatism is not an ideology.

Towards the end of the Reagan years, Liberals were pleased to term conservatism an ideology, that being a word that Liberals considered—for reasons I do not entirely understand—reproachful. Perhaps this is another case of what the shrinks call projection, for it is the Liberal who is the ideologue. Rather than being an ideology, conservatism is, as Michael Oakeshott has demonstrated, a disposition. From time to time almost everyone falls into its humors—even the fierce feminists, most of whom are ferocious advocates of reform. Yet, who among the women of the fevered brow would countenance the abolition of dessert or the finger bowl after dessert?

Throughout this book and in others I always capitalize "Liberal" when referring to the American varietal, my reason being that such Liberals are not consistently for freedom, reason, or any of the other values characteristic of the true liberal. To the liberal intellectual inheritance bequeathed us by our Founding Fathers, our Liberals have attached ideas, policies, and bugbears that make modern American Liberalism as different from liberalism as Dumbo the Flying Elephant is from Benjamin Franklin's kite. Today's Liberal is an ideologue with an agenda of statism in pursuit of utopia that is by definition an ideology. The American conservative is merely a political preservationist, preserving the Founders' creations. He is prodded not by ideological constructs but by his disposition to preserve.

As Oakeshott explains it, conservatism "is not an ideology and it cannot determine the engagements of a government; it is, rather, a set of general considerations in terms of which to reflect upon and appraise such engagements."[1] Given the right disposition, a Liberal can be conservative, and a conservative can be Liberal. Why have more students of politics not made this conciliatory point? It could have dispelled so much of the partisan rancor that has kept Liberals and conservatives at each other's throats. As noted in preceding chapters, intellectuals have a proclivity for violence, particularly when politics is at issue. Politics is to the intellectual what the cigar was to Dr. Freud. It is an emotional support or, as is now said, a "coping mechanism." Moreover, political partisanship gives intellectuals a sense of importance that they might not otherwise have. Consequently, it is the rare egghead who can revolve a political idea in his coco and not immediately reach for a neck to wring.

I view politics more amiably. It is obvious that the early conservatives tried and succeeded in differentiating themselves from regnant Liberalism. After World War II, the noble Liberal barque still had plenty of wind in its sails as it boldly traversed the world, Christianizing the heathens with statist Glad Tidings, economic planning, social planning, New Deals, Fair Deals, and tantalizing glimpses of utopia. American conservatives could take no more of it and went to the utmost lengths to separate themselves from statist Liberalism. In time, however, Liberalism fragmented as its constituent elements radicalized into enthusiasms desirous not of anything so substantial as Roosevelt's full employment but rather of such subjective matters as soothed feelings—those feelings of "alienation," of "rage," of "powerlessness." Now conservatism, too, had changed. The theorizing of the Hapsburg emigres had shut down. Most conservatives came to share the view propounded by their sagacious historian, George Nash, in his 1987 address to the Heritage Foundation. After establishing that the American experience "means equality of opportunity, increased popular partic- ipation in politics, and equal justice under the law . . . a social order that is not static and hierarchical but dynamic and future-oriented," allowing "technological innovation and a spirit of self-improvement." Nash con- cluded, "It is the duty of conservatives . . . to forge the internal checks and balances" that will preserve that experience.[2]

"What is conservatism?" asked Abraham Lincoln in his address at Cooper Union. "Is it not adherence to the old and tried, against the new and untried?"[3] In his time, Lincoln preserved the work of the Founding Fathers. In the 1980s, conservatism carried on Lincoln's work. The Found- ing Fathers had fashioned a set of liberal documents to secure liberty, and the American conservative will conserve their work. The conservative has no alternative. As Oakeshott writes, conservative conduct "is not a creed or a doctrine, but a disposition. . . . The general characteristics of this disposition are not difficult to discern. . . . They center upon a propensity to use and to enjoy what is available rather than to wish for or to look for something else; to delight in what is present rather than what was or what may not be. Reflection may bring to light an appropriate gratefulness for what is available, and consequently the acknowledgment of a gift or an inheritance from the past; but there is no mere idolizing of what is past and gone."[4] A few paragraphs later comes Oakeshott's famous assertion: "To be conservative, then, is to prefer the familiar to the unknown, to prefer the tried to the untried, fact to mystery, the actual to the possible, the limited to the unbounded, the near to the distant, the sufficient to the superabundant, the convenient to the perfect, present laughter to utopian bliss."[5]

Whether his source be George Nash or Abraham Lincoln or the En- glishman Michael Oakeshott, the American conservative's task is to pre- serve ordered liberty. For many years there have been conservatives and libertarians of a cantankerous turn of mind who have made this difficult task more difficult still by slamming the claims of virtue into the claims of liberty or vice versa. Theirs is a parlor game best played by those who are not really serious about participating in politics. Frank Meyer set them straight four decades ago. Liberty cannot endure in an atmosphere of license, and virtue is not virtue without the opportunity to choose it. The parlor libertarian would let the terms of liberty be set by the most extreme voice, whether it belong to a crank or a scoundrel. The parlor bluenose would let authoritarians stamp out liberty in the name of virtues, which may not even be virtues. Establishing the correct relationship between liberty and virtue is the trick, and for over two centuries Americans have done tolerably well at it.

Today, however, maintaining the relationship between liberty and virtue is problematic, for neither our liberal politics nor the conservative disposition is all that healthy. We have suffered an enduring Liberal Crack-Up that is rarely discussed accurately and is probably irresolvable within the Liberal camp, where inconsistency and extremism abound. (Within Liberalism, as aforementioned, the only consistently maintained value is neither liberty nor virtue but disturbing the peace.) As for conservatism's Crack-Up, it too is discussed inaccurately. In fact, neither Crack-Up is likely to be discussed adequately as long as the *Kultursmog* pollutes the public discourse, denying the fragmented condition of Liberalism and exaggerating every aspect of conservatism save its hold on the average Americano.

Mark it down as still more evidence of the *Kultursmog's* ability to contaminate our political discourse that when in 1987 I first wrote about a Conservative Crack-Up my formulation caught on pronto even among the bovine intelligentsia, though my more richly detailed treatise explicating Liberal Crack-Up in 1984 has rarely been mentioned outside scholarly circles. In 1987 the Conservative Crack-Up was still incunabular and ambiguous. In 1984 the Liberal Crack-Up's consequences were clearly visible and quite tragic. It had barred Liberals from the White House, created mayhem at Democratic national conventions, and, in general, made being a Democrat at the national level ticklish business. Yet Liberals dominate the *Kultursmog*, and so the subject of Conservative Crack-Up got the ready attention that Liberal Crack-Up did not—which is not to say that the conservatives' condition has been discussed adequately. Even such perspicacious writers as Charles Krauthammer get it wrong. They think it is a fragmentation brought on by the declining threat of communism.

Admittedly, anticommunism has been one of the bindings that has held conservatives together, but as can be deduced from Nash, Lincoln, and Oakeshott, conservatism is more fundamental to society than mere anticommunism. Moreover, anticommunism is not the only binding that has held together the conservative movement's traditionalists, libertarians, and anticommunists. All have shared antipathy to utopianism, to marplot reformers, to zealots, and to statists. And think of the long years during which they have been brothers in arms against a common enemy who is still out there, the New Age Liberal. The shared experience of battling against a common enemy must in itself provide some sense of cohesion. Those who believe a Conservative Crack-Up resulted from the decline of communism overlook recent social and intellectual history. Before there was Marx there was Burke, the father of modern conservatism. He was not concerned with communism, and a contemporary conservative can remain conservative long after the Marxist-Leninist has been removed from his neck.

The cause of the Conservative Crack-Up was not communism's evanescing challenge, nor was it simply the decline of Liberal reform movements. It was the conservatives' intrinsic disrelish for politics, for building political alliances, and for creating a fertile conservative counterculture. Hence, by the mid-1980s, conservatives began to fade from the political and cultural fields of battle. Some, like Irving Kristol and Bill Buckley, went into semi-retirement without telling us. Many of the traditional conservatives, such as Pat Buchanan, gave themselves over to an erratic grumpiness, taking on causes that have long been obsolete and frivolous, such as America First. They quarreled pointlessly with other conservatives, usually neoconservatives who are always eager for such intellectual exercises. (One of Buchanan's campaigns was to champion the paleoconservatives' complaint that other conservatives received more money than they—not a terribly edifying complaint from rugged individualists.) In none of these quarrels was there much that was new or interesting. All were reminiscent of past disputes between traditionalists and libertarians. They were about issues remote from the American mainstream or they were about hurt feelings.

In watching some two decades of political conversions, I have always been amazed at the thoroughness of the transformation. In the 1980s even the neoconservatives adopted the antipolitical proclivities of the conservative temperament. They, who had been raised among the hams of Liberalism, adopted the weakness for parochialism and the hankering for isolation that are forever a threat to the conservative public figure. The purveyors of the little magazines returned to polemicizing, as though just one more perfectly modulated essay would save the world. The think tankers returned to their laboratories to think and to lunch. They were joining a trend; conservatives in large numbers were either retiring from politics or going it alone, unmindful of the value of a conservative community. Most ominously, the politicians and activists seemed to lose interest in their movement's founding principles and contemporary ideas. "Ideas have consequences," they had been saying since olden times when Richard Weaver first uttered those words. But by the last years of the

Reagan Administration, the maxim had become an empty mantra to be repeated frequently and fervently in lieu of actually acquiring ideas.

In the course of a conversation with Milton Friedman in 1988, Peter Brimelow, a learned and astute Canadian writer, developed a theory about the then current phenomenon of the Stupid Conservative.[6] Peter mentioned to Milton that in the 1960s and 1970s he had never met a Stupid Conservative among the movement's intelligentsia. Milton agreed and added that they were rare in the 1940s and 1950s, too. Yet now there were multitudes of vacuous conservative activists and a goodly number of young intellectuals who confused pedantry with brilliance. Peter concluded that their presence represented the natural degeneration of an intellectual movement. The early conservatives of the 1940s were moved by audacity and exceptional intelligence to diagnose the flaws of a reigning orthodoxy. Natural selection seemed to be at work. The Stupid Conservative was never seen. In the rough-and-tumble of the movement's early days, no Stupid Conservative could survive. But by the time of the Reagan-Bush ascendancy, rhetoric came easy. One could be a parrot and pass for a conservative. Bright fellows were still around, but they were being overwhelmed by the Stupid Conservatives and it was usually the Stupid Conservative whom the *Kultursmog* would cite on those rare occasions when citing a conservative was useful.

Their presence was not all bad. They could provide a few laughs. I remember late in the Conservative Crack-Up, after Reagan had left Washington and I was again a bachelor, I would at carefully timed intervals attend soirees in Manhattan at the Lehrman Institute. They were hosted by the Vile Body, a group of young conservative writers who took their odd name from Evelyn Waugh's 1930 novel, *Vile Bodies*, about London's Bright Young Things. Some of these Bodies were very intelligent, contributing occasionally to *The American Spectator*, *Commentary*, *National Review*, and *The New Criterion*. Others, I am duty-bound to report, were insufferable pedants. Holding desperately to a scotch and water for support I would politely listen as they stuttered out their recent findings on feminism, the welfare state, or some other issue then of great moment. Their findings were all old hat, when they were not absolutely idiotic. What struck me most forcefully at these meetings was how little the pedants knew about the vastly more luminous writings of earlier conservatives and how unaware they were of the world around them. They were curiously unworldly.

After each session I usually headed off to one of the night clubs that were then so popular with Manhattan's real Vile Bodies. Every era has its fixtures worthy of scholarly concern, and in the late 1980s one such fixture was the hot Manhattan night club filled with Eurotrash, all timeless replicas of Waugh's original *dramatis personae*. One night en route to Au Bar, I stopped by the Lehrman Institute with a terrific date, literate, *soignée*, and physiologically well-appointed. We were polite, drank modestly, and brimmed with admiration at every abstruse discourse—then into the night we fled. Two days later came an astounding report from one of Vile Bodies' first-rate minds, Erich Eichman. He had received an indignant call from one of Vile Bodies' chief anti-feminists exclaiming that "Tyrrell arrived the other night with a hooker." Eichman is a true Renaissance Man; his explanation was brief but incisive: "When a Stupid Conservative takes out a beautiful woman he's usually paying by the hour." In assaying the problem of Conservative Crack-Up, experts are going to have to give a second look at the role played by the Stupid Conservative. Milton Friedman believed it would take decades to overcome their influence and to penetrate the *Kultursmog*.

Along with the decline of Communism and the rise of the Stupid Conservative, another partial explanation for the Conservative Crack-Up has been the existence of the various conservatives' doctrinal disagreements. Toward the end of George Bush's first term, a thoughtful Liberal political analyst, E.J. Dionne, saw these disagreements as portending disaster for conservatives. Actually, their importance has always been overrated. They led to squabbling that sapped energy and occasionally eliminated a talented individual, but they were always peripheral. They were usually about matters so remote from the real issues of the day as to be mere questions for speculation. They had no political significance. Libertarians argue for such policies as the privatization of public highways, but it will be generations before such questions get into the American mainstream, if ever. On those rare occasions during the Reagan-Bush ascendancy when an issue divisive to the movement did become a political issue, it never had lasting political repercussions.

Perhaps the most divisive issue settled during a recent Republican Administration was the Nixon Administration's implementation of the volunteer army. It was right out of the libertarian catechism, and traditionalists and anticommunists generally denounced it as a threat to national security. However, when the unexpected fallout from Vietnam suddenly made the volunteer army feasible and Nixon adopted it, conservative support for the Pentagon budget remained steadfast. Concern for the national interest was a stronger binding force than the quiddities of conservative

factions. Later, when Pat Buchanan led isolationist strains in the movement
into opposition to war against Saddam Hussein, he ended his opposition
the day hostilities began. Basically the Conservative Crack-Up was a consequence of two phenomena: the conservative temperament's antipathy to
politics and the *Kultursmog*'s ability to control the terms of public discourse, even the language of, and participants in, America's public discourse.

American conservatism has demonstrated its ability to govern America.
Its ideas have been effective in creating prosperity and peace. It has even
demonstrated a capacity for bringing aboard new groups, for instance, the
neoconservatives and the religious right. But as the retirement of the
religious right most vividly demonstrates, Americans of a conservative
temperament do not revel in the hurly-burly of politics. They prefer home
and hearth. The conservatives' major problem resides not in doctrinal
disagreements but in their personnel.

What is to be done if the conservative movement is to remain vital in
preserving what George Nash calls the American experience? How can
conservatives remain stalwart in a time when American Liberals no longer
compose a reform movement on the march but rather a mob of sectarians
all fighting for the usufruct of a secular religion in which no one really
has much faith? My mind returns to the 1970s. Then the radicalization
and fragmentation of Liberalism was in its first howls, the perspicacious
Liberals of an independent spirit recognized the chaos ahead and began
the great migration to the conservative camp. There they renewed conservatism, liberalizing it a bit, and creating that infamous conservative
sub-species, neoconservatism. In the 1980s this migration ended. The
Zeitgeist shifted. Liberals of independent mind either lost heart or could
not bear to support a president who embodied the Goldwaterism against
which they had remonstrated since 1964. Look at it from the Liberal's
point of view: Reagan might not be as embarrassing as a New Ager, but
he probably was going to blow up the world. No Liberal would willingly
be a party to an environmental mishap like that!

Today, however, a different *Zeitgeist* is whistling around the globe.
Gunnar Myrdal and Karl Marx, Jean-Paul Sartre and Che Guevara, and
all the other giants who, in the aftermath of World War II, inspired hope
worldwide have been rendered obsolete. Since the autumn of 1989 their
names have been forgotten almost everywhere save in the faculty lounges
of certain American cow colleges and perhaps among some inert minds
in the Ivy League. The platitudes of Ronald Reagan reign in lands where

the secret police once seemed indestructible; and Reagan has been followed by George Herbert Walker Bush, a politician built in conformity with Oakeshott's formulae.

Ronald Reagan had to think about the conservatism he adopted. For him it was a dozen or so principles he held in his mind's eye. George Bush grew up with the principles. They are a part of his character. As Vice President and as President he has been a guest of *The American Spectator*. I have observed him from afar and in close. His is the conservatism of the gentleman capitalist. His policies need the stimulation of a conservative counterculture, but the counterculture needs stimulation, too. It has languished without the reinforcement of fresh troops eager for public life. Now, with the image of Ronald Reagan no longer in the White House blocking their view of reality, Liberals of reasonable disposition can begin again their migration toward conservatism. Their relish for politics can be salutary, and as George Nash makes clear, today not that much separates reasonable Liberals from conservatives. Both have reason to preserve the American experience. In the presidency of George Herbert Walker Bush it is again possible for Liberals to become neoconservatives or to complete the transformations that neoliberals had begun. The Conservative Crack-Up is unlikely to end until the Liberals' political libido is brought to conservatism and the Liberal Crack-Up will not end until the Liberals shake their fanatics.

That Liberals and conservatives can be compatible was demonstrated by the neoconservatives, but the process of cross-fertilization began long before the 1970s, a fact that struck me with particular poignancy the night I became the first man to introduce the President of the United States to the music of Frederick the Great. You did not hear about that? Well, to be brief, I invited the President out to the house for dinner on July 26, 1988, to celebrate what was to be about the last hopeful observance of that day in Havana. (The Twenty-Sixth of July Movement is the name Fidel gave to his revolutionary organization in commemoration of his 1953 attack on the government's Moncada barracks.) At dinner I brought together ten of the conservative movement's most promising journalists and, as the dinner conversation turned from politics to politics and back to politics again, I was struck by the fact that everyone at the table had shed his Liberalism since the 1960s, except for two congenital Republicans and Ronald Reagan, who shed his Liberalism earlier and who turned out to be conservatism's greatest political leader.

The evening proved to be amusing, as the President probably anticipated it would be. His friendship with *The American Spectator* had never been occasioned by the kind of awful solemnity so prevalent in Washington.

I remember his amusement back in 1987 when I told him of a joke I played on a couple of humorless journalists in the White House right after he signed the INF treaty with Gorbachev. We were the first writers invited to interview the President, and as we waited outside the Oval Office the atmosphere was oppressive. My colleagues were devising questions which they presumed would trip the President into some unanticipated revelation. What would my question be, I was asked. Innocently, I explained that the occasion required originality; my question would be: "Mr. President, precisely what evidence have you that President Gorbachev is not a woman?" A look of terror crossed my colleagues' faces as they saw their opportunity to make history threatened by burlesque. This farceur Tyrrell was going to steal the show! Of course, in the end my courage failed me. But at a later date the story got a few laughs from the President. When he came to dinner he expected a few more. He lives up to the Aristotelian ideal.

The security shielding Ronald Reagan after one assassination attempt and repeated terrorist threats could put a damper on every social occasion. Bill Buckley's wife, the formidable Pat, would tell me of the many times she had felt impelled to tell the Secret Service to restrain itself, but I come from a Secret Service family. My great-great-grandfather, P.D. Tyrrell, U.S.S.S., broke a counterfeiters' plot in 1876 to steal Lincoln's body from its tomb in Springfield, Illinois. Since then, the Secret Service's place in family legends has been secure, and I was eager to cooperate with the colleagues of my great-great-grandfather.

A week before the President's arrival, the Secret Service stops by the house with a dozen White House personnel to arrange communications, security, and the President's cocktail. Then the Secret Service ingratiates you with the neighbors by interviewing every one of them about their personal arms caches. Next the Secret Service sends a swarm of helicopters overhead to photograph the neighbors' yards for missile silos and perhaps to get a shot of a nude Yuppie sunning herself by the pool—even the scar from her appendectomy is not missed by these powerful cameras, and she had cosmetic surgery on it! A grim note is struck when the Secret Service asks the location of the nearest hospital capable of landing a helicopter. For a week unexpected visitors ride through the neighborhood, and a day or so before "D-day" the telephone company begins putting in extra wires with the assistance of White House communications experts—twelve lines are needed.

The day of the dinner a team of cooks, waiters and butlers flew down from New York, for by this time my wife had forsaken home and hearth for the tennis court—later it would be law school. As a hostess she was becoming unreliable. An hour after the caterers' late-morning flight, LaGuardia is socked in by a furious rainstorm that is moving in on the entire East Coast. As the hours pass Teddy Forstmann, chairman of the *American Spectator's* publications committee, reports worsening climatic conditions that bar him from flying our New York guests down on his private jet. Teddy is a fiercely determined fellow; if he cannot get his plane in the air, the weather must be ghastly. Soon comes word that Nancy Reagan, too, is stranded in the Manhattan deluge. We scramble to find suitable standbys, as a last-minute flight from New York seems improbable.

The action picks up steadily through the afternoon. A military build-up is taking place in my neighborhood. By four o'clock twenty-five security cars filled with cops and dogs have parked along the streets by my home, serving as barricades lest terrorists aim an armored personnel carrier towards my living room. Checkpoints are set up to bar the unauthorized from the neighborhood. My house is evacuated as dogs search for bombs—and completely miss my son's fireworks. But they do not miss my house guest, John O'Sullivan, who is hustled out onto the lawn in the middle of shaving. His presence is making history, for on this day he will become the only man known to have begun his day in London taking morning coffee with Prime Minister Thatcher and ended it 3000 miles away in McLean, Virginia, over dinner with President Reagan—a feat made possible by the technology of Concorde and the politics of a spreading conservative movement.*

By five o'clock, radar and lights have been strung around the house. Seventy sharpshooters, Secret Service agents, and local police are in the walk-in basement, where we have set up a buffet and where the sharpshooters talk endlessly about the same topics then favored by university profs, to wit, real estate prices and personal incomes. The communications center is in the garage. The twelve telephones are there, in the library and in the guest room which is also fitted out for the "football," an attache

---

*John had arrived to become editor of *National Review,* and *The Washington Post's* story about him is an illuminating example of how the *Kultursmog* obscures a reality it abhors. The *Post's* Sidney Blumenthal was frequently reporting on conservatives in those days. In fact, it seemed that conservatism had become his beat. Here is how he keeps the dimensions of conservatism's ascendancy manageable: "On Tuesday morning, O'Sullivan has a long chat with British Prime Minister Margaret Thatcher in London. . . . In the evening he dined with President Reagan in Washington. . . ." Not Washington, Sidney, McLean, Virginia; and is there not a little more to this story for monitors of the conservative diableries?

case with the codes to activate our nuclear arsenal. Guests, rain-soaked and bewildered, are passing security checks and entering through the garage. Soon I will greet the President in this same inelegant room amongst bicycles and gardening equipment—the front door is deemed too exposed for entry by our guest of honor.

Trying to relax, my guests have drinks in the living room where I have arranged appropriate background music as we await the President. There are supercilious devotees of serious music who sniff at the idea of it being used as background music. They insist that it was written to be wept over and otherwise to exacerbate neuroses. This notion is, if you will allow me, doltish. Haydn wrote music, much of it in symphonic form, to be played while listeners performed such normal bodily functions as eating and gossiping. Other composers did the same. I had laid hands on the perfect background music for dinner with the liberator of Grenada and the pacifier of Libya, symphonies and flute concerti composed by Frederick the Great. Two years earlier, when I had Bill Casey and his wife to dinner to observe May Day, my twelve-year-old daughter, Katy, found an exquisite record to help us solemnize the economic miracles of Marxism-Leninism, a record of wolf calls entitled *The Music and Language of the Wolves*. Now I turned to the music of an enlightened despot.

As the sough of the orchestra radiates softly from the living room speakers, an importunate White House aide begins popping in, announcing the President's progress. "The President has left the White House." O'Sullivan orders his first American cocktail of the day. "The President is coming up the George Washington Parkway, Mr. Tyrrell." My guest, Lally Weymouth, becomes visibly distressed about the music. "He is fifteen minutes away, Mr. Tyrrell." "He is five. . . ." "Please," I say, "you are unnerving my guests"; whereupon the entire front of the house lights up. Helicopters thrash overhead. My wife and I hasten into the garage, where, through a steady downpour, we see acting White House press secretary Marlin Fitzwater and Chief of Staff Ken Duberstein holding an umbrella above a bemused Ronald Reagan. Rain splattering at their feet, all three are illuminated in a mysterious shaft of light. Behind them the presidential seal is resplendent on the door of a huge White House limousine. A similar car purrs behind it, a dummy to dupe would-be assassins. The caravan includes motorcycles (twelve of them, my son P.D. later reports), two ambulances, two vans with Secret Service agents, a van containing the night's press pool ("the death watch"), and overhead the source of that shaft of light, a helicopter, perhaps two. In a Washington rush hour made more impossible still by a monsoon, the cops have blocked traffic on the

George Washington Parkway, the Capital Beltway, and a nearby congested country road. All this so that I can introduce the President of our democratic republic to the music of Frederick the Great. My driveway is a chaos of police lights and revving engines from which I now extricate my distinguished guest. Into the quiet of my garage he comes with only half a dozen aides, including the White House doctor, the White House bartender (carrying the President's vodka and orange juice), and an Air Force officer (carrying "the football"). The other one hundred or so cops stationed from the checkpoint down the road to my front door and the seventy other security personnel in and around the house itself are not invited. Over a grease spot we shake hands, and President Reagan says, "Bob, I apologize for all this."

We deposit the President's retinue in the family room, and I lead the President through double doors that open down into a sunken living room. The doors slam shut. There is quiet. The melodies of a Prussian Emperor insulate us from the pandemonium outside. The President smiles at my guests, but before he sits down there is alarm in his eyes, and hastily he retreats through the double doors. I had been expecting it. The party is over. Quite unintentionally, I had led the President of the United States into a dangerous situation.

In the early spring, when he accepted my invitation, my house was relatively safe. Since then conditions had changed radically. A sadness that befalls over half the American population, and from which I had been miraculously exempt, had hit. For sixteen years my wife had been excitable, but during our brief time in Washington her volatility heightened. She resorted to tennis, then religion, and then psychotherapy. Finally she tried divorce—all common American coping mechanisms for navigating middle age. By the time of the President's dinner the divorce negotiations were in their final stages, but not even these intellectually stimulating negotiations had appeased her random wrath. She had placed high hopes on a notorious divorce lawyer to make the proceedings as public and ugly as possible, but all for nought. When, fifteen minutes before the family headed off to Palm Sunday mass, she confronted me with her plan to make public the usual lurid charges, now so plausible in our soap-opera drenched society, I remained serene, reminding her that through the years the editor of *The American Spectator* has been charged with multitudes of abominations. More false charges would not affect me. That was the end of her ugly public divorce, though not of my startled children's travail. It was also about the end of her lawyer, who was suspended temporarily from the bar for transgressions he had committed on behalf of some other victim.

Despite all the intellectual challenges that her divorce negotiations provided, my wife was in a poisonous humor the day of the President's dinner, and I was hopeful that the Secret Service had taken every precaution. Surely some were carrying tranquilizer guns in the event that she lunged for the President. She liked him very much, but then she once liked me too. At any rate, the President had left the room. Lally was sure it was the music. I took solace in knowing we had plenty of champagne on hand and good company, though I hoped the Secret Service would leave the tranquilizer guns.

As it turns out, my pessimism is unwarranted. Within minutes the President reemerges, explaining that his doctor has replaced a failing hearing aid battery—now he can really enjoy the music! The White House bartender brings him the presidential cocktail, a screwdriver. Frederick the Great's orchestra saws away from behind a bookshelf. And the conversation begins, along with the photographs—an American president goes no place without White House photographers. My wife was fine. In fact she was splendid, a reprise of days gone by. It was Lally who imposed on me to turn the music down.

A final guest, *The American Spectator*'s assistant managing editor, Andy Ferguson, sloshes into the room. He is one of our most gifted writers with a knack for the woebegone drollery. At the last minute he has been drafted to take the place of our grounded New Yorkers (Forstmann is still indignant and calls on the half hour to denounce the clouds), and the congestion caused by the presidential caravan has forced him to walk half a mile through the rain. Andy makes his ordeal sound like the Italian army's retreat from Caporetto. I hint to the President that we are slightly behind schedule, and that is all this most agreeable guest of honor needs; he hastily downs his second screwdriver and we enter the dining room, where again I am reminded of the Liberal's yen for politics and receive an early adumbration of the solution to both the Liberal and the Conservative Crack-Ups.

Around the table, the palaver is solely of politics. There is no talk of business. The speculation about real estate, so absorbing to the sharpshooters downstairs, is not heard up here. These are people engrossed in political acts, political ideas, and political animals. The President's first concern is the Soviet Union where he is convinced change is in the air, a change made imperative by both material *and* spiritual deprivation—let theologians contend with that contretemps! He is eager to get on the campaign trail for George Bush, though there are pundits who doubt his eagerness. He insists that the Democratic candidate, Massachusetts governor Michael Dukakis, is wrecking his state's economy and is incensed by Dukakis's charge that the Republican Party is the instrument of The Rich. He believes that his policies have made it the party of the mainstream while the Democrats have moved off to exotic parts—"I didn't leave them; they left me," he says, not for the first time and not for the last. But then he observes that "It's hard for people to give up party allegiance." He himself never became a Republican until 1962. He ran for the governorship reluctantly, but then "five or six months into the governorship I realized that politics is more exciting than anything I'd ever done."

Nothing Ronald Reagan said that evening was unexpected, but as he and the other lapsed Liberals at the table continued to dilate on Liberal excesses and conservative deficiencies I became aware that the solution to the twin crack-ups of Liberalism and conservatism was all around me that evening. The sober Liberal had been deserted by the Liberals of the New Age. If in the 1990s the sober Liberal will take the same walk that Ronald Reagan once took, American conservatism will get the lift it needs to continue its preservation work on our liberal constitution.

History has made it easy for sober Liberals to take such a walk. Ronald Reagan is no longer in the White House, reminding them of those Danger-on-the-Right alarums that they received so long ago. George Bush is an easier conservative to abide; and he will surely welcome them, gentleman that he is. The Cold War has ended. International dangers will arise not from Manichean geopolitics but from the ambitions of overarmed despots such as Saddam Hussein and from the decrepitude of the former Soviet empire, some of whose anarchic components are going to be seething at each other in precisely the same region where the decrepitude of the Hapsburg empire occasioned World War I. The old impulses and animosities that divided conservatives and Liberals are not so applicable now. Even domestic problems offer opportunities for a new alliance. In reviewing E. J. Dionne's argument that the old divisions between Liberals and conservatives are obsolete, political scientist Norman Ornstein notes that "We are starting to see real and meaningful debate over the civil rights agenda, along with a welcome coming together of liberal and conservative views on welfare reform, the earned income credit and other areas of welfare policy. There is in fact a growing common ground between left and right in many areas of domestic policy."[7]

What is more, today's conservatives are different from earlier conservatives—if not as different as night is from day, at least as different as dawn is from early morn. A fundamental problem with any cyclical theory of history that posits the great dumb pendulum of the cosmos, swinging right–left, right–left, is that it is based on the false notion that history repeats itself. It does not. Rather it approximates itself. No era ever replicates another. There are too many variables: long winters one year, wet summers the next, different technologies; different exigencies; a different *dramatis personae*. Could anyone, even a very great leader, ever precisely replicate Abraham Lincoln? Talleyrand walked the European stage through three distinct eras. His nature never changed. But in the changed ambience of three different eras his performance changed. Vicissitudes beyond human control make every Bourgogne vintage different and every historic era too. That which the conservative disposition wishes to preserve today is different from that which yesterday's conservatives preserved, and so today's conservatives are a little different, too. Even our principles have changed somewhat.

Reading over Clinton Rossiter's *Conservatism in America*, written in 1955, I noticed that today's issues have brought almost a complete reversal in positions once held to be conservative. In the 1990s, the conservative believes that the economy prospers best not with the high tariffs his forebears swore by but with low tariffs or none at all. Protectionism is now the policy of Liberals, though in the past free trade was a progressive policy in the hands of such New Dealers as Secretary of State Cordell Hull. Pursuant to economic growth, today's conservative has renounced his reverence for the balanced budget, while yesteryear's advocate of deficit spending, the Liberal, greets deficits as opprobrious (though his spendthrift ways continue).

The list of policy shifts goes on. In the 1950s conservatives denounced the all-powerful presidency while Liberals prescribed it as an instrument of good government. Today conservatives denounce congress and fight to preserve presidential power from congressional Liberals. Welfare is no longer so abhorrent to the 1990s conservative as it was in the 1950s, and their old states' rights cause passed away years ago. Today's conservative seems to be completely oblivious of his forebears' dread of the demos, and it is the Liberal who trusts elites to preserve progress from the mob. Even the university is appraised differently by today's conservative. There he calls for tolerance, diversity, and free speech while the Liberal, or at least the leftist, has taken a position not all that far removed from that taken four decades ago by William F. Buckley, Jr., in *God and Man at Yale*, wherein Bill advocates the inculcation of proper values on campus and the proscription of politically incorrect speakers. In a new era, even old actors adopt different lines. Buckley, the Nockian libertarian of the 1950s, today sounds very much like yesteryear's New Dealer as he calls for a national youth service in *Gratitude: Reflections on What We Owe to Our Country*. Burke was right. Societies grow organically, but only the Deity knows their genetic code.

The conservatives of the present, then, are not carbon copies of conservatives from the past. That should make them easier for Liberals to work with. By the 1990s, after a decade of hegemony over the presidency, these conservatives are all over the federal government. Today, people who came into government with the Reagan-Bush campaign are on government commissions here and abroad. One encounters them in the bureaucracy and, most importantly, in the judiciary. What is more, conservative concerns circulate throughout society, and with enduring vigor in those regions where the *Kultursmog* is weak. Now, however, the conservatives' passion for politics is cooling. They have power but are not eager to use it.

Someone is going to have to apply the proven ideas of modern conservatism to those areas of America in need of improvement. Our system of education needs a benign earthquake, the inner city needs a moral revival, the moribundity of the American family is going to multiply social pathologies until its causes are addressed—and one cause to be addressed is the abundance of frivolous divorces that leave children abandoned. Our banking system and our spendthrift government need a shake-up. The polity would be improved with term limitations, greater budget accountability for Congress, and tort reform to smite the trial lawyers. In the jittery geopolitics ahead, strategic defense is going to have to be adopted. And there is something sickly about American social and cultural life—both are shapeless and close to meaningless. In the conservative think tanks there remain policies applicable to all these problems. New Age Liberalism, with its contradictory promise of personal anarchy and a most intrusive variety of public statism, is no more likely to ameliorate these problems than the shouts of an idiot savant. Many Liberals must know this. But have they noted that, though conservatives are still abundant with ideas, the conservatives have no leaders?

The conservative temperament grows impatient with leaders. The passing generation of conservatives gave no thought to building a new generation of leaders. The sense of drama that I spied in Luigi a decade ago and the literary imagination that went with it were simply not prevalent among American conservatives. Liberals, of course, have always had these qualities—too much so at times. Let the Liberals again take to the path once trod by the neoconservatives. Let them bring imagination and drama with them. The conservatives need the Liberals' relish for public life. The conservative counterculture needs fresh troops too. Liberals say they are civic-minded. Some, such as Ornstein and Dionne, claim the old left-right grudges are obsolete. Well, let the great migration begin again as sober Liberals part from the utopia and unreason of the New Age and march back to the Founding Fathers' love of liberty and Republican Virtue. Let the sober Liberal join with the conservatives in the preservation of our founding principles. Surely, my old pal Luigi expected as much; he knew that a moment in history takes a long time.

CHAPTER 16

Epilogue: With George Bush and Lord Avebury

I Have Seen the Future and It Is Delicious!

I am having lunch in the little patio immediately adjacent to the Oval Office with the forty-first President of the United States, his chief of staff John Sununu, and a political adviser, Charlie Black—both long-time conservatives. Tall shrubs block out the din of the city and the noisy skies above. Millie, the President's springer spaniel flicks in and out of the shrubs in what President Bush calls "the Great Squirrel Hunt." He carries on two conversations, alternately talking with Black about campaigns all over the country and with me about the *Kultursmog*.

My moment in history has been different than I had anticipated. There has been more politics than I wanted and more government roles. *The American Spectator* has published more politics and less culture, but most of the pieces and their writers would never have been published up there in the *Kultursmog*, and much that has come out of our pages has made a mark. There have been grand times and sadnesses—lose a family, gain a nightclub. But one of the questions that I began the 1980s with has yet to be answered, how serious are these political intellectuals, both the conservatives and the Liberals? They are not like my old friends in sport. They never have to face the judgment of the stopwatch. They can pontificate on to eternity. Well, almost, as with Lord Avebury, someday we shall know how serious they are.

Surely you remember Lord Avebury. Believing that "anything biodegradable should be recycled," in the late 1980s his Lordship stimulated debate throughout the United Kingdom by vowing to bequeath his body to the chefs at London's Battersea Dogs Home "to give the doggies a good meal." Naturally there were protests. "Ugh, it's grotesque, oh, it's horrible," remarked an employee at the Battersea Dogs Home where Lord Avebury's generosity was spurned. Press coverage, however, was quite good. "A good meal on him," brayed the *Daily Express*. "The Liberal peer who wants to end his life as a dog's dinner," announced another London paper. The good-humored *Daily Telegraph* interviewed a lady at Britain's Pet Food Manufacturers' Association: "I've never heard of such a thing," she exclaimed. His Lordship persevered. He journeyed to the Battersea Dogs Home to press his case. "The dogs liked him all right," reported the *Daily Mirror*. "They licked him and seemed to enjoy the taste quite a lot." But after a photo session with two mongrel pups, Lord Avebury was asked to leave. Said Battersea's director, the banal Colonel Edward Sweeney: "I am sorry, but I have been told by my committee that you cannot walk around the kennels." With that, Lord Avebury moved the debate in a slightly different direction: he suggested being buried at sea where he might "enter the marine food chain," or in a coffinless grave beneath a tree that might thrive on his remains.[1]

Lord Avebury speaks very well and he obviously devotes careful thought to his projects. The same can be said for our Liberals and conservatives. But how serious is Lord Avebury about recycling his mortal remains? Well, someday we shall know, and someday we shall know how serious American Liberals and conservatives have been about their projects, perhaps by the time my little daughter Anne is a lady.

Notes

PROLOGUE

1. Ethan Bronner, *Battle for Justice: How the Bork Nomination Shook America* (New York: Norton, 1989), p. 99.
2. *Ibid.*, p. 295.
3. *Facts on File 1987* (New York: Facts on File, Inc., 1987), p. 738.
4. Bronner, *Battle for Justice*, p. 98.
5. Suzanne Garment, "The War Against Robert H. Bork," *Commentary*, January 1988, p. 25.
6. Mary Ellen Bork, "An Ordeal to Remember: The Attack on My Husband, Robert H. Bork," *Crisis*, May 1988, p. 8.

CHAPTER 1

1. George Jean Nathan, *The World in Falseface* (New York: Alfred A. Knopf, Inc., 1923), p. xii.

CHAPTER 2

1. Friedrich Hayek, *The Road to Serfdom* (Chicago: University of Chicago Press, 1944), pp. 3–4.
2. George Nash, *The Conservative Movement in America* (New York: Basic Books, 1976), p. 159.

298

3. Arthur Schlesinger, Jr., "The New Conservatism: Politics of Nostalgia," *The Reporter*, June 16, 1955, p. 9.
4. Nash, *The Conservative Movement in America*, p. 153.
5. Daniel Bell, *The Dispossessed* (New York: Anchor Doubleday, 1964), p. 42.
6. Nash, *The Conservative Movement in America*, p. 291.
7. Richard Hofstadter, *The Paranoid Style in American Politics* (New York: Knopf, 1965), p. 40.
8. Paul Bedard, "The Presidential Contest Grows Even Meaner," *The Washington Times*, October 25, 1988, p. 1.
9. Anthony Lewis, "What Is a Man Profited," *The New York Times*, October 27, 1988, p. A27.

CHAPTER 3

1. Russell Kirk, *Confessions of a Bohemian Tory* (New York: Fleet Publishers, 1963), p. 29.
2. Alonzo Hamby, *Liberalism and Its Challengers* (Oxford: Oxford University Press, 1985), p. 277.
3. *Ibid.*, pp. 261–62.
4. John Herbers, "Panel on Civil Disorders Calls for Drastic Actions to Avoid 2-Society Nation," *The New York Times*, March 1, 1968, p. 1.
5. Jack Rosenthal, "President's Panel Warns Split on Youth Perils U.S., Asks Him to Foster Unity," *The New York Times*, September 27, 1970, p. 1.
6. Peter N. Carroll, *It Seemed Like Nothing Happened* (New York: Holt, Rinehart and Winston, 1982), p. 28.
7. *Ibid.*, p. 50.
8. *Ibid.*, p. 14.
9. Susan Sontag, *Styles of Radical Will* (New York: Farrar, Straus and Giroux, 1969), p. 195.
10. "Transcript of President's Address to Country on Energy Problems," *The New York Times*, July 16, 1979, A10.
11. James Wolcott, "The Young Farts," *Vanity Fair*, June 1987, p. 22.
12. William Manchester, *The Last Lion* (Boston: Little, Brown and Co., 1983), p. 7.
13. *Facts on File 1970*, p. 646.

CHAPTER 4

1. "A Conversation with Irving Kristol," *The Alternative*, May/June 1969, p. 7.
2. Irving Kristol, "Why I Am for Humphrey," *The New Republic*, June 8, 1968, p. 21.
3. George Will, "George Bush: The Sound of a Lapdog," *The Washington Post*, January 30, 1986, p. A25.

CHAPTER 5

1. E. T. Bell, *Men of Mathematics* (1937, New York: Touchstone, 1986), pp. 125–126.
2. *Ibid.*, p. 227.
3. Peter Steinfels, "The Reasonable Right," *Esquire*, February 13, 1979, p. 26.
4. Peter Steinfels, *The Neoconservatives: The Men Who Are Changing America's Politics* (New York: Simon & Schuster, 1979), p. 1.
5. "Why Are There Neoconservatives?" Symposium, *Orthodoxy: The American Spectator Anniversary Anthology* (New York: Harper & Row, 1987), pp. 434–436.
6. *Ibid.*, p. 423.
7. Henry Miller, *The Colossus of Maroussi* (1941, New York: Penguin Books, 1982), p. 7.
8. *Ibid.*, p. 35.

CHAPTER 6

1. Arthur M. Schlesinger, Jr., "The End of an Era?" *The Wall Street Journal*, November 20, 1980, p. 26.
2. Jack Newfield, "Why Democrats Can't Stand Pat," *The Village Voice*. November 19–25, 1980, p. 7.
3. Warren Brookes, "The Silent Boom," *The American Spectator*, August 1988, p. 18.
4. Felix Rohatyn, as quoted by Arthur M. Schlesinger, Jr., *The Washington Post*, May 1, 1988, p. C4.
5. Martin Anderson, "The Reagan Boom—Greatest Ever" *The New York Times*, January 17, 1990, p. A25.
6. Editorial, "Job Poison," *The Wall Street Journal*, May 13, 1988, p. 18.
7. Robert J. Donovan, *Conflict and Crisis* (New York: W. W. Norton, 1977), p. 14.
8. Theodore H. White, "America's Problem: Trying to Do Everything for Everybody," *U.S. News & World Report*, July 5, 1982, p. 59.

CHAPTER 7

1. Quoted in Dinesh D'Souza, "Whatever Happened to Neoliberalism?" *National Review*, June 2, 1989, p. 34.
2. Hendrik Hertzberg, "The Tortoise: Dukakis's Slow Sure Bid for the White House," *The New Republic*, May 16, 1988, p. 15.
3. Editorial, "Job Poison," *The Wall Street Journal*, May 13, 1988, p. 18.
4. Randall Rothenberg, *The Neoliberals* (New York: Simon & Schuster, 1979), p. 21.

5. Richard Vigilante, "The Liberals' Halfway House," *The American Spectator*, January 1984, p. 48.
6. Interview, "Hart on El Salvador: It's Their War," *The Washington Post*, February 28, 1982, p. B3.
7. *Ibid.*
8. Richard Vigilante, "The Liberals' Halfway House," p. 48.
9. *Ibid.*
10. *Thomas Babington Macauley, Selected Writings*, ed. John Clive and Thomas Pinney (Chicago: University of Chicago Press, 1972), p. 37.

CHAPTER 8

1. Editorial, "The Goldwater Nomination," *The New York Times*, July 16, 1964, p. 22.
2. James Reston, "What Goldwater Lost," *The New York Times*, November 4, 1964, p. 23.
3. Roger H. Marz, "The Republican Party Has No Future," *The New Republic*, December 19, 1964, p. 11.
4. M. Stanton Evans, *The Future of Conservatism* (New York: Holt, Rinehart and Winston), p. 32.
5. *Ibid.*, p. 198.
6. David Broder, "Frustration on the Right," *The Washington Post*, February 19, 1975, p. A14.
7. Lou Cannon, "Can GOP Broaden Its Base?," *The Washington Post*, January 2, 1975, p. A12.
8. Everett Carll Ladd, Jr., "The Unmaking of the Republican Party," *Fortune*, September 1977, p. 98.

CHAPTER 9

1. Richard M. Nixon, "Remarks on Departure from the White House, August 9, 1974," *Public Papers of the Presidents: Richard Nixon, 1974* (Washington, D.C.: Government Printing Office, 1975), p. 630.
2. Peter Hannaford, *The Reagans: A Political Portrait* (New York: Coward-McCann, 1983), p. 9.
3. Robert H. Bork, *The Tempting of America* (New York: The Free Press, 1990), p. 1.
4. Interview, "A Conversation with Irving Kristol," *The Alternative*, May–June 1969, p. 7.
5. "The Sniper," *Time*, November 3, 1967, p. 80.
6. Michael K. Deaver, *Behind the Scenes* (New York: William Morrow and Co., 1987), p. 120.

CHAPTER 10

1. Anthony Lewis, "The Anderson Factor," *The New York Times*, August 25, 1980, p. A23.
2. Tom Wicker, "Catch-22 for Anderson," *The New York Times*, September 7, 1980, p. E19.
3. Editorial, "President Yesterday," *The New York Times*, October 26, 1980, p. E18.
4. John B. Oakes, "The Reagan Hoax," *The New York Times*, November 1, 1981, p. E21.
5. Anthony Lewis, "It's Morning Again," *The New York Times*, October 22, 1987, p. A35.
6. Robert Reich, "The Glitz is Gone," *The New York Times*, October 22, 1987, p. A35.
7. John Kenneth Galbraith, "The Toll of a 'Nonstop Binge': Five Respected Leaders Assess the Damage," *Newsweek*, November 2, 1987, p. 49.
8. Pete Hamill, "It's Time to Pay for Reagan's Party," *New York Post*, January 17, 1989, p. 2.
9. Laurence Barrett, "Going Home a Winner," *Time*, January 23, 1989, p. 14.
10. "The Wraps Are Off," editorial, *The Nation*, January 3, 1981, p. 3.
11. James Q. Wilson, "Politics Then and Now," *Commentary*, February 1979, pp. 39–46.
12. Jane Mayer and Doyle McManus, *Landslide: The Unmaking of the President 1984–1988* (Boston: Houghton, Mifflin, 1988), p. 393.
13. Ronald Steel, *Walter Lippmann and the American Century* (Boston: Atlantic-Little, Brown, 1980), p. 291.
14. Joseph P. Lash, *Dealers and Dreamers: A New Look at the New Deal* (New York: Doubleday, 1988), pp. 101–102.
15. Steel, *Walter Lippmann*, pp. 291–292.
16. George Wolfskill and John A. Hudson, *All but the People: Franklin D. Roosevelt and His Critics, 1933–39* (London: Collier-Macmillan, 1969), p. 7.
17. Ronald Reagan with Richard G. Hubler, *Where's the Rest of Me?* (New York: Duell, Sloan & Pearce, 1965), p. 139.
18. David Herbert Donald, *Liberty and Union* (Boston: Little, Brown, 1979), p. 83.
19. Rexford G. Tugwell, *The Art of Politics: As Practiced by Three Great Americans: Franklin D. Roosevelt, Luis Munoz Marin, and Fiorello H. LaGuardia* (Garden City, New York: Doubleday, 1958), pp. 222–223.
20. Richard Tanner Johnson, *Managing the White House: An Intimate Study of the Presidency* (New York: Harper & Row, 1974), p. 11.
21. Arthur M. Schlesinger, Jr., *A Thousand Days: John F. Kennedy in the White House* (Boston: Houghton, Mifflin, 1965), p. 686.

22. Johnson, *Managing the White House*, p. 9.
23. Mayer and McManus, *Landslide*, p. 21.
24. Francesco Guicciardini, *Selected Writings*, trans. Margaret Grayson; ed. Cecil Grayson (London: Oxford University Press, 1965), p. 23.
25. Claude M. Fuess, *Calvin Coolidge: The Man From Vermont* (Boston: Little, Brown, 1940), p. 306.

CHAPTER 11

1. Martin Anderson, *Revolution* (Orlando: Harcourt Brace Jovanovich, 1988), p. 72.
2. Lou Cannon, *President Reagan: The Role of a Lifetime* (New York: Simon & Schuster, 1991), p. 802.
3. *Washington Post*/ABC News poll, *The Washington Post*, January 18, 1990, p. A9.
4. Aaron Wildavsky, "President Reagan as a Political Strategist," *Society*, May/ June 1987, p. 59.
5. Anderson, *Revolution*, p. 164.
6. Warren Brookes, "The Silent Boom," *The American Spectator*, August 1988, p. 17.
7. Wildavsky, "President Reagan as a Political Strategist," p. 57.
8. Strobe Talbott, WUSA's "Inside Washington," September 21, 1991.
9. Margaret Thatcher, speech delivered March 8, 1991, Washington, D.C.
10. James Reston, "They'll Be Better Than Reston," *The New York Times*, August 1, 1988, p. A15.
11. Editorial, "On Loyalty," *The Wall Street Journal*, May 11, 1988, p. 20.
12. Terry Eastland, "Independent Counsels for Congress," *The Wall Street Journal*, September 20, 1988, p. 26.
13. Jacob Burckhardt, *Reflections on History* (Indianapolis: Liberty Classics/ Liberty Fund, Inc., 1943), p. 337.
14. *Ibid.*, p. 338.
15. Donald, *Liberty and Union* (Boston: Little, Brown, 1978), p. 165.

CHAPTER 12

1. Conrad Black, "Remarkable Reagan Passes the Test of History," *Sunday Telegraph* (London), February 3, 1991, p. 14.
2. Ambrose Evans-Pritchard, "My Fellow Americans . . . ," *The Spectator*, July 21, 1989, pp. 13–14.
3. Gregg Easterbrook, "Ideas Move Nations," *The Atlantic*, January 1986, p. 66.
4. Amy Moritz, "Conservatism's Parched Grass Roots," *Policy Review*, Spring 1988, p. 22.

5. Victor Gold, "The Coming Conservative Crack-Up," *The American Spectator*, September 1987, p. 19.
6. Jeane Kirkpatrick, "Dictatorships and Double Standards," *Commentary*, November 1979, pp. 34–45.
7. William F. Buckley, Jr., "Notes Towards an Empirical Definition of Conservatism," *What Is Conservatism?*, Frank S. Meyer, ed., (New York: Holt, Rinehart and Winston, 1964), p. 212.
8. Michael Oakeshott, *Rationalism in Politics*, (New York: Basic Books, 1962), p. 169.
9. George Orwell: *Homage to Catalonia* (New York: Penguin Books, 1962), p. 221.

CHAPTER 13

1. Irving Kristol, "Conservatives' Greatest Enemy May Be the GOP," *Wall Street Journal*, February 20, 1990, p. A24.
2. *Ibid.*
3. R. Emmett Tyrrell, Jr., "A Conservative Crack-Up?" *The Wall Street Journal*, March 27, 1987, p. 22.
4. William Simon, *A Time for Truth* (New York: Reader's Digest Press, 1978), p. 230.
5. David Shribman, "Conservatives Face a Bitter Struggle in Shaping Movement," *The Wall Street Journal*, April 29, 1987, p. 1.
6. Donald, *Liberty and Union*, p. 183.
7. Aaron Wildavsky, "The Media's 'American Egalitarians,' " *The Public Interest*, Summer 1987, p. 100.
8. "Notebook," *The New Republic*, November 14, 1988, p. 10.
9. Mary Belcher, "North Scoffed at Risk of Jail, Court Is Told," *The Washington Times*, March 9, 1989, p. 1.

CHAPTER 14

1. Paul Bekker, ed., *Gesammelte Schrifter uber Musik und Musiker* (Berlin: Wegweiser-Verlag, 1922), p. 22.
2. Gregg Easterbrook, "Ideas Move Nations," *The Atlantic*, January 1986, p. 66.
3. John Kenneth Galbraith, "Chronicles of Wasted Time," *The New York Times Book Review*, July 14, 1974, p. 1.
4. Richard Ingrams, "Muggeridge at 85," *The Sunday Telegraph*, March 20, 1988, p. 14.
5. Noel Annan, *Our Age: A Portrait of a Generation* (London: Weidenfeld and Nicolson, 1990), p. 167.

6. William F. Buckley, Jr., *On the Firing Line: The Public Lives of Our Public Figures* (New York: Random House, 1989), p.22.
7. Ian Hunter, *Malcolm Muggeridge: A Life* (Nashville: Thomas Nelson Publishers, 1980), p. 12.
8. Malcolm Muggeridge, *The Most of Malcolm Muggeridge* (New York: Simon and Schuster, 1966), p. 140.
9. Hunter, *Malcolm Muggeridge*, p. 160.
10. *Ibid.*, p. 131.
11. *Ibid.*, p. 158.
12. Malcolm Muggeridge, *The Most of Malcolm Muggeridge*, p. 148.
13. John B. Judis, *William F. Buckley, Jr.: Patron Saint of the Conservatives* (New York: Simon and Schuster, 1988), p. 14.
14. William F. Buckley, Jr., *Quotations from Chairman Bill* (New Rochelle, New York: Arlington House, 1970), p. 17.
15. Judis, *William F. Buckley, Jr.*, p. 267.
16. *Ibid.*, p. 232.
17. *Ibid.*, p. 372.
18. Constance L. Hays, "$39,000 Buys Global Flight with Buckley," *The New York Times*, March 31, 1989, p. B2.
19. Remarks at Thirtieth Anniversary Dinner of *National Review*, December 1985.

CHAPTER 15

1. Michael Oakeshott, "Scrutinizing the Conservative Disposition," *The Spectator*, July 9, 1988, p. 60.
2. George Nash, "Is the American Experience Conservative?" A Heritage Lecture, #136.
3. February 27, 1860. Reprinted in Mario M. Cuomo and Harold Holzer, eds., *Lincoln on Democracy.* (New York: Harper & Row, 1990), p. 166.
4. Michael Oakeshott, "On Being Conservative," *Rationalism in Politics* (New York: Basic Books, 1962), p. 168.
5. *Ibid.*, p. 169.
6. Peter Brimelow, "Why Liberalism Is Now Obsolete: An Interview with Nobel Laureate Milton Friedman," *Forbes*, December 12, 1988, pp. 161–176.
7. Norman Ornstein, "Nothing to Vote For," *The New York Times Book Review*, May 19, 1991, p. 7.

CHAPTER 16

1. R. Emmett Tyrrell, Jr., "The Continuing Crisis," *The American Spectator*, April 1987, p. 8.

Index

About the Author

R. EMMETT TYRRELL, JR., is founder of *The American Spectator*, and has been its editor-in-chief for the last twenty-five years. His weekly column, syndicated by King Features, appears regularly in the *Washington Times*, the *New York Post*, and papers in almost every major American city. He has written on politics, sports, travel, and the arts for *Commentary*, *National Review*, *Harper's*, *The New York Times*, the *Conde Nast Traveller*, the *Sunday Telegraph* (London), and *Le Figaro* (Paris). *Time* magazine has called him one of the "50 future leaders of America."

Tyrrell also makes frequent television appearances on leading opinion shows, including the "CBS Morning News"; the "ABC Evening News"; "Good Morning, America!"; "The MacNeil/Lehrer Report"; "Nightline" and CNN.

His previous books include *Public Nuisances* and *The Liberal Crack-Up*. He has also edited three volumes: *Network News' Treatment of the 1972 Democratic Presidential Candidates*, *The Future That Doesn't Work: Social Democracy's Failures in Britain*, and *Orthodoxy*, a collection of essays from *The American Spectator*.